Exploring English Character

EXPLORING
ENGLISH
CHARACTER

EXPLORING ENGLISH CHARACTER

by

Geoffrey Gorer

CRITERION BOOKS   NEW YORK

.

To the Memory of
My Parents
EDGAR EZEKIEL GORER
April 2nd, 1872–May 7th, 1915
RÉE ALICE GORER
June 13th, 1873–June 30th, 1954

ACKNOWLEDGEMENTS

I wish to thank Dr Henry Durant of the British Institute of Public Opinion for permission to republish some figures from the Gallup Poll which appeared in the *News Chronicle*.

I wish to thank Mr W. D. McClelland of the Research Department of Odhams Press Ltd. for permission to publish some figures from two surveys conducted by the Department he directs.

I wish to thank Chief Inspector J. L. Thomas of the City of Bradford Police for permission to quote from two articles by him.

Some of the material which follows has appeared (in slightly different form) in the *People, Encounter, The Observer* and *The Journal of Social Issues* (U.S.A).

CONTENTS

HOW IT BEGAN

I HAVE LONG felt it rather ridiculous that there was no study of the English character, comparable with the studies that my colleagues and I had made of the American, the Great Russian and the French characters.[1] It represented a major gap; and insofar as these studies were meant to be of use to politicians and political scientists—and this was certainly one of the major motives for making them—one of the sides of the square, one of the essential equations, was missing.

Though I was deeply conscious of this gap, I did not want to fill it myself. The difficulties of seeing one's own culture, of getting an adequate perspective on one's own inarticulate assumptions are very great, and psychologically disturbing. There are numerous advantages in being a foreigner to the society one is studying; one is unplaced socially, for one's foreignness masks the lesser differences of class or region; one's accent, or one's more or less halting employment of a strange language, mark one as a stranger, not as a rival, a superior or inferior to the people one is talking to; within the limits of one's enterprise and interest, the whole society, any portion of the society, can be open to one. And a foreigner is transient; one can talk to him freely and frankly for a few hours, as people talk to chance acquaintances on boats and trains, without the fears, or the hopes, that the chance meeting will develop into a longer acquaintance; many people will be far more open to strangers than they would ever be to neighbours.

All these advantages are lost when one is working in one's own society. As soon as I start speaking I am placed as a graduate of one of the major universities (Cambridge, as a matter of fact); and English people respond to this accent in a variety of fairly stereotyped ways. I am immediately recognized as belonging to the top percentile as far as education goes; and nearly all strange English people will therefore respond to me as a member of a class, as well as an individual. My manners, my gestures, my attitudes towards money are all class-typed; I can never be accepted in an English working class home, as I can in an American, or a French one. In both the latter I am an oddity, judged by my immediate behaviour at the time; in the former a 'toff', having to bear the attitudes developed over a lifetime to other 'toffs', to 'toffs' and 'snoopers' as a class, and quite possibly to political parties and stereotypes. I do not mean by this that acquaintance, and even deep friendship, is not possible between

1

members of different social classes in England; it is indeed, and I have been very fortunate in some of the friendships I have made. But it is an intensive, not an extensive relationship; it takes time to develop, probably longer than friendships within the same class. In the United States a casual encounter, a casual invitation has opened not only the house, but the hearts of people I have never seen before, and will probably never see again; and I know Americans who have the same happy experiences in England. But an invitation from one English person to another (or indeed from one American to another) is not given so lightly and easily, for it is a first step, which may well involve the future; the foreigner, in town for a couple of days, presents no such problems.

I could not learn the English, as I had learned the Americans, through a wide and varied personal experience, as a counterpoint to the numerous studies which specialists had made of different aspects of American life. Nor indeed did parallel studies exist; the self-analysis, self-criticism and self-discovery which so many Americans seem to find congenial and which is so amply supported by the sociology departments of many great Universities and the benefactions of the large charitable foundations for the pursuit of knowledge have no analogues in England. Since Mayhew there has been a certain amount of what may perhaps be called, without intending offence, 'slumming sociology', descriptions of how the 'other half' lives and works, books in which the word 'poverty' recurs, even in the titles, with monotonous regularity; but these are studies of ways and means, not of ideals or values or motives; and they emphasize the differences, not the similarities, between the people studied and the people likely to read the studies. There were hints a-plenty in the popular novels, the humour of music hall and radio, in biographies and autobiographies; but there was nothing approaching the mass of systematic work which I was able to take as my background for *The Americans*

Geographically, I know very little of England. When at home, I am naturally a sedentary type, preferring a country life; with Voltairean fervour, I cultivate my garden, and, latterly, my farm. As a boy I was taken for holidays to a wide variety of seaside and country places; but in recent years I have only been outside my home, or London, for short visits to friends or to various bodies who have been kind enough to invite me to address them; and few of these have been north of Oxford. I have no variety of personal experience, even of personal vision, to supplement, or replace, the non-existent sociological studies.

2

After the publication of *The Americans* English editors approached me from time to time with the suggestion that I write 'something like' that book on the English; but when I explained my ignorance, and the absence of other sources of information, so that quite a considerable amount of research would be needed before I would feel capable of writing anything on the subject, the proposal was quickly dropped This continued intermittently for two years, and seemed as though it would continue indefinitely, though probably at longer and longer intervals; but in the autumn of 1950 the suggestion was made once more by the editor of the *People*; instead of being frightened by my saying that research would be necessary, he blithely accepted the situation and said that the research department of Odhams Press would undertake the necessary work. I fear he did not realize quite how much that work would be

The *People* is a popular Sunday paper with the second largest circulation in Great Britain, passed only by the *News of the World*. As the tables published by the Hulton Readership Survey[2] show, it is widely read by every section of the community, though less proportionately by the first two socio-economic classes into which they divide the society ('The Well-to-do' and 'The Middle Class') the top 11 per cent of the population, than by the remainder of the community. According to this same survey, this paper is read by twelve million people, roughly three readers for each copy. Readers are scattered all over the country and are of all ages and both sexes; but, proportionately there is a slight falling off of readership in the South-East and North-West, and in old people aged over 65; male readers predominate. As will be seen, the sample follows the readership very closely, particularly in the lack of adequate representation of the top 10 per cent of the population, and of old people.[3]

The editors of the *People* had very clear ideas of the subjects which would interest their enormous audience, and the way in which it should be presented. Their editorial experience had determined that articles written in the second person were much more acceptable than articles written in the third person; and the original scheme outlined to me called for a series of six articles under the titles:

> You and Your Sweetheart
> You and Your Husband (or Wife)
> You and Your Children
> You and Your Boss
> You and The Law
> You and Religion

3

I did not feel that questionnaires were a suitable method for investigating the relationship between employer and employee, and I could discover no other adequate sources on this subject, so I suggested that 'You and Your Boss' be replaced by 'You and Your Neighbour'. This was agreed to.

The outlined scheme further suggested that I should write a preliminary article asking for volunteers from the readers of the *People*; that to them should be sent a questionnaire of my devising; and the coding of this questionnaire and the preparation of the resulting statistical tables should be undertaken by the Research Section of Odhams Press Ltd , headed by Mr McClelland with his assistant Dr Adler. They were fully equipped to carry out all social survey and market research work.

I hesitated some time before accepting this commission. Although I had, on many occasions, made use of statistical information derived from questionnaires, I had never engaged in such work myself; my preferred technique of research, and the one in which I felt most confident, was the interview, especially the multiple interview. I was far from certain whether questionnaires could provide the type of material, statements of conduct and ideals, which I needed for making hypotheses about the psychological motives shared by the members of a society. And, I must confess, I felt certain qualms about working for a paper which, however great its other merits, did not automatically command the respect of my colleagues nor, I suspected, of most of the people who read my books.

At the same time the commission was a challenge and an opportunity. It was a challenge to ingenuity to frame questions so that the answers would yield the type of information I needed; and it could also go some way to providing a convincing demonstration of the statistical validity of the concept of national character, which critics, not only unfriendly ones, had consistently questioned; and if convincing material could be elicited by questionnaires, it would enable far more people to do research in national character; the methods my colleagues and I had pursued hitherto relied too strongly on individual skills of interviewing and analysis, and the following of faint clues, to be teachable except by the equivalent of a prolonged apprenticeship.

It was, however, above all an opportunity, an opportunity to get a mass of data, which might otherwise never be forthcoming; for even if some learned institution were to consider undertaking parallel research, it would not (in England) have the clerical staff nor the machines to analyse such a volume of responses. For reasons that I

4

have already stated, I did not think I could successfully interview representatives of the mass of the English population; here I could get material from members of all classes which, though it would needs be limited, would not be distorted by the class-feelings of face-to-face interviews; and it would produce a wider geographical and social scatter than I could hope to achieve in the rest of my life, even if I abandoned all other pursuits.[4] This consideration finally outweighed my hesitations about working with a hitherto untried technique, under conditions and auspices which were not academically ideal.

A further drawback whose disadvantages I did not fully realize at the time was that the whole research had to be planned from the start, so that the total investment in time and money could be calculated; that meant that, instead of waiting for the preliminary results, and then deciding what further calculations and cross-correlations would be profitable, I had to make guesses on the basis of the questions, rather than the answers. This proved to be more of a loss for Odhams Press than for the work; there were a few cross-correlations which I think might have been significant which were not made; but quite a considerable number were made which were of very little interest. Thus, for example, I thought that it would be interesting to discover if the treatment of children were different in large and small families, and arranged for most of the questions about children to be cross-correlated with the number of children. As it turned out, there were so few parents with more than three children in the coded sample that the figures were hardly significant; but I didn't receive the basic table until most of the calculations had already been made.[5]

I asked for, and was generously granted, a couple of scientific safeguards to test the validity of the research; first a pre-testing of the questions on a small sample (a pilot survey, it is called technically), to make sure that the questions were understandable to all classes of respondents; this is standard procedure in questionnaires. It produced some illuminating and some curious results; I find it odd that few of the English working class recognize the word 'astrology' though, to a man and woman, they know the word 'horoscope'.

The second safeguard was more important technically, and incidentally much more expensive. Neither I, nor anybody else, had the remotest idea how many of the readers of the *People* would answer my request for collaboration, who they would be, nor how representative of the English people as a whole. To guard against the probability of major distortions, and to have a check on the representativeness of what we hoped would be the major group, the editors agreed that a field survey, based on a representative sample of the type which the Gallup polls have made familiar, should be made at the same time as the printed forms were sent out and with the same questions.[6] This concession was a remarkably generous one on the part of the editors, for it made practically no difference to the 'journalistic' aspects of the work, in which they were naturally the more interested; but it gave me far more confidence in the validity of the results, and provided a scientific check of major importance.

Once these arrangements had been agreed to, I went home and refreshed my memory of the various rules and recommendations for the formation of questionnaires which experts had published from time to time; and then I proceeded in a considerable number of cases to do just the opposite. It was recommended that written questionnaires be kept short and confined to one subject, or group of subjects, I made mine extremely long—the fullest questionnaires covered eight folio sheets and probably took about three hours to fill—and covered a great range of subjects. It was stated as an axiom that you would not get information on intimate or deeply felt subjects by this means; I asked for views on pre-marital sexuality and life after death, law-breaking and prayer, psychic experiences and child-training. Questions, it was said, should be neutral; but I wanted expressions of emotion, so I included such questions as 'What do you most disapprove of about your present neighbours?' 'If a husband finds his wife having an affair with another man, what should he do?' I thought that, in the great majority of cases, if people were going to bother to answer the questionnaire at all, they would do so honestly and fully, they were protected by anonymity;[7] and if I could not get information of the level indicated, the survey would be of little use to me.

Most of the questions were arranged in batches of 4 or 5 dealing with the same subject to avoid as far as possible fatigue or boredom; some subjects were recurred to after an interval. A few questions were put in because I thought people would enjoy answering them, and not because I expected to get much valuable information from them; for example, 'What do you consider your three best qualities?' 'What do you consider your three worst faults?' 'Do you think it is natural for young people to be shy?' and so on. The replies to some of these questions turned out to be surprisingly revealing, for the respondents were many of them extremely frank, and told things to their own discredit which I never expected to learn from such a source. I did not have a murderer among my respondents, nor did

6

anyone accuse him or herself of treason, simony or barratry; but I do not think there is another crime or misdemeanour on the calendar to which at least one respondent did not admit.

The project of avoiding fatigue by varying the topics of the questions was modified in two particulars. I wanted to get the views on marriage from those who had actual experience in marriage, and the views on child-rearing only from parents who could speak from experience; and consequently the questionnaires had to be arranged so that the questions on these subjects did not go to the inappropriate people. All respondents were asked to answer the first 45 main questions; 6 further questions dealing with marriage went only to those who were, or had been, married; 14 further questions dealt with child training and education and were sent to parents only. The questionnaires consequently came in three lengths Furthermore, certain questions were varied in their wording according to the sex of the respondent. Thus, for example, the question already quoted 'If a husband finds his wife having an affair with another man, what should he do?' was only sent to married men Married women were asked 'If a wife finds her husband having an affair with another woman, what should she do?' Consequently there were in all six forms of questionnaire, depending on the sex of the respondent, and whether he or she were single, married and childless, or married with children.

When these preparations had been made, I wrote the introductory article asking for the volunteers on whose goodwill and collaboration the success of the research so completely depended. The article was rewritten a number of times before what I wanted to say was successfully welded into the form the editors of the *People* considered desirable. The nub of the article read:

> Where can I find enough English people who will be willing to tell me their true ideas and experiences so that I can deduce the elements which make up the English character? This is where you can help me.

> Nowadays explorers and scientists do not work alone; they work in a team. I need a team to help me.

> From among my readers I want to form a study group to supply me with answers to questions which will give me the information I need on the way English people feel and behave.

> I should not need a very large group to get valuable results. If I could have 200 young men and 200 young women under 21, 200 men and 200 women between 21 and 30, 200 men and 200 women between 31 and 45, and 200 men and 200 women over 46 that would be sufficient.

All the members of my study group must be English, born in England of English parents, and should have spent all or the greatest part of their school years in England

One thing is very important Each member of the study group must answer all the questions by himself or herself without asking for any help.

Because I want the answers to be as true as possible, I am not asking anyone to sign the questionnaire or put their address on it

With the article was a coupon for volunteers, in which besides their name and address, they were asked to indicate their sex, age, whether they were married or no, and whether they had children, so that they should receive the appropriate form. The article appeared on December 31st 1950.

The figure of 1,600 respondents of both sexes and assorted ages, which I asked for in the article, was a purely fantasy figure, though I certainly could have done very little with fewer. It appeared to me possible that, by setting a rather small limit to the number asked for, I might attract some people by the appearance of exclusivity; and I was far from certain of getting even that small number.

In the first few days the applications came in a trickle; but this was soon transformed into a flood. We decided that no more questionnaires would be sent out after January 17th, by that date 14,605 had been despatched. There were more applications than this; some hundreds came from Welsh, Scots, Irish and nationals of other countries who were not suitable for this investigation. Even after the closing date applications continued to come in.

There were certainly enough volunteers. The stereotype of the withdrawn Englishman, resenting other people's prying into his business, received a severe jolt; I had got something approaching the rapport which, in foreign countries, I hope to achieve through interviews.

But what would be the relation between volunteers who sent for the questionnaire, and people who would take the time and trouble to complete them? The text-books indicated that a response of 25 to 30 per cent on a written questionnaire should be considered satisfactory; my questionnaire was a particularly long and intimate one (respondents occasionally noted the time it had taken them to fill it in; for single people it averaged about an hour and a half, for parents three hours or more); 25 per cent seemed all I could possibly hope for. This would give me about three thousand questionnaires; if the scatter was good, this would be adequate.

This forecast was wildly inaccurate. By January 31st, which we

8

had arbitrarily decided would be the closing date, 10,524 completed forms had been returned. A further 500 came in after this closing date, so that, in all, there was a return of 75 per cent of the questionnaires sent out, a response as far as I know unparalleled in the history of questionnaire investigations

This mass of material was actually something of an embarrassment. The coding of more than 10,000 questionnaires would be excessively expensive and time-consuming; and there was no reason to suppose that such a very large number was necessary to produce significant results. I decided that I would read each one for significant or apt information or illustrations; but consultation with statisticians suggested that 5,000 would be an adequate number to code, if they were selected at random.

The most completely satisfactory operation would probably have been to choose these 5,000 out of the whole mass without any principle other than randomness; but as they had come in, they had been sorted into six groups (dependent on sex and marital status) according to the six types of questionnaires returned. Much the smallest of these groups, both absolutely, and in proportion to the population as a whole, were those of married men (760) and married women (533) without children. It was therefore decided, (without, incidentally, consulting me) that all these groups should be coded, and that the remainder of the questionnaires, from the unmarried and from the parents, should be selected in random fashion in proportion to the total numbers of the groups in the English population, as these had been calculated by the registrar-general. This gave us 27 per cent unmarried, 26 per cent married and childless, and 47 per cent parents of living children, a parallel to the English population over 16, as far as marital status was concerned.[8]

Although the sample was correct maritally, this method of selection distorted it rather badly as far as age was concerned. A very considerable number of our childless married respondents were only recently married, and consequently the younger people, between the ages of 18 and 34, are heavily over-represented in these groups, and, consequently, in the sample as a whole; and people over 45, and particularly those over 65, are much under-represented. It is this skewing of the ages which make the comparisons between the sample and the field survey particularly tricky; in the field survey, as in the population as a whole, 31 per cent of the population over 16 is between the ages of 45 and 64, and a further 11 per cent over 65; in our sample only 21 per cent are between 45 and 64, and a mere 3 per cent over 65. The sample is also skewed for sex; we have

9

56 men for 44 women; whereas the true figures for the population are 47 per cent men and 53 per cent women. It will be remembered that the readership survey of the *People* showed that it was read proportionately more by men than women, and by the young and middle-aged rather than by the elderly. To that extent our sample of 5,000 mirrored the readership of 12,000,000 very closely.

It was gratifying to discover that geographically, according to region and town size, and also economically, our sample approximated very closely to the model of the country as a whole with variations in most cases of only 1 or 2 per cent;[9] as far as the gross criteria were concerned we had, on these levels, a truly representative sample.

The first six months of 1951 were devoted to arduous work on the part of the research staff of Odhams Press in coding this mass of information; and on my part in reading and making notes on over 10,000 questionnaires, and analysing the tables as they were delivered. In the hottest days of that summer I could not forget that the first fortnight in January had been wet and cold and that many people were ill with flu, nor that the papers and radio were much taken up with the hunt for the missing Coronation Stone The articles were written in August and September 1951.

NOTES TO CHAPTER ONE

1 For a full bibliography of current work on National Character see Mead and Métraux. *The Study of Culture at a Distance*, pp 455–74 (University of Chicago Press and Cambridge University Press, 1953)

2 *Patterns of British Life* (Hulton Research, London, 1950)

3. The actual percentages for readership given are
Classes. All classes, 32 8, A and B, 18 9, C, 29 2, D and E, 35 9.
Sex Men, 35·4; women, 30 5.
Regions. South-East, 31·6, South-West and Wales, 36 6, Midlands, 35 6, North-West, 32·1, North-East and North, 38 5.
Ages. 16–24, 33 7, 25–44, 33 7, 45–64, 33 9, 65 and over, 26 4

4 If one allows three hours for an interview, which considering the range of subjects covered is not excessive, the 11,024 informants would have taken something like 16 years to interview, working a 40-hour week, without taking into account the recording and subsequent coding

5. A second disadvantage, and this was a more serious one, was that the Research Section of Odhams Press, Ltd. were accustomed to doing all their work themselves, without consultations with any outside person between the deciding on the questions to be asked and the delivery of the answers This habit persisted in the work they were doing on my behalf; and on a few tables they established categories which failed to make the distinctions which I thought necessary Some useful information is permanently lost, unless all the questionnaires are rescored, and new cards punched; but it is, comparatively, so little, that it would probably not be worth anybody's expenditure of time and money.

HOW IT BEGAN

6 Although the questions asked were identical, it was not possible to ask all the questions in the survey in a face-to-face interview, and some of them were not suitable for fairly naive interviewers The field survey contained somewhat more than a third of the original questions and sub-questions, resulting in 55 tables, as contrasted with 134 tables from the main survey Every portion of the questionnaire was represented in part, except those which had been covered in recent surveys by the same, or parallel, institutions For a comparison of the results of interviews and of anonymous questionnaires see Appendix Two

7 On the top of the form 'IT IS NOT NECESSARY TO SIGN THIS FORM' was printed in capital letters, nevertheless a considerable number did so.

8. Absolute figures are single women, 607 (12 per cent); single men, 755 (15 per cent); married women without children, 533 (11 per cent), married men without children, 760 (15 per cent), married women with children, 1,044 (21 per cent), married men with children, 1,248 (26 per cent)

9 The following tables show the relationship in percentages between my respondents, who filled in the questionnaire, and the field survey based on figures derived from the census, the registrar-general, etc

REGIONS

	Questionnaire	Field survey
London and South-East	40	41
South-West	9	6
Midlands	17	15
North-West	15	18
North-East and North	18	17

TOWN SIZE

Over 1,000,000 inhabitants	22	22
1,000,000–100,000	27	24
100,000–10,000	29	29
Under 10,000	21	24

FAMILY INCOME

Under £5 a week	10	11
£5–£8 a week	42	36
£8–£12 a week	29	24
£12–£15 a week	10	9
Over £15 a week	7	10
No answer	2	10

CHAPTER TWO

ASSUMPTIONS

**The full questionnaire, as sent out,
will be found on pages 320 to 328**

A QUESTIONNAIRE IS not entirely like the proverbial Spanish inn, for one does get some surprises. information of a kind which was not foreseen; but by and large, the answers from a questionnaire are, quite inevitably, determined by the questions; and the questions in turn are determined by what the researcher assumes to be relevant, whether he has made these assumptions articulate or no. In the case of market research, on the one hand, or censuses on the other, these assumptions are usually quite clear; but in other types of polling or research the implications are not always so obvious. The well-publicized public opinion polls, for example, have the underlying assumption that all opinions—not merely political preferences where the evidence is fairly good—are to a great extent determined by a relatively few physiological and social variables—age, sex, income, place of residence, type of work or social class, and so on.

With an inquiry such as mine, which was attempting to discover factors or motives which underlay a variety of opinions and actions, the assumptions governing the choice of questions become very important; for many of the questions were designed to elicit attitudes as well as ideas or behaviour. Although I knew I didn't know enough to make any confident statements about English characteristics, nevertheless I had certain hunches or expectations of what I would be likely to find out, and what would be significant; without some such framework the answers to a questionnaire would merely be a barrage of irrelevant facts.

I did not (as I ought to have done) write down my assumptions at the same time that I drew up the questionnaire; only in that way could I have safely guarded against being wise after the event, of revising my assumptions in the light of later knowledge. I do have, however, some check on what my thoughts then were in the many letters I wrote to various people connected with the project before any of the results were available; and some twelve months earlier I had written a short article in the last number of *Horizon* 'outlining a few of the problems which I think a dynamic analysis of the English character ought to be able to answer.'[1]

12

To my mind, then—and I may add, still—the central problem for the understanding of the English character is the problem of aggression, to use the technical term, of pugnacity, quarrelsomeness, envy, cruelty, nagging, bad temper, irritableness, to name some of the behaviour in which psychologists see the manifestation of aggression. This may seem superficially a contradiction in terms, for in public life today the English are certainly among the most peaceful, gentle, courteous and orderly populations that the civilized world has ever seen. But, from the psychological point of view, this is still the same problem; the control of aggression, when it has gone to such remarkable lengths that you hardly ever see a fight in a bar (a not uncommon spectacle in most of the rest of Europe or in the U.S.A.), when football crowds are as orderly as church meetings, when all the frustrations and annoyances symbolized by queuing are met with orderliness and good humour modified, at most, by a few grumbles and high words, then this orderliness and gentleness, this absence of overt aggression, calls for an explanation if the dynamics of English character are to be effectively described.

This English gentleness would seem to be a comparatively new phenomenon. I am not a qualified historian, but the evidence from novelists and from contemporary travellers visiting England, seems to me to show beyond question that the English people, perhaps especially the Londoners, of the seventeenth and eighteenth centuries were remarkably pugnacious and violent, callous about the sufferings of others, which indeed they often found a source of hilarious amusement, or of pleasurable excitement, and thoroughly enjoying a good fight. Kastril, the 'angry boy' in *The Alchemist*, would appear to have been a figure of fun because he was so naive and exaggerated, because he wanted to learn how to quarrel instead of being 'naturally' quarrelsome. A proper man was mettlesome, and he showed his mettle by the readiness with which he responded to, or provoked, a fight. Men walked about armed, if not with swords, then with cudgels or life-preservers; one could not, it would appear, walk on foot without being prepared to fight.

No society in the world which I know of had such persistently cruel and violent amusements and diversions as the people of Elizabethan England; the bull-baiting, the bear-baiting, the cock-fighting, the public executions and floggings, the teasing of the insane in Bedlam, as well as the endless duels and battles, the scenes of cruelty, torture and madness which flocked so thick on one another on the English stage. The Grand Guignol has produced nothing more gratuitously savage than some of the scenes in gentle

13

Shakespeare, from *Titus Andronicus* to the blinding of Gloucester in full view of the audience ('Out, vile jelly!') in *King Lear*. Compared with the works of most of his contemporary dramatists, the plays of Shakespeare are 'gentle' in our meaning of the word, as well as in the Elizabethan sense Of the theatre I know of, only the Burmese drama of the second half of the nineteenth century approaches the Elizabethan in its search for horror.[2]

All novels can be read as documents, as well as works of art or entertainment, if they are describing the society in which the author lives. However conventional the characters, however stagy or contrived the plot, the background, the trivial incidents which occupy the paragraphs between scenes or those which set the scenes give a great deal of information about the way people ordered their day-to-day lives, about what the author and his readers think 'normal'. Read in this way, the great novels of the eighteenth century like *Tom Jones* and *Roderick Random* show an enormous amount of incidental aggression—cudgel fights, fist fights and so on—which don't develop the plot or illustrate character so much as describe agreeable everyday events, perhaps somewhat similar to the rôle of meals in the Russian novelists of the nineteenth century. Public life at that period was very violent and dangerous; there were the cut-purses and the gangs of highwaymen led by Jonathan Wild and his kin. When such criminals were caught, their punishment made a public holiday. But it was not merely against criminals that such violence was shown; read the letters of Voltaire, read the memoirs of Casanova. Almost as soon as Casanova arrived in London, he was advised always to carry two purses, one with a few guineas in to hand over to highwaymen, and a fuller one secreted about his person. Among other incidents, he tells of a visit to Drury Lane Theatre when:

> for some reason or other which I forget the play which had been advertised could not be given. The public started protesting The great actor Garrick, who was buried twenty years later in Westminster Abbey, tried to calm the audience but in vain; he was obliged to withdraw. Some angry people shouted *Sauve qui peut*, and then the king and queen and the rest hurriedly left the theatre, an hour later the whole theatre was wrecked except for the walls which withstood the anger of the people who did all this destruction for the sole pleasure of exercising their power. . . . A fortnight later, when the theatre had been repaired, Garrick came before the curtain to beg the public's indulgence. A voice from the pit cried 'On your knees', and this cry was taken up by a thousand voices; and Garrick . . . was forced to kneel and ask the public's pardon in this humiliating position. Then there was loud applause and all was over. This is what the English people are like, especially the

14

Londoners; they revile the king, the queen, the princes when they appear in public, consequently they seldom do so except on ceremonial occasions, when there are hundreds of constables to keep order.[3]

The opening of the nineteenth century saw little change in these violent pastimes and occupations. In 1800 six women were publicly flogged for hedge-pulling till the blood ran down their backs; and the *public* flogging of women was only made illegal in 1817, one year after the pillory was abolished. In the first decades of the century:

> Mondays and Fridays were the great days for bullock-hunting, an inhuman and brutal sport that throve in the neighbourhoods of Hackney and Bethnal Green [in London] with the sanction, if not with the connivance, of the peace officers of those parishes. The procedure of the bullock-hunters was as follows A fee having been paid to a cattle drover, an animal was selected from his herd, peas were put into its ears, sticks pointed with iron were driven into its body, and the poor beast, when mad with rage and pain, was hunted through the streets with a yelling mob of men, women and dogs behind it . . until the exhausted victim could no longer be goaded to any show of resistance or movement. . . .

> On Sundays the favourite resort was a field adjoining Bethnal Green Church, and here some hundreds of men and boys assembled during the hours of divine service to indulge in less exciting games, such as dog-fighting and duck-hunting . . .

> The Receiver of the Metropolitan police wrote to Lord Rosslyn in 1831 'It will hardly be credited that within the last five or seven years . . . people were robbed in open day . . and women, stripped of their clothes, were tied to gates by the roadside; the existing police being set at defiance'

> John Sayer, the Bow Street officer, stated before a Parliamentary Committee that there were streets in Westminster . . . so dangerous that no policeman dare venture there, unless accompanied by five or six of his comrades, for fear of being cut to pieces. . . .

> In 1812 the crime of murder was so common and so much on the increase that a Parliamentary Committee was appointed. . . . Spurious coin and counterfeit notes flooded the country (It had been calculated that at this time there were as many as 50 fraudulent mints in the metropolis alone; between 1805 and 1816 there were more than 200 executions for forgery) [4]

During the course of the nineteenth century this lawless violence, this pleasure in fighting and in witnessing the pain and humiliation of others, and the gratuitous suffering of animals almost completely disappeared. The most spectacular drop in criminal activities took

15

place in the decade 1850–1860;[5] and in 1824 that peculiarly English institution, the Royal Society for the Prevention of Cruelty to Animals, was founded. The consciences of the upper classes of society seem to have been somewhat disturbed by the merciless exploitation of children in the nineteenth century, as is shown by the various Royal Commissions on the employment of children and the like; but there is an interval of over sixty years between the founding of the Royal Society for the Prevention of Cruelty to Animals and the National Society for the Prevention of Cruelty to Children. This latter was founded in 1889; the first local Society for protecting abused children was founded in 1882 at Liverpool, when action was taken to establish a Home for Children instead of a Home for Dogs. At this meeting the local President said. 'I am here for the prevention of cruelty and I can't draw the line at children.'[6]

These societies for the prevention of cruelty are doubly significant in their implications; they show that there are large groups in the population much preoccupied with the horrid thought of cruelty inflicted on the weak and helpless, willing to give their time and their money to remedy this state of affairs, and to harrow their feelings by the vivid literature which describes the misdeeds; but they also imply the existence of another large group, who, from pleasure or callousness, inflict persistent and unnecessary sufferings and deprivations on the weak and helpless. Both the number of subscribers and the number of prosecutions bear out these implications; cruelty and aggression are English preoccupations.[7]

Readiness to fight, and approval of aggressive behaviour, would seem to have lingered longer in the working classes. There is the history of political violence all through the nineteenth century, from the Chartists and Tolpuddle to the great dock strike, but besides this there was the mockery and (on occasion) physical aggression against the more fortunate classes which Dickens symbolised in Trabb's boy. Up to the beginning of this century, probably up to 1914, well-dressed adults risked mockery, well-dressed children and adolescents assault, from the ill-clad. In the appropriate localities fights between 'town' and 'gown' seem to have been common, and by no means always provoked by the gown-wearers. Together with many of my contemporaries I can just remember the jeering of the 'rude boys' which the late George Orwell described so vividly, and the fear, probably not altogether groundless, which women felt at going about unaccompanied on lonely roads, or anywhere at all at night.

What has happened to all this aggression, this violence, combativeness and mockery? In other respects, so far as the novels and memoirs

16

and so on can be taken as evidence, the English people don't seem to have changed their character very much, and I don't think anybody would argue that the characters in Fielding or Smollett, Jane Austen or Dickens, could possibly belong to any other nation; but so far as public life is concerned, there does seem to have been this remarkable change from the Roaring Boys to the Boys' Brigade, from John Bull to John Citizen.

A psychologist dealing with a similar case in an individual would probably suspect that the aggression had changed direction, that instead of being manifested in public life, it was being discharged somewhere else; and this 'somewhere else' has three possible locations. It may be inside the family, behind the drawn window-curtains, where all is smooth outside, all in turmoil within; it may be dissipated in fantasy, in reading about, and dreaming about the misdeeds of others, or concentrated on some rarely seen or unseen scapegoat; or it may be turned inwards on the self, with a great deal of 'self-punishment' manifested in either the reproaches of an overly strict conscience, or in various illnesses or aches and pains which are now called psycho-somatic, and were earlier called functional. It is theoretically possible, of course, that it has just disappeared; but in an individual one would expect a number of other changes—an increase in gaiety and spontaneity, for example—to occur simultaneously with a real diminution of aggression This last does not seem to be the case for the English people as a whole.

Because this problem of aggression seemed to me so basic to an understanding of the English character, I framed a number of questions whose replies gave an opportunity for expressing aggression or attitudes towards it. The chief of these were:[8]

25. What do you most disapprove of about your present neighbours?

80. What do you think of the police?

56. What are the three chief faults wives (husbands) tend to have?

59. If a husband (wife) finds his (her) wife (husband) having an affair with another man (woman), what should he (she) do?

58. What do you think goes to wreck a marriage?

61. Generally speaking, do you consider children need more or less discipline than they get nowadays?

67. How should a really naughty boy be punished?

69. Are there any forms of punishment you don't approve of for boys?

68. How should a really naughty girl be punished?

17

70. Are there any forms of punishment you don't approve of for girls?

66. If you were told that a small child, say, between 3 and 8, had done something really bad, what would you think the child had done?

Of course, the answers to these questions also provide a great deal of information on the ostensible subjects; but I hoped that they would give me some leads as well as to the ways contemporary English people deal with the problems of aggression today.

A second assumption I made about the English character, is that most English people are shy and afraid of strangers, and consequently very lonely. This assumption was developed less from literature than from observation. I had also been much impressed by my visits to the Peckham Health Centre and the reports issued on the work of this pioneer institute.[9] The Peckham Health Centre was established in one of the residential areas of South London as a means of studying the incidence of health, rather than sickness, in the community. The building contained every sort of amenity for all ages and sexes, from nurseries to sitting rooms, from a swimming pool to a theatre, cafeterias and full medical equipment. Membership, which naturally included the enjoyment of all these amenities, was provided for a very small weekly subscription, but was limited to families living in a very restricted area (less than a square mile) around the Centre; the conditions were that only families—not individuals—could join, and each member should have a thorough, and free, medical examination every six months. Despite these numerous and great advantages, never more than half the families eligible for membership were actually members at any one time.

All the members came from the same small neighbourhood, in which many of them had lived for several years. Nevertheless it was altogether exceptional if a new member family, on joining, had any acquaintances or friends in the Centre. Most of them had no friends at all in the neighbourhood, many of them no friends, unconnected by kinship ties, in London. Even without medical treatment, many of the members improved dramatically in physical and psychological health during their membership; the inference was that the finding of congenial companions for sport or hobby, gossip or craft, and the loosening of the constricting bonds of isolated family life were chiefly responsible for this beneficent change.

There was no reason to suppose that Peckham was anomalous as far as the London suburbs were concerned. I partially accepted the stereotype that there might be less loneliness among the poor

18

and in the cities of the North; but I considered that, as far as practicable, it would be useful to discover the extent of loneliness, of sociability, and of community participation among the population. The chief of the questions designed to elicit this information were:

20. Not counting relations or in-laws, do you know most—a few—hardly any—no—neighbours by sight?

21. To speak to?

22. To drop in on without an invitation?

23. To visit for a meal or an evening?

19 Would you say that your best friends live near you (that is, within walking distance) a short distance away (say, a mile or so) or far away? Or some in all three?

26. Are there places outside your own homes or the street where you meet neighbours to have a chat? (*Please mark in the first column if you visit such places at all, and in the second column how often you have been this last month.*) Church or chapel meeting rooms: Men's club; Women's club or Women's Institute· Mixed club; Youth club· Gymnasium. Sports ground: Dance hall: Political club: Public house: Café; other (*please specify*).

24. Do you think you could rely on your neighbours in a pinch? Entirely—to a large extent—to a small extent—not at all—it depends.

33. If you wanted to spend a pleasant evening, what sort of company would you like to spend it in? (*Please mark in the first column the company you'd like best with '1', next best with '2' and so on; and in the second column mark the company which you had last Saturday evening.*) One man· One girl: A foursome (two couples) A group of men: A group of girls: A mixed group: With my own family: Alone: Working: Was ill.

35. Do you think it natural for young people to be shy?

36. Do you think you were exceptionally shy?

37. Are you less shy than you used to be?

38. Do you think shyness a good thing?

75. Do your children play with other children whose parents you don't know? Often. Occasionally: Never.

76. Do you tell your children not to play with some of the neighbours' children?

77. Do you forbid your children to visit some of the neighbours' houses?

If yes, what are your reasons?

I can find very little evidence from literature or other sources to show whether this shyness and fear of strangers has long been

19

a specifically English trait. For Jane Austen, such shyness is a sign of ill-breeding (Sir William Lucas and Maria, for example), but so was its opposite, 'ease' (perhaps Mrs. Elton's most damning characteristic); and for Dickens shyness was a sign of near-imbecility (Toots and Georgina Podsnap are striking examples), but there can be few people temperamentally less fitted to understand this emotion than Dickens was. On the continent in the eighteenth and nineteenth century the English milord had a great reputation for reserve, for *phlegme*; and this reserve is mirrored in a number of the characters whom Jane Austen asks us to admire, and quite a number of the aristocrats (Sir Leicester Dedlock, for example) whom Dickens asks us not to admire, at least not without many reservations. But this is usually portrayed as an aristocratic, an upper class, type of behaviour; and I wanted to know about the whole population.

One of the problems which bedevils the discussion of the English character—I suppose this should rightly be called another assumption—is that it is almost impossible to write three pages without mentioning Class; and Class today is almost a rude word, except for the militant working class, and we are all, myself included, excessively mealy-mouthed and embarrassed by the subject. We feel it to be an indelicacy to point out that there are differences between the classes; lip-service to democracy apparently entails not merely the admission that one man is as good as another (which is, in certain meanings of the word, undeniable) but reticence on the ways in which one group is different from another group within the population. But this reticence in a book about English character or English society is as ludicrous as the reticence about the organs of reproduction which can be found in some of the nineteenth century text-books of anatomy and physiology.

I was so convinced of the importance of social class that I had every question in the questionnaire analysed by these criteria. I also wanted to establish the pattern of English class structure, rather than impose one and asked:

> 7. If you were asked what class you belonged to, how would you describe yourself?

The answers are analysed in detail in a subsequent chapter;[10] but it may be said here that the vast majority of my respondents place themselves in one of six classes. Most of them call themselves simply 'middle class' or 'working class'; but some make finer distinctions and call themselves 'upper middle' or 'lower middle', 'upper working class' or 'lower working class'. None of my respondents called themselves 'upper class' with or without modification; so I have no evidence from this source to show whether the upper class is divided into one, two (as I suspect) or three sub-groups.

This is really a parenthesis. We were discussing the loneliness of the English, especially the loneliness of the urban lower middle class —there, it's out!—and working class as illustrated by the Peckham experiment. Is this a general urban phenomenon, a concomitant to life in big cities, wherever these cities may happen to be, London or Chicago, Birmingham or Berlin, Manchester or Calcutta, Shanghai or Liverpool?[11] Or is there something specifically English about it? I know of no evidence which could decide this problem conclusively; but my impression is that, though life in big cities everywhere has a tendency to isolate and, as it were, atomize the inhabitants, this process has been carried further, and for more people, in England than in any other country with which I am familiar. To the universal conditions of urban life the English brought the shyness which I assumed to be a widely spread characteristic.

Psychologically, shyness is a type of anxiety which is more or less, but never wholly, rational. With most people probably the fears, the anxieties, are not wholly articulate and may not be wholly conscious. It would seem that in most people these fears have several components. Probably the most generally recognized is the fear that strangers will reject one or treat one with contempt, because one is not sufficiently attractive or entertaining, well-educated or well-spoken, lacks the approved manners or the approved skills. When one fears one will be, or in fact has been, treated in this manner, the strangers are described as 'snobbish', 'swanky', 'pretentious', 'stand-offish', and so on. Another component of this fear is that strangers will corrupt or contaminate one, either by undermining one's moral principles and leading oneself or one's family into disapproved-of indulgences, extravagances or other bad habits, or by undermining one's social position and the esteem which one presently enjoys through association with people 'who don't know how to behave', who are 'no class', 'not p.l.u.'

Expressed in another way, both these fears can be described as fear that strangers will be aggressive, either fairly directly through rudeness and lack of kindness, or, more symbolically through attacking one's moral or social position. Shyness thus links up, at least in theory, with my first assumption of the importance of aggression; we impute aggressive intentions or potentialities to strangers and then avoid them by shyness, by 'keeping oneself to oneself', by 'being backward in coming forward'. But this is only half the picture;

21

we are ourselves strangers to the people who are strangers to us; other people impute to us the aggressiveness we impute to them. Is the charge as true about *us* as about them?

Most of us, I imagine, would indignantly deny the suggestion; we may not be particularly 'forth-coming'; but we certainly have no wish to hurt people, either directly or indirectly. On a conscious level this is probably true; on an unconscious level it may well be a different matter. From a theoretical point of view, the projection of bad intentions on to others nearly always implies the unconscious wish to act in the same way on the part of the projector; it is not the sinners who discover sin in the most unlikely places. If, on an unconscious level, most of us harbour the wish to humiliate or corrupt others, as we suspect others of wishing to humiliate or corrupt us, then that gives one more motive for our shyness and withdrawal. For we certainly don't consciously approve of these wishes; by 'keeping ourselves to ourselves' we avoid the occasion for temptation, we defend our strong moral principles from the sabotage which would result if our unconscious wishes were given free rein.

These strong moral principles are a third (or fourth) assumption I made about the English character. Nearly every foreign observer notes, either with approval or disapproval, that the English do not easily give way to their impulses; they are described as 'law-abiding' or 'restrained', as 'puritanical' or 'cold', 'sheepish' or 'disciplined'. I don't think there is much question that this stereotype contains some truth; the English as a whole do have high ideals of conduct both for themselves and for others, whether they are dealing with legal rights or duties or what is somewhat narrowly called 'morals', which means roughly all sexual activities outside marriage.

The ideals are almost certainly there; but what about the practices? I somewhat suspected that the multiplication of laws and controls under wartime and post-war rationing had weakened the general observation of the law; and, possibly, the strains of war and general military service had loosened the stringent sexual morality which had, reputedly, characterized the English of recent generations.

I had a considerable number of questions which would reveal ideals of conduct; but fewer from which I could hope to get a picture of actual practice. On respect for the law, the most important question asked for views about 'fiddling', the euphemism which has been very widely given to circumventions of the rationing and control systems. People were asked to choose among 9 statements on the subject, 3 of which were admissions, 1 an outright denial, 3 more conventional moralizations on the subject, and 2 'projections',

22

putting law-breaking on to outsiders, and implicitly rejecting it for one's own group. If people agreed with more than one statement, they were asked to give them a rank order; and this order should show whether people were consistent in their views or no. The question read:

81. There's a lot of talk about 'fiddling' nowadays. *Please mark which of the following statements most nearly represents your own opinion. If more than one do, please mark the most important '1', the next most important '2'—and so on*

Nearly everybody fiddles nowadays.
Most people fiddle occasionally, but not many do regularly
With all the rules and regulations, one can't help having to break a rule sometimes.
It is unpatriotic to fiddle
None of my family has ever got anything 'off the ration'.
It is wrong to break the law under any circumstances
Most fiddling is done by profiteers.
It is unfair to try to get more than others.
Most fiddling is done by foreigners.

Similar instructions were given for a group of sentences giving conventional explanations for the publicized increase in juvenile delinquency This question was devised chiefly to find out views on 'character formation', on what was thought to be the most important source of high moral principles; but it also throws some light on the way people think their own character was formed.

79. One reads a lot in the papers about the post-war increase in crime, especially among young people. *Please mark which of the following reasons seems to you most important. . . .*

People got into bad ways in the Forces.
Children whose fathers were in the Forces didn't have proper discipline.
Children who were evacuated weren't properly looked after.
Modern parents aren't strict enough.
Modern schools aren't strict enough
Young people follow the bad example of crime films and crime stories in books and on the radio.
Young people are neglecting religion.

These questions have the scientific advantage of being easily transferable to statistical tables; but I expected to get most insight from a very simple question indeed:

80. What do you think of the police?

I expected that views on sexual morality and sexual behaviour

23

would be more difficult to elicit. I devised one question to try to discover whether the belief in the decline of morals was generally held.

40. *Please mark in the first column the statement you most* AGREE *with and in the second column the statement you most* DISAGREE *with. (Only* ONE *statement for agree and* ONE *for disagree)*

There is much more immorality than there used to be
Human nature hasn't changed, but people are not so narrow-minded as they used to be.
It is right and natural for young people to want to make love.
It's other people's nasty minds which make all the mischief.
People are really more moral today than they were thirty years ago.

The following questions were also expected to elicit views on sexual morality, and to reflect, at least to a certain degree, individual practice.

49. Do you think a young man should have some sexual experience before he gets married? Yes: No. Don't know.

51. Why?

50. Do you think a young woman should have some sexual experience before she gets married? Yes: No: Don't know.

52. Why?

59. If a husband (wife) finds his (her) wife (husband) having an affair with another woman (man) what should he (she) do?

Two questions specifically asked about actual sexual behaviour:

47. Not counting marriage, have you ever had a real love affair?

45. Before you became engaged to your wife (husband) did you ever seriously consider marrying another woman (man)?

I had always accepted, more or less as a stereotype, the statement so neatly made by Somerset Maugham, and set out at such length by many other writers: 'The English are not a sexual nation and you cannot easily persuade them that a man will sacrifice anything important for love.'[12] This belief was on a rather different level to the assumptions I have discussed hitherto, for it was more about behaviour than about motives; though, if it were true, psychological hypotheses would have to be devised to account for it. First of all, I wanted the facts; and I had a number of questions which I hoped would throw some light on this question. The most direct was:

48. In marriage do you think sexual love is very important? Fairly important? Not very important? Not important at all?

24

In the Somerset village where I had lived for many years I had been struck with the suspicion—jealousy is perhaps too strong a word—with which the news of any tête-à-tête between two people of opposite sex, almost irrespective of age or condition, was nearly invariably greeted. If a male and female were known to have been alone, it could only be for one reason. In *Home and Beauty* Somerset Maugham treats such suspicion as judicial; the solicitor grumbles 'Why, the other day I came across [a judge] who wouldn't believe the worst had happened when a man and a woman, not related in any way, mind you, were proved to have been alone in a room together for three-quarters of an hour.' In my village there would have been no doubt at all, at least as far as the gossip value went: but I had no means of knowing whether this attitude was widespread.

Despite the watchful eyes of the neighbours, girls and young men did get together, mostly in the fields in the summer evenings; but the process of courtship and engagement seemed a slow one, often lasting years. To try to discover if this pattern were general I asked my married respondents:

46. How long had you known your wife (husband) before you were engaged?
How long was your engagement?

And I asked all respondents:

44. Do you think English people fall in love in the way you see Americans doing it on the films?

The pattern which I had in mind, and which I think most American films illustrate, is immediate attraction at first sight, courting behaviour at the first opportunity, ardour and impatience, at least on the part of the man, culminating fairly rapidly in a marriage founded on mutual attraction.

I thought it at least possible that English attitudes were very different, that love or attraction were less valued and other qualities more valued. So I asked:

42. Would you say you had ever been really in love?

43. Do you expect to fall really in love sometime?

39. How old were you when you first started being really interested in girls (boys)?

55. What do you think are the three most important qualities a wife (husband) should have?

56. What are the three chief faults that wives (husbands) tend to have?

25

I also expected to get relevant information from the questions I asked all my married respondents:

58. What do you think goes to wreck a marriage?

57. What do you think goes to make for a happy marriage?

My final inquiry on this aspect of English life was an attempt to discover the attitudes held by men and women on woman's sexual nature. Did they consider, as I believe the Americans and the French do to a considerable extent, that women have sexual feelings of the same urgency and nature as men? Or was the attitude promulgated by the Victorian novelists, that 'good' women were more 'spiritual' than men and, though they might respond to their husband, would feel no spontaneous urges or desires of a sexual nature, one which was still held by a sizable portion of the English population? I devised a question which would have given a quite unambiguous answer on the physiological level; but the editors thought that it might cause unnecessary offence. Although I doubted this myself, I was willing to yield to their greater experience; and so to my regret the question was taken out of the first draft.[13] It is only information on this level of concreteness which would permit the drawing of unambiguous conclusions; but I had to make do with such information as I could get on more generalized attitudes from the question:

53. *Please mark in the first column the statement you most* AGREE *with, and in the second column the statement you most* DISAGREE *with. (Only* ONE *statement for agree and* ONE *for disagree.)*

Most women don't care much about the physical side of sex.
Women don't have such an animal nature as men.
Women really enjoy the physical side of sex just as much as men.
Women tend to enjoy sex more than men.

With one important exception, the hypotheses outlined above represent the more important of the assumptions of which I am conscious which determined my choice of questions. There were a number of questions which were designed simply to elicit information which I thought might be interesting without thinking that psychological deductions could be inferred from the answers. I was interested in what sort of houses people lived in; how long they had lived in them; whether their parents lived with or near them; whether they lived near their own blood-relations or relations in-law. A second batch of questions was designed to discover the importance of wartime experience and comradeship in civilian life. People who

26

had been members of the forces were asked how many friends from the forces they had seen or written to in the past year, and so on. I asked a number of questions about belief in the occult or supernatural: whether people had mascots or lucky or unlucky days or numbers; if they could tell fortunes, and if so how; if they visited fortune tellers, and, if so, how often; whether they read horoscopes, and, if so, whether they believed them and followed the advice given; whether they believed in ghosts and, if so, whether they had themselves seen or heard a ghost, or knew a person who they believed had such an experience? These questions were intended as a pendant to the questions on religious beliefs and practices. I knew, from numerous reports, that a relatively small proportion of the population were constant church-goers, whereas every popular paper carries a 'horoscope' feature; and it seemed at least plausible that belief in revealed religion had given way to belief in magic or occult practices.

The one further assumption which was important in deciding what questions to include, was not specifically concerned with the English character. It is an assumption which lies at the base of the belief that character can be studied and analysed. Put very briefly, it can be called the historical concept of character formation. Except for identical twins, every infant is born with its unique constitution and genetically determined potentialities; but the way in which, and the extent to which, these potentialities are realized depends on what happens to the infant after birth, the order in which these experiences occur, and the customs and values of the society in which it is reared.

A simple example is speech. Only a tiny minority of human babies is born without the physical basis which will make the acquisition of speech possible; there is also another small unfortunate group born with physical defects, a cleft palate or disproportionately shaped tongue, which render impossible the production of some sounds. These defectives apart, all human beings are born with the potentialities of making any or all the sounds which occur in all human languages the world over. But in nearly all cases by the time a child has learned to speak it only makes the sounds used in its native language, the sounds made by its guardians and parents and people who have brought it up.[14] In large societies this range may well be more limited than that for the country as a whole; the child will acquire the sounds typical of its class or region.

As time goes on, the potential ability to reproduce unaccustomed sounds steadily decreases. Up to the age of about six or seven a

27

child can pick up a foreign language or dialect without conscious strain or falsification of the sounds; but with each year even this potentiality diminishes; and it is a very exceptional adolescent or adult who can learn to speak a foreign language without a trace of his or her native accent. As far as is known, this is in no way determined by heredity or physiology; it is the experiences the child has after birth which first determine the sounds which it will learn to make; and then subsequently makes it progressively harder to modify or change the original pattern.

Languages do not consist merely of sounds, of words. Each language has its own special syntax, its grammar, the rules by which words are organized into meaningful and relatively unambiguous sentences. Syntax is one of the most complex of human inventions, so complex that even today there are only about three languages for which a really adequate grammar, covering all the practices, has been prepared. Even learning the syntax of a closely related language, as for example French or German for an English speaker, is an arduous task, demanding considerable time and effort.

Nevertheless, every child learns the syntax of its native language without much conscious effort on its part, or much detailed instruction on the part of its elders. Minor faults may be arbitrarily corrected —'that's not the right word', 'you shouldn't say that'—but the underlying principles are seldom expressed or contravened. All French children learn to use gender, and no English child does; no English child uses the sentence order which seems so inevitable to all German children, and vice versa. People find the syntax of their native language 'natural', however complicated it may be for foreign speakers; and they learn it, with the numerous rules and exceptions, without being fully conscious of what they have learned. Complex habits concerning the arrangement and modification of words have been acquired without either teacher or child being articulate about what has been taught. And, in its more important outlines, this syntax will be identical for all members of the society which uses the language; slight variations may mark differences of class or region; but these are insignificant compared with the large body of rules which are universally accepted, and which do not recur in their entirety in any other language. Probably no item is unique; but the combination of items and the way they are patterned are unique for every human language.

This is more than an analogy with the formation of national character; it is an aspect of national character. The syntax by itself structures the world for its speakers. Ideas of time and sequence are

28

largely determined by verbal forms; languages which possess gender group objects together in a way which would not occur to speakers of gender-less languages. The thoughts we can have about the world are to a very great degree determined by the words our language possesses to express them.

In the same way and at the same time as the vast majority of human children are acquiring the vocabulary, syntax, and intonations of the language which will make them members of the society into which they were born and will enable them to communicate freely with other people who have acquired the same native language, they are acquiring the characteristics and motives, the values and the beliefs which will make them recognizable members of their respective societies. Nobody can tell whether a naked new-born baby is English or American, French or Danish, Russian or German; by the time that baby is six years old he or she is a recognizable national of a specific society, even without the identification of speech. Of course, the child is also an individual with its unique character and appearance; but this does not contradict the fact that he has also acquired the character of a member of his society. In the same way, the fact that we can nearly always recognize the voices of our friends, so that we immediately know who is speaking, does not contradict the fact that they all speak the same language with the same sounds and the same syntax. National character is a close analogue to language; the syntax, the sounds, the total vocabulary are common to all; intonation, choice of words, phrasing of sentences, style of speaking or writing vary to a certain extent with each person. National character is an attempt to isolate and identify the psychological equivalents of syntax and sounds, the shared motives and values and predispositions; it has as little to say about individual characters and idiosyncracies as a study of grammar has to say about individual styles of speaking or writing.

If the observation is true that the main lines of national character are acquired early in life—say, roughly, the first six years—then it is obviously valuable to know as precisely as possible what happens to infants and young children in any given society during those formative years. This knowledge is not essential; if you know enough about the adults your description can be adequate without delving into the experiences of childhood; and the knowledge of childhood experiences in isolation will never tell you how adults do develop, it will at most suggest ways in which they *can* develop. But if your knowledge of the adults is only partial, then information about the early experiences of life can be of the greatest assistance. If you can say 'Children with these sorts of experiences (among others) turn into adults with these sorts of characteristics (among others)', you can then develop hypotheses, in the light of psychological theory, which can link these two bodies of data and which may well suggest new possibilities which had before been overlooked.

Although people, and peoples, change they do not seem to do so very rapidly. Probably Adam and Eve were the first people to complain about the younger generation; and Cain and Abel the first to decide that they weren't going to make the same mistakes as, or grow up into the same sort of people as, the older generation. But societies are, relatively speaking, remarkably stable; people grow old and die, and a new generation takes their place without violent shocks; the institutions of the society, the society itself, maintain their character though the personnel changes; new inventions arise, material conditions alter, there are even occasional political revolutions; but these new inventions, or conditions, or political innovations are manned by people whose characters are already formed; and it seems as though more often people adapt the new conditions to their existing characters, rather then remould their characters to the new conditions. It is possible to write history, to trace the development of a society over generations; but would this be possible if there were not continuity between the generations, if the sons did not replace their fathers and the daughters their mothers, if character and institutions, not merely geography and natural resources, were not relatively constant?

Because of my assumption that information on the way children are reared is valuable in all studies of national character, I asked in all 23 questions of all the parents who answered my questionnaire. This is few enough for so complex a subject; and I had to choose with great care the areas where I thought indicative answers could be obtained. Many things which I should like to have known can better be discovered by observation than by questioning; on some subjects, such as infant feeding, there was luckily good and recent information which I would not need to duplicate.

With my initial assumption of the importance of the problem of aggression, I concentrated largely on questions of training and discipline, of naughtiness and punishment. The other major subjects which I tried to cover were religious education and some of the means by which, I thought, social classes might be differentiated.

I asked the very wide question:

61. Generally speaking, do you consider children need more or less discipline than they get nowadays? More: Less: The same.

30

This question had been asked in a survey conducted by Odhams Press Research Branch earlier in 1949, so that I would have a check on my results. I also asked the very concrete questions:

63. When should a young child start being trained to be clean?

62. Which is worse for the child, starting training too early? or too late? or doesn't it make much difference?

Cleanliness training is the earliest discipline which children have to undergo. Insufficient feeding, or feeding at times which do not correspond to the child's natural physiological rhythms of hunger, may provide earlier deprivations and feelings of anxiety or insecurity, but there is practically nothing the child can do about this; but cleanliness training depends on the child's disciplined control of its muscles, up to the limit of its powers; the demands made on, and the expectations held for, the child in this context could be expected to give a clear picture of the parents' attitudes to such subjects, and would cover an important part of the child's social learning in the earlier months or years of its life. Psycho-analysts have elaborated at great length the probable sequelulae of early or late training.[15]

On the subjects of discipline and punishment I asked, besides the questions already quoted[16] on the ways naughty boys or naughty girls should be punished, and what forms of punishment were not approved of for boys and girls:

64. Who is the proper person to punish a child who has done something really bad? Mother: Father: Teacher: Other (*please specify*).

65. Why?

Knowledge of who holds the disciplinary rôle in childhood gives important clues to the attitudes towards authority, and the types of authority figure which will be expected and respected in later life. I also suspected that there might be consistent differences in class or region concerning the rôle of the parents in the family. Finally I asked:

66. If you were told that a small child, say between 3 and 8, had done something really bad, what would you think the child had done?

This was, purposely, a vague question; I thought that by their answers parents might indicate the greatest fear they had for their own children, and possibly indirectly the greatest fear they had of their own impulses. I expected that there would be a certain amount of reminiscence or anecdote, which would of course be useful; but

31

I hoped to get some picture of what parents thought children would develop into if they were not disciplined.

I was interested in reward as well as punishment. I wanted to know if children were encouraged to act properly as well as punished for acting improperly; so I asked:

71. Should children be praised in front of others if they are good and helpful? Yes: No: Don't know.

72. Do you give your children regular pocket-money when they start going to school? Yes: No.

73. Do you give your children money or other rewards when they are useful and helpful? Always Sometimes: Occasionally: Never.

74. Would you let your children take money for doing jobs for neighbours such as running errands, watching babies, or helping them? Yes: No: Don't know.

These last questions about money had more implications besides the question of direct rewards. I wondered to what extent parents encouraged their children to early independence; and, taking the American practice as a model, it seemed as though allowing or encouraging children to earn money, whether inside or outside the home, as opposed to giving them 'unearned' pocket-money, might give a suggestive indication. Furthermore I suspected, chiefly on the basis of my own upbringing and that of my contemporaries, that there would be a major class difference between those who allowed their children to accept money 'from strangers' and those who did not.

I further thought that one of the major emphases of the upbringing of middle class children was the prevention of their associating with children of a lower class. Consequently I asked:

75. Do your children play with other children whose parents you don't know? Often: Occasionally: Never.

76. Do you tell your children not to play with some of the neighbours' children? Yes: No

77. Do you forbid your children to visit some of the neighbours' houses? Yes: No.

78. *If Yes*, what are your reasons?

Such then are the major assumptions which I held when I drew up the questionnaire. Subsequent chapters will show what I actually discovered.

NOTES TO CHAPTER TWO

1. Geoffrey Gorer 'Some Notes on the British Character,' *Horizon*, Vol XX, Nos 120–121, December 1949–January 1950.

2. Maung Htin Aung· *Burmese Drama* (London, 1937)

3. *Mémoires de Casanova* (Paris, Garnier Frères, n d. Vol. VI, p 350).

4 Quoted from Captain W. L. Melville Lee· *A History of Police in England* (Methuen, London, 1901), especially pp 196–222. This is a very well-documented history of crime and its control in England from Saxon times up to the end of the nineteenth century.

5 Lee, op. cit, p 337 See Chapter XV, p. 294, and Appendix One It is instructive to contrast the number of comic descriptions of physical mishaps, fights, etc, and the attitude to the law, in the earlier, and in the later novels of Dickens on the one hand, *Pickwick Papers*, *Nicholas Nickleby*, or *Oliver Twist*; on the other, *Bleak House* or *David Copperfield*

6 I am indebted to the Secretaries of the R.S.P.C.A. and the N S P C C. for the information above In the year ending February 1952, 101,767 children came to the notice of the National Society for the Prevention of Cruelty to Children, and 99,780 in the following year

7. This paragraph should not be interpreted to mean that the English are unique in either the practice or prevention of cruelty to children and animals. No single trait is unique I do not know whether investigations would show that, in proportion to population, there were a greater number of prosecutions for these offences than in other countries, though I suspect that, outside the mainly Protestant countries of Western Europe and North America, cruelty to, or neglect of, children is much less common, and cruelty to, or neglect of, animals much more common It is not the incidence of cruelty, but the preoccupation with it, to which I wish to call attention

8 The numbers are those provided for the tables and not those printed on the questions in the questionnaire form

9. Pearse and Williamson: *The Case for Action* (London, 1931). *Staff Report, Pioneer Health Centre* (London, 1938) Pearse and Crocker. *The Peckham Experiment* (London, 1943).

10. See Chapter Three.

11 See David Riesman *The Lonely Crowd* (Yale University Press, 1950).

12. W. Somerset Maugham: *Collected Plays*, Vol. III, Preface (London, 1932).

13. The question read: *Which of these statements do you agree with?* Women don't have the same type of sexual climax as men: Women have a climax very much like men do: Don't know

14 If a child has a nurse who speaks to it in a different language to its parents, or if, as was general with the Czarist Russian aristocracy, governesses or tutors speaking several different languages are in charge of the child, it will learn the sounds of the languages of all the people it is in contact with. These polyglot potentialities are developed in relatively few cases

15. See Otto Fenichel: *The Psychoanalytic Theory of Neurosis* (W. W. Norton, New York, 1945), and its exhaustive bibliography and references.

16 See p. 17.

CHAPTER THREE

PEOPLE AND HOMES

THE *average* English man or woman calls him or herself 'working class', finished full time schooling at 14 or under, is married, had (in January 1951) a family income around £8 a week, and lived in a terraced or semi-detached house, which had been his or her home for more than four but less than ten years in a town with more than 100,000 inhabitants. This is the average, the man in the street, something like half the population, the range, of course, is considerable.

Nine out of ten English people feel no hesitation in assigning themselves to a social class. Five of them call themselves working class and three middle class; of the remainder, two in a hundred call themselves upper middle class, seven lower middle class, three upper working class and one lower working class; one in a hundred says he or she does not believe in class; and a twelfth of the population either misunderstands the question, or says it doesn't know.[1]

The answers to the question about social class are not given frivolously; the added comments show that many people have thought seriously about the matter. Whether they have thought realistically, whether a person's own social placing would be the same as that given objectively by an analytical observer is another matter which will be discussed subsequently; but there is no question that class-membership is a most important facet of an Englishman's view of himself as a member of society; and the class to which he assigns himself is nation-wide, and not local or provincial as it is in some other societies.

Class is not directly correlated with income, certainly not with current income; this is a point which many people make. Thus, a prosperous married man from Colville says of himself: 'Though in the higher wages class—definitely working class'; and a well-off married woman of 38 from Leytonstone in Essex: 'I was born in the slums of London of working class parents and although I have attained a higher standard of living I still maintain I am working class.' By contrast, a 49 year old married man from Swindon writes: 'Middle class, trying to keep up home and appearance on inadequate wages'; and a young married woman from Yorkshire: 'Middle class farming stock reduced to living in a lower class industrial area.'

As the last quotation shows, the status of one's parents is of some importance for calculating one's own class position, particularly

34

perhaps for women. A fairly prosperous married woman from
Kentish Town says of herself: 'Through no fault of mine, I was born
of poor parents, hence, Working Class.' A well-off and well-educated
London woman described herself as. 'Upper middle; distinguishable
only from the upper class only by not having an old family and not
working land.'

The people who reject or 'don't believe in' class, mention both
birth and money as false criteria for measuring a person's worth.
A married woman from West Ham says of herself: 'Of no class for
there should be none. We should take a man for his worth and not
by birth accidents'; another from Darlington replies 'Wouldn't
know, as I do not think the *amount* you earn has anything to do
with it.'

Education is a major criterion for social status; but in many cases
it may well be a validation of the parent's class, as much as the
establishment of the children's. Relatively very few of those claiming some sort of working class status continued their full education
after the age of 16; and most of those who did call themselves
'upper working class.' The converse however does not hold; quite
a number of the claimants of middle class status left school at 14.[2]
Specialized education for a recognized profession would seem to
qualify without question for middle class status: thus, a 19-year-old
student from Mossley, Lancs, says: 'As I am studying to become
an Architect I should say Middle Class or mid-way between working
class and middle class.' The subtler derivatives of education, such
as accent or manners, would seem to be more important in this
regard than academic instruction; a young married woman from
St Albans describes herself as. 'Just ordinary working class; I can
look frightfully "bung-ho!" but must keep my mouth closed or else.'

Social class in England would appear therefore to have a number
of determinants. education, including manners and accent, position
of parents, income and occupation; these do not normally coincide
in a one-to-one relationship, with the exception of some occupations.
A professional skill puts its possessor nearly automatically in the
middle class, an occupation based on physical prowess or strength
places the worker in the working class. But a number of occupations
are quite ambiguous. For example, quite a few of my respondents
identified themselves as policemen or special constables, and as the
children, wives or kinsfolk of policemen. Out of 22 policemen or
women 9 described themselves as working class; 5 as middle class;
1 as upper middle class (he left school at 18); 2 as lower middle
class; 4 gave incongruous answers; and one did not answer the

question. Of the men who had served as special constables seven called themselves middle class and two working class; both military policemen called themselves working class. Twenty-two respondents were the wives or children of policemen; 10 of these called themselves middle class, 4 lower middle class, 1 upper working class, and 7 working class. Six respondents had a brother or son in the police; five called themselves working class, and one lower middle class. Finally 9 people identified slightly more distant relatives—uncles, nephews, brothers-in-law—as members of the police force; of these 4 called themselves working class, 3 middle class, 1 does not believe in class, and 1 did not answer the question. The identification of social class with occupation, which has been attempted by a number of English sociologists[3] would seem to ignore many of the complications inherent in the subject.

It was only by chance that I learned the occupation of my respondents or of their parents, for I had not asked for this information. I did however ask for their family income, and the number of years they had spent in full time education; and these answers show that though there is a marked tendency for higher class to be accompanied by higher income and more years of schooling, there are numerous exceptions. Forty-two per cent of those calling themselves upper middle class had family incomes of over £12 a week, a range reached by 25 per cent of the middle class, and 12 per cent of the working class; but 22 per cent of the upper middle class had family incomes of under £8 a week. Forty-three per cent of those calling themselves middle class had incomes falling in that range, 59 per cent of the working class and 76 per cent of the lower working class. With years of education the picture is similar but rather more marked. Twenty-eight per cent of those calling themselves upper middle class continued their education to the age of eighteen and beyond, as compared with 11 per cent calling themselves middle, 13 per cent lower middle, 6 per cent upper working, and 2 per cent working class. On the other hand, no less than 27 per cent of those calling themselves upper middle class left school at 14 or younger; 46 per cent of the middle class, 38 per cent of the lower middle, 54 per cent of the upper working class, 76 per cent of the working class, and 84 per cent of the lower working class had this minimum education

All these figures on class membership are on how people rate themselves, not, as in the various American surveys,[4] on how they are rated by their neighbours. Such information was unobtainable by this kind of survey. The only check on the validity of such self-rating is the somewhat impressionistic one of internal consistency.

The full questionnaire contains numerous clues, from spelling and hand-writing and vocabulary, to the expression of values and sentiments; I think it would be relatively seldom that English readers would be in doubt of the class of the respondents if they read a questionnaire with care, though they might not be fully articulate about the grounds on which they based their conclusion.

My impression, based on reading all the questionnaires, and that of some colleagues and friends who have read selected samples, is that the overwhelming bulk of the English people assign themselves to the same place in the class structure as their neighbours or an analyst would give them. There are however two exceptions to this generalization, neither of them bulking very large.

The first of these would seem to be a post-1945 phenomenon. Young people of high family income and prolonged education describe themselves as working class. 'I work for my living, so I am working class' is the typical phrasing: 'I do not believe that sections of the community fall into classes, but as a working member of society I presume that I belong to the working class' writes a 26-year-old Streatham woman, with a high family income and some secondary school education. It would seem as though this is a reflection of the egalitarian ethos of the Labour party (many of my better educated respondents were unwittingly recruited by the *New Statesman and Nation*[5]), which divides the population into good workers and naughty bourgeois (or idle rich); and perhaps describing oneself as working class may be a magical apotropaic device which would turn away the envy of the less favoured. This is a small group; and the device was not, as far as I noticed, adopted by anybody over 30.

Numerically more important, and somewhat more puzzling, are the poor women, mostly over 45, and unmarried or widowed, with a minimum of education, who call themselves 'middle class'. Many of these, going by internal evidence, would not objectively merit the ascription; and the reasons why they so describe themselves demand some investigation.

It would seem that, in England, women at home take their class position from their parents, and, after marriage, from their husbands: a married woman from a small town near Southampton describes herself as 'Low class by up-bringing (since marriage should say middle class)'; and a 20-year-old girl from Studley in Warwickshire, with some university education writes 'Middle class, i.e. I come from a decent family and have had a good (average) education. I have never worked in a factory not that I should mind doing so I am not snobbish.'

37

If a woman's social class depends on that of the man who is the head of the household, then what is the status of the spinster living alone or of the widow? It would seem to be indeterminate, and it is precisely from these groups that most of our claimants to middle class status derive. The figures are quite striking; whereas only 24 per cent of the married claim middle class status, 33 per cent of the single and 35 per cent of the widowed do so.[6] It seems possible that these solitary women are not very fully integrated into the larger society, and therefore rate themselves in relation to their immediate circle, rather than to the nation-wide hierarchy. This would have some resemblance to the American pattern, where at least three-quarters of the population call themselves middle class, because some are better, some worse off than they are.

The social position of women in England is puzzling in many respects. Far more women than men claim middle class status: 33 per cent of the women, compared with 21 per cent of the men in the main sample, 40 per cent of the women compared with 30 per cent of the men in the field survey.[7] But, at least in the main sample, women have consistently more secondary and university education than men; 31 per cent of the men and 40 per cent of the women have had some education beyond the minimum age of 14; and in each year, up to university level, women exceed men by at least 2 per cent. I have not got the figures which would show unambiguously[8] whether this illustrates an English pattern, or merely that it was the more educated women who answered my questionnaire; but it seems at least possible that about one woman in ten receives some vocational training in school for such jobs as secretaries, while their brothers are serving an apprenticeship in the works; and that, during this training, and in their subsequent pre-marriage employment in offices, they acquire an, as it were, professional middle class status which they may not always relinquish at marriage, even though their husbands call themselves working class, and which they cling to in spinsterhood and widowhood. The figures are quite unambiguous, even if the written questionnaire appealed to the more literate women, this would not have operated in the verbal interviews of the field survey.

A second variation in claims to higher social status which, though not quite so pronounced, is consistent, are the differences in the regions. The South-West region has much the highest proportion of those claiming middle class status, and the North-East and North much the lowest; there is a difference of 10 per cent in both the main sample and the field survey The other regions are between

38

these two poles, London and the South-East and the Midlands being nearer the South-West pattern, the North-West approaching that of the North-East and North. In reverse the same patterns are found for claims to working class status. It seems at least possible that this is a straight reflection of the differing social composition of the country; that there are fewer people of middle class status in the industrial northern regions, and more in the residential and relatively rural southern regions. It is worth noting that the same variation does not occur for town size; there are a few more middle class people in the big metropolises, with over a million inhabitants, and somewhat fewer in the large towns with between a million and a hundred thousand inhabitants; but the difference is only a matter of 3 per cent.

The middle class then, in our sample, contains more women than men, and proportionately more people from the South and centre of the country than from the North; the working class is more heavily masculine, and has a relatively large number of northcountrymen. These two classes make up more than three-quarters of the population; but though the remaining classes are small, relatively speaking, they are significant; and their composition merits a little attention.

At 2 per cent for both sexes the upper middle class is probably slightly under-represented for the country as a whole; but it is less in numbers than in composition that it fails adequately to represent the professional, higher administrative and land-owning portions of the English population. The respondents who place themselves in this category are overwhelmingly students or young people; there are very few of them over 35, only 1 per cent in each age group. Judging by the standards of family income and years of education it seems likely that nearly all of those who placed themselves in this group would be so placed objectively; but the fact that they are so young and that so few of them are parents (28 per cent, as contrasted with 39 per cent for the middle and 52 per cent for the working class) means that the governing, managerial and officer class—the group which so often thinks and writes of itself as 'representative' and which, by most foreign observers, is treated as 'typical'—is inadequately represented in this study. Without casting any aspersions on the thousands of my collaborators, one can say that this book is not to any appreciable extent about Ladies and Gentlemen.

Few of the people who called themselves upper middle class added any comments or explanations to this ascription.

The other group which is certainly under-represented, with 1 per cent of each sex, is the lower working class. Whereas probably the

39

major reason for the under-representation of the upper middle and upper classes is that relatively few of them read the *People*, I would guess that the reasons for the under-representation of the lower working class were primarily the fact that filling in the questionnaire put too heavy a strain on their literacy, and possibly a suspicion about other people's inquisitiveness.

The actual phrase 'lower working class' is used by few respondents. Mostly they use descriptive phrases: 'very modest', 'Fairly respectable working class', 'very ordinary', 'working class, humble, respectable', 'unskilled worker' and so on. Only occasionally is it doubtful whether the respondent should be put in the lower working or working class. The great majority of those in this category had the minimum education and are the poorest section of the community.

Although the top and bottom of the social hierarchy are represented by so few respondents (relatively speaking) their responses are significant in many ways. In many respects they differ markedly from the rest of the population.

One-tenth of our sample place themselves in the two intermediate classes between the large blocks of middle and working class. Seven per cent call themselves lower middle class and 3 per cent upper working class. These finer distinctions in class position are made more by men than by women (8 per cent of the men and 6 per cent of the women call themselves lower middle class, and 4 per cent of the men and 3 per cent of the women call themselves upper working class), and more by people over 25 than by younger people. Both these groups are relatively prosperous, and many of them have had some secondary schooling (62 per cent in the case of the lower middle class, and 46 per cent in the case of the upper working class). Their self-classification seems objectively justified in the great majority of cases. They are very evenly distributed throughout the country.

Nearly all the lower middle class think the term self-explanatory without further elaboration; but there are relatively few of the upper working class who do not justify their claim to this status. 'Upper working class living comfortably within our means'; 'a little above average working class'; 'working class with a desperate urge to better myself'; 'of the labouring class with lower middle aspirations' and so on.

Most of the English recognize and accept their class position, occasionally defining it with humour and good humour. 'We are working class—the sort that call the mid-day meal "dinner",' writes a 32-year-old married woman from Bournemouth. 'One of the people, an ordinary everyday worker'; 'Usually known as working class or manual workers'; 'Average lower paid worker, who you

40

would see at any football match or at the local'; 'I am a typical working class man, I go to work in the morning and come home at night and I take my £5 10s. a week, and that's how it goes on week after week, just like anyone else'; 'middle class, professional, though wage earner'; 'Middle, middle class'; 'Middle class (something not quite human—a school teacher)'.

This good-humoured acceptance is general; but there is a small group which views their class position as political rather than social, and they are inclined to make remarks with a slightly bitter under-tone. My impression is that these bitter remarks come somewhat more often from the middle class; the 'lower than vermin' epithet produced by a Labour party politician is repeated quite frequently, and also such modifications as 'extinct middle class', 'former middle class' and so on. The politically minded working class are more truculent: 'Exploited Producer of Wealth Just a So-called Common Worker'; '£6 a week working class that all other classes of the country depend upon to make this country's fortune'; 'Hard Working Class'; 'Working Class and Proud of It'; 'Working class—the only portion of the population which contributes anything'; and the like. When people define their class position in this way it tends to colour their views on every sort of subject. Thus a North country 'militant working class' man says of the police 'I hate the police and every-thing they stand for, which is, among others, the subjugation of the working classes, so that the idle rich may live their worthless lives in comfort and security'; and a middle-aged 'vermin middle-class' man from Egham says of his neighbours 'I dislike to have to put it so forthrightly, but as they are the labouring class, they and I have nothing in common.' It is only small groups however who display such political passion.

As has already been said, current income is no clear indication of social class; there are some members of each class in each income group. There is a tendency however towards clusters. More than three-quarters of the lower working class have family incomes of under £8 a week, and half have incomes under £5 a week (many of these are pensioners); half the working class have incomes between £5 and £8 a week, and another three-tenths between £8 and £12; the upper working class have two-fifths between £8 and £12 a week and a third between £5 and £8; they are slightly better off on the average than the lower middle class, who have a third in the £5 to £8 a week group and another third in the £8 to £12, almost exactly the same figures as those for the middle class; the middle class has a quarter above £12 a week whereas the lower middle has only a fifth;

41

the upper middle have two-fifths above the £12 a week level, and are much the most prosperous group.

One of my major surprises was the extent to which people were willing to disclose their incomes. I had expected some of the prudery or secrecy about money matters which characterized my own family and that of most of my friends. My experience of the upper middle and middle class is that almost the last information to be confided to friend or relative is current income; and that questions on this subject are more resented than almost any other. With this anticipation in mind, I had purposely framed my question as discreetly as possible, and had even consciously permitted a certain ambiguity. People whose family income was precisely £8 or £12 a week could mark two categories equally correctly; thus £8 a week could be inserted either in the space marked for £5–£8 or £8–£12, though I would expect it mostly to be in the latter. I thought however that if I particularized to shillings and pence—say a category of £5–£7 19s. 11d.—I might excite hostility and suspicion which would overweigh the greater exactness.

I think these fears were unfounded, and that I could have been more precise. For less than 2 per cent of the people who wrote in left the question unanswered, whereas 5 per cent refused to tell their age; asked the same questions by interviewers 7 per cent refused to answer, and 3 per cent said they didn't know, both groups predominantly women. This is one of the many cases where more complete information was obtained from the anonymous questionnaire.

In England in January 1951 the median family income was just about £8 a week. In the main sample 52 per cent had incomes below, 46 per cent incomes above, that sum. The figures are almost identical for the field survey, if the 10 per cent of no answers be distributed at random; 47 per cent had incomes below, and 43 per cent incomes above, £8 a week. In more precise figures 10 per cent had incomes of under £5 a week, 42 per cent £5–£8, 29 per cent £8–£12, 10 per cent £12–£15 and 7 per cent over £15.[9]

The incomes are randomly distributed as far as the regions are concerned (there is a little more poverty in the South-West), but there is a tendency for the poor to live in small towns and villages, and the well-off to live in the metropolises. The poorest section of the community are the old, particularly widowed or divorced or separated women; the best off are the single men under 24, presumably because in most cases there are at least two earners in the family; also, as already pointed out, many of my better-off collaborators were connected with a university.

42

The English are the most urban people in the world. Only a fifth of my respondents (21 per cent) lived in towns and villages with fewer than 10,000 inhabitants; almost exactly the same proportion lived in metropolises, London, Birmingham and their conurbations (22 per cent). The remaining three-fifths are nearly equally divided between large towns, with between a million and 100,000 inhabitants, which comprise half the population of the North-West and North-East and North, and smaller towns with between 100,000 and 10,000 which are evenly distributed throughout the country, except for London and the South-East.[10]

Although England is so overwhelmingly urban, it seems as though most English people picture their country as rural ("There'll always be an England while there's a country lane'); and gardening is far and away the most popular leisure occupation of English men (to a lesser extent English women).[11] It is presumably to gratify this passion that the architects of England's cities and suburbs have covered so much ground with houses in terraces (both sides touching their neighbours) or semi-detached (only one side touching a neighbour) with a little piece of ground in the front, and a larger piece at the back, hidden by trellis from passers-by and usually fenced or hedged. The disadvantages both national (through the destruction of much potentially valuable farm land) and individual (through the greatly added expenses of heating and keeping in repair such small, and often shoddily built, dwellings) are presumably thought to be no excessive price to pay for a piece of land of one's own.

Two-thirds of the population of England live in semi-detached or terraced houses; in the two Northern regions this figure reaches four-fifths.[12] The total figures may even be slightly higher, the questionnaire offered a choice of eight types of dwelling and a further rubric 'other—please specify'; quite a number of the 7 per cent who filled in this section specified precisely 'corner house in a terraced row'.

Ten per cent of the population live in detached houses, chiefly from the smaller towns and villages of the two southern regions; this is one of the instances where the richest and poorest resemble one another more than either resemble the intermediate grades. Though a cottage and mansion differ in many ways, they both stand by themselves. In the middle ranges of income 9 per cent live in detached houses; on the highest level 18 per cent, and on the lowest 13 per cent do so.

Nineteen per cent of the population do not have a complete house to themselves. Five per cent live in each of the three following categories: self-contained flat or maisonnette in a converted house,

43

unfurnished rooms (these particularly the lower working class) and furnished rooms; 3 per cent live in flats in a block of flats (particularly in London) and 1 per cent in hotels or boarding houses. This fifth of the population, as will be shown, is untypical and unfortunate in many ways besides being deprived of the opportunity of working a garden.

Once English people have got a house they tend to stay in it; this is probably one of the biggest contrasts between the living habits of the English and the Americans Even with the relatively young group of the main sample, nearly a third had lived at the same address for between 10 and 20 years and 10 per cent even longer. In the field survey just on half the population had lived at the same address for more than 10 years.[13] Nearly a third of the main sample have been in the same address for 2 years or less; these are predominantly young married (or divorced) people under 34; 15 per cent have lived in the same place between 2 and 4 years, and 18 per cent between 4 and 10; despite the turmoil of war and the destruction of the blitz considerably less than half the population has changed its residence since the end of hostilities. Particularly in the Northern regions, it would appear, it is only the exceptional who move house after marriage. Men move a little more than women.[14]

Fifty-five per cent of the main sample (and 56 per cent of the field survey) have children; and, in the greater number of cases, the young children live with their parents; though there are a few unfortunate cases where housing difficulties have broken up the family. For example, a woman in Staffordshire says she 'lives in a workshop with two of the children in a home, three with my mother-in-law, and one in digs.'

People are children as well as parents; in the main sample the fathers of half of them, and the mothers of two-thirds were alive, when they filled the questionnaire I asked those who had living parents whether their fathers and mothers lived in the same house or the same town as they did, or no.

Two out of five people with living parents lived in the same house as their father and mother; these were mostly the young, the unmarried, divorced, or separated, and the better off. However 11 per cent of the married couples whose fathers were living and 12 per cent whose mothers were living shared a house with these older parents. Roughly one household in twenty has a resident father- or mother-in-law.

Nearly half the parents of adult children who do not share a home with them live in the same town; a little more than half live ın a different community. This is the pıcture for the country as a whole; but the distribution is by no means even. In the two Northern regions, particularly in the North-West, in large towns of between a million and 100,000 inhabıtants, in the workıng and lower working classes nearly two-thirds of the population live in the same town as their parents; in the two Southern regıons, partıcularly in the South-West, in the small towns and vıllages, in the upper middle class and with people with weekly ıncomes of over £12, barely a third do so. The figures are similar for both parents, and almost certainly mirror a real regıonal difference; whereas the doublıng up of households ıs evenly distributed over the whole country, geographical, as contrasted with residential, separation varıes greatly with regions and social class.[15]

These figures are significant. A great deal ıs spoken and written about the contemporary break-up of the family, which is meant to ınclude more than the break-up of marriage; and these figures show that, though this is overwhelmıngly true for the better-off and the members of the upper middle classes, to which so many of the writers and speakers belong, and of the small towns and villages in the Southern half of the country, in whıch so many of them lıve, it is not true of the urban workıng classes in the manufacturing towns of the Midlands and North to anything like the same extent.

When it comes to other blood relatives—brothers, sisters, married children—the regional differences are much less marked, though the class difference is still sıgnıficant. Just a quarter of the populatıon said that they had such relatıves living near them, within, say, five mınutes walk. There is only a dıfference of 3 or 4 per cent between the different regions and town-sizes; but 28 per cent of the working class answer in the affirmative, in contrast to 18 per cent of the upper middle and lower mıddle classes.[16]

The answers to the question 'Do your parents-in-law, brothers-in-law or sisters-in-law lıve near you—within, say, 5 minutes walk?' produced some interesting ınformation; ıt demonstrated the hitherto undocumented fact that there is a marked tendency towards *matrilocality* in the Englısh working class. Matrilocalıty is a technical term from social anthropology sıgnifyıng that the man at marriage moves to his wife's community, so that the children are brought up among their mother's kınfolk; when the wıfe moves to the husband's community the term is patrilocality. Wıth complete patrilocal residence all the women would live near their in-laws and none of the men; and the reverse with matrilocalıty. We do not have complete matrılocality, but 28 per cent of the men live near their in-laws and only 19 per cent of the women, a difference of real significance. Twenty-nine per cent of the working class in contrast with 18 per cent of the middle class, 28 per cent of those with incomes of £5–£8 a week, contrasted with 17 per cent of those with incomes over £15 and under £5 a week do so. This pattern is commonest in the Midlands and Northern regions and least common in the South. Considerably more men live near their wives' relatives than near their own parents.[17]

I thought further insight might be gained if these questions about living near blood relations and relations by marriage were correlated with the amount of time people had lived in the same address. The figures are quite conclusive. Nearly a third of the people who have lived in the same house ten years or more have brothers, sisters or married children living near them; barely half that number do so who have lived in their house a year or less. When it comes to living near in-laws, the figures vary comparatively little with length of residence, with the peak with those who have lived less than ten years in the same address. This confirms the hypothesis that, when English men do move house (and most presumably do so at marriage) they tend to move away from their own family and near to that of their wives.

Social anthropologists distinguish between the nuclear family—a husband and wife and their children—and the extended family, which are the other relationships by blood and marriage which are socially recognized In most primitive societies the extended family is of major importance in providing help and support for the individual, and these functions are of some importance in all societies. By practically every criterion, the break-up of the extended family has proceeded much further in the South of England than in the Midlands and the North. Kinsfolk are most scattered in the South-West, even more than in London; they are most closely knit in Lancashire and the other North-Western counties. In the small towns and villages of rural England the break-up has gone furthest; the very poor, with incomes under £5 a week, and the prosperous, with incomes over £12 a week, both tend to live isolated. In the middle income groups, in medium-sized towns (under a million population) and among the working class such isolation is much less common.

The assumption about the loneliness of the English, which I had in mind when I framed the questions, has therefore to be modified at least in part. People in the working class outside the Southern counties of England do tend to live near kinsfolk; it is the people in the South, especially the middle class—the regions and class with

46

Figure I

Question 10 by Question 17

10. How long have you lived at your present address?
17. Do any of your brothers or sisters or married children live near you—within, say, five minutes walk?

Question 10	Question 17			
	Yes	No	No answer	Total
Under 6 months	15	79	6	100
7–12 months	13	81	6	100
1 1–2 years	20	71	9	100
2 1–4 years	22	70	8	100
4 1–10 years	26	61	13	100
10 1–20 years	32	54	14	100
20 1–30 years	33	50	17	100
30 1 years and over	41	50	9	100
No answer	20	61	19	100
Total	25	64	11	100

Figure II

Question 10 by Question 18

10. How long have you lived at your present address?
18. Do your parents-in-law, brothers-in-law, or sisters-in-law live near you—within say, five minutes walk?

Question 10	Question 18			
	Yes	No	No answer	Total
Under 6 months	21	72	7	100
7–12 months	24	69	7	100
1.1–2 years	22	68	10	100
2.1–4 years	27	65	8	100
4.1–10 years	26	60	14	100
10.1–20 years	25	55	20	100
20 1–30 years	24	56	18	100
30 1 years and over	24	62	14	100
No answer	20	57	23	100
Total	24	62	14	100

which I am most familiar—who are most often separated from their kith and kin and therefore depend on friends and neighbours for help and companionship.

NOTES TO CHAPTER THREE

1 In the questionnaire the question on social class followed immediately after the question 'How old were you when you finished full-time school?' and a certain number, overwhelmingly the young under 18, answered the question as if the word 'class' referred to their class at school, and named the highest school class they had reached

The figures of self-ascription by class are remarkably similar in the main sample and the field survey, except that the members of the middle class interviewed made fewer distinctions than those who wrote in The actual percentages are

	Main Sample percentage	Field Survey percentage
Upper middle	2	1
Middle	28	35
Lower middle	7	4
Upper working	3	—
Working	50	47
Lower working	1	1
'Any class'	1	2
Miscellaneous	3	1
Don't know	4	9
No answer	1	—

The British Institute of Public Opinion has asked on three occasions since 1945 (March 1948, November 1949, and June 1952): 'If you had to say which social class you belonged to, which would you say?' These questions were asked of a sample from the whole of Britain, and not merely of England No distinctions were recorded within the working class. The pattern of answers during these five years remained remarkably constant, with variations of at most 1 per cent The survey nearest in time to mine is that of November 1949, which gave the following figures:

	Total %	Men %	Women %
Upper class	2	2	1
Upper middle	6	6	7
Middle	27	26	28
Lower middle	15	15	15
Working	45	47	43
Don't know	5	4	6

Although the contrasts are less, it is worth noting that compared with men, more women put themselves in the middle class and fewer in the working class; more women are uncertain of their class position

2 Seventy-six per cent of the working class and 44 per cent of the middle class finished full-time schooling at the age of 14 or earlier

3. A considerable number of articles in *The British Journal of Sociology* deal with the relationship between occupations and social class Particularly relevant are. *Social Grading of Occupations*, by John Hall and D. Caradog Jones (March 1950), *Social Class of Cambridge Alumni*, by Hester Jenkins and D Caradog Jones (June 1950), *Prestige of Occupations*, by A F Davies (June 1952)

4. See the numerous publications by Professor Lloyd Warner and his associates, especially the *Yankee City* series and *Structure of American Life* (Edinburgh University Press, 1952)

5. The *New Statesman and Nation*, the organ of the left-wing intelligentsia, runs a feature entitled 'This England' which consists of short excerpts from the Press which can make its readers feel superior or amused. A part of the editorial blurb for my introductory article in the *People* was reprinted under this rubric, besides, presumably, amusing the many, it induced a few readers to send for the questionnaire. Many of my higher educated and upper middle class respondents were recruited from this source, and from the students in the sociology and psychology departments of a number of the universities.

6 The figures are paralleled for the field survey, except that there the widowed and married are not listed separately Thirty-three per cent of the married claim middle class status, compared with 42 per cent of the single.

7. The actual figures of self-ascription of class by sex is as follows.

| | Main Sample | | Field Survey | |
| | Men | Women | Men | Women |
	%	%	%	%
Upper middle	2	2	1	0
Middle	21	33	30	40
Lower middle	8	6	4	3
Upper working	4	3	1	0
Working	53	46	54	40
Lower working	1	1	1	1
'Any class'	1	1	3	1
Miscellaneous	4	3	1	3
Don't know	4	3	5	12
No answer	2	2	x	x

It is worth noting the large number of women in the field survey who say they 'don't know'

8 The following figures, derived from the Census returns of the *United Kingdom* (not England alone), were supplied through the Ministry of Education, by the courtesy of Ben S Morris, Esq , of the National Foundation for Educational Research Of the Occupied Males, 13·6 per cent continued education beyond the age of 16, and of these 2·25 per cent continued beyond the age of 20; of the occupied females (excluding those who had already married or retired), 17·3 per cent continued education beyond the age of 16, and of these 2·85 per cent continued education beyond the age of 20.

The sample is not the same as mine, for it includes Scotland (with its marked emphasis on education), Wales and Northern Ireland as well as England. It does appear to confirm the findings of my survey that women tend to have more secondary education than men, a difference of just under 4 per cent for all education over 16. For the same amount of education my figures show a difference of 5 per cent, 14 per cent of my women respondents and 9 per cent of my male respondents finished full-time education after 16.

9 For the field survey see Chapter One, footnote (9).

10. For comparison with the field survey, see Chapter One, footnote (9).

11. See *Patterns of English Life* (Hulton Press, Ltd., 1950)

12 It is remarkable that if these two types of houses are taken together the main sample and the field survey practically coincide, 67 per cent for the main sample, 68 for the field survey. Separated however there is quite a discrepancy; the main sample has 36 per cent living in semi-detached houses, the field survey 26; for terraced houses the main survey has 31, the field survey 42 per cent. It seems at least possible that this is an artifact of the interviewing situation; that it is easier to find the type of person the interviewer needs in a terrace than in more widely separated houses The same principle may account for the other major discrepancy in the two groups; the main survey has 5 per cent living in flats (in a block of flats) and 5 per cent in unfurnished rooms; the field survey has 2 per cent of the former and 1 per cent of the latter. These

49

people would presumably be the most difficult to reach for a personal interview; but it is also possible that they are slightly over-represented in the main sample. These types of dwelling are much used by the widowed, divorced or separated, and it may be that these lonely people took special interest in filling up the questionnaire For all other types of dwelling the figures in the main sample and the field survey are either identical, or differ only by 1 per cent

13 That this difference between the main sample and the field survey is entirely an artifact of the method of selection (described on p 9) is demonstrated by the fact that, if the residences of the single only are compared, the figures are practically identical It is the overstressing of young childless married people which swell the figures in the main sample for those who have lived at the same address for four years or less.

14 As stated in the previous footnote the differing composition of the field survey and the main sample make it desirable to separate the answers of the single from those of the married The following table gives the percentages of the answers to the question 'How long have you lived at your present address?' from the field survey, the corresponding figures from the main sample being in brackets and italics

Period	Total	Single	Married
Under 6 months	7 (9)	8 (6)	7 (11)
7–12 months	5 (9)	4 (5)	6 (11)
1 1 to 2 years	7 (11)	7 (7)	7 (12)
2 1 to 4 years	11 (15)	7 (10)	13 (17)
4 1 to 10 years	21 (18)	18 (18)	22 (18)
10 1 to 20 years	32 (27)	38 (39)	28 (23)
20 1 to 30 years	9 (7)	11 (10)	8 (6)
Over 30 years	7 (3)	6 (4)	8 (2)

15 Further evidence that this is not a statistical artifact can be found if the answers are analysed by age If one omits the under 18's, who are mostly still living at home, and the over 64's who have few living parents, the positive answers to the question 'If your father (mother) is alive, but not in the same house as you, does your father live in the same town as you?' are as follows

	Father %	Mother %
18–24	40	43
24–34	43	49
35–44	43	44
45–65	41	44

16 This question was also asked in the field survey with practically identical results.

17 Fewer people questioned in the field survey had in-laws living so near them— 20 per cent of the men and 16 per cent of the women; but the patterns of distribution are very similar.

CHAPTER FOUR

FRIENDS AND NEIGHBOURS

ONLY AFTER PEOPLE have lived at the same address for ten years or more do they consider that their best friends live near them, within easy walking distance. Probably for most peoples in the world moving to a new dwelling means moving away from old associations; but the English appear exceptional in the length of time it takes them to knit new bonds During the first four years most of their emotional ties are elsewhere and their best friends live 'far away'; and it takes a further six years before friends are concentrated in the near neighbourhood Since marriage usually entails setting up a new home, it also tends to remove people from their friends; three times as many married men and women, particularly the younger people between 25 and 44, say that their friends live far away, compared with those who say they live near. The young and the old, the single and the widowed are more likely to have their friends near at hand.

Besides marriage, membership of the small social classes tends to separate people from their friends. People who consider themselves upper middle class, lower middle class and upper working class are likely to consider their best friends live at some distance from them to a significantly greater extent than those who consider themselves middle or working class without qualification.[1]

People in the big cities, perhaps particularly London, tend to be separated from their friends (when they have any: some pathetic creatures wrote across this question 'I have no friends'); but what is perhaps surprising is that the next loneliest type of community, judging by this criterion, are the small towns and villages. This is one more indication[2] that the atomization of English life is proceeding from both ends, that both in the country and in the metropolises most people tend to isolation and loneliness. It is chiefly in the middle-sized towns, above all in the Northern regions, that English people find friends among their neighbours. This is especially true of the people who live in terraced or semi-detached houses, that most congenial type of English home; people in detached houses are nearly as much separated from their best friends as the people who live in rooms. Most isolated of all are the guests in hotels and boarding houses.[3]

I asked a considerable number of questions about people's relations with their neighbours, in an attempt to get a picture of the amount of

Figure III

Question 9 by Question 19

9. Would you describe your home as

19 Would you say that your best friends live near you (that is, within walking distance), a short distance away (say a mile or so), or far away?

Question 9	Question 19					
	Near	Short distance away	Far away	Some in all three	No answer	Total
Detached	9	19	32	43	1	104
Semi-detached	12	23	23	46	1	105
Terraced	14	25	19	45	1	104
Self-contained flat in house	8	24	26	44	1	103
Flat in block of flats	12	21	23	45	2	103
Unfurnished rooms	11	25	30	33	3	102
Furnished rooms	7	25	34	36	2	104
Hotel or boarding house	2	16	34	50	2	104
Other	8	19	30	46	2	105
No answer	11	20	27	46	3	107
Total	12	23	24	44	1	104

social life in the local group, to compare with the information about the family and chosen friends. I am accustomed to using the terms 'neighbours' and 'neighbourhood' to mean all the people living within a fairly small area and I had thought that this meaning was general I now consider that I was probably using the terms as a dweller in the country does; nearly all my respondents are town-dwellers, and they tended to interpret the terms more narrowly and precisely; usually they only included the people living in the adjacent houses, or just opposite to them; or, for people who lived in multiple dwellings, some or all of the other inhabitants of the same building.

The typical relationship of the English to their neighbours can probably best be described as distant cordiality. Some two-thirds know most of their neighbours well enough to speak to; but not one in 20 know them well enough to drop in on without an invitation; and it is very exceptional for neighbours to entertain one another for a meal or to spend an evening together. Two-thirds of my respondents pay no formal visits to neighbours in this fashion; and nearly all the remainder fall between 'a few' and 'hardly any'.

One very curious point emerged in the answers to these questions: quite consistently people claimed that they knew more neighbours to speak to than they knew by sight! It seems possible that this is a point of sex differentiation, that men will pass a word with their neighbours but not look at them. Analysing the negative answers, there is only a difference of 2 per cent between men and women who say that they know hardly any or no neighbours to speak to, but one of 7 per cent between men and women who know hardly any or no neighbours by sight.[4]

The stereotype of the lack of neighbourliness in metropolises or big towns is amply confirmed, though it is only a relatively small group—less than one-sixth—which does not pass a word with the neighbours even in the biggest towns; but the regional stereotype of the greater friendliness of the northern regions, is not similarly borne out. The people living in London and the South-East have fewer relations on all levels with their neighbours than the rest of the country; and it is consistently the (predominantly rural) South-West which has the highest figures for neighbourly intercourse. The rest of the country falls between these two extremes, with only slight variations.

The small groups who do visit their neighbours, either formally or informally, can be defined with some precision. They are either at the top or the bottom of the economic scale, with incomes of under £5 or over £15 a week, who live in detached, semi-detached or terraced houses which they have inhabited for four years or more. The patterns of formal entertainment are established relatively quickly, so that there is little change after four years until you get to the old-established residents who have lived nearly all their life in the same house; the amount of informal visiting increases all the time, though it is still always a minority who drop in. Incidentally, the stereotype of the woman popping round next door is not borne out; two-fifths say they know no neighbours well enough to visit without an invitation, and another fifth know hardly any; parallel figures for men are very slightly higher.

As far as the English are concerned, easily the most important factor controlling the amount of contact people have with their neighbours is the type of dwelling they live in. The differences in social class, income and region pale into relative insignificance when compared with house-types.

It is perhaps understandable that the lessees of furnished or un-furnished rooms, or the inhabitants of hotels or boarding houses should have little contact with their neighbours, since most of them are liable to be transients; but this would not necessarily seem to be the case for people who live in flats. Yet flat-dwellers have little

Figure IV

Question 9 by Question 20

    9 Would you describe your home as

    20 Not counting relations and in-laws, do you know neighbours to speak to?

Question 9	Question 20					
	Most	A few	Hardly any	None	No answer	Total
Detached	71	22	5	—	2	100
Semi-detached	68	26	4	0	2	100
Terraced	69	25	5	1	0	100
Self-contained flat in house	36	41	19	3	1	100
Flat in block of flats	48	35	13	2	2	100
Unfurnished rooms	35	39	20	4	2	100
Furnished rooms	27	43	18	12	—	100
Hotel or boarding house	27	18	27	23	5	100
Other	57	25	10	5	3	100
No answer	58	34	4	2	2	100
Total	62	27	7	2	2	100

Figure V

Question 9 by Question 22

    9 Would you describe your home as

    22 Not counting relations and in-laws, do you know neighbours to drop in on without an invitation?

Question 9	Question 22					
	Most	A few	Hardly any	None	No answer	Total
Detached	9	35	24	30	2	100
Semi-detached	6	29	25	37	3	100
Terraced	8	25	25	41	1	100
Self-contained flat in house	1	17	25	54	3	100
Flat in block of flats	5	20	23	48	4	100
Unfurnished rooms	1	14	15	67	3	100
Furnished rooms	1	15	12	70	2	100
Hotel or boarding house	5	11	7	70	7	100
Other	7	21	22	48	2	100
No answer	2	24	27	44	3	100
Total	6	26	23	43	2	100

more contact with their neighbours than do transients; but what is perhaps suggestive is that people who live in a flat in a block of flats have more contact with their neighbours than those who live in a self-contained flat or maisonnette in a converted house. If the ideal of distant cordiality is correctly phrased, then it would seem that one's co-lessees in a converted house were too close for the desired distance to be maintained, since such buildings usually lack the relatively large and impersonal halls, lifts, etc of buildings designed for flats; and therefore the cordiality is sacrificed so that the distance can be maintained. The old saw claims that an Englishman's home is his castle; as soon as he does not have the building to himself he is, as it were, dethroned, and no longer appears to feel free to mix with his neighbours. It must need quite a lot of self-restraint not to know by sight nor to speak to people who share the same front door.

In ordinary life one keeps the neighbours at a distance· but could one count on their help in a crisis? could one rely on them in a pinch? This question produced a wide scatter of answers, but it is only a minority who feel they can rely on their neighbours' help. Eight per cent felt they could rely on their neighbours entirely, and another 27 per cent to a large extent; 10 per cent felt they could not rely on their neighbours at all, and 32 per cent only to a small extent The remainder—just on a quarter—would not commit themselves, and said that 'it depends'.

Trust in one's neighbours' helpfulness is greatest among the middle-aged and elderly who live in small communities, and lowest among the inhabitants of big cities, between the ages of 35 and 44. The answers to this question upset a number of my presumptions. There is no more reliance on neighbours' help in the Northern regions than there is in London; it is in point of fact the rural South-West which voices the greatest trust in friendliness. Secondly there is greater reliance among the well-to-do, the members of the middle classes. than there is among the poor; the greatest proportion of negative answers come from those with incomes of under £5 a week, and who call themselves lower working class The middle class has repeated for generations the cliché that it is the poor who help the poor; the poor themselves seem to doubt it.[5]

The neighbourhood, the local group, is not only the area of associations which may be more or less voluntary and more or less friendly; it is also the area in which many annoyances and disagreements can be focused. In an attempt to find out the nature and extent of these annoyances and disagreements I asked: 'What do you most disapprove of about your present neighbours?'

Five per cent of the population—one in twenty—know nothing at all about their neighbours; these are chiefly the younger married people, up to the age of 44, living in the big metropolises (particularly London) in the £8 to £12 a week income range; by all indications this is the most isolated group in the country. The older people and the somewhat better off are the chief components of the sizable group—nearly a fifth of the population—who have no complaints to make about their neighbours; and among them also are found the small group (3 per cent) who have positive praise for their neighbours. 'Maybe I am lucky, but I can think of no way of disapproving of my neighbours' writes a schoolmaster from Cornwall; a young married man who had moved to Liverpool says 'I have no complaints, being a southerner I found all Lancashire people sincere, understanding and hospitable', and an upper working class man from High Wycombe writes 'Neighbours on either side are ideal (they keep away)'.

The reserve which is so highly commended in High Wycombe is stigmatized as unfriendliness by many other respondents. The majority—more than two-thirds of the population—have specific complaints to make about their neighbours of one kind or another; and 8 per cent mention unfriendliness, men making this complaint somewhat more than women, and those under 34 slightly more than their elders. Except in the first few months in a new home, when it is presumably not expected that neighbours will be other than distant, this complaint seems to vary little with length of residence. It is made somewhat more by those who live in the Southern regions in medium sized towns, and slightly more by the upper middle, lower middle and lower working classes than by those who consider themselves middle or working class without classification.

The incidence of this complaint does appear to bear out the stereotype that the Northern regions are more friendly than the rest of the country, and a number of respondents explicitly make this point. Thus, for example, a 43-year-old working class woman now living in South Kensington writes that her present neighbours are:

Fair weather friends, any time you are up against it, trouble illness, you can count them out. Not like the North.

Similarly, a middle class woman from Ilford:

I myself, am from Lancashire were neighbours are warm and friendly, moved to Ilford during last war, southern people treat us as foreigners, and refuse to be friendly no matter how one approaches them

56

And a 31-year-old man from Bromley (Kent) who describes himself as 'very definitely working class' writes:
> On the whole they tend to keep to themselves, I notice this because I
> am a northerner (Lancs).

By way of contrast, a 40-year-old skilled workman, now living in
Bradford, complains of:
> their unwillingness to accept us as anything but 'foreigners' as we are
> from southern England

The treatment of immigrants from a different county or region as
alien would seem to be fairly widespread A 35-year-old 'upper
working class' woman writes of her neighbours·
> Most of them very 'close' but at the same time 'nosy' It is rather the
> other way round, we are 'foreigners' (Cheshire cats), but are now
> accepted by our immediate neighbours. We have been friends all the
> time we have lived here, but there's always that sense of restriction—
> one can go so far—and no farther That barrier is now crumbling

Or from Gloucestershire:
> Being a residential district most, if not all, of them are old people
> and appear to view strangers with suspicion (typical of Glo'ster!)

A woman from Grantham (Lincs):
> They are waiting for me to speak and be friendly, but I am waiting
> for them to speak and break the ice.

A few people describe really deplorable lack of charity on the part
of their neighbours. A Southampton seaman says:
> Whilst I am away there is no one who is interested in my wife or boy.

A working class married man from Richmond
> Little practical help. My wife cannot walk Lost a limb many years
> ago, arthritis in the other leg Only one neighbour comes in to offer
> a helping hand, we manage all right but an offer would be welcome.

A 38-year-old Halifax woman who calls herself middle class:
> I disapprove of my next door neighbour because I had no-one at
> Baby's birth, husband at work. She said I could knock on the wall and
> she would come but added 'I arn't forced to hear you! ! !', which for
> me speaks volumes

Merging into the complaints of unfriendliness, are the complaints
of snobbishness, of the neighbours considering themselves better
class, looking down on the respondents and so on. How for example,

should the complaint of a well-educated spinster from Streatham be classified·

I do not really disapprove of anything, but do not feel I have much in common, added to which they are given to conceit and pretence.

or that of a working electrician from Essex:

Neighbours on one side always finding fault with everyone, neighbours on other side call me 'Mr.' and not by my Christian name

Some 6 per cent of the total population complain unequivocally about their neighbours' snobbishness; the complaints being mostly voiced by middle-aged, middle-income married people of the working classes. Fairly typical is a 31-year-old worker from Crawley:

They speak with an *Oxford* accent but work, perhaps in a better paid job, but have to work to live as I do, but they make you think that they are just that bit above you.

A rather admirable 36-year-old woman from Edgware who said of her education 'I rarely attended school, my two eldest daughters taught me to read and write' complains:

I work from 6 a m to 4 30 p.m , in a day nursery and have no time to spare and know my neighbours think they are superior to me

Somewhat rarer is what one might call reversed snobbishness, typified by a 24-year-old Nottingham woman, separated from her husband, who writes·

I do not care for my neighbours at all, because they belong to the labouring classes, and I have absolutely nothing in common with them They are far too apathetic and care only for beer, fish and chips, football pools and racing They seem quite content merely to exist and seem to have no desire to educate themselves or to acquire a better standard of living

Similarly, a 35-year-old widow from Reigate who describes herself as 'extinct middle class' writes:

I do not disapprove of my neighbours at all—I am the square peg—I disapprove of the system of living that necessitates me living in a neighbourhood where I have so little in common with others

The complaints that the neighbours 'lower the neighbourhood' by their untidiness or unsanitariness, neglect of their houses, their gardens or their persons, their manners or their morals may sometimes be motivated by class feeling; more often it seems to reflect deplorable conditions. Four per cent of the population mention such objections; there are slightly more women than men in this group, and they tend to be people who have moved fairly recently into the neighbourhood they deplore, but otherwise they are very evenly scattered throughout the country. Thus, a serious married working-class man from Newcastle-on-Tyne writes:

> Upper half of my street, about 8 houses, is occupied by Prostitutes in furnished rooms and pimps etc We do not bother them, but their language in there frequent rows isn't the type I want my son aged three to repeat

A 28-year-old married man from Fulham who describes his class position as 'very modest' (he left school at 15 and has a weekly income of £8—£12) writes:

> This is a near slum neighbourhood, people neglect themselves, their children and their houses, spending too much time and money in public houses.

This type of stricture is repeated with a number of variations.

There are two further subjects of complaint which tend to bulk more heavily in the first years of residence· complaints about noise, and about failure to control children and pets. Six per cent of the population complain that their neighbours are noisy and inconsiderate of other people's rest and quiet, that they play their radios or rev. their cars at unsuitable times and so on Men make this point somewhat more than women, especially the younger, the unmarried, and the moderately well-off. A young Dorking man speaks for many when he mentions 'noisy radio, shouted directives to children.'

Five per cent mention the failure to control, or neglect of, children and animals. It is particularly new residents, in the first months of their occupation, who complain of the animals; thereafter ill-controlled or neglected children bulk larger; after ten years of residence in the same house both complaints die down.

The grounds for complaints so far discussed do not necessarily entail any contact or intercourse with the neighbours objected to. With the remaining sources of neighbourly ill-feeling this is less likely to be the case. One can, presumably, resent the neighbours' inquisitiveness without knowing anything more about them than that they are inquisitive; but this seems less probable than resentment about their noisiness, for example.

Thirteen per cent of the population complains of the neighbours' inquisitiveness; and it seems worth analysing with some minuteness the categories of people who make this complaint with most emphasis. It is the young, under the age of 24, the unmarried (followed by the divorced and separated), the people of medium income living in the smaller communities and who consider themselves lower middle or lower working class who are particularly liable to think they are being spied on, and to resent it. The complaint comes somewhat more frequently from the Northern regions, and least from London and the South-East. It is a complaint made hardly at all in the first two years of residence in a house; and it drops out again among the old inhabitants, who presumably think everybody knows everything anyhow.

The complaints are made with considerable vehemence and repetitiveness. Thus, a 27-year-old married middle class woman from Southport (Lancs):

> I have only lived here two years, but I think my neighbours know more about me than I do.

and, from the other end of the country, a woman of similar age and class of Woolacombe (Devon):

> They know more about my affairs, than I do myself, what they don't know, they make up.

A 50-year-old 'middle class Trades person' from Steyning (Sussex):

> They know more of my business than I know myself, and Her Voice.

A middle aged male artisan from Alsager (Cheshire):

> Their noses are longer than their arms They cannot live their own lives for watching and meddling in others Curtain shakes.

Almost the same words are used by an 18-year-old Eccles youth·

> They snoop too much, that is to say they are always peeping through the windows, also they mind other peoples businesses (instead of their own).

A 16½-year-old Liverpool girl:

> Nosiness and keeping you talking when you are in a hurry Peeping at people from behind their curtains, noting the time that everyone gets in at night.

Inquisitiveness would not be so objectionable perhaps, if it did not lead to gossip; and 13 per cent of the population also object to this neighbourly habit It is not altogether the same group who object to gossip as object to inquisitiveness, though again it is specially stressed by the young and single. It is a complaint made somewhat more often by women than by men, and its incidence increases steadily as income declines. The regions where this complaint bulks highest are the South-West and North-East and North; it is relatively low in the Midlands. It is mentioned somewhat less often by people living in the metropolises. As far as length of residence is concerned, it only starts to become important as a source of annoyance after people have spent four years in the same house; it never dies down What a 20-year-old Hereford student calls 'the proverbial "village pump" attitude and conflicts' seems to bedevil the life of many.

Five per cent of the population, remarkably evenly distributed, complain specifically that their neighbours are stupid, parochial, narrow-minded or old-fashioned; and a further 1 per cent object to their neighbours' religious or political views. The small group who make these objections are extremely emphatic about them, and show very little tolerance; they are almost entirely composed of the older residents, people who have lived in the same house for at least ten years It is from this same long-established group that the complaints about borrowing or cadging arise; it is made by 3 per cent of the population, distributed very evenly, though slightly concentrated among the married and more prosperous. A rather humorous worker writes. 'I have run out of tea, sugar etc., can you let me have some, I will return it later '

Finally there is the largest group of all, some 14 per cent, who have quite concrete complaints to make about their neighbours' morals, behaviour or character which show the most detailed knowledge. This knowledgeable group is concentrated among the older inhabitants, people who have lived at least 10 years in the same house, and who consider themselves middle class or working class without qualifications These specific complaints are made more by the poor than by the prosperous (complaints going up as income goes down), more by the inhabitants of small than of larger towns (concentration of complaints varying inversely with town size) more by the very young (under 18) and by the middle aged than by the young or old. Regionally the greatest number come from the South-West, followed by the Midlands. London and the South-East have the fewest. In short, the patterns of knowing neighbours, and of knowing something to their discredit, follow one another fairly closely.

The complaints cover every variety of behaviour and type of character from the ludicrous to the revolting. Neighbours disregard the Sabbath or are hypocritical, smoke too much, drink too much, make too much display, work in their gardens too much, are insincere or inconsiderate, feckless, extravagant, dishonest, immoral, two-faced or quarrelsome The complaints range from the lower middle class man of Enfield who says:

> One has no faith in doctors with a result that his crippled daughter cannot walk at 18, nor has been trained to do anything for herself. The other impovishes his home by excession of drinking

61

to the 30-year-old Wigan woman who complains:

Being endowed with good looks, an unusually good figure—their inclination to think that I would stop at nothing to get their husbands.

from the Nottingham worker who writes:

One of his is strictly Religious, but swears like a Trooper and talks about neighbours behind their backs They would not help a Lame Dog over a style

to the pathetic plaint of a 35-year-old policeman

Having lived in this neighbourhood all my life I disapprove of the manner in which they talk to me as tho' I am still going to school

from the 58-year-old Staffordshire villager (who describes himself as 'fairly respectable working class') who complains:

His undying devotion to his garden, Hail rain or sunshine, and which prompts my wife to say Mr. So and So is in the garden you could find something better to do than sit by the fire.

to the young middle class man from Worsley (Lancs) who deplores that:

When you drop in to see the older folks it is a job to get away and when you do they go into tears

Nearly every aspect of neighbourly ill-feeling is illustrated.

There are two small groups within this major category which call for a little comment. It would seem as though, among the younger married people, there is some articulate disapproval of, and pity for the parents of more than two children. Quite a few respondents write comments similar to the 26-year-old 'ordinary working class' Londoner:

They seem to regard us as poor things, owing to the fact that there are children of 2 and 6 respectively and we do not get out to enjoy ourselves as much as others of our ages

or the man from Leeds:

Their so called pity because we have 4 children and another due.

Secondly, it would seem as though people going up in the world are disturbed by the belief in their neighbours' jealousy at their relative success It is not possible with the evidence available to say whether this jealousy actually exists, or is a mildly paranoid projection; in at least some of the cases, particularly among the group calling themselves upper working class, the psychological explanation seems probable, taking their other answers into account. Thus, a 55-year-old North-countryman:

Their obvious dislike of our working hard which has resulted in our owning our own house and car, also their dislike of my having been elected to two local authorities

A married woman from Doncaster (Yorks):

They show they are jealous because I make a success of my finances and I don't tell them all I am doing.

A Yorkshireman ('Hard Working Class') from Barnsley:

The way they begrudge what we have and the way they spend their money on drink and gambling and sending the children with bets to the bookie

Improving one's position is not without dangers in England.

NOTES TO CHAPTER FOUR

1 The small group of 'lower working class' reverse this trend, and say that their best friends live near The poor, with under £5 a week, who are to a certain extent the same group, make the same claim

2 See p. 45

3 I asked a number of questions to try to discover to what extent friendships formed in the armed services persisted in civil life. Two men out of three, and one woman out of eight, had been in the services; and these people were asked if they had seen or written to service friends in the past year (1950), and if so how many, and whether they had attended a regimental reunion The analysis of the answers gives some rather curious results. Briefly, it may be said that associations formed in the 1914–18 war remain important for quite a number of men more than thirty years after demobilization; for their sons the associations made in the 1939–45 war seem of much less lasting importance For the young women on the other hand life in the auxiliary services meant a major expansion of interest and continuing friendship; thus nearly a third of the women, but only a seventh of the men who had been in the services wrote to three or more ex-service friends during the previous year. The attachment to old comrades is particularly strong among the men aged 65 or over, the poor (presumably pensioners) and the well-to-do; it also corresponds inversely with the extent people make friends with their neighbours Thus the metropolises and the small towns and villages in the Southern regions are the areas in which service links remain strongest, medium-sized towns in the Northern regions the areas where they are weakest The unmarried keep up the connection with ex-service friends more than twice as often as the married It would seem that only for the relatively small groups of elderly men and young women has comradeship in the forces meant a lasting enrichment of their post-service life

4. It is possible that an undiscovered semantic point exists here, and that 'knowing by sight' has a different significance for my respondents to what I intended. It is not a statistical artifact, nor one derived from the make-up of the questionnaire, the same questions were asked in the field survey, with a very similar pattern of answers Indeed, with one exception, all the answers of the written and field survey are very similar, and disclose a consistent pattern People were asked if they knew 'most', 'a few', 'hardly any' or 'no' neighbours, by sight, to speak to, to drop in on without an invitation, or to visit for a meal or an evening. The interviewed answered 'most' more and 'a few' less than the writers; but if these two ill-defined groups are added

together the figures are practically identical Tone of voice on the part of the interviewer may have contributed somewhat to this result, but, there is a consistent tendency for people being interviewed to exhibit more friendly feelings than for people filling in anonymous questionnaires See Appendix Two

5. This question was also asked in the Field Survey and the answers contrast somewhat markedly with the main sample An eighth of the people interviewed (12 per cent) refused to commit themselves in any way, much the highest figure of abstentions on any question in the field survey More than any other questions asked in the interviews, the question 'Do you think you could rely on your neighbours in a pinch?' suggested the possibility of 'unfriendly' answers, and all the evidence from this study suggests that, when English people are interviewed, they tend to present themselves in what they consider a good light, or else refuse to answer In the field survey there is a very marked contrast in the answers given by men and by women, which is not paralleled in the main sample, and has not, I think, a rational explanation Although the gross figures are so different, the distribution by age and area are similar in the two samples The percentages in the main survey are given in brackets and italics

'*Do you think you could rely on your neighbours in a pinch?*'

	Total	Men	Women
Entirely	28 (8)	21 (7)	34 (9)
To a large extent	22 (27)	24 (26)	20 (27)
To a small extent	17 (32)	16 (33)	18 (31)
Not at all	15 (10)	18 (10)	12 (9)
It depends	6 (23)	8 (24)	5 (23)
Don't Know and No answer	12 (—)	13 (—)	11 (1)

CHAPTER FIVE

GOING OUT

IN THE PECKHAM experiment[1] one of the aspects which struck me as most remarkable was the apparent unwillingness of something like half the local population to take advantage of this neighbourhood amenity; and I thought I would try to find out to what extent people availed themselves of such facilities as the neighbourhood provided for gatherings which could, at least potentially, be social. To stress this aspect I phrased my question: 'Are there places outside your own homes and the street where you meet neighbours to have a chat?' and then listed eleven possibilities and left a blank for 'other (*please specify*)'. The eleven possibilities which I listed were voluntary associations (men's club, women's club or women's institute, mixed club, youth club, political club), church or chapel meeting rooms, gymnasium and dance hall, sports ground, public house and café. The omnium gatherum of 'other' found members of dramatic societies, boy scouts and girl guides, territorials, allotment gardeners, and a number of similar associations and accounted for a quarter of the women and a sixth of the men The question seems to have been understood without ambiguity by those who gave an answer; and therefore it seems probable (though too much stress can never be placed on negative evidence) that the quarter of the population who left this question unfilled take no rôle in community life, whether organized or unorganized.

This quarter of the population is heavily concentrated in the metropolises and big towns, in London and the South-East, followed by the Midlands and North-West. The married and widowed are heavily represented, the single much less, there are four women for three men in this category. Under twenty-four the solitaries are relatively few; the highest concentration is in the 25–34 groups. The poorer are slightly lonelier than the better off, with £8 a week as the dividing line With one exception, social class seems to make no difference· the exception is that those who consider themselves upper middle or upper working class belong to associations far more than the rest of the community After 10 years of residence in the same house the numbers of the isolated tend to fall slightly. The people who belong to no associations tend not to know their neighbours informally either.

These negative figures confirm in general the Peckham picture:

it is the younger married people, especially the wives, living in big towns on small incomes, who are the loneliest members of English society, without even the faint friendliness of pub or café.

The remainder, three-quarters of the population, engage in some sort of social life, however attenuated; some of the people participate in a number of social institutions. I asked if people visited them at all, and also how many times they had gone in the last month (for most respondents December 1950); and I correlated such participation with type of house, how long it had been their home, and their opinions of their neighbours It is most convenient to deal with each institution separately and summarily.

One-fifth of the English population visit their *church or chapel meeting rooms*. a quarter of this number are zealous in their attendance, going more than once a week, another quarter go weekly. These regular and zealous visitors are predominantly women, in most cases poor, often unmarried, and either young or old, rather than middle aged. Only two-thirds as many men as women use these meeting rooms; they are used less by the married than by the single, and least of all by the divorced or separated They are little used by the inhabitants of the metropolises; and visiting increases as town size decreases The Western regions, both North-West and South-West, make more use of these facilities than the rest of the country; London and the South-East make least. Socially, those who call themselves working class, without qualification, make markedly less use of their church or chapel meeting-rooms proportionately than those of other classes; it seems possible that the poor, ill-educated women who call themselves 'middle class'[2] consider that their church or chapel going gives them higher status.

The people who use these facilities tend to live in detached or semi-detached houses which they have inhabited for 10 years or more. Transients and new-comers, people who live in flats or furnished or unfurnished rooms, or who have lived in the same house for 4 years or less are very sparsely represented, suggesting that since the war churches and chapels have failed to get into touch with new residents. The only other institution which so concentrates on old inhabitants is, somewhat surprisingly, the youth clubs. It is perhaps not surprising that the people who are assiduous in their visits to church or chapel meeting rooms should be particularly censorious about the moral faults and failings of their neighbours. Very few of them complain about neighbourly inquisitiveness.

Eleven per cent of the population belongs to some sort of *men's club*. Membership, particularly among regular club-goers, rises with age and income, with the higher concentration in men aged 45 and over. Socially the biggest concentration of members is in the upper working and working classes; there are fewest in the middle class. Regionally, men's clubs are by a significant figure most popular in the North-East and North followed by the South-West; London and the South-East have the fewest. The smaller the community, the larger the membership of such clubs.

It is uncommon for a man to join a club unless he has lived at the same address at least 2 years; and the greater number of members are old-established residents. The chief complaints that club members make about their neighbours are their religious and political views and their habit of borrowing.

In contrast to men's clubs, women who join *women's clubs or women's institutes* are likely to do so shortly after settling into their houses. Membership is chiefly drawn from the middle aged and elderly, the poor, the married or the widowed. They tend to claim either middle class status or else to be very confused about their class position Membership is predominantly from the smaller communities, and is highest in the rural South-West. Since this is chiefly (it appears) a phenomenon of country life, it is perhaps not surprising that nearly all members live in detached or semi-detached houses. The club or institute is used very intermittently; one-third of the membership only makes a monthly visit, and less than a quarter go three times a month. Members of women's clubs are particularly inclined to be appreciative of their neighbour's good qualities; when they do complain, it is about the failure of the neighbours to keep their houses, their persons, or their domestic animals in approved fashion. Five per cent of the total population belong to some sort of women's club.

Just twice the number belong to a *mixed club*, but it is a very different group of people; the members of mixed clubs are predominantly young (under 24), predominantly single, (followed by the divorced and separated) and predominantly well-off. Town-size and region make very little difference though such membership is lightest in the North-East and North; the upper middle class and upper working class are largely represented. Many members go once a week, a small number more frequently. They find their neighbours noisy and unsociable. Nearly all members of mixed clubs have lived in the same house at least 10 years, most of them all their lives.

The concentration of old established residents is even more marked in the membership of *youth clubs*; more than half the total membership has lived in the same house for more than 10 years, most of

67

them all their lives; and these houses are mostly detached or semi-detached. Newcomers or transients, people living in flats, furnished or unfurnished rooms, hotels or boarding houses are considerably under-represented. As far as this evidence goes, youth clubs do not reach the new arrivals, the young people without friends or connections in the neighbourhood.

Nearly one in four of the under eighteen's belong to some sort of a youth club, and one in eight of the 18–24's; the proportion steadily rises with family income. Regionally the biggest proportion is in the North-East and North, and the most assiduous members come from there; there are fewest members in the North-West. Socially, members of youth clubs tend to place themselves as upper middle or upper working class, there are proportionately few working class or lower middle class members, and rather more lower working class. A fifth of the members are regular weekly visitors, and another fifth go even more often Most members of youth clubs have positive praise for their neighbours, some however complain of their inquisitiveness and their reserve

Seven per cent of the population, slightly more men that women, belong to a *political club*, though most members make little use of them; one monthly visit is general; less than a fifth go once a week. Length of residence makes little difference to membership of a political club, for the small minority who are interested enough to join the facilities are immediately available. By nearly all criteria the politically interested are scattered evenly throughout the population; there is a small concentration in the medium-sized (100,000–10,000) towns; but otherwise area, age, marital status and income appear to make but little difference. There is only one point of contrast, but that is a marked one members of a political club tend significantly to put themselves in the upper section of their social class, there is nearly twice the proportion of upper working class to working class, and a third more upper middle than middle It suggests that people who join a political club feel themselves representative of, or leaders of, their respective social classes. Members of political clubs are, understandably, very opposed to the political views of their neighbours; the only other complaint on which they concentrate is gossip

If one groups the membership of all clubs and voluntary associations together, a marked and interesting contrast between the different regions of England appears. The North-East and North easily leads in club membership; 46 per cent of the population belong to some sort of association. Next comes the South-West with 44 per cent, followed by the Midlands with 40 per cent; lowest are the North-West with 36 per cent and London and the South-East with 33 per cent. This is one of the fairly numerous situations in which North-East and North-West are strongly contrasted.

To become a member of a club implies to a certain extent an intention to associate with the other members, and so can be considered an act with social implications; with the other institutions, now to be considered, this social implication is less certain. A pub can be as much a social meeting place as most clubs; or a visitor can be completely anonymous, slaking his thirst among strangers Similar ambiguity attaches to visitors to cafés, sports grounds, or dance halls.

Two men and one woman in five make at least occasional visits to *public houses* Among the casual visitors, the people who go once a week or less often, there is not a very marked discrepancy between men and women visitors—twenty men to thirteen women; but with the frequent visitors, the 'regulars', there are fifteen men to two women. Among the 'regulars' there is a high proportion of the divorced and separated, and slightly more unmarried than married; they tend to come from the somewhat better-off section of the community. There is a slight concentration of such 'regulars' in the South-West and Midlands; but they are fairly evenly scattered throughout the community except that they are proportionately somewhat fewer in the metropolises, in the South-East and North-West, and among the old people. A noticeable factor about these regular drinkers is that they seem to have very considerable difficulty in placing themselves in the English social system; to a very marked extent they answer the question about their class position by saying that 'they don't believe in classes', or that they don't know or by incongruous replies. Frequent visits to the pub apparently have a tendency to confuse status.

Taking all the pub visitors together, both occasionals and regulars, there is some concentration of the lower middle, upper working and working classes, though the differences are slight. The amount of visiting increases regularly with income, until £15 a week is reached. The largest number of pub-goers is found in the Midlands in the large cities, but there is not much difference between regions or town-size, except that London and the South-East and the metropolises have proportionately somewhat fewer visitors than the rest of the country. Pub visitors are drawn from all types of dwelling, but there is a slight tendency to visit pubs more in the earlier years of residence than after one has lived 10 years in the same house. More than the users of any other type of social institution, pub visitors say that they do not know their neighbours; such complaints as they do make emphasize borrowing, and the neglect of children.

Although it is a very different group, as far as age and sex goes, that visit *cafés*, they too have a slight tendency to be new-comers to their houses, to live in all types of dwelling[3] and not to know their neighbours. Cafés are used by 21 per cent of the population, 19 men to 23 women. They are used predominantly by the young (under 24) and the unmarried, the divorced and separated, and relatively little by the married and widowed. The richer use cafés more than the poor, and the upper middle, middle and upper working classes considerably more than the others [4] Cafés play a lesser rôle in metropolises and in London and the South-East generally (though when people from these areas do use cafés, they tend to use them with regularity); they are most used in the South-West and Midlands; the North-West uses them even less than London.

Three men and one woman in ten visit *sports grounds;* but for most people this is only an occasional outing. One in ten go more often than once a week, and these are predominantly young men who are probably players; the remainder go once, twice, three or four times a month in almost equal proportions. People in the North-East and North are far the keenest on sports, with over a quarter of the population going to sports grounds; London and the South-East is the lowest with proportionately a third less, the rest of the country is in between Except for the metropolises, watchers come from all town sizes equally; and this is one of the few activities in which length of residence in the same house makes no difference, and type of dwelling practically none, though flat dwellers are a little under-represented. With a weekly income of under £8 a week people apparently can't afford to spend money on sports; above that sum income makes little difference. Class is much more important; members of the upper working and working classes are much the most assiduous visitors; the upper middle classes go least. Sports fans—presumably, particularly since this was winter, football fans—make up a very representative cross-section of the English working class (with a partial exception of the lower working class); in income and habits, in type of residence, in their attitudes towards their neighbours, the sports watchers do not differ significantly from the population as a whole.

Very different are the small group—4 per cent of the men and 2 per cent of the women—who frequent a *gymnasium*. They are mostly

70

young—under 24—unmarried, prosperous, with slight concentrations in the upper working class and, regionally, in the Midlands. Most of them are gymnastic enthusiasts, going once a week or more often. They tend to be long established residents in detached houses. They are particularly censorious of their neighbours' moral faults, laziness, gossip, and inability to control their pets. The regular use of a gymnasium would seem to develop not only the muscles but also a feeling of moral superiority in the gymnasts.

Nearly a fifth of the population visit *dance halls*, the majority being under 24 and unmarried, and women more than men, in the proportion of five to four. The biggest concentration of dancers occurs in the big towns with a population of a million to a hundred thousand, and regionally in the North-West, followed by the Midlands and the North-East and North. There is least dancing in the metropolises, and in the whole South-Eastern region. Visiting dance halls is directly correlated with income, the most assiduous visitors coming from the groups with family incomes of over £12 a week; but it is even more highly correlated with social class. Those who put themselves high in their social class—upper middle or upper working class—go in considerable numbers to dance halls; those who put themselves low—lower middle or lower working—have less than two-thirds as many visitors. Only a very small group, and those mostly under 18, go more than once a week; nearly a quarter only go once a month and most of the remainder less than once a week. There is a slight tendency for newcomers to the area to be visitors to dance halls; once again the dwellers in flats or rooms are slightly under-represented. Dancers are particularly resentful of their neighbours' inquisitiveness and gossip; they also complain that their neighbours are noisy.

This review of the use the English people make of social facilities could give no indication whether they made use of these facilities alone, or in the company of other people. In an attempt to find out the smaller units of association, I asked 'If you wanted to spend a pleasant evening, what sort of company would you like to spend it in?' and further 'What sort of company did you have last Saturday evening?' in an attempt to discover to what extent people achieved the company they desired. For most of my respondents the Saturday described would be either January 13th or January 20th, 1951. They were presented with eight choices: one man, one girl, a foursome (two couples), a group of men, a group of girls, a mixed group, with own family, and alone. For the question about the specific Saturday

71

evening, two further categories had to be added: 5 per cent were working (7 per cent of the men and 3 per cent of the women, very evenly scattered throughout the population); and 6 per cent were ill (8 per cent of the women and 4 per cent of the men). These invalids were concentrated in the North-West, and were predominantly old and poor; there was apparently a flu epidemic in that area at the time.

Seven per cent of the population spent the Saturday evening alone; these solitaries come from every section of the population, but there is a heavy concentration among the old and poor, the widowed and divorced. Two per cent of the population would prefer solitude to any company; many of these are young, unmarried and call themselves upper middle class, they may perhaps be students. Some of the old and poor also choose their own company; and these hermits are represented in every category.

Eighty-five per cent of the population had some company on the January Saturday; 97 per cent of the population desires some sort of company for a pleasant evening.

A quarter of the population prefers the company of their own family to that of all others, a respectable choice which confirms previous observations about the relative lack of sociability among the English. As can be expected, it is the married who make this choice most frequently, followed by the widowed; it is made relatively little by the single. Significantly more men than women, in the proportion of four to three, choose their family's company. Regionally there are only slight differences; a smaller proportion of people from the North-West, and a larger proportion from the North-East and North choose their family, the smaller the township, the more the company of one's own family is preferred. This preference increases steadily with age, and to a certain extent decreases with income; with a family income of over £12 a week alternative company is largely preferred. The people who call themselves upper middle or upper working class have less taste for their family's company than those of other classes.

On the Saturday in January, considerably more people spent the evening with their own family than would have chosen to do so; it was the fate of 36 per cent, though the choice of only 25 per cent. It is above all the young and unmarried and the prosperous who were unwillingly at home; and there is a marked contrast between the regions, in the South-West and South-East (including London) considerably more people were with their family than in the rest of the country.

Second choice—made by a fifth of the population—is for a 'mixed group', a party; 23 per cent of the women and 17 per cent of the men opt for this type of entertainment. This is markedly a middle class preference; the percentage is higher in all three groups of the middle class, than in any of the working class groups, with upper middle leading. It is interesting to note that this is one of the fairly rare cases where response by income and response by social class differ very noticeably, the response is nearly identical for all income groups. The taste for parties is slightly higher among the under 18's; thereafter there is little difference until the age of 65 There is a slight preference in the bigger towns; and the figures are slightly lower for the two Western regions

In January there were fewer parties given than people would have liked; 14 per cent were actually in a mixed group, compared with the 20 per cent who would have liked to be. In practice income makes more difference than it did in choice; the number of party goers increases regularly with income, and varies relatively little according to class. People living in the two Southern regions went to parties less than did the rest of the country

The limited party of a foursome—two couples—is chosen by 16 per cent, 15 men to 18 women. This seems to be the first choice of two groups—the under 18's who presumably find it is a cover for their shyness, and the young married group of 25–34; the married choose this combination somewhat more than the single. It is particularly preferred by the more prosperous members of the lower middle and upper middle classes in the metropolises and big towns.

A relatively small group—only 6 per cent—actually spent their Saturday evening in this way; but those who did so mostly came from the groups who prefer this combination, especially the younger married people.

Sixteen per cent of the population as a whole prefer the company of one man. Thirty per cent of the women and 5 per cent of the men make this choice. It is made least by the married, but even here 13 per cent would like it; the same percentage of choice is made by the 25–34 age group, after which the figures rise slightly. It does not seem an unfair deduction that the older married women sometimes yearn for an evening out with another man. The poor make this choice considerably more often than the better off.

Nearly the same proportion—15 per cent—would prefer to go out with one girl, a choice made by 25 per cent of the men and 2 per cent of the women; but the distribution is markedly and interestingly different. The highest proportion comes from the unmarried

73

under 24; far fewer married or widowed men would choose the company of one person of the opposite sex than is the case with women of similar standing. After the age of 24 the interest in the company of one girl drops off sharply and continuously; there is no recrudescence of interest after the age of 35, as there is with women. The desire for the company of one girl mounts dramatically with income; twice the number of those with a family income of over £15 a week desire the company of one girl compared with those with a family income of under £8 a week; this reverses the picture with women, and suggests that the habit of the man paying all the expenses when a couple go out is almost universal in England. Only the richer men can contemplate taking a girl out; and for the poorer girls being taken out by a man is the only possibility of spending a pleasant evening. There is a curious lack of fit in the class picture; the middle class women are the most interested in going out with a man, the upper working and lower working class men most interested in going out with a girl. Regions and town size do not seem to make any significant difference.

On the Saturday evening in January fewer people spent the evening in the company of the opposite sex than would have chosen to do so. Eighteen per cent of the women, and 5 per cent of the men were out with one man; 14 per cent of the men and 5 per cent of the women were out with one woman. The economic aspect of what is, at least potentially, courting behaviour is once more confirmed; the going out with a girl rises consistently with income, whereas the poorest girls go out with men as much as their wealthier sisters, and indeed slightly more than most of them. It is interesting to note that there is least of this potentially courting behaviour in the South-West; there is a little more in the North-West than in the other regions, but the difference is slight.

Nine per cent of the men and (perhaps slightly unexpectedly) 2 per cent of the women would choose a group of men for company; but no men, and only 2 per cent of women would choose a group of girls.[5] The choice of all-male company is low (3 per cent) in the 18–24 age group; thereafter it rises steadily with age. It is most marked in the North-East and North, and lowest in the North-West[6]; otherwise it seems to be a characteristic of all the other regions and all town-sizes and income groups. It is lowest in the middle and highest in the lower working and working classes. So few women choose the company of a group of other women for an evening's entertainment that little can be said about the distribution; there is a slight cluster among the young and poor.

Six per cent of the men and 1 per cent of the women actually enjoyed the company of a group of men 'last Saturday', none of the men and 2 per cent of the women spent the evening in a group of women. The distribution is very even, though this pattern is slightly more common in the Northern regions and the Midlands; there is a concentration, for which I can find no explanation, of all-male groups in the £12–£15 a week income group.[7]

It does seem worth emphasizing that 14 per cent of English men prefer the company of their own sex, when given a completely free choice; only 4 per cent of the women would choose to be with other women. All the figures seem to bear out the generalization that in England women are more likely to express heterosexual interest than are men.[8]

NOTES TO CHAPTER FIVE

1 See p 18

2. See p. 37.

3. Only with the pub, the café, and the sports ground, do the dwellers in flats, furnished and unfurnished rooms, hotels or boarding houses use the facilities in proportion to their numbers in the population

4. It is perhaps relevant to recall that many of my upper middle class respondents were students, which may account for the apparently high use of cafés by members of this class

5 It seems possible that the emphasis on the time of the day has somewhat falsified the picture of the amount of pleasure English women take in the company of their own sex. It appears probable, though I have no material to demonstrate this, that women enjoy the company of other women during daylight hours, for lunch or tea, but prefer male company after the sun has set.

6. See page 302.

7. The questions about the company which would be chosen, and the company actually enjoyed on the Saturday evening were also asked in the field survey The contrast between interviews and written questionnaires can most conveniently be demonstrated in tabular form, the percentage for the written survey being in brackets and italics.

	Would choose			Last Saturday		
	Total	Men	Women	Total	Men	Women
One man	7 (16)	4 (5)	10 (30)	5 (11)	3 (5)	8 (18)
One girl	7 (15)	12 (25)	2 (2)	4 (10)	6 (14)	3 (5)
A foursome	11 (16)	10 (15)	11 (18)	3 (6)	3 (7)	2 (5)
Group of men	6 (6)	12 (9)	1 (2)	5 (4)	10 (6)	— (1)
Group of girls	0 (1)	0 (0)	1 (2)	0 (1)	0 (0)	1 (2)
Mixed group	26 (20)	21 (17)	29 (23)	15 (14)	15 (13)	15 (14)
With own family	40 (25)	37 (28)	42 (21)	48 (36)	43 (37)	52 (34)
Alone	3 (2)	3 (3)	3 (2)	8 (7)	6 (6)	10 (9)
Working	—	—	—	7 (5)	10 (7)	4 (3)
Was ill	—	—	—	2 (6)	2 (4)	2 (8)
No answer	0 (1)	1 (1)	1 (1)	2 (4)	2 (4)	2 (5)

The most immediately striking contrast between the answers from interviews conducted by young women, in contrast to anonymous questionnaires, is the great increase in devotion to one's own family, and the great decrease, even in preference, for the company of a member of the opposite sex This would appear to be an artifact of the interviewing situation. As has been noted before (see Appendix Two), the English seem to have a tendency in face-to-face interviews to present themselves as friendly, domestic, and good neighbours to a much greater extent than they do in a non-personal situation. The field sample is somewhat older than the main sample, but if the table is inspected for the choices and reported behaviour of the young and unmarried the discrepancy is still most striking. I would suggest that the professed lack of interest in a companion of the opposite sex is an artifact of modesty.

The relative lack of invalids in the field survey is presumably due to the fact that convalescents were difficult to get at for interviews, whereas many seem to have found filling-in the questionnaire an agreeable pastime during convalescence. The greater number of Saturday workers in the field survey seems to result from the selection of interviewees in Birmingham, the big concentration is in the Midlands and in the largest cities.

Although there are the marked differences in absolute quantities, the rank order is the same, and many of the distributions are similar, for example, parties or four-somes are directly correlated with income, and there is a similar preference from the poorer girls and the better-off young men for a companion of the opposite sex

8 I suspected that this preference of English men for the company of their own sex would be demonstrated, and I devised two further questions which I hoped would further illuminate this aspect of English character The questions were not well designed, and not a very great deal can be learned from the answers

One of these questions read 'Which of these statements do you agree with Friendship is more important than love Love is more important than friendship Love and friendship are equally important?' Everybody answered this question, but four-fifths (79 per cent) chose the answer 'Love and friendship are equally important', 76 per cent of the men and 84 per cent of the women making this choice Nineteen per cent of the men and 11 per cent of the women thought love more important than friendship, 7 per cent of the men and 6 per cent of the women thought friendship more important than love There is one curious regional difference; the South-West depreciates friendship (4 per cent) and appreciates love (20 per cent), whereas the other regions stay close to the national average The very young and the very old, the poor, the upper middle and lower working classes value friendship highly, otherwise the distribution is very even It is problematical whether members of some other societies would plump so heavily for the equal importance of love and friendship

The second question was 'Do you think a man and a woman can have a real friendship without sex playing any part?' And the alternative answers given were yes, no, don't know In gross figures 54 per cent said 'yes' (52 per cent men and 55 per cent women), 37 per cent said 'no' (40 per cent men and 35 per cent women); 8 per cent marked 'don't know' (7 per cent men and 9 per cent women); 1 per cent did not answer.

Here again it seems to be the general pattern which is significant, rather than minor variations More than half the population think that a cross-sex friendship can be sexless, which would surely not be echoed in many other societies If one takes, somewhat arbitrarily, a difference of 3 per cent from the national average as significant, then the following groups are particularly prone to believe in the possibility of a friendship between a man and a woman having no elements of sex in it the unmarried, people under 24 and over 65, those with an income of under £5 a week and the lower working class Groups which stress the impossibility of a friendship between a man and a woman without sex playing any part are· the divorced and separated, the inhabitants of metropolises, people between the ages of 25–44 and the lower middle class Uncertainty is most evenly divided, with three exceptions the under 18's haven't made up their minds (12 per cent), and very few of the widowed (4 per cent) or the lower working class (2 per cent) are uncertain With these few exceptions more than half the English population expresses belief in the channelling of sexual feelings

76

CHAPTER SIX

GROWING UP

SLIGHTLY MORE THAN half the population of England consider that
they themselves were 'exceptionally' shy, two-thirds of the population think that it is 'natural for young people to be shy'; but barely
a quarter of the population consider shyness 'a good thing' Two-
thirds disagree that shyness is desirable. Four-fifths think they are
less shy than they used to be

The distribution of these beliefs and attitudes is remarkably
regular and consistent whichever way the population is analysed.
The sexes differ only in that somewhat more men than women
consider shyness a good thing There is slightly less acceptance of
shyness in the two Western regions; and members of the upper
middle and upper working classes are significantly below the national
average in their beliefs in the naturalness or desirability of shyness,
and in thinking that they themselves were exceptionally shy. These
social groups, and the young—under 24—are the only groups in
the population of whom less than half think they were exceptionally
shy.

These are surely remarkable figures, especially in their implications.
Stated schematically, the typical English position would appear to
be. Shyness is a natural but undesirable, condition of youth, from
which many people suffer severely, but which most eventually get
over.

This background of shyness must be kept in mind in considering
the answers to the question 'How old were you when you first
started being really interested in girls?' (or. in the case of women
respondents, 'in boys?' This was one of the questions which were
phrased differently according to the sex of the respondents). Only
3 per cent of the population did not answer this question; and we
have therefore a picture of the conscious awakening of heterosexual
interest for a sample at least as large as any collected on this subject
in any country, and with a far larger proportion of working class and
lower middle class respondents than have ever been gathered before.
The implications of these answers seem sufficiently interesting for
the table to be analysed in considerable detail.

The gross figures are as follows. No answers were indicated on
the questionnaire, and the figures have been grouped in what seems
the most convenient way.[1]

77

Age of awakening interest	Total	Men	Women
Before 13	15	14	16
13 1–14	12	12	13
14 1–15	12	11	14
15 1–16	19	18	19
16 1–17	12	12	13
17 1–18	11	12	9
18 1–19	5	6	3
19 1–20	4	5	2
Over 20 1	5	7	4
Not interested	2	1	2
No answer	3	2	5

The first deduction that can be made from these figures is a statistical confirmation of the well known fact that women mature (at least emotionally) earlier than men. Between the ages of 14 and 17, there is a preponderance (in the neighbourhood of 6 per cent) of girls who are interested in boys over boys interested in girls. For England, it would seem that mixed groups of adolescents would be more harmonious if the boys were a year older than the girls. A second deduction of considerable interest is the difference between the divorced and separated on the one hand, and the married on the other, in the age at which interest in the opposite sex reaches awareness. Among the married, 59 per cent say they were interested in the opposite sex at 16, but only 43 per cent of those whose marriages have broken were interested The figure for the unmarried is 60 per cent, so that this is almost certainly not a statistical artifact. This pattern continues consistently. By the age of 17, 72 per cent of those whose marriages have endured were interested in the opposite sex, compared with 58 per cent of the divorced and separated. A year later, at 18, 85 per cent of the married were interested in the opposite sex, compared with 69 per cent of the divorced and separated. On these figures it seems clear that an English man or woman who is not aware of interest in the opposite sex by the age of 17 is a rather bad bet for an enduring marriage.

Thirdly, the rate of maturing at least emotionally, if not physically, seems to vary consistently with town size, with income, and with social class. The premature, those who are interested before 13, are heavily concentrated in the metropolises, among the well-to-do; members of the middle classes, the big towns, and the rural South-West mature earlier than the rest of the population. With the categories employed, the age nearest to the median is 16, when 58 per cent of the population say that their interest has been awakened. This figure rises to 60 per cent or above for the South-West, towns with more than 100,000 inhabitants, people with incomes of over

£8 a week, and members of the upper middle, middle and lower middle classes. It falls below 56 per cent only among the widowed, the divorced and separated, the upper working class, and those with an income of under £5 a week. The contrast between people of different income levels (ranging from 49 per cent of interest at 16 from those with an income of under £5 a week to over 60 per cent in the higher levels) suggest that poverty and different nutrition play a major rôle in development, but this is partly masked and partly seconded by differences in class behaviour; the difference in numbers between all members of the middle classes, and all members of the working classes (although only a matter of 5 or 6 per cent) is completely consistent, which would not be the case if income were the only determinant.

The most marked contrast of all depends on the present age of the person answering; and this would seem to be susceptible to a number of explanations, none of which can be checked by the facts at present available. At the median age of 16, 83 per cent of those under 18 said they were interested in the other sex, 71 per cent of those between 18 and 24, 59 per cent of those between 25 and 34, 55 per cent of those between 35 and 44, and 49 per cent of those over the age of 45.

It seems possible that the youngsters, especially those under 18, had no adequate criterion for being 'really' interested. This interpretation is made more likely by the fact that a number of respondents underlined the word 'really', and quite a few made uninvited but elucidating comments. Thus, a 41-year-old working class man from Derbyshire replied: '17. I must admit I was too shy and did not go out with one until I was 19.' And a 20-year-old middle class girl from a Warwickshire village: 'I responded to the difference in sex at the age of about 5. I can remember falling in love at that age. However, at 20, I still do not feel sufficiently attracted to boys to become a wife. Possibly about 18 I am not sure.' A couple of young men added rather facetious comments; a 23-year-old working class bachelor from Stepney writes: '12 or 13 years, school run out of Footballs owing to the war'; and a 28-year-old married working class man from Prudhoe, Northumberland: 'About 16, though the soccer pitch outwayed them every time.'

Even allowing for the possible confusion among the adolescents and post-adolescents, there is still the phenomenon that as age increases so does the recollection of the time of onset of sexual interest. Does this represent a real historical change or is it merely a difference in recollection? Did people now over 45 develop their emotions later than those now under that age? Or is there a tendency among English people, as they go towards their physiological decline, to increase in fantasy the number of years when they were still 'innocent' and 'uninterested in sex'? It seems at least possible that both elements are involved. Respondents over 45 who were born at the beginning of the century or earlier mostly grew up without the constant stimulation to 'love' and 'romance' which is so incessantly supplied to their juniors by the films, the radio and television and the lyrics of popular songs. Consequently, when the impulse was not particularly strong, there was much less propaganda to induce the young to attempt to manifest interests which they did not strongly feel; and the confused notions of 'psychological health' and the relative undesirability of one-sex groups had no currency. On the other hand, it does seem likely that the middle aged and elderly tend to deny their own early sexuality and to establish, even in an anonymous questionnaire, the picture of the absence of sexual feelings, as well as experience, before marriage which was, and still to a great extent remains, the English ideal. The men and women who place the development of their interest in the other sex after the age of 19 are predominantly over 45. Apart from the under 18's, the small group who say that they are 'not interested' in the other sex are very evenly distributed; quite a number of these volunteered the statement that they were homosexual

I asked a question intended to discover whether there was a general belief in a change in sexual morals over recent years Unfortunately, the form of the question was one in which many respondents found difficulty in following the instruction. They were presented with five sentences and asked to mark the one which they most agreed with, and the one they most disagreed with. Very few respondents were willing to confine themselves to marking only one sentence; so instead of 100 per cent answers (this is one of the questions which less than 1 per cent did not answer) we have 184 per cent positive choices and 123 per cent negative choices. There is no group in the population which did not give more answers than were called for; the most garrulous were the poor, the old, the widowed and the lower working class.

Fortunately this question was also asked in the field survey, with the added safeguard that cards were printed with the sentences in different arrangements, so that there would be little likelihood of the position of the sentence in the list determining the choice. In the interviews people could only make one choice; and there is therefore less chance of obscurity in the resulting pattern. Except for one instance, the pattern and distribution in the two surveys appear very similar.

The sentences offered for agreement or disagreement were:
    (i) There is much more immorality than there used to be.
    (ii) Human nature hasn't changed, but people are not so narrow-minded as they used to be.
    (iii) It is right and natural for young people to want to make love.
    (iv) It's other people's nasty minds which make all the mischief.
    (v) People are really more moral today than they were thirty years ago.

The most approved-of statement is (ii). 'Human nature hasn't changed, but people are not so narrow-minded as they used to be'. This is selected by over a third of both groups. In the field survey second choice goes to (iv) 'It's other people's nasty minds which make all the mischief,' again with nearly a third; and third choice is (iii) 'It is right and natural for young people to want to make love' chosen by a little under a sixth In the written sample both the order and comparative weight of these two statements are reversed. Only one in eight hold that there is much more immorality than there used to be; and a tiny group—one in 25—consider that people are really more moral today than they were thirty years ago.

The disagreements are perhaps even more revealing. Over a third repudiate the statement that 'People are really more moral than they were thirty years ago'; and nearly the same number repudiate the statement that 'There is much more immorality than there used to be' Two-thirds of the population of England deny that there has been any change in sexual morals. Only small groups rejected the other sentences; an eighth rejected the importance of censoriousness, a tenth the decrease in narrow-mindedness, and a twentieth the naturalness of young people wanting to make love. A tenth did not answer the negative questions.

To the extent that this survey is reliable, the English people strongly repudiate the belief, enunciated by so many preachers and writers in the popular press, that the present generation manifest a licence and lack of moral standards unprecedented in earlier generations. Even when the views of the older people are analysed separately, the same picture appears. They do, it is true, stress the increase in immorality somewhat more than their juniors, but not enough to effect the rank order of the choices.[2]

We are of course dealing all the time with statements and not with behaviour, with what people say and not necessarily with what they do. It is assumed that there is some relationship between what people

81

say and what they do; and the frankness of so many of the answers give some grounds for assuming that the discrepancy between ideals and behaviour is not unduly great. By internal checks the picture is very consistent; the younger generation—those under 24—are just as strict in their views of desirable and undesirable sexual behaviour as their elders. There seems every reason to believe that the sexual morals of the English have changed very little in the present century.

NOTES TO CHAPTER SIX

1. This question was also asked in the field survey, but owing to the rather gross categories imposed, the answers are only very roughly comparable They also appear to be inherently improbable, and indicate that this is one more area in which modesty, and a desire to present oneself in a light the interviewer will think favourable make face-to-face interviewing unrewarding with English respondents. The figures with the categories used are as follows

Age of awakening interest	Men	Women
Up to 10 years	2	2
11–13 years	6	5
14–16 years	33	38
17–19 years	34	37
20–22 years	12	10
23–25 years	4	2
26–30 years	3	0
Over 31 years	1	0
Not interested	3	3
No answer	2	3

2. In the very few interviews which Dr. Kinsey administered to the old (*Sexual Behaviour in the Human Male*, pp 226–7, 235–8, 319–35) he also found no evidence for a change of sexual mores in the interviewees' lifetime

CHAPTER SEVEN

LOVE

SLIGHTLY MORE THAN three-quarters of the total English population, and nearly 90 per cent of the married, consider they have been 'really in love' The meaning of this phrase is far from precise, though some attempts will be made to elucidate it later, but whatever the understanding the English give to it, it does represent an important emotional event in the lives of the greater part of the community.

Being 'really in love' would seem to be an experience of the prime of life, between 25 and 34. Under the age of 18 barely a quarter of the population claims this experience; between the ages of 18 and 24 two-thirds do so; between 25 and 34 the figure reaches the maximum of nearly nine-tenths. Slightly more than half the unmarried claim this experience, also; a little more than a third do not, and the rest are undecided.

It is interesting to note that one married person in twenty (with the widowed, a slightly higher figure) say that they have never been 'really in love'; the other groups who say that they have not had this experience in marked excess of the national average are the top and bottom of the economic and social scales· members of the upper middle and lower working classes, those with incomes of under £5 and over £15 weekly. There is no appreciable difference between the different English regions or sizes of towns.

For most people this experience is apparently expected to be unique The question 'Do you expect to fall really in love sometime?' was a clumsy one to put to the total population, though I would have thought it meaningful for the single. My respondents did not; nearly a fifth refused to answer (much the highest figure of refusals); and among the unmarried more than a quarter refused. Nearly half marked 'don't know'.

A tenth of the married and a fifth of the widowed expect to fall really in love in the future (presumably for a second time); slightly more than half the unmarried have a similar expectation. Except for the very poor, the hope for future falling in love increases steadily with income; the reverse pattern is equally consistent; the poorer one is, the less hope one has of a future 'falling in love'. This is one of the cases where income appears to be a more positive determinant than social class.

A slight insight into the English conception of love was afforded by the answers to the question: 'Do you think English people fall in love in the way you see Americans doing it on the films?' Although the question is fairly vague, the pattern referred to is not, I think, unclear. In many American films the principal boy and principal girl are portrayed as being strangers to one another before the start of the story, attraction is immediate ('at first sight') followed by a speedy wooing of persiflage and endearments which leads to marriage as soon as the obstacles are removed—the chief obstacle being usually the necessities of the plot. The English are vehemently of the opinion that this does not represent typical English behaviour; more than three-quarters say 'no'; a mere 7 per cent say 'yes', and these are mainly young girls, with a slight concentration in the upper middle and lower working classes and in the high income groups [1]

Some further insight into the pattern of love in England can be deduced from the replies given by married men and women about the antedecents to their marriage; for it seems a reasonable deduction to make that, in the great majority of cases, the people who said they had 'really been in love' married the person they were in love with. This supposition is enhanced by the fact that two-thirds of the married men and a half of the married women answered in the negative the question whether they had seriously considered marrying another person before becoming engaged to their spouse; just over a quarter of the men (27 per cent), and slightly under half the women (44 per cent) had given serious consideration to other possible partners. Six per cent did not answer

As the gross figures show, English women are much more likely than English men to contemplate alternative partners. These women can be identified somewhat more precisely. They are likely to be prosperous (family incomes of over £12 a week) members of the middle classes living in the two Southern regions under the age of 34. Such people are found in all groups, but it is here where the biggest concentrations occur. Conversely the people, predominantly men, who marry their first choice are likely to be members of the working classes (particularly upper working class) with a family income below £12 a week, and particularly concentrated in the North-West, though the Midlands and North-East and North are also slightly above the national average. Such constancy is somewhat more stressed among the middle-aged and elderly.

The people thus chosen, whether they be first or subsequent choice, are likely to be acquaintances made in adult life. Only a very small group—less than 10 per cent—know their future spouses 8 or more years before becoming engaged; the pattern of childhood friends (or, for that matter school-fellows) marrying would appear to be a rare one in England; where it does occur it is mostly in the two Northern regions, especially in the North-East and North. Slightly more than a third (36 per cent) of English people become engaged after less than a year's acquaintance; just on a quarter (23 per cent) after less than 2 years; the remaining quarter (28 per cent) knew their future spouse more than 2 but less than 8 years before betrothal, with the greater concentration in the shorter periods.

It does look as though there has been a slight change in custom in recent years; compared with their elders, people under 35 are much more likely to become engaged in the first year of acquaintance; this is particularly true of members of the upper middle and middle classes. People in the Southern counties and in the metropolises are more likely to marry relative strangers than people from the North. The figures suggest that there is some truth in the adage 'Marry in haste and repent at leisure', for 40 per cent of the divorced or separated got engaged after less than a year's acquaintance, compared with 36 per cent of the married; if the acquaintance has lasted more than a year, the subsequent marriage is more likely to endure

I can say little about the length of engagement, for this is one of the situations[2] where thoughtless codification made the figures practically meaningless For slightly more than half (56 per cent) the betrothal period is less than a year; for another fifth (22 per cent) less than 2 years; for another 12 per cent some period between 2 and 5 years. Some 10 per cent of the population, chiefly the poorer members of the working classes from the Northern regions do not have a formal engagement, apparently on account of the expense of an engagement ring and a formal party.[3]

The English patterns of love which lead to marriage can be briefly summarized as follows. A young man meets a young woman, becomes attracted to her, courts her for between 1 and 2 years, and then may have an engagement lasting less than a further year. If the young man is a working lad from the Northern regions his future wife is likely to be the first girl by whom he was seriously attracted; if the girl is of the middle classes and from the big cities or the Southern regions she is more likely to have considered other young men before allowing herself to become seriously attached. There is little here of whirlwind romance, or of playing around before finding Miss or Mr. Right; there is also little of the in-group marriage of old acquaintances which characterizes some settled communities. It would seem to steer a middle way between these two extremes.

This is the pattern which leads to marriage; but even in the most sober of communities one would expect that sometimes love doesn't lead to marriage. When I asked 'Not counting marriage, have you ever had a real love affair?' I was quite uncertain what kind of answers I should get; after reading 11,000 questionnaires I think that the vast majority of the answers were completely frank. Seven per cent of the population refused to answer this question; these reticent people were the poor, the elderly and the widowed; the remainder divided up almost evenly, 43 per cent admitted to a love affair outside marriage, 3 per cent made qualified answers (not really—not a real affair); 47 per cent gave an uncompromising No.

Region and town size make remarkably little difference to the distribution of the answers; whatever the relationship of the answers to the facts, the answers seem to represent a true cross-section of English attitudes. The answers are almost exactly equal for the two sexes. Marital status makes a greater and expectable difference; the divorced and separated have the greatest number of admissions with 58 per cent, followed by the single with 47 per cent; 40 per cent of the married say that they have had a real love affair outside marriage, 50 per cent that they have not. The figure for the widowed is slightly lower than for the married, but there was so much reticence in this group that it would be risky to make deductions

Age makes little difference except for the predictable lack of experience in the under 18's, and the reticence of the over 65's; there is a climax in the age-groups 25–34, but they are only slightly more numerous than their juniors and seniors.

Class position and income appear far more decisive; members of all the middle classes claim to, or admit, more experience than all the members of the working classes; and economically the big dividing line is a family income of £12 a week; above that sum more than half have had some experience outside marriage, below barely two-fifths, a difference in the neighbourhood of 10 per cent. This is remarkably consistent with the picture[4] already given of the connection between income and the choice of one member of the opposite sex as a companion for a pleasant evening.

What did my respondents mean by 'a real love affair'? The question was vague, and quite purposefully vague; no answer was indicated and quite a lot of space was provided for any comments they cared to make. My intention was that the question should refer to pre-marital or extra-marital sexual relationships and the detailed answers make it quite clear that the majority of the respondents so understood it. The frankness and detail of the replies can only be demonstrated by a rather massive series of quotations; but lest these give a misleading impression of the sexual morality of the English, I should like to emphasize once again that half the married population of England, men and women alike, state that they have had no relationship, either before or after marriage, with any person other than their spouse, and that the numbers are even greater in the working classes. My personal impression—and it is backed up by other material to be described subsequently—is that this is a very close approximation to the truth; and although there are no extensive figures available comparable to these[5] I very much doubt whether the study of any other urban population would produce comparable figures of chastity and fidelity.

A number of respondents have such strict views of sexual morality that they included the anticipation of marriage under the heading of 'a real love affair outside marriage'; there is no way of counting in how many cases this applies; but the amount of promiscuity is obviously even lower than the gross figures would suggest. The following answers are typical of many:

A married working class woman from Hornsey:
If by 'real' you mean illicit—no except with my husband before marriage.

A prosperous 18-year-old girl from East Croydon:
Yes but with fiance which is really just anticipating marriage.

A 28-year-old lower middle class man from near Manchester:
Does this mean including sexual experience? If so—Yes with my fiancee

A working class man from near Nottingham:
When I was courting my present wife.

A 47-year-old Londoner:
Yes, twice and in both cases have married both these ladies.

A 22-year-old professional woman from near Portsmouth:
"Yes, with my ex-fiance (3 years ago); casual 'affaire' under unusual circumstances recently (was travelling abroad).

With some of these answers, particularly from the younger people, it is not at all clear what exactly is involved. A 23-year-old single woman from Herne Bay makes the distinction clearly:
Was unofficially engaged once (to wrong man). If, by 'real' love affair intimicy is implied then I never had a 'real' love affair It was the starry-eyed variety on my part.

A charming picture of the 'starry-eyed variety' is given by a 20-year-old middle class man from Evesham:

"Yes, It happened to me at 9.45 p m. on January 4th, 51, at a 'dance' A lightening of the heart, a feeling of utter joy. It's been that way ever since. Her name is Gladys, she's a Nurse here.

But one doesn't quite know what to make of the 19-year-old Leicestershire girl who writes:

I am having one now with marriage next Sept. have been in love two years.

or of the 23-year-old unmarried working class Yorkshireman·

Yes, the one I am having now and which has reached the stage of planning for marriage.

Similar ambiguity is found in some of the other replies. For example, the 24-year-old man from Thorpe-next-Norwich who writes.

Many times before my marriage I thought I was in love, but now I realize what I took for love was merely infatuation, probably brought on by the fact that the girls wanted to experiment in sex affairs as much as I did.

A lower middle class man, 44-year-old, from a village in Leicestershire·

Difficult to say. Seemed like it at the time and then evaporated.

A 42-year-old Middlesex woman:

My very first love affair was and always will be the only real one but we didn't marry.

A 37-year-old working class man from Christchurch.

Yes, but sex was forbidden by the lady.

An 18-year-old working class lad from Leicester:

An awkward question; people seem to think a boy of 18 cannot know what love is, For over a year I've been in love with a young girl: So much in fact that if I could afford it, I would like to marry her."

A 23-year-old miner from County Durham:

I have gone out with charming young ladies for periods ranging from 2 months to 6 months, but I don't think I could class any of them as *real* love affairs.

Quite a number make sufficiently explicit distinctions so that they can be placed in the 'not really' category:

A 23-year-old lower middle class man from a village near Great Yarmouth.

Numerous flirtations and affairs lasting sometimes several weeks Never had sexual intercourse.

A 33-year-old married woman from Hove:

Yes, several before marriage but never (physically) went far. I was too frightened and sex seemed very unromantic.

An unmarried working class girl from Swindon, aged 22:

Yes, twice One at 18 not very seriously, second time last year when I went out with a parson (C. of E) for some considerable time. After consideration he felt he was called to be celibate Reason—'God first partner second'.

A 25-year-old bachelor from Fulham

"Yes, with a girl employed by NAAFI during the War Though when I realized she was a willing party to sexual Intercourse I stopped seeing her. (I have never seduced any girl)

In the majority of the answers there is no ambiguity at all. Thus, a 47-year-old unmarried woman from Hampshire

Yes, two neither reached actual marriage standard, one only had two sex relationships."

A 59-year-old married woman from Newton Abbot:

Yes, was considered a fast young lady I loved a fellow previous to my husband.

A 21-year-old working class girl:

Yes, with an American when I was sixteen

A miner's wife from Essex:

Yes three years ago with a married German Prisoner of War

A 19-year-old middle class girl from Manchester:

Yes, I have lived with a Polish man and intend to marry him *this year*.

A 24-year-old working class girl in Ilfracombe·

Yes, since I came to Ilfracombe with a German who realizing we were getting serious told me he had no room for marriage in his plans.

A 42-year-old married woman from Enfield:

Yes when I was 27, lasting several years (during a separation from first husband)

A married woman, 30-year-old, who describes herself as 'ordinary working class':

Yes 2 affairs since being married

Another woman of the same age from North Kensington who places herself as 'working class (I think)' and is separated, says simply:

Yes I am still living with him.

A 24-year-old married woman from Rochdale who describes herself as 'respectable working class':

Yes, it ended up with me giving birth to a child. He married someone else

A 23-year-old middle class woman from Lincolnshire

Lived with a doctor for a few weeks A few hotel weekends with a medic (Both professions more important than marriage.)

A 37-year-old woman, twice married, from London

Yes at $17\frac{1}{2}$ I had a child before marriage, did not marry the father.

A divorced middle class woman from Southport

Yes, with the one person with whom I thought I had everything in common, we would have married but he is too jealous of my children.

A 31-year-old married woman from London:

Yes, six years ago with a married man. Girls take a chance and nearly always pay for their experience with a baby, like I did, while the wolf goes free.

A 38-year-old unmarried working class woman from East Ham:

Depends what you mean by 'love'. ? sexual experience without affection—yes, once, ? Platonic—yes

A widow from Weybridge:

This is difficult I was *really* in love before meeting my husband I loved my husband. Now I'm having an 'affair' but not sure if its love or loneliness

An 'average English working class' woman from Devonshire, unmarried and 23 years old:

Yes, and it is still continuing with my present boy friend who is awaiting a divorce But although we are very much in love I regret it but I should never tell my boy friend so.

A 44-year-old woman from Norfolk:

I met two men both of which promised to marry me. Both left me to face the world alone with two babies

A 54-year-old married woman from Macclesfield:

I was alone in the world that is why I married I had my first baby with my husband before I married him, then he went to war and left me, so I married him three years later.

90

A trained nurse from a South coast resort:
Lived with a soldier during the war. He was killed before we could marry.

A 49-year-old married woman from Lincolnshire·
Yes! When I was 19. He married someone else Nothing else mattered any more.

A 21-year-old North Country University student:
Yes there was a coloured medical student from a backward country, who is to be that country's 1st native doctor. We love each other but his and my parents disapprove of our marrying and for the above reasons he must return home, where my presence might prejudice his people against him and indirectly against modern medicine We decided it was selfish to put our happiness before the good of his people.

Few of the men's replies are as dramatic or as tragic as a number of the women's, though the working class man from Stockton-on-Tees has a sad story:
I am in love at the moment—the moment has lasted four years—but the lady is the other side of the iron curtain.

A 40-year-old man from Southend says tersely:
Yes, more pleasurable than marriage.

A married miner from Newcastle:
Yes, I once lived with a woman 10 years my senior, of good class and in a top neighbourhood, where we defied convention and were really in love. I still regret its termination 12 years afterwards

A 19-year-old youth from Burton-on-Trent:
Yes, with a married woman who has two children, but is separated, she lives with me now at present address, also quite often with various people.

A 40-year-old man from Yateley in Hampshire:
Having lived with a single woman for five years, before I was divorced.

A middle class civil servant from Reading·
Yes, several—one before marriage and two affairs at least during my married life.

A 30-year-old man from Stoke-on-Trent who describes himself as 'average working man who likes to live quietly'·
Yes with the girl who will be my wife as soon as I get a divorce from my present wife.

A 65-year-old general foreman in a public works in East Anglia:
Yes, after I separated from my first wife, and shall I confess, yes, I committed bigamy but parted after 14 years

A 32-year-old skilled craftsman from London:
Yes, I am separated from my wife although I have marked for marriage. I am actually living with the person concerned.

A 27-year-old married working class man from Wealdstone:
Yes—With a widow in South Africa but absence dulled it after leaving and meeting someone else

A 27-year-old working class man from the West Riding of Yorkshire:
Yes, on quite a few occasions I think couples appreciate each other more when they are not married to each other.

There are also a number of more fugitive relations. A 20-year-old single working class man from Chorley Wood:
Yes, I slept with a girl regularly every weekend for 4 months on the continent.

A lower middle class man from Cottingham in Yorkshire:
Not a love affair only sexual.

A black-coated worker from Newcastle-on-Tyne.
Not to the extent of intercourse with an English girl As a soldier abroad I was 'with' women. I had never been anybody's 'lover' in the affectionate sense as well as the other sense. Briefly *No*.

A 23-year-old working class man from East Finchley:
If you mean intercourse, yes, but was not in love with the girl.

A 26-year-old unmarried shop-keeper from Bletchley.
No, not in that sense of an adult relationship with a whole person (woman).

An unmarried 41-year-old Bournemouth man:
No Not a LOVE affair I have had women. I usually pay them.

A 33-year-old married man from Leeds:
Not normal love affair.

A 23-year-old working class man from Ipswich:
Yes, but there was no love in it! Happened in Athens 5th May 1945. It was disappointing and have never ceased to regret it.

A 28-year-old Devonshire man:
Yes (but I have different instincts to the normal man) I am abnormal —homo.

Only by such a barrage of quotations, which could be multiplied many times, is it possible to convey the impression of overwhelming honesty and truthfulness which a reading of the questionnaires produces I feel convinced that, within the limits of an anonymous questionnaire, my respondents were being as truthful about themselves as they could

I think it worth calling attention to the frequent appearance of foreigners as partners in these non-marital sexual relationships. I would suggest that this is a cross-cultural phenomenon, rather than a reflection on the sexual habits of most peoples other than the English. The foreigner is less 'dangerous', less likely to be censorious; and foreign techniques of courting and flirtation, with their greater apparent aggressiveness and confidence, may well be more successful with the 'exceptionally shy' English than they would be in their own countries.

NOTES TO CHAPTER SEVEN

1 This question was also asked in the field survey with identical figures for the answers

2. See p 10, note 5

3 In April 1952, the British Institute of Public Opinion asked a sample from the whole of Britain 'How long were you engaged?' with results very close to those given above Seven per cent did not have an engagement, 25 per cent one of less than 6 months, 28 per cent 7 months to 1 year, 14 per cent 13 to 18 months, 14 per cent 19 to 24 months, 12 per cent more than 2 years

4. See Chapter Five, especially pp 73–4

5. The sample used by Dr Kinsey in his *Sexual Behaviour in the Human Male* is in no way comparable

CHAPTER EIGHT

IDEAS ABOUT SEX

MOST ENGLISH PEOPLE'S views on sexual morality are more rigid than their personal practice; quite a number condemn their own lapses from their own high standards of complete chastity before marriage and complete fidelity after: 'I did, but I wish I had not' is a recurring theme.

This does not mean that the English tend to underestimate the importance of sexual love inside marriage. To the question: 'In marriage do you think sexual love is: very important; fairly important; not very important; not important at all?' 55 per cent answered 'very important' and 36 per cent 'fairly important'; the small group of 6 per cent who answer 'not very important' consist predominantly of the very young, the old and the poor; and the tiny group who say it is not important at all or don't answer are almost entirely old women.

Men, particularly between the ages of 18 and 34 in the medium income groups, stress the major importance of sex in marriage; women, particularly those under 18 and over 45 in the upper middle and lower middle classes, and also the unmarried, are more likely to qualify it as 'fairly important' with other components playing a major rôle

Despite the importance that the majority of English people give to sexual love in marriage, the majority think that both sexes should approach marriage with no prior sexual experience. Slightly more than half the population in the case of men, and nearly two-thirds in the case of women, disapprove of any sexual experience before marriage. Roughly an eighth say that they do not know. A third of the population in the case of men, and just under a quarter in the case of women, are in favour of some sexual experience before marriage.

In the case of both sexes, men are markedly more in favour of some pre-marital sexual experience than are women; 40 men to 26 women approve of a young man having some experience, and 30 men to 14 women approve of a young woman doing so. As will be discussed at some length later, quite a number of woman support a 'double standard' of sexual morality in which what is sauce for the gander is taboo for the goose; men are much more likely to invoke a 'single standard' in which they will not deny to others what they claim for themselves.

The most numerous advocates for sexual experience before marriage are the divorced and separated; and many of them advance their own unhappy stories of ignorance or maladjustment to justify their choice. The single are slightly, but only slightly, more in favour of such experience than the married; the widowed are least in favour.

The very young tend to be more severe in their ethical judgments than their elders, though nearly a quarter of the under 18's have not made up their minds; the height of permissiveness is reached by the people aged between 25 and 34, but it is only a small difference; people between the ages of 18 and 24 are just as severe in their moral notions as people 20 years older. The old people, aged 65 and over, tend to be very non-committal; they have markedly fewer advocates for sexual experience before marriage than their juniors.

With one exception, social class makes remarkably little difference to the views on the desirability or otherwise of experience before marriage: a far higher proportion of the lower working class are in favour of sexual experience before marriage than of any other group. It is only in this group that there is an absolute majority in favour of pre-marital experience for men; and a third are in favour of it for women too. There is a folk tradition that in some of the metropolitan and rural groups of the lower working class marriage normally follows pregnancy; and it is possible that these figures echo this alleged practice. The upper middle class have the greatest number of undecided respondents; it will be remembered that many of this class were students.

Far more determining than social class is family income. Here there is a steady and marked increase in permissiveness directly correlated with the increase in income, ranging, in the case of men, from 25 per cent in those with incomes of under £5 a week through 35 per cent in the £8–£12 to 42 per cent with incomes of over £15 a week. Parallel figures for young women are 18 per cent for incomes under £5, 24 per cent for incomes £8–£12, and 30 per cent for incomes of over £15. Here once more we find evidence of the determining influence of money on the English ideas about and attitudes towards sex.

In the case of young men, town size makes a marked difference in the incidence of permissiveness, with 38 per cent in favour in the metropolises and only 20 per cent in the small towns and villages; the intermediate size towns, between 1,000,000 and 10,000 inhabitants, are on the national average. This difference practically disappears in the case of women, suggesting that the 'double standard' is almost entirely confined to the inhabitants of London and Birmingham

95

and their conurbations. The Midlands are by a small degree the most permissive region for both sexes, followed by London and the South-East, the North-East and North is by a small degree the most severe region.

My respondents were not only asked for their views, they were asked to give the reasons why they advocated them: after both questions appeared the word *Why?* with adequate space for any answer they cared to give. The great majority availed themselves of this opportunity; in the case of young men 13 per cent gave no answer and a further 2 per cent said they did not know; in the case of young women 12 per cent were silent and 1 per cent had no opinion. All the remainder made some sort of answer, though, in the case of 3 per cent for each sex the answer was the non-committal one that it depended on the people concerned.

People were given no sort of guidance as to the way in which their answers should be phrased; after a preliminary analysis I established twenty-six categories into which all the answers fitted adequately, though some of these had very few respondents. Nine reasons are advanced why some experience before marriage is desirable, and sixteen reasons why it is undesirable. It is interesting to note that, as far as this questionnaire is any guide, English people appear to be more prolific in arguments against a given course of action than in arguments in favour of it.

Fifty-two per cent of the population, it will be remembered, are against any sexual experience for young men before marriage and 63 per cent against any experience for young women; the following are the reasons advanced for this judgment:[1]

Reason given	Percentage for young men	Percentage for young women
(i) Marriage should be a new experience	13	12
(ii) Man wants virgin wife	0	9
(iii) Man should be pure because he wants wife to be	6	1
(iv) Against morality	7	6
(v) Against religion	4	4
(vi) Not necessary—Nature teaches	4	5
(vii) People should have self-control	2	2
(viii) Unfair to girl	2	1
(ix) Degrades girl	2	8
(x) Danger of pregnancy	2	6
(xi) Danger of V D	2	1
(xii) Danger to health or future children	0	1
(xiii) People wouldn't marry if they could get it without doing so	2	1
(xiv) Leads to promiscuity after marriage	1	1
(xv) Husband may bring up later	0	1
(xvi) Danger of invidious comparisons	0	1

The following are the nine reasons advanced why some experience before marriage is desirable, they apply to 34 per cent of the young men and 23 per cent of the young women.

Reason given	Percentage for young men	Percentage for young women
(xvii) To avoid ignorance, maladjustment, etc, on honeymoon	13	7
(xviii) To make certain marriage not based on physical glamour	4	3
(xix) To avoid woman's fear or disgust	0	2
(xx) Makes for fidelity after marriage	1	0
(xxi) With future husband or wife only	2	3
(xxii) Not to include intercourse	3	3
(xxiii) For good effect on character—makes more mature, etc	6	3
(xxiv) For physical or psychological health	2	1
(xxv) It is normal and natural	5	2

Before these reasons are examined in greater detail, the list itself seems to call for a few comments. What seems to me most note-worthy is the high seriousness with which the great majority of English people approach and regard marriage. Whether pre-marital experience is advocated or reprobated, the effect on the future marriage is the preponderating consideration Secondly, the high valuation put on virginity for both sexes is remarkable and, I should suspect, specifically English. Thirdly, it is interesting to note that what might be dubbed the hypochondriacal attitude towards sexual activity has apparently achieved very little currency. This hypochondriacal view, derived from assorted popularizations and vulgarizations of psychology and psychiatry, connects sexual activity with physical and mental health, so that abstinence becomes, as it were, a rather more dangerous type of constipation and sexual activity a kind of prophylaxis. In some other societies, this view would appear to be very widely held.

The argument (1) that marriage should mean a new experience, a new 'thrill', that intercourse should be confined to marriage, is one that is advanced considerably more by women than by men for both sexes; it is particularly stressed in the lower middle, upper working and working classes, and is mentioned relatively little by the lower working class. It is an argument whose use decreases consistently with the increase in income, and is relatively little advanced by people with incomes of over £12 a week. In the case of young men the rural South-West finds this argument particularly cogent; and it is advanced from this region too slightly more in the case of young women than elsewhere. The replies advancing this view vary relatively little; the same form of words recur with great regularity

The high evaluation of virginity in women (reason ii) is advanced slightly more by men than women, and finds some concentration in the middle income groups, and the upper working and working class; the lower working class advance this relatively little. A great number of synonyms are used for this desirable state, many of them metaphors from merchandizing—'new', 'not second hand' 'not shop-soiled' and so on The converse, that a man should be pure because he wants his wife to be a virgin (reason iii) has very similar distribution for income and social class, with the exception of the well-off and the upper middle class, who advance it even less than the lower working class. Women advance this argument slightly more than men, but it has its relatively numerous advocates in both sexes. Thus, a 20-year-old middle class man from North London:

Some sexual experience may be necessary and is useful but I, when I marry want a pure girl, so the least I can do is to be the same myself.

A 23-year-old bachelor from Stockton-on-Tees·

Why should he? What good can it possibly do? If I ever marry, I would like my wife to be a virgin—is it fair to expect this if I haven't been chaste myself?

A 41-year-old married working class man from East London·

From my own experience, I'm glad I only had mild petting flirtations. Which I'm not ashamed to tell my wife

A 42-year-old working class man from Sutton-in-Ashfield.

I can only answer this It was a joy on my wedding night to know this was my first experience.

A 38-year-old working class man from Penrith:

Because I married a virgin as I always hoped I should, that is why I never had sexual intercourse before marriage.

A 28-year-old working class married man from Prudhoe, Northumberland:

He enjoys his sexual experiences to the full with his wife if he is still a virgin and he will never wish to wander from her Variety may be the spice of life but it can be fatal in this instance Secondly it can also be fatal as regards V.D I was at sea at the age of 17 yrs and have been in all the 'spots' and had lots of chances yet I remained a virgin & so bought no 'spots'.

A 24-year-old bachelor from South-West London:
It's my belief that a man should be content to wait. I personally would feel shame for myself, and a slight contempt for the girl. (if it happened before we married.)

A 27-year-old married working class man from Dudley:
He should keep himself to himself until he gets married. Should not like to think some man could point out my wife

A 25-year-old married working class man from Dartford:
If he has ideas of finding a virgin he should do likewise

A 19-year-old middle class bachelor from Liverpool:
Every man expects to marry an untouched woman therefore should not have any sexual exp. himself I think all women should be married in white and can't do so if she has had sexual exp with men.

A 35-year-old labourer from Huddersfield:
A man likes to be first and marry a virgin. I did. I learned my sex experience the dirty way. In the mills, My father died when I was ten."

A 27-year-old married woman from Bishops Waltham:
Men of today expect the best when they marry so should be prepared to give the same.

A 50-year-old married woman from Croydon:
In my opinion my husband and I were 18½ years of age and we fell madly in love and having no other experience our marriage has lasted.

A 29-year-old working class wife from Birmingham:
Should imagine no decent man would ever regain his self-respect. May I say that though sorely tempted during engagement I never did and have never regretted it."

A 31-year-old married man from Streatham:
I did, but I wish that I had not, because I think this experience should only be had at the peak of a love match, namely a honeymoon.

A 45-year-old working class man from Southend-on-Sea·
I did have that experience and regretted it, one loses self-respect and also respect for the girl.

A 21-year-old bachelor from Lincolnshire:
Would not like my future wife to have had sexual experience with other persons prior to our marriage. Matter of principle also.

A 23-year-old working class bachelor from Tilbury:
I think it is wrong for anybody to gain experience at the expense of somebody else. I should hate to think somebody had tried married life out on my wife to be.

Besides the arguments about the intrinsic value of virginity there are also appeals to the rules of morality and ethics and mistaken views of common law (reason iv); and, for a small group. an appeal to the prohibitions of religion (reason v). The argument from ethics is advanced much more by women than by men, and is particularly favoured in the rural South-West; it is little stressed by the upper and lower working classes In its application to women, the married stress it more than the single, and the older more than the young. The appeal to religious sanctions is advanced nearly equally by both sexes, but chiefly by the elderly and by members of the lower middle class, it is hardly used at all by members of the upper middle or lower working classes.

An interesting point is that the appeal to religious principles is often advanced by people whose practice would appear to be agnostic; thus a 42-year-old married man from Enfield who says flatly 'Sexual experience before marriage is not Christian' practically never goes to Church or prays, nor does he believe in a future life. In similar case is a young single woman from near Portsmouth who says 'It is against the law of the Country and the Church and leads to moral degeneration of the community.'

A middle class married woman of 39 from Chippenham in Wiltshire·

> Sex should be regarded as sacred by both sexes An affair before marriage could lead to one after marriage [for young women?] Again for sacred reasons A girl seldom goes 'scott free' and an easy woman does not usually mean she makes a good wife and mother Pre-marital sexual experiences leaves one with a tainted mind and guilty conscience

A 29-year-old married middle class woman from North London:

> Promiscuity in either sex can never be right, in any case, sex is not always 'all it is cracked up to be'.

A twice-married 47-year-old London man:

> If a man *really* loves a Lady, he doesn't necessarily or shouldn't expect sexual experience, for my part it wouldn't worry me if I never did any more I know I am 47 yrs. now but it never has worried me much anyway [for young women?] I say, again, if a couple really love one another that shouldn't worry them, if one of the couple says No, then the other shouldn't ask or expect it. Again for my part, I've honestly never had or expected it before marriage and wouldn't lower myself to ask for it, from a Lady.

The belief that experience is unnecessary, because 'nature teaches' (reason vi) is one particularly favoured by the upper middle class

100

and completely rejected by the lower working class. Otherwise it finds its advocates in nearly every category, approximately equally. Thus, a 39-year-old married working class man from Bradford:

> Sex is an instinct which everyone is blessed (or cursed) with therefore it does not need a 'tryout'.

The appeal to self-control (reason vii) is in many ways similar to the confidence in nature, and to the appeal to ethics; the actual phrasing is different to the extent that it does imply that there are some emotions to control; it is used somewhat more by the middle aged and by the well-off. A typical statement is that of a 36-year-old working class married woman from Sendon, Derby: 'He should respect women and curb his desires till married.' Or a separated woman, 43 years old, from Evington: 'If control is not obtained before marriage, it certainly will not after.'

There are three closely related reasons (viii, ix, and x) for abstaining from all sexual experience before marriage; these are all connected with the effect on the girl involved. The fact that it is 'unfair' to the girl is advanced as a reason for male abstention; and many of the male respondents refer specifically to their own sisters or daughters as a reason why men should be chaste. This argument is somewhat favoured by the lower middle class, and is not used at all by the upper middle; otherwise the distribution is very even.

Thus an unmarried working man from Runcorn:

> I don't think it is really fair to the girl he is going to marry (although I should not talk because I have and am now sorry).

A 45-year-old working class man from Southend-on-Sea:

> I have two daughters of my own (verb sap)

The argument that such experience degrades the girl and cheapens her, makes her feel tawdry or second-hand, and destroys her self-respect and the respect of others (argument ix) is advanced more by women and for women than it is by or for men; but it is invoked for both sexes and by all groups, though least of all by the young people, under 24. For the lower working class it is easily the most important reason for restraint. The danger of pregnancy (reason x) which can be considered the physical complement of the feelings of degradation is much more stressed by the married than by the single, and by the upper and lower middle classes. It is little advanced by the lower working class.

A number of the women who advance this latter argument bolster

101

it up with their own distressing experiences; thus, a 16-year-old girl from Birmingham:

> A girl might have a baby, she has the worry and disgrace the man just has his fun. Marriage should last and she should be pure. Anyhow I am illegitimate, but my mother had four children before me, legitimately.

A 25-year-old married woman of the working class from Shropshire:

> We had been married 3 months when our oldest boy was born and though we love each other very much we both realize that we behaved foolishly Not only does it mean sorrow for the boy and girl, but their families too. We were lucky Our folk helped us.

A 31-year-old married woman from London:

> She takes a chance and nearly always pays for her experience with a baby, like I did, while the wolf goes free.

A married woman from Sheffield:

> In these days of womens clinics it is not needful to try before you buy. From my childhood I made up my mind I would never marry a man who had sexual relations with me before, my mother was pregnant when married and hated my father for it

The other physical danger, venereal disease (reason xi), is advanced more by and for men, particularly younger men, than by women; the group is not large, but it does suggest that the anti-venereal-disease campaign has on occasion been too successful and created unrealistic phobias.

Thus, a 22-year-old working class bachelor from South-East London:

> In my opinion it is immoral to have sexual experience before marriage, thus creating V.D.

or the 21-year-old Bristol bachelor·

> It seems to me that this sort of thing lowers the general moral tone of the populace Also, I think it a crime to be responsible for congenital syphilis in children.

This fear runs into the obscure fear (reason xii) that such conduct will in some way cause harm to future children; only a small and scattered group takes up this attitude.

There is a small group which has the odd idea (reason xiii) that nobody would get married if they could have sexual intercourse outside marriage; these people are barely represented in the more

102

prosperous groups, the upper middle or lower working class. Thus, a separated lower middle class woman from Nottingham:

If a husband has some sexual experience before marriage he really has nothing to look forward to, and there is no point in his getting married.

A 29-year-old spinster from Putney:

If he finds he can gain this before marriage he naturally doesn't want to get married. Also a man seems to lose respect of the woman in question.

A 30-year-old married woman from Sunderland (Durham):

If young men had it women should too, I think they should start off together at marriage. If women had sexual experience before hand most women I know wouldn't have been married.

The lower working class are among the most convinced that experience before marriage leads to promiscuity after (reason xiv); but a few of all groups, except the young and unmarried, advance this argument. Thus, a 40-year-old married woman from Thorpe-next-Norwich:

Its moreish, the more you have the more you want. Because he rarely marries the girl he has his experience with, and has nothing to lose, so just continues from one to another.

A single woman from Putney, aged 29.

She is liable to become loose with every man. Also men talk about these things to one another and in this way a woman can lose her good name forever.

It is chiefly from the upper middle class (followed by the lower working class) that the arguments are advanced (reasons xv and xvi) that pre-marital experience could be inconvenient after marriage, either because the other spouse would use it as a reproach, or because he or she might draw invidious comparisons between lover and spouse. Thus, a single girl of 21 from London who describes herself as 'a member of a well educated family who have known better times':

As far as women are concerned, once having had this experience, one always wants it and it is injurious to health and the wife may become impatient with her new husband if he could not satisfy her as did her previous lover

A national service man whose home is in Merton Park:

Every man wishes to marry a virgin. Also there is danger of comparison when married. (Comparison between husband and other man.)

A 46-year-old working class man from Romford
> If you were not so satisfying for them, they would, one day, tell, how nice so and so did it

A single middle working class man from East London, aged 21:
> If she has she would tend to compare her sexual experience with her present husband and so might be unsatisfied.
> I shouldn't like a woman to have sexual intercourse before marriage and therefore nor should the male

Among the smaller group who do advocate some experience before marriage, far and away the most important reason advanced for this is the desire (reason xvii) to avoid ignorance, maladjustment or clumsiness on the honeymoon. Nearly one man in six and one woman in ten advances this as a reason why men should have some previous experience; nearly one man in ten and one woman in twenty-five advance this as a reason why women should do so—one more example of English men being more in favour of female emancipation than English women This is an argument whose use increases consistently with income and decreases with town size, as far as men are concerned; it has its most numerous advocates in the upper middle and lower middle classes and in the age group 25–34. As far as young men are concerned the single, married and divorced have similar figures; but for young women, the married and divorced have twice the number of advocates that the single do. The lower working class, followed by the upper working class, stress this argument in the case of young women.

A number of respondents cited their own unfortunate experiences to justify the course they advocated. Thus, a 37-year-old married woman from Barnshurst:
> My own husband made such a mess of it, we ceased relations after the first year.

A 31-year-old divorced working class man from Greenwich:
> I had no sexual experience before my marriage and I'd never want to experience my wedding night again

A 32-year-old married working class man from Essex:
> I had none myself and my marriage is now a physical failure

A 27-year-old middle class man from Strood:
> The failure of my own marriage was lack of sexual knowledge

A 41-year-old married woman of the middle class from North London:
> My personal experience with a virgin husband was most distressing.

A 26-year-old divorced woman from North-West London:
My marriage was recked mainly through a lack of sexual knowledge.
My husband had never had an affair before marriage. [for young
women?] Yes, because one can be disillusioned or shocked by sex—
and to be afraid can have a bad sycological effect if one does not know
what to expect

A 24-year-old married woman from West Bromwich:
A man should have had some experience because a woman expects a
man to be able to love make I was bitterly disappointed when I married
I had to teach him. Sexual experience teaches you things about each
other you can't possibly know otherwise.

A 41-year-old married woman from Walsall:
The cause for much unhappiness for myself was because my husband
had no sexual experience before marriage.

A 49-year-old re-married man from Willesden:
Lack of sexual experience was the cause of my first marriage break-
down.

A 40-year-old separated man from Yateley (Hants.):
Because I got married myself without any sexual experience whatsoever, to my sorrow. [for young women?] To help young men as unfortunate as myself as I have written about.

A divorced man, middle class, from Leigh-on-Sea, 45-year-old.
I didn't and my marriage went on the rocks from the beginning
through shyness and ignorance of women.

A 30-year-old divorced working class man from Coventry:
My own failure in marriage was due to a lack of sexual experience.

Quotations with the same underlying theme could be continued
over several pages, they strongly suggest that ignorance, particularly
on the part of the men, is a major hazard in English marriages.
A 36-year-old married worker from Nottingham says 'I met men
in the forces who were Married and were dead ignorant about sexual
Matters'. A great deal of my evidence bears out his observation.
 The argument that experience before marriage will make for a more
rational choice of marriage partner (reason xviii) is an argument
advanced twice as much by men as by women, and (understandably)
is particularly favoured by the divorced and separated It also finds
advocates particularly among the younger people and members
of the upper working and working classes; it is not employed at all
by the upper middle class

A 27-year-old separated working class man from Shipley:

He has some idea what he is about when first married and he is less likely to be landed into marriage and disappointment to find in a few months there is no love as he thought at first.

A 20-year-old betrothed middle class girl from Birmingham:

Not necessarily 'should' but it's sometimes wisest You see, I can quote at least one instance where a couple married and then the woman found she just couldn't stand him touching her, although she loved and trusted him.

A 25-year-old unmarried working class man from Hounslow.

The result is inevitably disappointing and he is thenceforth able to take a more rational view of marriage—stripped of its false glamour and accent on sex.

A 65-year-old working class man from Rainham·

For one thing it is natural and he's not likely to fall for the first pretty face and/or pair of lovely legs, the latter I think most English men fall for.

A widow from Weybridge:

A man should have experience, but not with the woman he chooses to marry It is well for him to know whether such experience is worth marrying for. He is likely to be in less hurry to marry, thereby choosing wisely and ensuring future happiness.

A women's instinct will tell her whether she will enjoy the experience or not. If she intends to marry she should wait for fear what she or parents should suffer through unforeseen circumstances. If she doesn't intend to marry (or re-marry) she may provided she remains utterly true to one man.

A 26-year-old unmarried woman from Streatham:

Many young men marry from only physical attraction as the basis for their desire to marry. Sexual experience helps to curb that desire, he does not marry so young, and chooses much more wisely someone with whom he can be really happy, as well as sexually suited.

In a way the reciprocal to the avoidance of marriage based on glamour is the avoidance of women's fear or disgust at intercourse or physical intimacy (reason xix). This argument is most advanced by the divorced and separated, and by members of the working classes. Although not mentioned by very many, this, like male ignorance, seems a hazard of English marriage.

A 42-year-old working class married woman from Bradford writes:

Not knowing much about the facts of life before marriage, it came as rather a shock to my nervous system.

A 44-year-old married woman from a Norfolk village (who herself had two babies before marriage):

I knew a home that was nearly wrecked through a young woman that got married. She was disgusted when her husband suggested intercourse. She thought he married her to cook and keep his house clean

The 46-year-old middle class woman from Folkstone may, or may not, be in a similar case; she writes:

A difficult question as I really loathe sexual experience. This has only happened since my marriage, as my husband was almost a sexual maniac.

A further small group argues that experience before marriage makes for fidelity after marriage (reason xx). This argument is chiefly used by the more prosperous women. Thus a 34-year-old married woman of the middle class from Carlingham (Yorks).

It is better to sow wild oats before, and not after, marriage Some women cannot reconcile themselves to that side of marriage Better to break an engagement than a man's heart.

A 17½-year-old working class youth from near Nantwich:

Quoting from my own experience of my father, what experience he's missed before marriage he will make up for after marriage elsewhere.

A 28-year-old woman, once widowed, once divorced, and now happily married:

I would sooner a man do it before marriage because after marriage he may feel he has missed something and start out *then* to sow his wild oats

A 51-year-old lower middle class widow from London:

To sow a few 'wild oats' within reason helps him in experience when he gets married, and make things pleasanter for the wife; and if a woman 'tastes before she buys' there would not be so many broken marriages through incompatibility, or disappointment through couples being unsuitable to one another, as in my own case.

The group who favour intercourse with the betrothed only (reason xxi) are extremely evenly distributed. A 25-year-old betrothed man from Birmingham:

If the fellow is engaged to the girl and all is on the up and up I think it is an extra bond.

A working class married woman from Yorkshire:

A girl should not, because I did—with my husband and I've often wished we'd waited Neither of us ever refers to it and we are very happy in our marriage even so.

107

A 34-year-old married woman from London S E.:

I did myself, fortunately to the man I really love my husband, I became pregnant. I wish now that we had been sensible and got married first If my husband hadn't loved me I would have borne an illegitimate child and 'labelled' easy to get (We had been engaged 2 years when this happened).

A 49-year-old separated woman from Chelsea:

They might suit in everything but not in sexual love, if sexual love goes wrong everything goes wrong. Marriage is three parts sex.

A 30-year-old 'ordinary working class' married man from Leicester:

Because it means a lot in married life and its nice to know if you can get on alright with your lover [for young women?] My reason is the same as above. But I don't mean they should go around trying whoever comes along It should only occur if you intend to marry for love.

The five arguments so far advanced are all concerned with the success of the marriage subsequent to the pre-marital experience. Together they account for nearly two-thirds of the reasons advanced for young men having some experience before marriage, and nearly three-quarters of the arguments for young women The remaining reasons are concerned with various theoretical views concerning 'human nature' and the effect of sexual intercourse on health and character, none of which are very widely spread, the position of the 3 per cent who would exclude intercourse from pre-marital sexual experience is however somewhat ambiguous.

Sexual experience without intercourse is presumably the English equivalent of what the Americans call 'heavy petting'; and it is probably significant that the advocates for these practices are heavily concentrated in the upper middle class, followed by the lower working class. The upper middle class emphasis follows Kinsey's finding[2] that in the U.S.A. this custom is most widespread among the college-educated portion of his sample.

Examples of this attitude are a 19-year-old middle class youth from Leicestershire·

My answer 'no' stands definite if by 'sexual experience' you mean intercourse. I have no objection to moderate 'pretence' love-making or 'fair-play' kissing

A working class youth from Reading of the same age:

If by sexual experience it means sexual intercourse, this is wrong as I believe that a man should enter marriage 'clean'. I do think there is nothing wrong with 'love making' before marriage provided both parties are sensible about it

A 31-year-old married lower middle class man from Manchester·

Whilst not condoning pre-marital intercourse, I do think 'petting' can be a great help. My reason is that for the first few months of my marriage I had a lot of difficulty in this direction, most of which could have been avoided had my wife and I had some previous experience.

A 19½-year-old middle class Liverpool girl·

Don't know Can't make up my mind about this but I am sure I would never hate a boy for this as if I loved him I know I should want to as I think Nature is a beautiful thing. [for young women?] Don't know. Again I am uncertain as my boy friend has often asked me often and as I love him very much to me it does not seem wrong. Its just that I am afraid as I do not want to hurt my family

A prosperous upper working class girl aged 18 from East Croydon:

It helps him to be more gentle and understanding. I do think, however, that he should not go the whole way until he meets his future wife. [for young women?] Really the same as for a man. When people have had a little experience they know how to make their loved one happy and content without too much misunderstanding, shyness, etc

An upper middle class 18-year-old youth from Berkhamsted (Herts):

I don't really think a young man should experience actual intercourse before marriage; a certain amount of passionate love-making and possibly homosexuality are not harmful.

The argument that sexual experience has desirable effects on the character, by making the experienced more mature or more confident or with a broader outlook finds slightly more advocates among the women as far as male experience is concerned; this pattern is reversed (though the numbers are barely half as many) in the case of female experience. This argument is most heavily pressed by the divorced and separated; it is also favoured by the younger groups (especially the under 18's) and members of the middle class. The lower working class advance it hardly at all, and the upper middle very little.

A 28-year-old unmarried man from Mitcham of the lower middle class:

It broadens a chaps mind. It has a Psychological effect on a young man, it fetches out the manliness No woman likes to think that she is going around with an inexperienced overgrown schoolboy.

What might be called the therapeutic attitude to sexual experience —the belief that it will ward off physiological or psychological disturbances if taken regularly—has very few advocates among the English and these are significantly concentrated in the most prosperous groups of the middle and upper middle classes living in big cities. These small groups presumably represent the extent of the impact of diluted psycho-analytic thought and simplified versions of mental health on an English audience, it seems probable that such reasons would be advanced by a far greater portion of the population in the United States

This viewpoint is typified by a 58-year-old married working class man from Morecambe and Heysham (Lancs):

> Nature cannot be hidden—the natural tendency is ever prominent and perversion can be averted by practical experience with a young woman with the same desires [for young women?] As above and for both male and female sexual desires are far better eased by intercourse than by personal actions

The periphrasis employed above occurs with some regularity. An attempt at plainer speaking by a 61-year-old working class man from East Kirby (Notts) resulted in: 'Yes. Its either that or mastication'.

Finally there is the group (5 per cent in the case of men, and 2 per cent in the case of women) who consider pre-marital experience 'natural' and 'normal'. I was myself surprised at how small this group turned out to be. This view of human nature is held much more by men than by women, and finds its greatest proportion of advocates in the lower working class, followed by the working and middle class. It is advocated very little by the upper working and lower middle classes; it is a relatively popular idea in the Midlands, but is little held in the South-West, or North-East and North. Thus a married coalminer aged 45, from West Melton, Yorks.

> Yes, Because he cant help reacting to nature and I dont think there are many who dont [for young women?] Dont know. I think I would have to change sex to be able to answer this truthfully

A 30-year-old Surbiton bachelor who describes himself as 'A low paid relic of the Bourgeois Intelligentsia'.

> A man's nature demands sex satisfaction before he is sufficiently mature to contract matrimonial responsibilities.

A 61-year-old married middle class woman from Margate:

> For men, yes, because it is natural and men are made of a different kind of ruling [for young women?] No, because when a girl goes to the altar a virgin she can hold up her head and tell her husband to go to hell if she had due cause to in the case of ill treatment.

A 27-year-old married man from Wealdstone (Mddx):

> Yes, because it is normal and providing precautions are taken not to get the girl in trouble, in the same way for women though I didnt touch my wife until we were married.

110

A 36-year-old miner from Barnsby.

It is only natural, whenever anything Bird, Beast, or man decide to become mates they have to have that experience, i e. you would hardly buy anything without taking a look at it first.

Presumably the same argument was advanced for the unfortunate 17-year-old girl who writes.

Recently I was sexually assaulted it was horrid and for a few weeks after I thought sex was a shameful thing but now I understand it isn't, it was just the way this man approached me.

In this review of the reasons given for and against sexual experience before marriage, I have not, except incidentally, paid attention to different respondents' views of the relationship between what is considered appropriate conduct for young men and for young women. In current phraseology the term 'double standard' is used for the view that sexual experience before marriage is suitable for one sex (typically and almost universally, men) and not for the other; 'single standard' is used when the same rules of conduct are applied to both sexes.

Cross-correlations show that the vast majority of the English population employ a single standard of sexual morality. The only significant exception is that slightly under a third of those who are in favour of pre-marital experience for young men are against such experience for young women, and this is barely 10 per cent of the total population. There is a tiny (and somewhat inexplicable) group of less than one in a hundred who reverse this preference, and would allow experience to the woman but not to the man. For nine English men and women out of ten what is sauce for the goose is sauce for the gander.

My impression—for this cannot unfortunately be completely substantiated with the figures at my disposal—is that it is the women who tend to advocate the double standard, whereas the men (albeit often unwillingly) opt for the single standard.

The women, whether married or unmarried, who advocate the double standard do so with a view to achieving greater happiness, or avoiding unhappiness, in marriage. Thus, an unmarried upper middle class woman from Godalming, aged 23:

[for men?] Yes, because I can imagine little worse than two complete novices on a wedding night! [for women?] No, in most circumstances no.—I intend to be really in love with, and love, the man I marry and would prefer to keep myself for him.

A Liverpool girl of not quite 17:

I think yes because until a man has such an experience he really

111

Figure VI

Question 49 by Question 50

49 Do you think a young man should have some sexual experience before he gets married?

50 Do you think a young woman should have some sexual experience before she gets married?

Question 49	Question 50				
	Yes	No	Don't know	No answer	Total
Yes	66	25	6	3	100
No	1	98	1	0	100
Don't know	1	31	66	2	100
No answer	5	15	3	77	100
Total	23	63	11	3	100

Figure VII

Question 50 by Question 49

50 Do you think a young woman should have some sexual experience before she gets married?

49 Do you think a young man should have some sexual experience before he gets married?

Question 50	Question 49				
	Yes	No	Don't know	No answer	Total
Yes	97	2	1	0	100
No	13	80	6	1	100
Don't know	20	4	75	1	100
No answer	24	11	7	58	100
Total	34	52	12	2	100

cannot define LOVE as anything particular, because men fall victims to their emotions much more easily than women [for young women?] No, because although I am a woman and believe in Equality of the sexes, I am still old-fashioned enough to believe a woman should be perfectly pure before she enters into matrimony.

A 33-year-old married woman from Hove:

On the husband's success at love-making depends his bride's physical *and* mental pleasure A hesitating, shy man would be terrible. [for women?] No, because she must have lost a certain self-respect, and also may be tempted to marry purely for physical reasons Also an old fashioned maybe, but deep rooted prejudice.

112

A 23-year-old unmarried working class woman from Exeter:
I should think he would be much more considerate to his wife due to previous experience. [for women?] No, because most men prefer a pure wife, and it must be nice to know you are that.

A 25-year-old unmarried working class woman from Southampton:
I would rather have my husband know what he is doing, but for a girl I do not consider this necessary as she takes more risks.

This combination of arguments occurs with considerable frequency; it also has some, but fewer, male advocates. The reverse argument, as has been said, is advanced by very few and seems to be idiosyncratic. A 45-year-old working class man from a village in Leicestershire (who considers his major good qualities poaching, gardening and hard work) writes:

[for a young man?] It is unnecessary, as love will find a way as soon as a man and woman get to bed together [for a young woman?] She can easily spoil her life through ignorance, she will also know what to expect on her wedding night

A 28-year-old 'middle working class' woman from Bromley:
[for a young man?] I think no because a man soon learns quick enough, if he has experience before marriage he wouldn't want to get married. [for a young woman?] Yes, here I think yes to save disillusion. A woman nearly always wants to marry for so many reasons beyond sexual love

A single man from Bootle:
[for a young man?] It is not absolutely necessary. [for a young woman?] Yes A woman is different they go for the man but a man does not go for a woman

A 49-year-old married woman from Gainsborough:
[for a young man?] uncertain. [for a young woman?] Yes. Then she realizes what marriage means.

The advocates of the double standard seem to have as their major value their own happiness, or the success of marriage in general. The advocates of the single standard of complete pre-marital chastity for both sexes (and it is worth recalling that this is far and away the most widespread English attitude) presumably have as chief value the categorical imperatives of morality, according to their views. Similarly many of the advocates of the single standard, permitting pre-marital experience to both sexes, seem also to have as their chief value moral considerations, in this case justice or equity, which often over-ride deep-felt attitudes and prejudices. Emotionally,

113

many of the men respondents would prefer a double standard; but since they claim licence for themselves, their sense of justice will not allow them to deny the same licence to others (women). This lively sense of justice seems to me one of the most admirable, as it is also one of the most widespread, of English characteristics; and it seems worth while calling attention to it in this context, where it is in patent conflict with another aspect of morality.

These attitudes become apparent in the answers which men give to the question whether young women should have sexual experience before marriage, when they have already answered positively in the case of young men. This type of answer is fairly stereotyped, and a small selection can stand for the whole group. Typical is a 29-year-old lower middle class man from West Wickham.

It seems unfair to deny to a woman a right which I claim for myself, and yet I know I should be upset to marry a girl other than a virgin

A lower middle class bachelor from Wallasey, aged 25:

I am torn between natural desire to marry a virgin, yet feel selfish if I say 'no' in view of my answer for men.

A 21-year-old bachelor from Halifax, middle class·

I am tempted to answer, a young woman should not have sexual experience prior to marriage—but if I agree that men should, then in my opinion it goes equally for both sexes.

A married man 'sort of lower middle class' from Sheerness (Kent) aged 41:

I've said 'yes' in the young man's case, so equal rights etc gives me yes here, yet wishing I could put No.

A married working class man from Lincoln, aged 33:

Anyone who tackles a big job should be trained for it marriage and sex life is a big job, and for women my answer obviously has to be the same, but I suggest a woman does not obtain her training from too many teachers.

Besides the hypothesis just advanced that English men tend to place ethical principles first and English women more practical considerations, there is another possible explanation for women giving support to a double standard of pre-marital sexual morality, and men to a single one; this is the difference in views which English men and women appear to hold about the nature of women's sexuality. Stated briefly, English men tend to the belief that women's interest in sex is as great as, or greater than, that of men; English

114

women on the contrary consider that the physical aspects of sex mean less to them than to their menfolk.

These statements have been phrased rather tentatively, because they are derived from the answers to a question with the type of instructions which apparently[3] are too difficult to follow accurately. Respondents were asked to mark *one* of four statements which they most agreed with, and *one* which they most disagreed with; but more than a third of the population were unable to restrain themselves to a single choice in each column; and so, instead of the base-line of 100 per cent, there are 134 per cent of agreed statements and 127 per cent of disagreed. Men and women over-mark in nearly equal numbers.[4]

The sentences among which respondents were asked to choose were:

  (i) Most women don't care much about the physical side of sex.
  (ii) Women don't have such an animal nature as men.
  (iii) Women really enjoy the physical side of sex just as much as men.
  (iv) Women tend to enjoy sex more than men.

Sixteen per cent of the men and 26 per cent of the women agree with the statement 'Most women don't care much about the physical side of sex'; 55 per cent of the men, contrasted with 39 per cent of the women disagree with it. The agreement is most concentrated among the poor, the middle aged and elderly, members of the lower working class and especially the widowed; it finds fewest advocates among the young (under 34), the more prosperous, members of the upper working and lower middle classes, and quite markedly, the Midlands. Disagreement with this sentiment follows much the same pattern, with a concentration among the unmarried under 24, the more prosperous, and the upper working, middle and working classes.

The other sentiment repudiating female sexuality—'Women don't have such an animal nature as men'—shows much the same pattern. Forty-eight per cent of the women but only 38 per cent of the men state their agreement with it; 13 per cent of the women but 21 per cent of the men their disagreement. Once more it is the poor, the middle aged and elderly, the widowed and the lower working class who stress this notion most; they are joined with—though to a lesser extent—the upper middle and middle classes, the divorced and separated, and the two Northern regions. The idea is most vehemently rejected by the young, the unmarried and the more prosperous; it is very little mentioned by the inhabitants of small towns and villages (presumably because they know something about animals).

The pattern already discernible continues with the egalitarian statement 'Women really enjoy the physical side of sex just as much as men'. Sixty-three per cent of the men agree with this statement, compared with 51 per cent of the women, a mere 10 per cent of the men, but 18 per cent of the women, reject it. Acceptance is markedly higher among the unmarried, aged between 18 and 24, the prosperous, especially the £12–£15 a week group, the upper middle class and, once again, the Midlands; it is lowest among the poor, the middle-aged and elderly, and the widowed. It is the same group which actively rejects this statement the most.

Fifteen per cent of the men, but a mere 4 per cent of the women, state their agreement that 'Women tend to enjoy sex more than men'; 39 per cent of the men, but 57 per cent of the women disagree with it. This rather surprising belief is particularly held by the young and unmarried, it may be a reflection of the difference in the conscious awakening of interest in the opposite sex already noted.[5] It is particularly held in the North-West, followed by the Midlands. It is little advanced by the widowed, or by members of the upper middle or lower middle classes. Its most emphatic rejection comes from the middle aged (35–64), the widowed, the poor and the upper middle and lower working classes.

These remarkable figures—and they do seem to me remarkable —allow some tentative conclusions. Among the young, the unmarried and the more prosperous, especially in the Midlands, there is a belief, held more strongly by men than women, that women's sexual feelings are as strong as, or stronger than, men's; this belief diminishes with marriage, increase in age, or decrease in income. Putting the tables together, one might hypothesise that thirty years ago there was a fairly widespread belief in the 'lesser animality' of women; and secondly that many women find disillusionment, at least on the physical level, in marriage around the age of 35.

The last two chapters have analysed in considerable detail some English attitudes towards love and sex. A number of cross-correlations were made to attempt to discover to what extent the views expressed were internally consistent; and also in the hope of finding out what other characteristics distinguish the minority who depart from the English pattern of complete chastity before marriage and complete fidelity thereafter.

On the basis of these correlations, it can be said quite unambiguously that the greatest influence making for pre-marital chastity is the active practice of religion Correlating the questions about

116

the desirability of pre-marital experience for young men or women with attendance at religious services there are nearly double the number of advocates for pre-marital experience from those who never go to Church, or only for weddings and funerals, as compared with those who go once a month or more often. The figures become even more marked if the questions are correlated with private devotions, where those who never say prayers, or only in peril and grief, have more than double the advocates for pre-marital experience compared with those who pray daily or more frequently. Religion, particularly private religion, appears the strongest bulwark of the austere English sexual morality.

Figures VIII and IX

Question 84 by Question 49

Question 84 by Question 50

84 Do you attend Church or religious services?

49 Do you think a young man should have some sexual experience before he gets married?

50 Do you think a young woman should have some sexual experience before she gets married?

	Figure VIII					Figure IX				
	Question 49					Question 50				
Question 84	Yes	No	Don't know	No Answer	Total	Yes	No	Don't know	No Answer	Total
More than once a week	17	70	9	4	100	14	75	8	3	100
Once a week	24	59	14	3	100	17	69	10	4	100
Less than once a week but more than once a month	24	63	10	3	100	16	73	8	3	100
Less than once a month	29	55	14	2	100	21	66	10	3	100
Once or twice a year	34	53	11	2	100	23	64	10	3	100
Only for weddings and funerals	42	44	12	2	100	28	57	12	3	100
Never	40	43	16	1	100	29	54	14	3	100
No answer	—	20	13	67	100	—	13	—	87	100
Total	34	52	12	2	100	23	63	11	3	100

There is also some evidence for the often promulgated belief that the influence of American films tends towards the loosening of the bonds of English morality. It was only a very small group (7 per cent) who said they thought that 'English people fall in love the way you see Americans doing it on the films'; but this group are

117

Figures X and XI

Question 85 by Question 49

Question 85 by Question 50

85 Do you say private prayers?

49 Do you think a young man should have some sexual experience before he gets married?

50 Do you think a young woman should have some sexual experience before she gets married?

	Figure X					Figure XI				
	Question 49					Question 50				
Question 85	Yes	No	Don't know	No Answer	Total	Yes	No	Don't know	No Answer	Total
More than once a day	22	60	13	5	100	16	69	9	6	100
Daily	25	60	12	3	100	16	72	9	3	100
Only in peril or grief	42	44	13	1	100	28	59	11	3	100
Very seldom	36	50	12	2	100	25	60	12	3	100
Never	46	39	12	3	100	34	50	13	3	100
No answer	24	53	9	14	100	21	62	7	10	100
Total	34	52	12	2	100	23	63	11	3	100

Figures XII and XIII

Question 44 by Question 49

Question 44 by Question 50

44 Do you think English people fall in love in the way you see Americans doing it in the films?

49 Do you think a young man should have some sexual experience before he gets married?

50 Do you think a young woman should have some sexual experience before she gets married?

	Figure XII					Figure XIII				
	Question 49					Question 50				
Question 44	Yes	No	Don't know	No answer	Total	Yes	No	Don't know	No answer	Total
Yes	45	42	11	2	100	31	56	10	3	100
No	35	53	11	1	100	24	65	9	2	100
Don't know	25	52	21	2	100	17	61	19	3	100
No answer	24	32	7	37	100	11	36	6	47	100
Total	34	52	12	2	100	23	63	11	2	100

Figures XIV and XV

Question 42 by Question 49
Question 42 by Question 50

42. Would you say you had ever been really in love?

49. Do you think a young man should have some sexual experience before he gets married?

50 Do you think a young woman should have some sexual experience before she gets married?

Figure XIV   Figure XV

Question 42	Question 49					Question 50				
	Yes	No	Don't know	No answer	Total	Yes	No	Don't know	No answer	Total
Yes	34	53	11	2	100	23	65	9	3	100
No	34	49	15	2	100	23	61	13	3	100
Don't know	35	40	24	1	100	22	53	22	3	100
No answer	14	28	4	54	100	9	27	4	60	100
Total	34	52	12	2	100	23	63	11	3	100

Figures XVI and XVII

Question 43 by Question 49
Question 43 by Question 50

43. Do you expect to fall really in love some time?

49 Do you think a young man should have some sexual experience before he gets married?

50 Do you think a young woman should have some sexual experience before she gets married?

Figure XVI   Figure XVII

Question 43	Question 49					Question 50				
	Yes	No	Don't know	No answer	Total	Yes	No	Don't know	No answer	Total
Yes	40	41	14	5	100	28	52	13	7	100
No	30	57	11	2	100	20	69	9	2	100
Don't know	31	57	10	2	100	22	66	9	3	100
No answer	35	48	16	1	100	23	63	13	1	100
Total	34	52	12	2	100	23	63	11	3	100

119

markedly more in favour of pre-marital experience for both sexes than are the majority who do not consider American films representative of English habits.

There seems no connection at all with the experience of having been 'really in love' and views about pre-marital experience; but those who expect to 'fall really in love some time' are consistently more in favour of pre-marital experience than those who do not. The relevant question was not asked, but it looks as though there are two groups in the population, one of which believes that falling in love is a unique experience in life, normally culminating in marriage, and the other that falling in love is a repeatable performance; for this latter group, with its expectations of the future, experiment in the past would appear permissible.

There is also a convincing correlation between the attitudes to female sexuality described above and the desirability of experience before marriage. Those who think women's enjoyment of sex is equal to or greater than men's are markedly more in favour of experience before marriage than are those who consider that women do not care much about the physical side of sex, or do not have such an 'animal' nature as man There would appear to be a connection between viewing men and women as equal or similar, and permissiveness concerning sexual experience before marriage. This does not however seem to apply to love affairs outside marriage; when the question about women's sexuality is correlated with the question 'Not counting marriage have you ever had a real love affair?' no discernible pattern emerges.

A possible explanation for this rather surprising result might be that the main motive for extra-marital love affairs is lack of satisfaction with the sexual aspect of marriage; in which case the unsatisfied women, or men with frigid wives, though they may have affairs outside marriage, would not be particularly inclined to agree with generalizations that women get as much or more pleasure from sex than men. This explanation is given some backing by the fact that those who have had 'a real love affair' outside marriage are more likely to answer the question 'In marriage do you think sexual love is very important?' emphatically than those who disclaim such experiences

An attempt was made, within the limits of cross-correlation, to check a couple of psychological hypotheses. Dr Kinsey and others have stated that early onset of puberty and high interest in sexual activity are related, so I correlated the question about the importance of sexual love in marriage with the reported age of onset of

120

IDEAS ABOUT SEX

Figures XVIII and XIX

Question 53 by Question 49
Question 53 by Question 50

53. Please mark the statement you most agree with

49 Do you think a young man should have some sexual experience before he gets married ?

50 Do you think a young woman should have some sexual experience before she gets married?

	Figure XVIII					Figure XIX				
	Question 49					Question 50				
Question 53	Yes	No	Don't know	No answer	Total	Yes	No	Don t know	No answer	Total
Most women don't care much about the physical side of sex	27	55	14	4	100	18	68	10	4	100
Women don't have such animal natures as men	30	55	12	3	100	20	67	9	4	100
Women really enjoy the physical side of sex just as much as men	36	50	13	1	100	26	60	12	2	100
Women tend to enjoy sex more than men	47	42	9	2	100	34	52	10	4	100
No answer	19	45	18	18	100	10	59	13	18	100
Total	34	52	12	2	100	23	63	11	3	100

Figure XX

Question 47 by Question 53

47. Not counting marriage, have you ever had a real love affair?

53. Please mark the statement you most agree with·

Question 47	Question 53					
	Most women don't care much about the physical side of sex	Women don't have such an animal nature as men	Women really enjoy the physical side of sex as much as men	Women tend to enjoy sex more than men	No answer	Total
Yes	20	41	60	10	1	132
Not really	18	38	62	10	1	129
No	20	43	57	11	2	133
No answer	28	50	51	11	5	145
Total	21	43	58	11	1	134

121

Figure XXI

Question 48 by Question 47

48 In marriage do you think sexual love is very important?

47 Not counting marriage, have you ever had a real love affair?

Question 48	Question 47				
	Yes	Not really	No	No answer	Total
Very important	46	3	46	5	100
Fairly important	42	3	49	6	100
Not very important	32	2	54	12	100
Not important at all	26	2	57	15	100
No answer	7	11	15	77	100
Total	43	3	47	7	100

Figure XXII

Question 39 by Question 48

39 How old were you when you first started being interested in girls (boys)?

48 In marriage, do you think sexual love is very important?

Question 48	Question 39					
	Very important	Fairly important	Not very important	Not important at all	No answer	Total
Up to 10 years	57	34	4	1	4	100
11, 12 and 13 years	62	32	4	1	1	100
14, 15 and 16 years	59	35	5	1	0	100
17, 18 and 19 years	50	41	7	1	1	100
20, 21 and 22 years	48	39	9	2	2	100
23, 24 and 25 years	47	40	10	—	3	100
26 years and over	43	39	11	2	5	100
Not interested	35	42	16	2	5	100
Don't know	50	33	6	3	8	100
No answer	49	38	6	1	6	100
Total	55	36	6	1	2	100

real interest in the opposite sex. The result is marked and consistent; there is a marked decline in the value given to sex in marriage by those whose interest in the opposite sex developed after the age of sixteen.[6]

A second hypothesis tested was that advanced by psychoanalysts on the relationship between early training in cleanliness and general

122

rigidity of character. The questions about the permissibility of pre-marital experience were correlated with the answers to the question 'When should a young child start being trained to be clean?'[7] The results are an extremely neat confirmation of the hypothesis. In the two ambiguous categories 'as early as possible' and 'as soon as

Figure XXIII

Question 49 by Question 63

49 Do you think a young man should have some sexual experience before he gets married?

63 When should a young child start being trained to be clean?

Question 49	Question 63										Total
	From birth	As early as possible	Up to 2 months	2–6 months	7–12 months	1–2 years	2–3 years	3–4 years	Over 4 years	As soon as it understands	No answer	
Yes	16	12	8	17	16	11	2	1	2	11	4	100
No	18	12	11	19	15	8	1	0	1	12	3	100
Don't know	17	11	12	19	16	7	1	—	1	11	5	100
No answer	20	15	14	8	19	3	2	—	—	13	5	100
Total	17	12	10	18	15	8	2	0	1	12	5	100

Figure XXIV

Question 50 by Question 63

50 Do you think a young woman should have some sexual experience before she gets married?

63. When should a young child start being trained to be clean?

Question 50	Question 63										Total
	From birth	As early as possible	Up to 2 months	2–6 months	7–12 months	1–2 years	2–3 years	3–4 years	Over 4 years	As soon as it understands	No answer	
Yes	15	12	7	17	15	11	2	1	1	12	6	100
No	18	12	11	18	15	8	1	0	1	12	4	100
Don't know	17	10	10	19	16	7	2	1	3	12	2	100
No answer	21	12	11	13	18	5	3	—	—	10	6	100
Total	17	12	10	18	15	8	2	0	1	12	5	100

it can understand' the percentages for and against pre-marital experience are equally balanced. Those who advocate that cleanliness training should start after the child is twelve months old are also markedly permissive about pre-marital experience; those who advocate training from birth or during the first two months of life are more rigid in their attitudes towards sexual experience before marriage. Those who advocate the starting of cleanliness training between the age of two and twelve months are nearly evenly divided though with a little more permissiveness in those advocating the later start. The English attitudes towards sex fall more fully into focus when the factors involved in the training of an English man or girl are taken into account.

NOTES TO CHAPTER EIGHT

1. A few respondents gave more than one reason, which accounts for the slight discrepancy of the total

2 *Sexual Behaviour in the Human Male*, pp 345–7, *et passim*

3 See Appendix Two, p. 318

4 It is interesting to note that there is no social group, however high their income or social class (which on the whole correspond with education) which did not have at least a fifth of its members failing to follow the instructions, though the number of excessive responses are greater among the poor, the working and lower working class, the middle aged and old

5 See p. 78

6. Unfortunately the answers to the question about the onset of interest in the other sex had (for the purposes of this table) been rather clumsily categorized in groups of three years, consequently the contrast in the figures is, if anything, too blatant, and the variations do not come out as subtly as they probably would have done if the answers had been categorized by single years.

7 See Chapter Eleven

CHAPTER NINE

MARRIAGE I: HOPES AND FEARS

As a generalization it may be said that what English men most value in their wives is the possession of appropriate feminine skills, whereas what English women most value in their husbands is an agreeable character. This seems to be true both for the married and the single, and for all classes and regions. Neither sex pays any appreciable heed to the aesthetic qualities of their spouse; beauty or strength, good looks or good figure are very seldom mentioned, and then chiefly by the single; and it is also a very small group (less than one in twenty) who mention specifically sexual characteristics —being a good lover, staying sweet-hearts and so on

No answers were suggested to the question: 'What do you think are the three most important qualities a wife (or husband) should have?', and originally the answers were divided into 28 categories. It was found however that, apart from the qualities which only apply to one sex (for example, being a good mother) there were some qualities mentioned by so few people that they could be ignored. Besides beauty and good looks and being a good lover, gentleness, trusting one's husband or wife, and helping in the house were mentioned by less than 5 per cent;[1] and, as will be seen, some qualities which bulk very high for one sex, drop to practical insignificance for the other

Before the lists are detailed, it may be helpful to explain a few blanket terms I employed. I used the phrase 'moral qualities' for those traits which in a religious context might have been called virtues; good principles, sincerity, integrity, Christian principles, 'a good honest outlook', 'honesty to be straightforward', and so on. The phrase 'personal qualities' refers to traits with social or physical rather than moral significance· 'to keep oneself attractive and smart', 'cleanliness', 'always clean and tidy in the home', 'good conversationalist', 'good manners and good company', 'well dressed' and so on. The phrase 'equanimity' covers all the variations of tact, good temper, not getting angry and so on.

English men look for or admire qualities in their wives in the following order:

(i)	Good housekeeper	29 per cent
(ii)	Personal qualities	26 ,, ,,
(iii)	Understanding	23 ,, ,,
(iv)	Love	22 ,, ,,

(v)	Faithfulness	21 per cent
(vi)	Good cook	21 ,, ,,
(vii)	Intelligence	18 ,, ,,
(viii)	Good mother	18 ,, ,,
(ix)	Sense of humour	16 ,, ,,
(x)	Economical	16 ,, ,,
(xi)	Moral qualities	13 ,, ,,
(xii)	Patience	11 ,, ,,
(xiii)	Tolerance	9 ,, ,,
(xiv)	Share husband's interests	8 ,, ,,
(xv)	Love of home	7 ,, ,,
(xvi)	Equanimity	7 ,, ,,

As can be seen, five of the first ten qualities refer to skills as housewife and mother; in the first ten qualities which women list, only the tenth refers directly to the husband as provider and father. The qualities looked for and admired in their husbands by English women are:

(i)	Understanding	33 per cent
(ii)	Thoughtfulness	28 ,, ,,
(iii)	Sense of humour	24 ,, ,,
(iv)	Moral qualities	24 ,, ,,
(v)	Faithfulness	21 ,, ,,
(vi)	Generosity	19 ,, ,,
(vii)	Love	17 ,, ,,
(viii)	Tolerance	14 ,, ,,
(ix)	Love of home	14 ,, ,,
(x)	Fairness	13 ,, ,,
(xi)	Good father	13 ,, ,,
(xii)	Personal qualities	12 ,, ,,
(xiii)	Good worker	12 ,, ,,
(xiv)	Treat wife as person	11 ,, ,,
(xv)	Equanimity	10 ,, ,,
(xvi)	Intelligence	8 ,, ,,
(xvii)	Virility, strength, courage	8 ,, ,,

With relatively few exceptions, the experience of marriage does not much alter the importance given to the different qualities. The single put more stress than the married on intelligence and understanding; and the small demand for beauty comes chiefly from the unmarried. Marriage teaches men to put greater value on their wives' skills: personal qualities are mentioned very considerably more by the married than by the single; to a lesser extent, so are being a good housekeeper, being economical and being a good mother. The only trait which married women mention significantly more than their unmarried sisters is thoughtfulness.

For what the observation may be worth, the qualities of understanding, love, faithfulness, thoughtfulness and generosity were listed as first choice much more frequently than as second or third. This may imply that these qualities are valued more highly than those which bulk larger in second or third position; these are sense of humour, intelligence, moral and personal qualities, being a good worker, helping in the house, treating wife as a person, sharing husband's interests, being a good mother, and being economical.

For most of the qualities distribution by region, age, income or class does not seem to be significant; there are however a certain number for which the variations are suggestive. Thus, the naming of personal qualities is most marked in the North-East and North, followed by the North-West; from people between the ages of 25 and 64 with incomes of £5–£12 a week, in the middle, upper middle and working classes. Being a good housekeeper is stressed by men in the Midlands, North-West, North-East and North, with incomes of £8–£15, in the upper working, working, and lower working classes. Being a good cook is most stressed by men from the North-East and North, followed by the Midlands, in the £5–£8 income group in the working and lower working classes Being a good mother is once again most stressed in the North-East and North, followed by the Midlands, by men in the £5–£12 income group, concentrated in the upper middle and upper working classes. From these figures it does seem that one of the major regional differences in England is the attitude towards women;[2] and that women's skills are more highly valued in the North-East and North (followed by the Midlands) than in the rest of the country, particularly by the middle income working class. With a single exception, there is no parallel regional variation in the qualities women demand of their husbands; understanding (which, it will be remembered, was highly valued by both sexes) is quite markedly stressed in the South-West. This quality is particularly valued by the young; mention of it decreases steadily with age.

A second quality which is particularly demanded by the young is intelligence, with the bulk of those naming it being under 24. The demand for this quality increases with income, with a marked jump when income passes £12 a week. The upper middle and (rather strangely) the lower working classes particularly stress intelligence

Two qualities which are more stressed by the middle aged than by the young are faithfulness and thrift. The demand for thrift comes more from the median income groups than from the very poor in the working classes.

Moral qualities are most stressed by the upper middle, middle and upper working classes, and by the very poor as well as by those with over £12 a week.

It can, I think, be deduced that English spinsters think more, and

127

more seriously, about marriage than do English bachelors Seven per cent of the unmarried did not answer the question: 'What are the three chief faults husbands or wives tend to have?', and three-fifths of these abstainers were men. A number, who had listed the qualities desirable in a wife, wrote to the effect that, not being married, they knew nothing about wives' faults; a similar reticence is rare on the part of unmarried women. Consequently, the base line for percentages is 285 per cent, rather than 300 per cent, which it would have been had everybody answered.

The list of faults is (as might be expected) considerably longer than the list of qualities; but there are 11 which are mentioned by such small groups (less than 3 per cent of either sex) that they can be listed and then disregarded. The most surprising item on this discard list is infidelity or flirting; women mention it a little more than men, but it hardly appears at all. Other minority complaints made by both sexes are· neglecting the spouse for the children; not sharing interests of spouse; hostility to spouse's parents or friends, always being dissatisfied; sexual difficulties. Only very few husbands complained that their wives were vain or thought too much about clothes, that they were bad cooks or spoiled the children. Only a very few wives complained that their husbands went out too much alone, thrust too many responsibilities on their wives, or saw too much of their mothers and compared their wives unfavourably with their mothers.

A few of the blanket terms used in the list can profitably be expanded. 'Moral faults' are the converse of 'moral qualities'—such attributes as irresponsibility, lying, stubbornness, greed. A number of synonyms are gathered under the term 'Lack of intelligence'. lack of interest, illogical, mentally lazy, narrow-minded, dull, boring etc. etc.

The faults that English men find in their wives are as follows:

(i) Nagging, scolding, fault-finding	29	per cent	
(ii) Lack of intelligence	24	,,	,,
(iii) Gossip	21	,,	,,
(iv) Extravagance	17	,,	,,
(v) Domineering, bossiness, hen-pecking	16	,,	,,
(vi) Selfishness	16	,,	,,
(vii) Letting herself go, slovenly, dress badly, etc.	13	,,	,,
(viii) Over-anxious, always worrying	13	,,	,,
(ix) Jealousy, lack of trust	12	,,	,,
(x) Bad temper	11	,,	,,
(xi) Moral faults	11	,,	,,
(xii) Bad housekeeper	10	,,	,,
(xiii) Too houseproud, too tidy	8	,,	,,
(xiv) Making invidious comparisons, run down husband, etc	6	,,	,,
(xv) Making herself a martyr, being too self-sacrificing	6	,,	,,

128

The faults which women find in their husbands are very different; only six items appear in both lists; and the women concentrate on one single fault—selfishness—in a fashion which is quite different to the wider scatter of the men. These are the faults which English women find in their husbands:

(i) Selfishness	56 per cent	
(ii) Lack of intelligence	20 ,, ,,	
(iii) Taking wife for granted	18 ,, ,,	
(iv) Lazy, sleepy, won't help in house	18 ,, ,,	
(v) Untidiness	17 ,, ,,	
(vi) Complacency, conceit, self-opinionated	16 ,, ,,	
(vii) Bad temper	13 ,, ,,	
(viii) Moral faults	13 ,, ,,	
(ix) Mean with money	10 ,, ,,	
(x) Forgets anniversaries, doesn't appreciate wife	10 ,, ,,	
(xi) Domineering, possessive	9 ,, ,,	
(xii) Childishness, fussiness, helplessness	9 ,, ,,	
(xiii) Drinking, gambling, smoking	8 ,, ,,	
(xiv) Jealousy	8 ,, ,,	
(xv) Won't entertain wife, take her out, converse	7 ,, ,,	

The contrast in the faults found in the opposite sex is not so marked as was the case with the qualities sought; but it is worth remarking that in the faults named by 10 per cent or more of the men, only one refers to the professional skills of the wife, and the remainder to her character; whereas, in the women's corresponding list at least three refer to domestic deficiencies on the part of the husband—laziness, untidiness and meanness with money. Somewhat over-simplifying the picture, one might say that in English marriage character makes for the woman's happiness and the man's un-happiness, and domestic behaviour and skills excite the man's approval and (to a lesser extent) the woman's condemnation.

There are only three faults which bulk larger in the imagination of the single than in the experience of the married; they are moral faults, nagging, and taking one's wife (or husband) for granted. Nine faults are the sad fruits of experience, which occur significantly more often in the lists of the married than of the single, and it is interesting that the majority of these are among the complaints men make about their wives. This is perhaps a further indication that English girls are more realistic in their approach to marriage than English men. Single men don't envisage the complaint that women may make themselves martyrs, and few suspect that they may be over-anxious or bad housekeepers. Dislike of gossip increases with marriage; so do complaints of extravagance, bad temper, lack of intelligence and selfishness. The only specifically female complaint

129

against husbands which increases appreciably after marriage is untidiness

If rank order signifies the importance given to a complaint, the following faults, which occur more frequently in first than in second or third place, would seem to be of major importance. nagging, domineering. selfishness, taking spouse for granted, jealousy, over-anxiety, meanness with money. Lack of intelligence, extravagance and bad housekeeping are more frequently in second or third place The remaining faults are evenly distributed

As with the qualities, the majority of faults are evenly distributed among the complainers of different regions, ages, income levels and social class; but, in contrast to the qualities, where there is a significant difference in distribution it is more often by social class than by geographical region.

As far as these figures are any guide, the most unsatisfactory English marriages are in the lower middle. upper working and lower working classes The upper middle class only stress the husband's selfishness and lack of appreciation of the wife and the wife's extravagance; and the middle classes the husband's selfishness and laziness. In the lower middle class most of the complaints seem to be directed against the wife: she is said to be nagging and domineering, to let herself go and neglect her personal appearance; both spouses complain of the temper and lack of intelligence in the other. The upper working class is fuller of complaints than any other: wives are nagging and domineering, extravagant and bad house-keepers; husbands are selfish; and both sexes are bad-tempered and lack intelligence. In the working and lower working classes dislike of gossip and the naming of specific moral faults come to the fore. Working class wives also complain of their husbands' laziness, and both sexes stress the bad temper and lack of intelligence of their spouses. The lower working class husbands complain that their wives nag, are extravagant and bad housekeepers; the wives complain that their husbands don't appreciate them. Although the trend is not very marked, it does seem as though there is a shift from complaints about the husband to complaints about the wife as one descends the English social scale

Each of the regions stresses one or two bad qualities; but in most cases the emphasis is slight. The North-East and North is emphatic in its dislike of gossip, and also stresses extravagance. Selfishness is very much complained of in the North-West. followed by temper. The only complaint specially stressed in the Midlands is extravagance. Extravagance is also emphasized in the South-West, but not so

130

strongly as is bad temper. London and the South-East concentrate their complaints on domineering and selfishness. It is possibly significant that the men of the North-East and North, who are so appreciative of women's skills are also the most critical of women's failings; and that in the North-West, where women have so much influence,[3] the emphasis falls on masculine faults.

A few complaints seem to vary consistently with income or age. Thus, selfishness is most complained of by people with family incomes of under £8 a week. whereas nagging and lack of intelligence are more blamed with incomes over that sum. Extravagance, perhaps understandably, finds its chief spokesmen in the £8–£12 a week income range, much the same range as complains of gossip. The most prosperous complain of domineering and of the wife letting herself go It is the poorest and the richest and also the very young (under 18) and the old (over 65) who are most specific about moral faults. It is particularly the middle-aged (over 35) who complain of domineering, selfishness, gossip and extravagance; the complaint that wives let themselves go comes more from the husbands under 34. The complaints about the husband's laziness decrease steadily with increasing age; it is mentioned by 12 per cent of those under 18, 10 per cent 18–24, 8 per cent 25–34, 9 per cent 35–44, 6 per cent 45–64, 1 per cent over 65. The figures are slight, but they do suggest that there has been a marked change in the expectations of the help which a husband should properly give in a household, with the dividing line among those who were born in the first decade of this century or earlier. Observation suggests that the young husband, particularly of the middle classes, is expected to help a good deal more in the household than was his father; and this situation may be reflected in these figures.

There are two complaints which seem worth discussing in this context, though neither of them ranks high in the lists; they are both however referred to a great deal in the answers to the questions· What makes for the success or failure of a marriage? These are financial and sexual difficulties.

By financial difficulties I do not mean absolute poverty, but the distribution of money within the family, typically the amount of his wages or salary which the husband hands over to the wife. These complaints are somewhat concentrated among women in the Southern regions; and although I cannot substantiate this from the tables, it does appear that there is a difference in pattern between the Southern and Northern (particularly North-Western) regions in the working classes. In the North it would seem that not infrequently

131

the husband hands over his unopened pay packet to his wife, who then gives him back a portion for his private expenses; in the South it seems customary for the husband to 'give' a portion of his wages to his wife for all household expenses and to keep the remainder for himself. The relevant questions were unfortunately not asked; but a number of inferences suggest that in the North, where the domestic skills of women are highly esteemed, budgeting has an important place among these skills.

The complaints follow a fairly typical pattern. 'They give out the housekeeping money as if it were a gift' (a 54-year-old middle class wife from Weston-super-Mare); 'Treat their wives as paid house-keepers. Not let his wife know how much money he has' (a 30-year-old wife from Wigan), 'Meanness or rather hard over money matters. This refers to my husband' (a 49-year-old working class wife from Bury St. Edmunds), 'Refuse to acknowledge right of woman having little of his money to call her own' (a 34-year-old lower middle class widow from North London); 'Spending too much on cigarettes, betting and the "local" when the wife needs it more for the home and the children' (a 29-year-old lower middle class wife from Bromley); 'They never want to allow a woman "pocket money"' (a 35-year-old working class wife from Bishops Stortford, Herts); 'Unequal division of income especially in times of rising prices for weekly necessities' (a 49-year-old professional woman, divorced, from Chesterfield); 'They do not understand high cost of living. They do not go shopping with their wives to find out where money goes to' (a 30-year-old Birmingham wife); 'Most of them do not disclose how much salary they have. It *should* be a partnership' (a 30-year-old wife from the Birmingham district); 'Many men deliberately keep wives short of money on pretense of saving for old age. but nothing makes a woman age quicker than having to scrape and do without when children are young' (a 56-year-old middle class woman from Birmingham); 'Seeing husband indulge, while wife has to stint and scrape to make housekeeping money do' (a 52-year-old middle class wife from South Harrow), 'I can have all my husband has and he can always rely on me for help of any sort, that I think is love' (a 59-year-old working class woman from Rochdale, Lancs.); 'Each to his own task, the man for wages, the woman for "exchequer" work' (a 38-year-old 'labouring class' man from Salford, Lancs.).

The sexual difficulties centre around the wife's unwillingness for intercourse when her husband desires it. The men usually describe this in a single word—coldness or frigidity—but the actual phrases employed have revealing implications. Thus, a 39-year-old husband from Eastbourne: 'Excuse of tiredness when husband desires sex privilege'[4] 'Complaining she has pains at bedtime' (a working class husband from Lancashire, aged 37); 'Reasonable sexual intercourse (approximately once or twice weekly)';[5] (a 49-year old middle class separated man from Eastbourne).

Most of the complaints about sexual difficulties come from the wives. A 47-year-old lower middle class woman from Shrewsbury complains of husband's 'Brutality (claiming their "rights" when a woman is ill or tired)' A 29-year-old lower middle class wife from Bromley: 'Treating their wives like servants instead of partners, and being very selfish and demanding in sexual matters'. A 39-year-old lower middle class wife from the Isle of Ely: 'To make love only when they feel desire'. A 28-year-old working class wife from Castleford, Yorks. 'Expect a woman to submit to love-making because it is "their duty" whether they like it or not'.[6] A 22-year-old middle class wife from Hereford· 'Takes me for granted when it comes to the physical side of marriage'.[7] A separated mother of four, aged 35, from Maidenhead who describes herself as 'A typical housewife of the Working Class': 'Excessive sexual demands. A wife should be entitled to say no if she wants to, and not be forced'. A 45-year-old wife from Liverpool· 'Thinking their wives should like the sexual part of married life as much as they do themselves'. A 33-year-old middle class wife from Hove: 'Taking wives for granted. Wanting intimacy without much love making first. Not troubling if wife is sexually satisfied or not'.

As can be seen, a number of respondents use these questions for autobiographical comment or for comment on their husbands or wives. A few of the young men also achieve considerable epigrammatic neatness. A 21-year-old working class bachelor from Stamford defines the qualities of a wife· 'Good cook in kitchen. Little lady in Parlour. Mistress in bedroom'. And a married hairdresser from Fulham: 'Look after herself. Look after her children. Look after her home.' A 25-year old Dagenham bachelor defines the faults of a wife. 'A whore in the kitchen; a cook in bed'.

Most of the autobiographical comments are critical, though with some of the men this does not exclude appreciation. Thus, a 25-year-old Southern working man, now living in Liverpool, complains of his wife·

> Giving the family her rations and going without herself. Always finding the odd copper for her husband's cigarettes (You going without) Cold feet in bed.

A 34-year-old middle class husband from Eccles.

Too much self-sacrifice in favour of their homes, children and husbands. Too much unhappiness when unable to 'keep up with' neighbours and friends. A tendency to overcriticize husband's actions.

A 47-year-old divorced working class man from North-West London:

Not known of other wives, only own nagging, coldhearted, untidy.

A 42-year-old working class Londoner:

Having made an analysis of my wife's faults only I cannot hold judgment on others—House proud, No interest in any social functions or evenings out Failing these two I do not think there is any other criticism to make.

A 25-year-old schoolmaster from the Midlands.

(I don't know much about other men's wives These remarks apply to mine) Lack of understanding Drabness of spirit Lack of 'joie de vivre' Mulishness

A hairdresser from Fulham:

If upset she brings up old sores of 25 and 30 years ago. She saves goods for the future, when needed they are useless She puts things away and never knows where to look for them after a certain lapse of time

Women are inclined to be more specific, and (I have the impression) more full of complaints about their husbands. A 46-year-old working class wife from Bishop's Castle, Shropshire

My husband not generous with money. Prefers billiard room and pub Unreasonable quick temper.

A 31-year-old working class wife from a village near Tamworth, Staffs:

They still hang on to their bachelor day liberties They go out to work and so (they say) are entitled to all the freedom they need, heedless of how things are at home They take too much for granted

A 43-year-old working class wife from Hounslow.

Putting their mothers before their wives Making up to other wives and expecting their own wives to be so loyal Not being interested in planning any pleasure for wife and taking her too much for granted.

A 35-year-old working class wife from Barnsley.

Dilatoriness Married life seems to have made my husband forget how to enjoy himself and give me a good time. After gazing at some venus like figure in the Sunday paper my husband will insist on telling me I am getting fat forgetting of course that am nearing middle age and have had a family.

A 28-year-old working class woman from Sheffield:

Speaking from personal experience a great disinclination to do essential odd jobs. When being asked to do same, giving the stock answer 'Don't Nag' Arriving home late from work, thereby spoiling nice meals (Though I admit this is often not his fault)

A 27-year-old working class wife from Cornwall·

My own is selfish, Doesn't help at all, smokes and drinks.

A 48-year-old 'wife of an employer' in Canterbury:

Giving the business too much time Trying to turn me into a Methodical, systematic Unit. Crunching hard sweets in bed.

A 41-year-old working class wife from West Bromwich:

They are always right or think they are (so let them think it). If you ask them to do a job they are just going to do something else. Work (my husband seems to work so many hours).

A 53-year-old woman from the centre of England who says:

I have never been married but my four children do *not* know this and never will if I can help it. Read the papers and be annoyed if you say one word Sleep as soon as Sunday dinner is finished Try to make you think they don't hear you speak when you know they must do.

A 28-year-old working class wife from Enfield.

Afraid of being thought a cissy (mine hates people to know he helps at all in the house Wont push pram) Some neglect their jobs as father. Leave their wives most evenings to go out to enjoy themselves.

Occasionally these depressing pictures are lightened by a husband or wife using the opportunity of the anonymous questionnaire not to denigrate but to praise their partner. Thus a 35-year-old Huddersfield man:

[*qualities of wife?*] Maternal Instinct Towards Children
Cooking With Materials and Not a Tin Opener.
Cleanliness and Administration of the House.
[*faults?*] It Depends on the Wife I Perhaps Could Find Lots of Faults with Somebody Else's Wife, But For My Own, She Does a Good Job of Work, Faultless

A 20-year-old middle class husband from Dinkley, Lancs.:

[*qualities of wife?*] Devotion and fidelity.
Trust in her husband.
Sensible house sense and motherhood Cook.
[*faults?*] Apart from cold feet in bed I have never been able to find fault with my wife.

A 33-year-old working class husband from Heanor, Derby:

The one and only fault I have with my wife is, she does not take care of herself when she is ill.

135

A 43-year-old upper working class wife from Enfield:
[*qualities of husband?*] To be able to meet the family budget
To be as interested in the family as the Mother is
To be a friend as well as a lover
[*faults?*] If a wife complains or grumbles on rare occasions to use
that awful word dont nag
Mine is not too bad I can not name three faults (don't tell him)

A 58-year-old wife from Wolverhampton
[*qualities of husband?*] To be a good husband, To be a Good father
and Provide a good home He has done all three, given my son a good
education and he is a very good man to live with
[*faults?*] Working when he should be resting Evenings
Worrying about getting up early for work.
Cross if tea isn't ready when he comes in but he soon gets over it

A 46-year-old working class wife from Hayes:
[*faults of husband?*] lack of understanding (in men whom I have met)
I am afraid I can say little to this ? as my husband is a good man and
I have no complaint to make

NOTES TO CHAPTER NINE

1 Since three qualities were demanded, the base line is 300 per cent, or rather
291 per cent, since 3 per cent, mostly those under 18, did not answer this question

2 See also Chapter Fifteen, p 302

3 See Chapter Fifteen

4 'Privilege' seems to be a most important concept in English thought. See especially
Chapter Twelve

5 No direct questions were asked on frequency of intercourse or similar concrete
sexual questions Quite a few individuals, however, volunteered such information
No informant was more demanding than the one quoted above, the minimum advocated is once a month, 'otherwise the wife will get suspicious'. A few middle class
respondents describe in detail the abandon they would wish from their wives a
38-year-old husband from Richmond, Yorks· 'lack of reticence during intimacy and
ability to indicate desires', a 45-year-old man from Wallington, Surrey 'No inhibitions
whatever re sex, and a willingness to enter into all bedroom games, and use freely
all the words her husband wants her to ' Some respondents used these questions to
detail their erotic fantasies

6 This woman names as first quality in a husband. 'Use restraint in the physical
side of marriage.'

7 This woman names as a quality in a husband 'To know when his wife is tired
and does not want to be made love to '

CHAPTER TEN

MARRIAGE II: EXPERIENCE

(NOTE· *This chapter is founded entirely on the answers
of respondents who are or have been married.*)

ENGLISH HUSBANDS AND wives are agreed that there are about a
dozen factors whose presence makes for the happiness, and whose
absence for the unhappiness, of marriage. Men and women vary
somewhat in the weight they give to the different factors; and in a
great many cases the presence or absence of a factor are quite
differently esteemed. Thus, for 15 per cent children make for a
happy marriage; no children is only considered the cause of an
unhappy marriage by 4 per cent. Conversely, not having a house of
one's own or living with in-laws is named by 21 per cent as a reason
for a wrecked marriage, only 6 per cent name a house of one's own
as a factor in a happy marriage.

The factors mentioned besides these two are give-and-take
(sharing 50–50), understanding, love, mutual trust, equanimity,
sexual compatibility, comradeship, a decent income, mutual interests,
happy home life and no money difficulties, their converse are
selfishness, neglect, lack of love. lack of trust, bad temper, incompatibility. conflicting personalities, poverty, outside interests, bad
housekeeping. and disagreements about money. Two factors are
named with some frequency which make for unhappiness in marriage,
which have no direct converse in a happy marriage; they are drink
and infidelity Mutual help (the husband helping in the house and
the wife with the accounts, for example) is mentioned as a component
in a happy marriage; but the absence of this practice is not particularly noted.

A certain number of other factors were mentioned by such small
groups that they do not seem to need any discussion Marriage in
the same class or religious or national group is mentioned almost
exclusively by members of the upper middle class as a cause for
happiness, and mixed class or religion as a cause for unhappiness.
Agreement on the number and education of children finds slight
mention as a cause for marital happiness, disagreement on this
subject, too many children, or one partner wanting children and
the other not finds a few more advocates as causes of unhappiness.
Going out together, or conversely no outside interests or boredom

find occasional mentions Two or three per cent mention religious principles, the spouse maintaining his or her appearance or smartness, and the absence of a boss in the family as factors making for a happy marriage; too hasty a marriage is mentioned, particularly by the divorced and the most prosperous, as a reason for subsequent misery.

The gross totals and ranking given to the factors are as follows Nearly all respondents listed two or more causes for marital happiness or unhappiness, the women being consistently more voluble than the men, positive factors have a base line of 251 per cent, negative 229 per cent. Less than one married person in fifty refused to answer this question; it is a subject on which nearly everybody has views which they are most willing to propound.[1]

Making for a happy marriage

Give-and-take	39 per cent
Understanding	35 ,, ,,
Love	24 ,, ,,
Equanimity	24 ,, ,,
Mutual trust	23 ,, ,,
Comradeship	15 ,, ,,
Children	15 ,, ,,
Shared interests	13 ,, ,,
Sexual compatibility	11 ,, ,,
Financial security	10 ,, ,,
Happy home life	8 ,, ,,
House of one's own	6 ,, ,,
No money difficulties	5 , ,,
Mutual help	4 , ,,

Making for a wrecked marriage

Lack of trust	33 per cent
Selfishness, no give-and-take	28 ,, ,,
No house of one's own	21 ,, ,,
Temper	20 ,, ,,
Sexual incompatibility	18 ,, ,,
Poverty	16 ,, ,,
Neglect	15 ,, ,,
Infidelity	14 ,, ,,
Drunkenness	10 ,, ,,
Conflicting personalities	8 , ,,
Money disagreements	8 ,, ,,
Each going own way	8 ,, ,,
Lack of affection	6 ,, ,,
No children	4 ,, ,,
Bad management of home	3 ,, ,,

Men and women vary slightly, and in a pattern which is now familiar, in the importance they give to these different factors Women stress the importance for a happy marriage of good temper and companionship, and, to a lesser extent, give-and-take, understanding and love; men put more value on sexual compatibility, a decent income, and, most markedly. children As causes of unhappy marriages women emphasize bad temper, neglect, and, to a lesser extent money disagreements; men stress not having a house of one's own, poverty, and incompatibility. Once again, we find the English woman's emphasis on the overwhelming importance of character; whereas for men concrete circumstances play a major rôle

It seems understandable that the divorced or separated should put more emphasis than the married on sexual compatibility and understanding as causes for marital happiness; and infidelity, lack of sexual compatibility and too hasty marriages as the chief causes for marital unhappiness. Those who remain married put more emphasis on temper, selfishness and outside interests for unhappiness, and good temper, give-and-take and love for a happy marriage.

There is remarkably little difference in the emphasis placed by the middle class and the working class on the importance of the various factors which make for marital success or failure. The other classes, however, all present idiosyncratic patterns of over- and under-emphasis which provide something like a synoptic picture of the differential components of English marriages.

Thus for the members of the upper middle class, sexual compatibility and mutual interests are the most stressed positive factors, followed by a decent income, love and understanding; mutual help is not even mentioned, and having a house of one's own and give-and-take are rated low. Sexual incompatibility, selfishness, lack of trust, temper and sharing a house are much mentioned as causes for marital unhappiness; but lack of affection is little regarded; and money quarrels, neglect, and conflicting personalities are relatively seldom mentioned.

In the lower middle class good temper and mutual interests are most heavily stressed, followed by mutual trust, sexual compatibility and children; understanding is less valued and so are mutual help The most important causes of unhappy marriage in this class can all be expressed negatively lack of trust, lack of love, lack of money, no mutual interests, sexual incompatibility; too many outside interests is a relatively uncommon complaint

In the upper working class understanding is given pride of place when the factors making for a happy marriage are considered, this is followed by love, sexual compatibility, give-and-take and mutual trust, in this class comradeship plays a significantly small rôle, and so do mutual interests. Neglect plays a major rôle in unhappy

139

marriages, together with infidelity, lack of trust, lack of love and no mutual interests.

The lower working class only stress three positive factors, but these are all of major importance for them mutual help, children and good temper. They pay little attention to sharing a house, love, sexual compatibility, absence of money differences, give-and-take, or mutual trust. They also concentrate heavily on four negative factors drink, no children, neglect, and lack of love; infidelity, sexual incompatibility, poverty, living with in-laws, selfishness, lack of trust, temper and too many outside interests are all reckoned relatively low.

Drink and infidelity are almost entirely problems of the poor and the old. Of the positive factors the poor most stress good temper, love, and give-and-take The prosperous (over £12 a week) make much of sexual compatibility and incompatibility, and the people with the highest incomes (over £15 a week) are also the people most pre-occupied with financial matters—the absence of debts or extravagance. The more prosperous also consider the presence of children important.

Children and a decent income are the factors which the early middle-aged (35–44) think particularly important for a happy marriage; and they find poverty and too many outside interests the most potent negative factors. For the younger married people love. understanding and give-and-take rank highest positively, and sexual incompatibility and lack of trust negatively.

With the partial exception of the rural South-West, the regional variations are slight. In London and the South-East drink and bad house-keeping play very little rôle; in the Midlands drink is an important negative factor, as mutual trust is an important positive factor. The people in the Midlands pay little attention to poverty or selfishness. Both Northern regions stress the importance of a happy home life; the North-East and North also values highly give-and-take, and finds too many outside interests an important negative factor. This region mentions relatively little either love or bad temper; and in the North-West comparatively little importance is attached to a decent income. The South-West stresses the importance of love, understanding and mutual interests on the positive side and lack of trust on the negative; compared with the rest of the country they pay little attention to give-and-take and conflicting personalities. The inhabitants of small towns emphasize the importance of mutual interests and infidelity; in the metropolises comradeship is the most stressed positive, poverty the most stressed negative factor.

A great number—perhaps the majority—of the respondents answered these questions autobiographically. Inevitably, there is a great deal of repetition in these answers, but a certain number are so poignant, or so heart-warming, that they seem worth reproducing for their intrinsic interest.

The following are examples of unhappy marriages:

A 66-year-old working-class man from Hebburn, Durham:
In my wife's case—careless spending and domineering I was the one who always gave way until I had reached the limit—then I became hard as H—— unfortunately for my youngsters whom I loved.

A 33-year-old divorced school teacher from E. Yorkshire.
The easiest way to wreck a marriage is for the man to let the wife provide the income, run the home, bring up the child, and nag her all the time. I know—I've had it.

A 42-year-old working class man from Manchester:
Finding out you are unsuited when it is too late, such as after a child is born. Couples tolerate each other because they love the child or children . . Many couples have been called a happy couple, simply because people don't know what happens between them in private, and actually they'd be glad to part.

A 31-year-old agricultural labourer from a village near Malvern:
(to much nagging) my wife says I'm always nagging her and is always going to leave me. I tell her she's free to go, and that I can soon get a housekeeper if she goes.

A 54-year-old Leeds working class man:
Believing untruths as in my case, my wife was a widow with a child, whom I love as my own, until she accused me of a serious offence but not until 3 years before she had got to the age of going out with young men. Although at the time she was sleeping in the same room as her grandmother We separated after 7 years and I have lived alone. Bothering with no one of that sex since

A 22-year-old middle class housewife from Essex:
Been cruel, bad tempered, drinking, mean with money, demanding too much, i.e not giving enough (you see it has happened to me).

A 48-year-old woman from Birkenhead:
Losing interest in each other, selfishness, heartlessness. Here I think I'd better explain more fully If a husband tells his wife there is nothing in having a baby when she is having her first, and ends it by saying women make themselves invalids out of the most natural of all things, and refuse share the little fears and ridicules her when she wants most

141

of all to show off the little things that are needed for baby when it comes
Well love just goes and it never returns and without love marriage is
an existance.

A 52-year-old working class woman from Manchester:

For myself, I married a very hasty-tempered boy, very argumentative
and dominating, but at times, the kindest hearted person that ever was
born. In 30 years I've hidden a lot of heartbreak behind a smiling face
I've had few friends and have always given people to understand my
Husband is one of the best. Had we both been of the same nature our
marriage would not have lasted more than a week

A 45-year-old upper working class woman from Folkestone:

In my case my husband is lazy. He wont work and keep my little boy
and myself and because I work and keep my husband he left us. He was
very plausible but underneath it all he was dishonest and untruthful
and disloyal and selfish. Since my baby was 10 weeks old Ive worked
for us both
We don't know where he is. WE DON'T CARE

A 28-year-old woman from North London:

I could not say what makes for a happy marriage as mine is not happy
and never has been and never will be as I have a bad husband.

A Sutton Coldfield man aged 73½

In my case (which nearly became a wreck) leaving my wife alone
(when we were married first) in the home and stopping out drinking all
hours, but seeing that our happiness was at stake luckily gave it all up
and went home and spent the hours at home and I have since become
a home bird

A 59-year-old working class man from Penge:

Well I upset my home when I joined the British Legion and the
Discharged Soldiers Federation then I was out almost every night as
I was a good darts player I was picked to play too often Also held many
positions on the Committees Gave it up three years ago. [for a happy
marriage?] 'be equal' help to wash and dry dinner plates etc. but do
not spoil them that is the wife, take her out with you occasionally where
you know she will be happy

The happily married have a slight tendency to give instructions
from their own experience. Thus, a 27-year-old husband from
Edlington:

What makes for a happy marriage is 'Any two persons with the same
temperament as my wife and myself Accept each other at face value.
Do not pry into each others past. Never be afraid to discuss problems
of any nature Dont be afraid to put your arm round your wife's shoulder
in public'.

142

A 55-year-old working class man from Beeston, Notts·

Firstly you both must have no secrets, and if any affairs do come along be straightforward and have a round table talk. . . If you or your wife do have any flirtatuse affairs do keep each other fully informed. it has proved in our case a happy marriage in our not having any secrets

A 62-year-old 'common worker' from East Ham:

Myself I am lucky, my old Dutch has been through all my adversitys an Angel without Wings. My two sons nearing 40 *years old age* (Still Single)

A 37-year-old middle class man from a village near Devizes:

A man and wife do not love each other when they are married first, this comes with being married to each other in years and being completely open and above board with each other and by courting each other all the time and not being ashamed to sneak a kiss. . . Allow the wife the same scope as you like yourself let her know how much a week you get.

A 45-year-old coal miner from a village near Rotherham, Yorks:

What makes for a happy marriage is All that made our courting days pleasant. I find they are still life's main pleasure and raising a family etc.

A 30-year-old working class wife from Westoning, Beds:

Make allowance for hubby's hobbies When it is too cold outside in the shed, let him play with his pliers and spanners etc in the living room. Don't nag Let him come and go without asking too many questions. Trust your husband and he will never betray your trust

A 28-year-old middle class wife from Tiverton·

You get in a rut at times, everyone does regardless of what they say Most people think when they get married I've got him or her, and that's that, but it's all wrong After marriage I think it's harder to keep a man than before because really you should try to be as attractive as the day he married you and even with children Always have his meals *ready*, nice clean house and home, listen to all his troubles about what a horrid day he's had, even if yours has been dreadful, a housewife can stop and rest for half an hour, but a man can't Above all, look clean and attractive yourself

In the three quotations which follow, three husbands of different generations give remarkably succinct pictures of happy married life.

A 62-year-old man from Cannock:

Well each going 50 ; 50 in everything we have been married 38 years if my wife wants anything she has it I don't grumble, if I want anything I have it she doesn't grumble, we have always had little tifs but we get over them.

143

A 42-year-old working class husband from London, S.E. ·

When you are out of work with a couple of youngsters, been trying hard to find some, and when you reach home, the woman greets you with a smile, and says, how are your poor old feet No recriminations for having nothing but hope for the following day (Thats how a woman should be)

A 24-year-old 'ordinary working class' husband from Newcastle:

A Loving Husband A nice Home, Loving wife to look after him and the Husband who comes from work and puts his pay packet on the table and kisses his wife and says Darling I love you.

Having to share a house, and interference from in-laws, is one of the causes most frequently given for the wreck of a marriage. In reading through the questionnaires, I had noted that, with remarkable frequency, the people who made such complaints were in fact living with their own parents; and it seems that, in England, the marriage of a child turns the parents almost automatically into in-laws.

It consequently seemed worth while making a correlation between the causes listed for success and failure in marriage and sharing a house with one's own parents. Twelve per cent of the married sample live in the same house as their father, and 14 per cent in the same house as their mother; these of course are not entirely separate groups, as some may have both parents living with them. Nevertheless, the figures do suggest that it is the presence of a mother or mother-in-law which is the disturbing factor, as has always been maintained in the traditional music hall joke. When the house is shared with the father, no house of one's own is listed fourth in the causes for a wrecked marriage, and having a house of one's own third as a reason for a happy marriage When the house is shared with the mother, on the other hand, sharing a house is listed first as cause for an unhappy marriage (though four other defects have the same percentage); and having a house of one's own is listed first as a factor making for a happy marriage. The percentage differences are slight, but would seem to be significant; the pattern of English life can accommodate two men, but not two women, in the same household.

One of the biggest surprises which I received from this investigation was the very small rôle accorded to infidelity as a cause for marital unhappiness. Fidelity was rated fairly high as a desirable characteristic in a spouse, particularly by men; but infidelity was eighth in the list of factors wrecking a marriage, only mentioned by 14 per cent. In my own experience in the rural South and South-West, it had

144

seemed to me that people were very markedly preoccupied with jealousy and suspicions of sexual straying, often on what seemed to me the most tenuous and improbable grounds; but in view of the results of this research, I think maybe what I took for jealousy was a sort of bitter marital game not taken really seriously; the scenes provoked would perhaps be described as 'nagging' and 'lack of trust' and 'temper' rather than infidelity.

It was the memory of these scenes and gossip which prompted me to ask the question of all my married male respondents 'If a husband finds his wife having an affair with another man, what should he do?'; for the female correspondents the sexes in the question were suitably transposed.

This is a question which nearly all the respondents took seriously and answered at length; only 2 per cent of the men and 1 per cent of the women refused to answer, and these silent people were concentrated in the elderly. Many of the respondents advocated more than one course; consequently the base line for the percentages is 163 per cent. Women were somewhat more voluble than men (once again); they have 170 per cent of answers, the men 158 per cent.

Less than a third of the men and barely a sixth of the women consider that infidelity should automatically terminate the marriage; and only a very small group contemplate violence. The replies admirably illustrate that aspect of English behaviour which is called 'civilized' by those who admire, and 'cold' or 'unemotional' by those who dislike it. A sense of fairness and a most lively conscience are, for the majority, far stronger than passion, either passionate love or passionate jealousy. There is however the interesting correlation that those who consider sexual love 'very important' in marriage are much more likely to consider terminating the marriage if the spouse is discovered to be unfaithful than those who consider it 'fairly important'.

Although the general pattern for husbands and wives is fairly similar, the sexes differ in the emphasis they place on different solutions and to a certain extent in their phraseology. The course most frequently advocated by both men and women is talking the matter over with the erring spouse; and in second place they recommend finding out what ego has done to make his or her partner stray. Men state this directly more often than women; women tend to assume that the reason for their husband straying is that they have lost their physical attractions, and that they can win him back by smartening themselves up. It would be interesting to know whether this rather pathetic belief that an erring husband can be

145

Figure XXV

Question 48 by Question 59

48 In marriage do you think sexual love is very important?

59 If a husband finds his wife having an affair with another man, what should he do?

Question 48	Question 59												
	Divorce	Separation	Divorce as final resort	Separation as final resort	Physical violence on erring spouse	Physical violence on intervener	Verbal reproach to erring spouse	Talk it over	Examine self	Forgive	Try to win back	Preserve marriage for sake of children	Total
Very important	13	18	13	12	6	9	7	23	21	7	11	6	159
Fairly important	9	16	14	13	4	9	6	28	20	10	11	6	159
Not very important	10	24	9	8	8	9	3	27	20	2	5	2	140
Not important at all	14	33	—	14	1	10	14	—	5	5	5	10	130
No answer	12	35	—	6	3	6	6	12	15	—	6	3	125
Total	12	18	13	12	5	9	7	25	20	8	10	6	159

Figure XXV

Question 48 by Question 59

48 In marriage do you think sexual love is very important?

59 If a wife finds her husband having an affair with another woman, what should she do?

Question 59	Question 48														
	Divorce	Separation	Divorce as final resort	Separation as final resort	Verbal reproaches to erring spouse	Verbal reproaches to intervener	Ignore passing fancy	Talk it over	Examine oneself	Forgive	Try to win back	Do nothing	Preserve marriage	Make self more attractive	Total
Very important	5	8	11	11	6	8	5	29	15	11	16	9	7	24	176
Fairly important	4	9	9	11	5	9	8	30	14	9	16	8	8	21	173
Not very important	6	16	3	15	6	8	5	23	10	4	8	7	8	15	147
Not important at all	—	24	—	—	—	6	6	41	—	24	12	6	—	6	131
No answer	6	4	2	4	2	6	6	22	16	12	14	18	4	20	144
Total	5	9	10	11	6	8	6	29	14	9	15	9	7	22	170

reclaimed by a new hair-do and smarter clothes has any foundation in fact or experience, or whether it be entirely the product of skilful advertisements and the women's magazines which carry them. Very few men indeed believe that improving their own appearance would be of any help.

The rank order of the solutions offered is as follows:

Men	%	Women	%
Talk it over with wife	24	Talk it over with husband	29
Examine self	20	Make self more attractive	22
Separation	18	Try to reconcile	15
Divorce as last resort	13	Examine self	14
Divorce	12	Separation as last resort	11
Separation as last resort	12	Divorce as last resort	10
Try to reconcile	10	Separation	9
Physical violence on other man	9	Forgiveness	9
Forgiveness	8	Do nothing	9
Verbal reproaches to wife	7	Verbal reproaches to other woman	7
Preserve marriage	6	Preserve marriage	7
Physical violence on wife	5	Verbal reproaches to husband	6
Verbal reproaches to other man	3	Ignore passing fancy	6
Ignore passing fancy	3	Divorce	5
Do not know	3	Do likewise	3
Do likewise	1	Do not know	3
Do nothing	1	Have innocent good time	1
Make self more attractive	1	Physical violence on other woman	1

The categories divorce or separation as 'last resort' are in all cases second choices, to be adopted if the first suggestion for preserving the marriage fails

Discussion, talking it over with the other spouse, is the most popular of all solutions in all branches of the community except the lower working class; it has somewhat more numerous advocates among the young, under 34, people with incomes under £12 a week, and markedly in the upper working class

Self-examination, is, as has been noted, particularly popular with male respondents. It is mentioned most often by people between the ages of 25 to 44, in the upper middle, upper working and lower working classes. It finds relatively few advocates in the Midlands, among the very young or the old and the poor. It is especially among the more prosperous and socially successful men that this feeling of responsibility is most highly developed. Usually the phraseology is fairly stereotyped; but this seems to be such an idiosyncratic reaction as to be worth illustrating at some little length.

A 30-year-old middle class man from Worksop:

First and foremost he should discover what it is in himself that has turned his wife away from him and try to put it right. He should then confront first wife and then lover and thrash it all out.

147

A 27-year-old Doncaster man.

He can either laugh or cry, because the blame rests on his own head.
If he gave his wife proper care and attention and praised her good
points she would not go astray. My wife doesn't feel like going elsewhere after I've done with her

A 46-year-old working class man from Kentish town·

If he, himself, is free from guilt, he should find out why she has gone
adrift. If he is to blame there is not much he can do about it

A 25-year-old working class man from Portsmouth:

Try to find out where he failed To keep his wife content put that
right and win her back

A 41-year-old middle class man from Barking:

Be very considerate, at first look for own faults and try to help her.
It may be a very difficult phase for her

A 66-year-old working class man from Hebburn, Durham:

Consider whether or not he is free from blame Consider (well) if
they have kiddies

A number of women who employ this argument use the metaphor
of looking in a mirror. Apparently for many English women the
mirror tells the unpleasant truths about character and behaviour as
well as appearance.

Thus, a 36-year-old middle class wife from Newcastle-on-Tyne:

Look in a mirror—mentally and otherwise.

A remarried middle class wife from Ely, aged 29·

Take a good look at herself in the mirror! Then find out if possible
what the attraction to the other woman is—and develope that quality
herself Above all do not 'nag or rave' at him. If possible make him a
little jealous also.

A 26-year-old middle class wife from a village near Rugby:

Firstly—look into her mirror, and then answer one question If he
loved her once, why does he now seek another woman? A woman loses
her husband generally through her own neglect

A 38-year-old working class woman from Sunderland, Durham:

I suggest she stands in front of the mirror and examines her reflection
in detail, then she should examine her conscience carefully, and finally
review her attitude towards her husband. Inevitably she will find the
fault lies within herself and as soon as she remedies it, her husband's
affair will cease.

A 25-year-old working class wife from Bristol:

If she loves her husband she should find out what is lacking in herself and endeavour to rectify it, but if he is a blaggard to her I would say that she is lucky to have found sufficient evidence for divorcing him.

A divorced working class woman from Batley, Yorks:

In my own case I went to see the other woman and pleaded with her for the sake of my two babies who were only 6 months old I went back through my own marriage to see where I had gone wrong and found that we mustn't have been physically suited.

A 42-year-old 'middle working class' wife from Peterborough:

I suppose the first thing to do would be to try and find the reason why and if she finds herself to blame remedy it

A 35-year-old widow from Reigate:

Find out where she may be at fault herself make herself as attractive as possible, then go out as much as possible with her best girl friend. Meanwhile living as sweet as possible to her husband, and treating his affair with amused lenience.

This widow's advice shades into the woman's panacea of making oneself more attractive The belief in the efficacy of this behaviour is strongest among the younger people in the middle, lower middle and upper working classes, especially in the South-West and North-West in medium and small towns. It is relatively little advocated by the elderly, the most prosperous and lower working class; and it has fewer advocates in the metropolises. For some reason, which I confess to finding obscure, a permanent wave is considered particularly efficacious in bringing a straying husband back to the fold.

A 30-year-old woman from St. Helens, Lancs:

First of all discuss it calmly with him, then do nothing but wait. Let the affair die a natural death and the man will return. In the meantime she can buy some new clothes and have her hair permed, make herself as attractive as she can. Spend more on herself than on the house.

A 33-year-old middle class wife from Shepperton:

1st. New clothes, undies, hair styles: 2nd Start going out, make company if possible (see he knows it) be hard to get, with husband. If possible go away for a spell leaving him with children to care for (only short time perhaps a sick mum?) Come back all fresh and charming. Try not to show grief, or to discuss other woman When he cannot see *her*, do not let him fall back on you! If he finally really loves other wench—retire as gracefully as you can, indulging in grief only when alone.

A 42-year-old working class wife from Wembley:

Ignore it, and make herself and home attractive enough to compete with and beat the other one Actually it happened to me, and I wrote to the other woman, she was miles away (He met her in the Forces). Told my husband to choose. It all finished, and has never been mentioned since.

A 'struggling middle class' wife from Sheffield.

Firstly try to keep it to yourself, then have a sort of competition with the other woman, by going to unusual lengths to improve your appearance, and make kindly remarks about the husband, and treat him as if you were courting again

The beauty treatment ploy is a specifically feminine gambit to preserve the marriage. Both sexes also advocate reconciliation without detailing the means by which this should be achieved, men somewhat more than women, particularly the young people (under 34) in the more prosperous middle and upper working classes in the two Southern regions, especially in London and the small villages. Another group, only slightly smaller, recommends preserving the marriage for the sake of the children, though this does not necessarily imply full reconciliation. This is not a solution which recommends itself to any extent to the more prosperous or to members of the upper middle class; and the under 24's barely mention it, but relatively few of these have children. This course finds its most numerous advocates in the upper working class.

A 50-year-old separated wife from London

These days if there is a child or children one has to forgive and forget, but when I came up against it, 22 years ago, I would do neither I turned him out and have regretted it ever since.

A 48-year-old separated man from Hucknall, Notts:

Well it happened to me, as I had two dear children, I gave her another chance, which I realize was wrong, but it happened again and we separated.

A 38-year-old working class wife from near Bury St. Edmunds·

My husband has had affairs for the last 17 years I have taken no notice, because I have had children, but my advice to another woman leave him then, when you are young. Not wait as I have done till my children are older. Always quarelling

A 25-year-old middle class man from Benfleet·

As in my personal experience, to try and keep the Family together for the Childrens sake, and not to go all out for a divorce unless there are no Children.

There seems to be more than a semantic difference between reconciliation and forgiveness; the latter implies both open acknowledgement of the situation and generosity; the former does not necessarily imply either. Forgiveness finds its advocates in every stratum of the society, though they are slightly more numerous among the young and in the middle class.

A 34-year-old middle class husband from Northolt:
Rather hard for me to answer. My wife had a child while I was overseas. I forgave her and we have been very happy.

A 29-year-old middle class man from Darlington, Durham:
To tell the true I would not know what I would do until it happened to me But a man who can forgive is in my opinion a real man.

A 24-year-old working class man from Newcastle:
I think a man should have a talk with her and try to make up. I think a Husband who really loves his wife would do that. I think I would

A 65-year-old working class man from Coalpool, Staffs:
It is best to be a better Man than the other. Tell her she has gone far enough and that unless she stops the home and all belonging to it must be broken up That with all her faults you love her still, and that all is forgiven.

A 63-year-old middle class man from Leicester.
Point out the risk of ruining both their lives, promise her a thrashing if it continues, then take her into town, buy her a new frock, take her to a good Hotel have a slap-up dinner, then on to a show to demonstrate what a damned good husband she has, and promptly dismiss the affair from my mind, *and tell her so*

A 59-year-old divorced working class man from Leominster, Herefordshire:
Pray to God in Heaven above to forgive her, as God, for Christs sake forgave him (I've done this and IT PAYS.)

A 22-year-old middle class woman from Essex·
Some women may forgive, but I could never forgive I would feel he didn't belong to me any more. You see it has happened to me and I cant forgive.

A 36-year-old middle class woman from Halifax·
Well having had that experience during the war, in which it hurt very much I forgave him and since we had our little boy things have been different, but I shall never forget time heals all things.

There is a group of women whose forgiveness is modified by a refusal to maintain or continue marital relations. I failed to make a special category for these partial forgivers; but my impression is that they are not numerous.

A 51-year-old wife from Morley:
I have never been put to the test, but I have always made it known to my husband that should such an occasion arise our personal relations would cease

A 36-year-old woman from Shrewsbury:
If he is only infatuated and realizes he has made a mistake I think the wife could forgive, as we all make mistakes once, but if the husband has other affairs, I think they are better without them unless there are children and then the wife has to consider them, because if parted, the men don't always pay the maintenance money regular, then live with them but as a lodger.

A 49-year-old woman from Gainsborough:
I should not mind so long as he allowed me a decent sum of money to live on. I should refuse myself to share the same bed with him.

The indifference of this last respondent finds a number of echoes from those who advocate ignoring the passing fancy and doing absolutely nothing. These are predominantly solutions offered by women of the upper middle and middle classes, with a slight concentration in early middle age. They are not solutions which commend themselves to the lower working class.

A lower middle class woman from Blackfield, Southampton·
I think it depends on the age mostly. If I had been in that position when young I should simply have left my husband But now I am 39, I don't think I would take it so seriously

A 34-year-old lower middle class wife from Rawmarsh, Yorks:
Depends on his age and time he's been married. If after 10 years marriage leave him alone except to let him know you know about it. Its usually a mild affair and it gives him a kick to feel he's still attractive

A 47-year-old middle class woman from Newbury:
Ignore it and take into consideration that men like change but not many break up their home and married life if they are fairly happy. I cant speak from experience as have never suspected anything of this of my husband, he is more interested in talking to men about mens interests.

A 48-year-old married woman from Birkenhead:
I don't know what others would do, but I'd let him get on with it as long as he didn't trouble me.

A 36-year-old lower middle class woman from Weston-super-Mare:
Do as I *did*. Let him know that I know about it, then ignore it and him. When he thought I didn't care, then *he* started worrying.

A 42-year-old lower middle class wife from Teignmouth:
This depends on the circumstances. If any other woman fancied my husband she'd be welcome, as long as he provided for me and my children properly But if I loved him, I cannot imagine what I should do.

A 36-year-old upper working class man from Peckham:
To my idea if it was in my case, I don't think I should do anything. I should say that my wife was finding the other man more interesting than me for the present and should let her carry on until the affair fizzled out or otherwise developed into a real love affair I do not believe in putting on a false front to win her back.

A 38-year-old man from New Malden, Surrey:
Nothing, if it fades out and she realizes that her husband, dull as he may have seemed is the best after all, she will be a chastened and better wife If it doesn't fade out the husband certainly hasn't got what the other man has, and he must accept the fact.

A 46-year-old working class man from Romford.
Shake his hand, because if husband isn't man enough to satisfies his wife, then I should think the other man is doing him a favour, as long as he doesn't take the wife away from you

A small group of women recommend that the wife should take advantage of the situation to have an innocent good time herself. This suggestion finds no favour in the rural South-West, nor in the upper middle class. Similarly the upper middle class has no advocates for the suggestion that the other spouse should go and do likewise; this is recommended by a scattering from all other classes and regions, 2 per cent of the population who seem to think the other's error condones their own.

A 42-year-old wife from Billericay, Essex:
Completely ignore gossip, find another male companion and tell husband and also introduce them, writing from experience, I have him back and happier from his escapade.

A 42-year-old working class man from Leicester·
Have an affair with another woman if it suits him.

A 42-year-old middle class woman from East Dean, West Riding:
As I did, tell him if he can have an affair, so can I, and really mean it, then they find why it hurts them when they find somebody wanting you so they make it up again.

A 35-year-old working class woman from Stockton-on-Tees:
> Try to say nothing, but this is very hard for a woman. Personally when I was younger and married under five years I used to create a scene and weep Now I start an affair with another man, it upsets my husband more than a scene.

Three per cent of the population state at some length that they have no idea what they would do in such a situation; but this uncertainty never seems to involve breaking the marriage. Thus, a 28-year-old wife from Sheffield:
> I think this depends on her love for her husband and on the happiness or otherwise of her married years. If this happened to me, I honestly don't know what I should do, I know my life would be shattered.

A 39-year-old middle class man from Leicester:
> FAINT—at least I should because it would be such a surprise that she was interested in men.

A 27-year-old working class wife from Kingston-upon-Hull:
> I cant imagine mine doing so because he's so critical of other women. If it ever did happen I know in my case I'd never get him back because she'd have to be something in the first place to come up to his standards.

A 39-year-old working class man from High Wycombe:
> Very difficult to answer people's temperament vary. I detest, personally, those intrigues and affairs. But should it happen to my family, I hesitate as to whether I would walk out, talk to both or what! It could happen in rare cases for a person to be happily married and then meet The 'Dream Girl' or 'Dream Man' Tough luck, then.

All the solutions so far discussed have the implicit or explicit assumption that adultery, real or supposed, should not terminate the marriage (if that can possibly be avoided) and does not justify the wronged spouse in adopting violent and aggressive behaviour. I think this can be described as the typical English response, covering as it does the views of more than half the men, and nearly three-quarters of the women. Thirty per cent of the men and just half that number of women advocated taking immediate legal steps to end the marriage (a further 25 per cent of the men and 21 per cent of the women contemplate this as a last resort if none of the devices described above have been successful); and 14 per cent of the men contemplate violence against the wife, or the lover, or both, but only one woman in a hundred considers going for the other woman.

This typical gentleness or reasonableness is susceptible to a variety of explanations or qualifications. It does seem fairly certain that an English man or woman's 'honour' is no longer involved in the chastity or fidelity of his or her spouse, as would appear to have been the case in the historical past, and still occurs in a number of societies today. For the English majority 'honour' would appear to inhere entirely in one's own character and behaviour; and, as has been shown, there is at least as much tendency to blame oneself for a spouse's dereliction as to blame or punish the offending spouse.

Secondly, I would suggest that such attitudes imply a relatively low valuation of 'love' and a very high valuation of the institution of marriage, a point which has already been previously documented. It is interesting to note that there is practically no mention of what might be called the ethical attitude to divorce, the feeling that it is morally wrong to keep bound to one a partner who prefers another; such an ethical attitude seems to be relatively common in the United States, where 'love' is, apparently, very highly valued.

It is perhaps worth recalling in this context that 40 per cent of the married sample stated that they had had 'a real love affair' outside marriage;[2] as far as men are concerned this is as high a number as admit, or advocate, experience before marriage, and for women it is nearly twice as high. Although it cannot be directly demonstrated from the figures available, I have the strong impression that extra-marital sexual experience is considerably commoner in England than pre-marital experience, although it still involves only a minority of the population; that, in the greater number of cases, both parties are married; and that the affairs are in most cases of relatively little emotional importance.

There does remain however the minority whose tendency is to react with violence, a small group who would use physical violence or upbraidings, and the more considerable group who would call in the resources of the law. My impression from reading the comments of the men and women who advocate these courses is that sexual jealousy is a comparatively uncommon emotion among the English; where anger is felt and expressed in such a situation it is more likely to be vindictiveness, a desire to hurt rather than a desire to avenge.

Those who threaten or consider violence are predominantly the younger married men (under 34) with a very heavy concentration in the lower working class, particularly from the Midlands. Such courses have advocates in all groups of English society, but they are markedly fewer in the middle class, among the most prosperous and poorest and in the North-East and North.

A 38-year-old upper working class man from Farnham:
If she has been unfaithful—kill her If she has not been unfaithful seek a settlement A clean break either way with husband or 'other

155

Man'. I believe in divorce before infidelity occurs—but not after it happens

A 31-year-old working class man from Hull:
Regarding myself I would kill my wife as my whole life would be shattered and I wouldn't want to live. I'm not being dramatic I'm sincere.

A 30-year-old middle class man from Dinkley. Lancs.
Quite personally I should be inclined to take her life and suffer the consequences I would not be able to forget or forgive the wrong to myself and children.

A 53-year-old working class man from Salford, Lancs:
If there are no children, kill her.

A 32-year-old remarried man from Leicester:
This is an unanswerable question. I was *very* nearly guilty of murder; but I can assure you what happened was *natural* It is *not* a question one can answer.

A 31-year-old divorced working class man from Greenwich.
Do as I did personally, give her a good hiding but unfortunately led to the wrecking of my marriage and my wife now lives with the man I caught her with 6 years ago.

A 65-year-old separated man from Rainham, Essex:
Like myself, try and point out where it will lead to and be forebearing for a while and try to win her back, look into yourself and see if you are to blame in any way, but not like me, take an axe and decide 'doing both in' if found together, lucky I did not, or I should not be writing this.

A 22-year-old man from Walthamstow:
First he should kill the man and when the husband goes too the gallows for the murder the wife will have the death of her husband on her mind for the rest of her life also pays the penalty

A 37-year-old middle class man from a small town in Wiltshire:
Tip her up and pull down her knickers and spank her till it hurts her. I found my wife just off to the pictures with another man I knew, this is what I did to her. We had been married 3 years then She is the best and most lovable wife a man could have now

A 51-year-old working class man from Epsom:
Reason with her—Explain the wreckage she is liable to make both of her own and his life, also see the man and reason with him. Personally I knocked 'seven bells' out of him, but it did no good

156

A 43-year-old lower working class man from Gravesend:
Give his wife three children periods of 18 months.

A 36-year-old miner from Barnsby:
Take a good hold of himself and make sure he's not seeing things then
Bolt the doors, get hold of anything heavy lash the pair of them to
practically unconsciousness then inform the police

Very few women advocate using violence, and not a single one
of my respondents imagined committing murder, which could
theoretically equalize the usual disparity in physical strength. A
28-year-old Cheltenham wife who describes herself as 'educated
working class' advises:
Hit him with something hard when he least expects it Cook a jolly
good meal and eat it all in front of him

A 43-year-old Croydon woman who describes her class as
'Intellectual':
Threaten both of them with physical violence—I've tried it and it
worked, and advised it and it worked (also tell husband other woman
boasts she has a lot of influence over him—this is a lie with grain of
truth and he recoils. Husband glad wife cares so much—other woman
gets scared she would not fair favourably if it got to a court case. She
slinks away—realises she is cause of large amount of aggravation)

A 62-year-old middle class woman from Cottingley, Yorks:
I dont Know but I think I should make it hot for both of them, no
woman would take my man without a fight, but my man never wanted
another woman, so I didn't have that trouble, my husband died, just
12 months ago.

Although there are so few female advocates for physical violence,
quite a number contemplate a 'scene', either with the husband, or
more usually the other woman, where the violence would remain
on the verbal level. Some men also consider this technique. It is
particularly favoured by the lower middle and upper working
classes, by the middle aged and, once again, in the Midlands.

A 29-year-old working class woman from Bath:
In my own experience, play up holy moses, pack your bag & prepare
to leave him with the small kiddies, also threaten to go to see the other
woman. Unless he is utterly heartless—it usually works.

A 42-year-old middle class wife from London, N.W.:
I had just this problem to deal with once After being nearly frantic
with worry—I decided to show him that he was making a fool of himself
—and no man likes to be thought a Fool—it worked.

157

A 36-year-old working class wife from Spondon, Derby·

Providing she has done nothing to cause it, she could get the other woman and her husband together and talk it over, this can make them both feel so guilty they would break it up (This is from my own experience)

A 28-year-old working class woman from Tiverton:

Well this may not sound good advice to you but it happened to me whilst I was in hospital and I said I would more or less scratch the other woman's eyes out when I got out and my husband was delighted, and has been the good husband ever since I did fight for him by post but that's all

A 41-year-old working class woman from the North of England:

If she finds out before it is too late, before he becomes a bigamist as mine did. She could talk things over with the other woman. Then they can decide what to do with him themselves

A 41-year-old divorced middle class man from Birmingham:

If it has been going on for any length of time there is *nothing* he can do as they would still do it. It happened to me and I approached the man and appealed to him in a straightforward way to stop it as he was also a married man He said he would but continued it My wife left home to go with him and now they have parted and she has gone to her mother in South Africa. She wants to come back but the eldest girl who looks after the house will *not* have anything to do with her and says *no*.

A 27-year-old man from Bethnal Green who describes himself as 'ordinary working man in the street'.

Shake the other man by the hand for showing him the type of woman his wife really is.

Finally, there are the people who would end the marriage legally, by divorce or separation. People in the Midlands favour divorce markedly more than those of any other region; as far as this survey is any guide, people of this region are somewhat freer and more expressive in all aspects of sexual life than the inhabitants of the rest of the country. The people of the South-West produce the fewest advocates for legal remedies. The most prosperous and the members of the upper middle class refer the most to legal proceedings, followed by the lower working class; divorce is somewhat more favoured by the middle aged, separation by the elderly, which probably reflects the changing pattern of English legal practice, and the availability of divorce for poor persons. As already stated, twice as many men as women advocate so drastic a course

The comments and advice about such courses are mostly straight-forward enough; but many of them are remarkable for the bitterness they illustrate Many of these comments are autobiographical.

A 43-year-old working class man from Horsham
If the husband had a little more sense than I had at the time he would divorce her.

A 32-year-old remarried 'average type of working class man' from Dorking·
Get himself free as soon as possible very few women go straight if with another mans company. Personal experience had my former wife return 4 times.

A 29-year-old man from Doncaster, W. Yorks, who describes himself as a 'moderate scholar'.
He should kick her out I should go insane with jealousy, probably break my heart. Soft talk for a grown man Just cannot bear to think of it

A 41-year-old working class miner from Ilkeston, Derby.
Divorce her I have only ever had one girl in my life and I married her. Never have I had intimate relations with any one else.

A 35-year-old lower working class man from Newent in Gloucester:
Well if it ever happened to me if my wife can find a better one than me good luck to her I wouldn't do her in as I have told her but she could go—I should be finished with her but I would see she went with the other man but I would have the kids they are mine

A 43-year-old working class man from Southampton.
Pack his traps and depart graciously leaving his wife and the other man in peace to 'vork out their own destiny Scenes are horrible anathema to me Love can be extinguished as well as kindled.

A working class man from Leigh, Lancs:
I should take my son and all our belongings and disappear. I should find another more trustworthy and leave the other man to keep her

A Cirencester man:
If it was me I should tell her to get out and not come back but I dare say I would take her back after a bit because I am still in love with her.

A 25-year-old working class man from Manchester:
If it was my fault, I'm uncertain, as we are now I should want her to go, but I should want our son.

159

A 27-year-old working class man from Shipley, Yorks:

Use his discretion from my experience I found it wise to take legal action against my wife even though she was a good mother and wife except for being faithful to me I find if they once start having affairs they will continue to do so except in very rare cases.

A 46-year-old woman from Malvern.

I, unfortunately, did discover my husband having an affair with another woman; she was married with a husband in the forces. My husband and she had a child before I suspected, although he was very unkind to me, and neglected me and our 2 children. . . . As I am a R.C I do not believe in divorce so there is a Judicial Separation. I am fairly happy—the woman in the case died soon after of T B. so my husband is now alone.

A 34-year-old woman from Macclesfield

Well have a divorce of course, but I am alright as I am. I work and I have 3 11. 0 and in for another 6/- next month so I'm alright, my husband has never fulfilled his payments to me for 15 years so why should I let him go free with a divorce

A 65-year-old woman from Coventry:

Tell him about it but don't nag and don't leave home & children through it, I did once and have always regretted it

A 49-year-old working class woman from Leeds:

If I found my husband having an affair with someone else, I should say, if she can get more out of him than I can she is welcome to him and leave it at that he would soon tire.

A 59-year-old working class woman from Nelson, Lancs:

That depends on the wifes position if there are young children. In my own experience I would ask him to go to the other woman and good riddance!!

A 32-year-old working class woman from St Albans:

It seems to me most women forgive for the sake of the children but not me. I'd get a good lawyer and hope to be rid of him bag and baggage, as I wouldn't want to try to hold him, but I'd see him in hell before he took my house.

A 27-year-old wife from Bishop's Waltham, Hants:

Pack his case and show him the way out. I haven't a forgiving nature.

A 30-year-old woman from Darlington, Durham·

Try to find out if it is true first, and how far it has progressed. Then do something about it. If I couldn't forgive or keep on loving I couldn't live with someone I hated or despised even for the children.

A 30-year-old married woman from Birmingham·

I would find out if I was letting myself go, if so, try to smarten up, keep myself young as possible, otherwise I would let him go. I don't think I would plead and cry, only on behalf of my two children, they love their daddy.

The spate of quotations—though only a fragment of those available—in the last two chapters have I hope illustrated the great importance for English men and women of the institution of marriage and the seriousness with which they consider it. It is marriage itself which is important, not. I think, love or sexual gratification; and marriage is living together, making a home together, making a life together, and raising children Perhaps even more for English men than for English women, parenthood is the greatest joy and greatest responsibility of adult life.

NOTES TO CHAPTER TEN

1. In January 1951, the British Institute of Public Opinion asked a sample of the whole of Britain 'What do you think is the secret of a happy marriage?' The answers are somewhat differently categorized to mine, but are strictly comparable Only in one instance is there a difference of more than 2 per cent between the sexes, 19 per cent of the men and 22 per cent of the women mention understanding, tolerance

Give-and-take	38 per cent
Understanding, tolerance	21 ,, ,,
Sufficient money	9 ,, ,,
Mutual trust	6 ,, ,,
Marrying for love	5 ,, ,,
Children	5 ,, ,,

The following factors are only mentioned by 1 or 2 per cent· wise choice of partners, good housing; good cooking, happy physical relations common religion Six per cent of the answers were not classified under these categories, and 10 per cent said there was no 'secret'. People answering this poll were, apparently, only allowed to name one factor.

2. See p. 86.

CHAPTER ELEVEN

CHILDREN I: BENDING THE TWIG

(NOTE. *The material in this and the following chapter is founded
entirely on the replies of parents of living children.*)

IN A SOCIETY as complex and diversified as contemporary England,
there are relatively few areas in which two-thirds or more of the
population share the same attitudes and practices. This is indeed
a matter of common observation. and is the major argument
advanced against the hypothesis of a national character, which
postulates the existence of shared motives and ideals underlying the
many varieties of observable behaviour within a society. It therefore
seems highly significant that there should be a whole cluster of
common attitudes concerning the proper way of rearing and training
infants and young children from birth onwards which almost
completely override the differences of region and town size, social
class and income.

Studies of national character have generally assumed the existence
of very widely shared patterns of treating the newborn members
of a society so as to form characters similar to those of the parental
generation. This assumption has been based firstly on detailed
observation of primitive societies, in which the treatment accorded
to every infant and child could be watched over a considerable
period; and subsequently, for large and complex societies, by intensive interviewing of socially disparate individuals, supplemented
by a little observation of young children, by photographs and by
pediatric literature. It is therefore theoretically gratifying that the
statistical results of interviews from two large samples should bear
out this fundamental hypothesis so adequately.

In the main sample, 2,328 respondents (47 per cent) were parents;
of these 791 (34 per cent) had only one child, though this included
many of the younger respondents whose families might be unfinished,
and 773 (33 per cent) had two children. Of the remaining third 349 (15
per cent) had three children, 146 (6 per cent) four, exactly the same
number five or more, and 123 people didn't answer; these non-
respondents are partly made up of a very few people who left blank
the whole of the inside page which included these questions, and a
considerable number of the widowed and divorced who may have
been sent the inappropriate forms.

The points on which there is this large consensus of opinion are that cleanliness training should be started before the baby is a year old (more than two-thirds of the mothers say before it is six months old), that more harm is done to the child if training is started too late than if it is started too early, and that children need more discipline than they get nowadays.

It would be possible to subsume these three points into one more general statement. 'The formation of a good English character depends on the parents imposing suitable disciplines as early as possible, the child's character will be spoiled if the discipline is insufficient or not applied soon enough.' A metaphor employed with considerable consistency is the training or pruning of a tree or plant, which will grow misshapen or sport back to its wild origins if not timely treated and formed. It is probably significant in this connection that English is, as far as I can trace, the only European language which has a single word, nursery, for the place where both children and plants are reared. In both senses the usage is long established.[1]

Implicit in this statement is the assumption, which quite occasionally becomes articulate, that there are innate tendencies of an undesirable nature in all newborn babies which will develop unless appropriate training is applied at the proper time, a lay echo of the religious concept of the Old Adam, and, as a corollary, that the parents, pastors and masters are to blame in the last resort if the child is of bad character, ill grown. There is very little belief in childish innocence[2] or in the innate goodness of children, views which are strongly held in some other societies. Somewhat less articulate, but nevertheless apparently strongly held, is the belief that discipline, habit training, is good in itself, and valuable for the formation of a good character, almost without regard to the habits trained or imposed. This is of course somewhat of an exaggeration; but it seems remarkable that nobody queried the meaning of the question 'Generally speaking, do you consider that children need more discipline than they get nowadays?' This is one of the very few questions on which nobody thought it necessary to write uninvited comments.

Sixty-eight per cent of the population consider children need more discipline, 28 per cent that present discipline is sufficient; 2 per cent that they need less discipline; and a further 2 per cent did not answer. The tiny group who think children need less discipline are predominantly young prosperous men from the metropolises; the non-answerers are chiefly the old and widowed.

There is no difference between men and women in the demand for more discipline, or in satisfaction with the present practice; but the widowed and divorced demand significantly more discipline than do the married. Satisfaction with the *status quo* is slightly more marked in the two Northern regions, in the medium sized towns, in the upper working and working classes, and most markedly in the young parents under 24 who are most engaged with small children. Demands for more discipline come most from the Midlands, from people aged over 65, and from the top and bottom of the economic and social scales, those with incomes of under £5 and over £15, from the upper middle and lower working classes. The variations however are very slight, with the exceptions of the young married couples who are divided almost equally between being satisfied and demanding more discipline; and on the other hand the upper middle class who have 83 per cent of its members demanding more discipline, which is possibly a reflection of the relative absence of disciplining nurses and governesses in households where the parents had been reared by professionals.[3]

A very similar pattern arises from the answers to the question: 'Which is worse for the child, starting training too early—or too late—or doesn't it make much difference?' This question followed immediately after 'When should a young child start being trained to be clean?'[4] and it is to be presumed that for most respondents 'training' in this question means cleanliness training. Seventy-eight per cent of the parents consider that starting training too late is the more harmful, 12 per cent starting training too early; 8 per cent considers it makes little difference, and 2 per cent (again predominantly the old and widowed) do not answer.

There is some conflict between the views of fathers and mothers on this question: 10 per cent more fathers (82 per cent to 72 per cent) consider late training more harmful; 7 per cent more mothers (16 per cent to 9 per cent) consider that too early training may be harmful. Parents from the North-East and North and the middle aged (over 45) are particularly insistent on the danger of postponing training; the younger group, particularly those under 24, and members of the upper middle class, followed by the upper working class, stress the harm of too early training.[5]

It would seem possible that we have here a synoptic demonstration of a change in cultural patterns. Modern pediatric advice tends to consider that early cleanliness training is physiologically useless and possibly psychologically harmful; and it would appear that the young mothers of the upper middle and upper working classes have attended

164

pre-natal clinics and taken the advice offered there. If this be the case, a table taken 20 years ago would show even fewer people aware of the dangers of too early training, and one taken 20 years hence might show a very considerable increase in the holders of this view This would in turn entail alteration in the generally held views of human nature (or at any rate childish nature) and the duties and responsibilities of parents, with all the internal and external repercussions that that would involve. The first lessons in the principle of gradualism which English men and women learn would appear to be these early months or years of training which can only very slowly become effective, and the patient parents in their turn learn again that Rome wasn't built in a day, more haste less speed, and all the other proverbs and apothegms that establish slow and gradual development as a law of nature and society.

The phrase 'trained to be clean' could of course be understood to refer to washing rather than toilet training, and it seems possible that a small group (5 per cent of the fathers and 1 per cent of the mothers) have so understood it, since they name some period between 2 and 5 years. A considerable number of men (17 per cent) and a few women (6 per cent) use the ambiguous phrase 'as soon as the child understands'. This phrasing is little used by members of the upper middle or middle classes, by the youngest married couples, or by the rural South-West, it is especially favoured by the middle-aged and elderly, members of the upper working class, the most prosperous people, and the two Northern regions. This phrase differs from any others used in that it takes the child's development rather than a schedule into account; but since it is so much favoured by the older and more prosperous men, it may well be a rational statement dating from a period when fathers paid relatively little attention to their infants Some 3 per cent, mostly middle-aged and lower middle class, do not answer the question.

Ten per cent of the fathers, and 7 per cent of the mothers name some period between 1 and 2 years; and this seems to be part of the group, referred to above, who have adopted modern pediatric notions. They are heavily concentrated in the young couples under 34, in the median income groups (£5–£12 a week) in all classes except the upper and lower middle, but since a child nearing the age of 2 might be capable of washing this category is still slightly ambiguous. This is not the case for all periods prior to twelve months of age.

Eighty-four per cent of English mothers and 60 per cent of English fathers consider training should start before the child is a year old; 69 per cent of the mothers and 45 per cent of the fathers

165

before it is 6 months old. The group who name a period between 6 months and 1 year are almost certainly those following contemporary advice; they are heavily concentrated in the under 34's, in the upper middle class followed by the lower working and working classes; on income they reach two peaks, in the £5–£8 a week and the over £15 a week groups. Relatively few of the poor or the elderly name this period.

Four categories were fixed for early training, chiefly dependent on the actual phrase used. Just a quarter of the mothers and half that number of the fathers state flatly 'from birth'. This is particularly favoured by the middle-aged mothers, between 35 and 64 in the upper middle, middle and upper working classes. The slightly more ambiguous phrases 'as early as possible', 'it's never too early', and so on are used considerably more by men, especially older men, than by women, 15 per cent men and 8 per cent women. There is some concentration in the smaller towns in the North-West. This group may well be identical with that which names a period under 2 months, very often 'as soon as the mother comes back from hospital' or 'as soon as the mother gets up'; this more precise phrasing is used twice as often by mothers as by fathers (14 per cent women and 7 per cent men), and is again somewhat more favoured by the middle-aged and elderly. If these two groups of phrases are treated as identical, both referring to some period shortly after birth but less than 8 weeks, and the two columns put together we find that fathers and mothers express similar views; that there is some preference for this early start in the two Northern regions and the upper middle class, particularly among the middle-aged and elderly.

Another 23 per cent of the mothers, and 14 per cent of the fathers name some period between 2 and 6 months, usually with considerable precision, but occasionally saying as soon as the baby can be held in a sitting position. This period, which is physiologically perhaps the most senseless of all, is barely mentioned by the upper middle class and little by the upper working class, it is favoured by all the others, particularly the middle and lower middle. It is mentioned relatively seldom in the North-West or by the elderly.[8]

Although the questionnaire called for no elaboration, quite a number of respondents added illuminating comments. The absolute moral value given to early training is illustrated by the 33-year-old working class father from Leicester, who wrote that training should start 'as soon as he or she can understand the difference between good and bad'; and, rather more ferociously, by the 32-year-old Surbiton

166

mother of two, who describes herself as 'The £6 a week working class that all other classes of the country depend on to make this country's fortune':

From the very first time of its life, if you are going to let it live, let it live the correct way from the first and not let it do one thing at a given time and later make it change its habits

A middle class mother from Lower Standen, Henley.

From the time it is born, but I am not saying how much luck you have, you just have to keep trying

A 32-year-old lower middle class mother from Enfield:

As early as possible in my experience in spite of the psychologists who say cleanliness before a year—18 months is more luck than judgment.

A working class father from Slough:

From birth then it comes naturally and all it needs is patience

A working class mother of four from Hastings·

A very tiny baby soon knows what is required of him when he is 'potted' after a feed I should say about 6 weeks

A 39-year-old working class mother from Halifax·

It should be trained patiently as early as possible but no bullying Praise and co-operation are essential.

A 54-year-old father from Darfield:

At four weeks old. Start holding the child out to do its motions without napkin at set times each day This is the foundation of cleanliness.

A working class mother of two from Honiton.

From one month but don't be disappointed if no results until the child can talk.

A 28-year-old mother from Farnley:

I should say as soon as possible though results do not often come quickly.

A working class mother from Derby.

Usually about 6 weeks is soon enough, but often then it is only good luck.

A working class father from Kidderminster.

When the mother has the time to waste periods of up to about an hour holding it out. Otherwise when the child can be sat on a comode.

A 40-year-old middle class father from Liverpool:

At 6 months it becomes clean parrot like.

It would seem as though, for most English people, the desirability of early training is so highly charged with emotional and moral values that they are incapable of learning from experience Indeed, parents of larger families (three or more children) are slightly more insistent than the parents of one or two children on the dangers of postponing training. A very few parents showed that they had learned from experience.

Figure XXVI

Question 60 by Question 62

  60 How many children have you?

  62 Which is worse for the child?

Question 60	Question 62				
	Starting training too early	Or too late	Or doesn't it make much difference	No answer	Total
1	17	75	5	3	100
2	14	75	10	1	100
3	12	78	9	1	100
4	7	85	5	3	100
5 and more	7	79	10	4	100
No answer	12	78	8	2	100
Total	12	78	8	2	100

Thus, a working class mother from Birmingham

I found with my oldest I started her at about 3 weeks and I couldn't do anything with her until she was 2½. The other I started at 12 months and she was no bother at all.

A 32-year-old working class father from Colyton, Devon:

I didn't think a child could be trained too early to be clean, but my experience (only a year's) proves otherwise; so I would say from 1 year old.

A 42-year-old middle class woman from Colne:

I 'potted' mine, on a pot on my knee, for a very short time at regular intervals daily, from birth. Tho' they didn't always perform then' Many people don't bother until a year or so later; either training can be successful if you don't fuss.

These parents, it must be repeated, are very exceptional. For the vast majority of English mothers and fathers, the physiological development and potentialities of the child do not seem to be taken

168

into account The first duty of a responsible parent is to impose the discipline of cleanliness at the proper date, the first lesson of a properly brought-up child is to respond.[7]

Until a baby can walk its training is inevitably almost entirely in the hands of its mother, even though fathers may have very definite ideas how the baby should be trained. When it acquires physical independence, and before it goes to school, it will in most cases spend the greater part of its time with its mother alone, since nearly all fathers are away at work during week-days; when it starts school many of its waking hours are spent under the supervision of teachers. Habitually, the child spends relatively few hours in the week with its father.

This pattern is of course common to the greater number of families living in technically complex societies; but within this pattern there seems to be a number of possibilities of variation in the authority and rôles of father, mother, teacher and possibly other publicly appointed figures. On theoretical grounds these variations can be expected to be of considerable importance, since the conscience (the conscious portion of the super-ego) would appear to be largely formed by the incorporation of some aspects of the dominant figure or figures of authority in childhood, so that most people approve and disapprove of themselves and others in the light of the standards they have introjected in their formative years.

Parents and parent surrogates demonstrate their authority by establishing rules of conduct which the child should follow, by punishing transgressions from these rules and (at least on occasion) rewarding obedience. Within the limits of a questionnaire only one facet of this complex and significant problem could be studied directly, though the answers to many other questions can be considered partially relevant; and the question I asked was: 'Who is the proper person to punish a child who has done something really bad?' I gave the alternatives: 'Mother. Father: Teacher: Other (*please specify*)'. I also asked Why? the reason for the choice made; but this was the unique occasion where insufficient space was provided on the printed questionnaire, and a third of the sample did not answer, presumably because they had not noticed that the query was there. My reasons for asking about punishment rather than reward were manifold; the power of authority is shown in the last resort by the ability to inflict sanctions; and although love, and the rewards which flow from it, are of inestimable importance in forming character, I considered it improbable that respondents would ascribe more love to one parent than to the other

169

On gross figures, three-fifths of English parents (61 per cent) think the father should be the chief source of authority in the home, and one-third (35 per cent) the mother; one in twenty (6 per cent) name the teacher, and one in fifty (2 per cent) some other figure, typically a policeman. The total is a little over 100 per cent as some parents named more than one punishing authority, the old and poor advance the view that mothers should punish their daughters and fathers their sons, the more prosperous members of the lower middle class especially consider that father, mother and teacher are equally appropriate, and another small group with some concentration in the upper middle class demand that the odium of punishment be shared, so that neither parent shall be disliked more than the other.

Quite a number of the fathers of the lower middle class, particularly the middle-aged and elderly. would grant chief authority to the teacher; as will be shown later[3] members of this class seem particularly willing to concede authority to 'the state'. No members of the upper middle or lower working class name the teacher. A few of the lower working class, particularly the youngest mothers, name the policeman, who again is not mentioned by the upper middle class.

Taking the country as a whole, three-quarters of the fathers (72 per cent) consider that fathers should do the punishment, and one-quarter (27 per cent) that mothers should: mothers are divided very nearly equally, with a slight preponderance (49 per cent for fathers, contrasted with 46 per cent for mothers) in favour of paternal authority. These figures were minutely analyzed in a number of ways, with a rather interesting result: men's opinions of the rôle of the parents vary quite considerably in different regions, and to a certain extent by town size and economic level, but with a couple of exceptions (mothers from the South-West and in the £12–£15 income range claim much less authority for themselves than do the women in other regions or income groups) women's views of the different parental rôles are remarkably stable This leads me to hazard the generalization that the differences between the characters of the different English regions (as opposed to such characteristics as accent, vocabulary, or regional cooking) are to a considerable extent based on the differing attitudes held by men about women.[9]

The fathers in the North-East and North, followed by the Midlands, are the most insistent on paternal authority; those from the North-West and South-West are least so. Men from the metropolises conceded slightly more authority to their wives than do those in the smaller communities. As family income goes up the father claims more and more authority, from the poorest groups (under £5 a week) of which only half claim paternal authority, to the most prosperous (over £15 a week) where it is claimed by four-fifths. Maternal authority is lowest in the lower middle class (except for the Midlands) and the lower working class (except for London and the South-East); paternal authority is somewhat weaker in the middle class, contrasted with the working class in London and the South-East and in the Midlands; in the remaining regions there is little difference.

It seems as though there are a number of influences somewhat modifying the general English picture of paternal authority in the family. The most marked is the regional, where the mothers in the two Western regions, above all the North-West, are conceded more influence than in the rest of the country, they also have more authority in the big towns than in the rest of the country. In the poorest families, and among the elderly the mother's authority equals that of the father; as income and social position improve, so does the mother's authority decrease, reaching its nadir in the lower middle class and in the £12–£15 income group. There is a slight recrudescence in maternal authority among the most prosperous and (to a lesser extent) in the middle and upper middle classes which would have the tradition, if no longer the practice, of boys and girls both being under feminine discipline (nurses and governesses) for a number of years. It seems possible that the resemblance in some traits between the upper middle and lower working classes (in contrast to the intermediate groups) may in part derive from the greater influence of women in the earlier years of the lives of members of both these classes.

In the few families in which there are more than three children mothers are more likely to do the punishing than they are in smaller families.

As has already been said, the answers to the question why one parent or representative of authority should be chosen was to a great extent vitiated by the faulty lay-out of the questionnaire, with the result that the figures are only illustrative, though failure to answer is pretty evenly divided among all the categories. A quarter of those who did reply used the space to modify rather than explain their answer—to suggest disciplinary rôles for the parent or teacher not named in the answer to the first part of the question. Thus, some 8 per cent, heavily concentrated in the more prosperous groups of the lower middle class, consider that father, mother and teacher

171

Figure XXVII

Question 60 by Question 64

60 How many children have you?

64 Who is the proper person to punish a child who has done something really bad?

Question 60	Question 64					
	Mother	Father	Teacher	Others	No answer	Total
1	34	62	5	2	0	103
2	35	63	8	2	0	108
3	33	64	5	2	1	105
4	38	59	5	3	1	'06
5 and more	44	58	9	1	1	112
No answer	37	48	7	1	9	102
Total	35	61	6	2	1	105

should each punish in their own sphere. Typical of this attitude is
the 37-year-old middle class father from Southend-on-Sea:

All three are required, I do not consider I should punish a child for
anything done in my absence or after the 'crime' has been committed.

Another 4 per cent, chiefly composed of the poor and elderly,
again somewhat concentrated in the lower middle class, advocate
that fathers should punish the boys and mothers the girls, on account
of the possible pathological implications. An example of this attitude
is the 47-year-old middle class father from London.

Father or mother each to each sex, to prevent any sexual aberration
in later life.

A small group of 2 per cent think that both parents should take
the onus of punishment to prevent one being turned into an ogre or
bug-bear; this is advanced somewhat more by fathers, particularly
the younger fathers, than by mothers A young working class mother
from Sheffield writes:

I think Mother and father equally. Because this job is too often (in
our household at any rate) left to mother giving the child a false impression of his parents.

Similarly, a 26-year-old middle class mother from Henley:

I think mother and father should punish because if not it gives the
child a one-sided affection if one person does the punishing

There are two arguments (with a total of 5 per cent in each case)
which are much more advanced by the mothers than by the fathers:

172

that punishment should be given immediately by whichever parent is present, and that discipline is more effective if it is administered by both parents. Apart from the sex distribution advocates of the first argument are very evenly divided, except that no members of the upper middle class advance it; they advance the second argument in considerable numbers; and this argument (that shared discipline is more effective) in general finds far more favour in all three middle classes and the upper working class, than it does in the working class, and it is not mentioned by the lower working class. As far as these incomplete figures can be taken as a guide, it would seem that the concept of multiple authorities is far more congenial to the middle classes, than it is to the working classes, who tend to favour a single figure of authority This is true even for the small group who think that all authority should be given to the teachers.

Twenty-eight per cent of the respondents provided explanations for father being the punisher, and 14 per cent for mother; these figures are of course very considerably less than those advanced for choosing either parent (61 per cent and 35 per cent respectively) but the proportions are not dissimilar.

The most important argument for paternal authority is that the father is the legal head of the household, the boss; 18 per cent of the fathers and 14 per cent of the mothers advance this view, with a heavy concentration in the younger parents of the two Northern regions in the upper working and working classes, followed by the lower middle; very few in the upper middle class hold this view. The argument that father makes more impression (10 per cent fathers and 7 per cent mothers) is particularly favoured in the lower working class; but it has advocates in all categories So too does the argument that father is the juster or fairer parent, with the exception of the youngest married group (under 24).

Fathers repeat, sometimes simply, and sometimes with elaborations, the statement that 'father should be the head of the house'. 'Father should be head of his household and therefore settle *serious* things' (a lower middle class father from Peterborough); 'One usually gets punished by "the boss", and, begging Mum's pardon, Father is the boss of the house!' (a 31-year-old lower middle class father from Bristol); 'The father as head of the house is responsible for his or her actions' (a 28-year-old 'poor working class' father from Farnworth, Lancs); 'A child should for his own sake have to answer to one authority—and by the very nature of things that authority ought very properly to be the child's father' (a lower middle class

173

father from Peterborough); 'Father's position at home is like a headmasters at school. Severity meets with severity' (a 'reasonably middle class' 29-year-old father from Hereford).

Besides this widespread concept of the father's legal position and rights, there is also a fairly widely diffused view of 'human nature' which makes father the 'natural' figure of authority. Thus, a 41-year-old miner from Cullercoats, Northumberland writes 'Father should punish on account of herd instinct, he is the leader', and then adds, in parenthesis, 'I prefer my wife to punish my children and not as some mothers telling their children just wait till your Dad comes home'!

On the father's greater justice or impressiveness, a 24-year-old working class father from Culcheth, Lancs, represents many when he writes.

> After punishment by mother, the child is usually smothered in kisses and told in a sweet voice that he or she has been naughty and must not do it again, the effect of the punishment being nil

A 28-year-old 'average working class' mother from London:

> Mother scolds all day, so they take more notice of father, if he only punishes when they are really bad

A 44-year-old middle class father from London

> Children have a hearty respect for Dad if they know it is going to hurt if they do not do as they are told.

A working class father of six from Hucknall, Notts.

> I think that most children today fear father more than mother.

A retired gardener from Lincolnshire:

> Father is the figure head who all look up to.

Three reasons are given why the mother should do the punishing·that she understands the child better; that she is less harsh or heavy-handed; and that she is always around It is only this last reason which is much advocated by men (5 per cent fathers and 3 per cent mothers); this argument has no advocates in the upper middle class, possibly because it does not apply to that section of the community The argument that mothers understand their children better is advanced by 11 per cent of the mothers to 4 per cent of the fathers, particularly the younger mothers (under 24) whose children are likely to be tiny, and with some concentration among the poorer members of the upper and lower working classes. Regionally it has most advocates from the North-West and fewest from the North-East and North. A working class mother from Hull speaks for most who use this argument in stating: 'Mother really knows the child's nature and can punish accordingly.'

The greater gentleness of the mother, advanced by 5 per cent of the mothers and 2 per cent of the fathers, has a rather odd distribution, with a heavy concentration in the upper middle class, followed by the lower working class, and in the Midlands. This may perhaps be an artifact of the imperfect responses. A 36-year-old working class wife from Shrewsbury.

I think a Father is too harsh, I think a Mother explains better and if she smacks, her hands don't come as heavy as a man's

Finally there is a small group—almost entirely male as far as this sample goes—whose reason for choosing one parent rather than the other as punishing agent is the amount of pain or humiliation the child will receive, rather than any of the ideas of law or justice, understanding or tenderness which inform the vast majority of the respondents. A few quotations will fortunately be sufficient to illustrate this attitude.

A prosperous father from Beckenham with one 2-year-old girl·

Daughters—Father should punish as it would be more affective as by a natural tendency daughters seem to adore their Father's more than their Mother's.

A middle-class father from Stockport, Cheshire, with two daughters:

Mother should punish because women are always the best torturers.

A building trades worker from London S.E. with six children:

Mother should punish because being closest to the child she upsets the child more

A lower middle class father, unwillingly living in Egham after having been blitzed from the North country:

Father should punish the child and hurt the child's pride first by denying it something it most desires, or send it to bed whatever the time of day and lock up its clothes so that mother cannot appease the child during father's absence.

Because a child, like a rose bush, if untrained, will 'sport back' to its early beginnings—for example a 'wild rose'.

This respondent considerably over-ran his space to outline his ideas on suitable punishments for boys and girls:

If a boy is naughty, First offence—an explanation of why he is naughty, and a good reason why his offence should not be repeated.

Second offence—a reminder of what he was previously told and a warning of what 'may' happen if the offence is repeated a third time.

175

Other offences—Determination on the part of the parent or teacher to prove to the naughty boy that *his* will will not prevail, and that he must fit into the general scheme of life.

There was nothing whatever wrong with the forms of punishment in my youthful days and I have never borne any ill-feeling towards the masters who administered them to me, for, on reflection, I must have earned it On the contrary, I am certain that I preferred them the more because they 'knocked' into me much schooling which otherwise I would not have paid attention to.

Girls should be punished by imposing a stronger (your) will on hers, and not weakening in your desire to make her a 'decent' citizen by weaning her away from undesirable friends and contacts A mother should make a 'friend' of her daughter and by that means guide her on the right path

Most girls have a 'point of honour' which a father, for instance, can quickly assail by challenging her that she has let him down badly by showing such a nasty attitude to her mother, who is always prepared to do such a lot for the girls welfare and happiness, that he is ashamed of her This works generally.

This respondent has been quoted at such length, because he is particularly articulate about one facet of English character which would appear to be fairly widespread the preoccupation with the moral duty of punishing children and the pleasures of severity.

NOTES TO CHAPTER ELEVEN

1. *Oxford English Dictionary* 'The apartment which is given up to infants and young children with their nurse' (1499), 'A piece of ground in which young plants and trees are reared until fit for transplantation' (1565)

2 See p. 178

3 The same question had been asked in December 1949 by Odhams Press Research Section of 488 men and 566 women, a sample which included the unmarried as well as the married and widowed The sexes did not differ in their answers which were, for the whole population, 78 per cent demand more discipline, 20 5 per cent saying the same and 1 per cent saying less Of the married respondents with children, who are strictly comparable to my sample, 74 per cent said they needed more discipline, 25 per cent the same, and 1 per cent less In this group also the demand for more discipline increased with age

4 See pp. 165–169.

5. The figures from the field survey are quite strikingly parallel 80 per cent of the parents interviewed think starting training too late is more harmful to the child, 8 per cent starting too early, 9 per cent that it doesn't make much difference and 3 per cent no answer. In the field survey those against early training are concentrated in the upper middle class, and mothers outnumber fathers, in contrast with the main sample there is a certain concentration of advocates of late training from London and the South-East In the main survey the only regional difference is that of the North-East and North, referred to above. There were 996 parents (56 per cent) in the field survey.

6 The answers to the field survey are categorized somewhat differently, apparently in part because the interviewers demanded an answer of some time period. There is so much difference in the views of fathers and mothers in the field survey that it is preferable to list them separately Corresponding figures for the main sample are given in brackets and italics

Period	Percentage of mothers	Percentage of fathers
From birth	39 (*24*)	22 (*12*)
Within first 6 months	32 (*45*)	21 (*36*)
7–12 months	19 (*15*)	22 (*16*)
1 year–5 years	8 (*8*)	23 (*15*)
Over 5 years	1 (–)	3 (–)
Don't know	1 (*2*)	9 (*3*)

As far as the mothers are concerned, the pattern revealed by the field survey and the main sample are very similar, the absence of a category for the return from hospital puts a somewhat higher percentage in the period 'from birth' and a slightly lower one in the period 'within 6 months', but the sum of these is practically identical The figures for fathers, on the other hand, suggest that the training of babies is far too delicate a subject to be discussed with a female interviewer, obviously many of them interpreted the question to refer to washing, and a tenth refused to answer at all

In the field survey, the demand that training should start at birth was concentrated in London, with respondents from the lower middle and lower working classes, it was relatively little demanded from the South-West, from parents under 35 and from the upper middle classes. Within the first 6 months is particularly stressed in the North-East and North, in the youngest married groups, and by the more prosperous (over £12 a week), it is little mentioned by upper middle, lower middle and upper working classes The upper middle and upper working classes have the greater number of proponents of the later periods; 7–12 months is particularly favoured by the parents aged 25–34

7 I did not consider it appropriate to ask for details about infant feeding in this questionnaire, moreover, extremely good recent material on this question is available in the survey *Maternity in Great Britain* (undertaken by a Joint Committee of the Royal College of Orthopaedists and Gynaecologists and the Population Investigation Committee (Oxford University Press, 1948)) This impressive study covers the children of all the women, some 14,000 in all, who were born in England and Wales during a specified week in 1946 Eight weeks after delivery, 45 per cent of the mothers were wholly breast-feeding their babies, 12 per cent were giving supplementary feeds, and 43 per cent were feeding entirely from the bottle. According to this survey, the establishment of breast-feeding is closely correlated with adequate ante-natal advice; and, since the ante-natal services are in most areas fairly recent it seems probable that, if there has been a change in recent years, it has been in the direction of more breast-feeding This survey does not cover the question whether the child is fed to a schedule or 'on demand', but such observation as is available to me suggests that schedules are customary.

8. See p 298

9. See also pp 190, 302–3

CHAPTER TWELVE

CHILDREN II· PUNISHMENT AND REWARD

THE BAD TENDENCIES, the undesirable instincts, the wrong behaviour which most English parents feel it their duty to uproot or eradicate or control in their young offspring are overwhelmingly concerned with some aspect of aggression· destruction of property, theft, cruelty to animals, cruelty to other children and so on There are of course other aspects of childish behaviour which many view with grave disapproval lying, swearing, wanton disobedience, and, for a very few, sexual or excremental misdeeds, but these are usually supplementary to, rather than contrasted with, acts of aggression in the minds of those parents who envisage any kind of serious childish misbehaviour.

The question asked was. 'If you were told that a small child, say between 3 and 8, had done something really bad, what would you think the child had done?' Some 5 per cent, mainly concentrated among the middle aged and elderly and the widowed, did not answer this question, and 6 per cent, to a large extent the same group, said they couldn't think of anything. One parent in eight, 12 per cent of the total, denied that a child of that age could do anything really bad, the remaining three-quarters of the population named some childish misdemeanour, most of them more than one, so that the base line figure is 123 per cent, rather than 77 per cent, as it would have been if each parent had only named one misdemeanour. Eighty-six per cent name some type of aggression.

The upholders of childish innocence are significantly concentrated in the middle-aged and elderly, who are likely to be no longer in contact with young children, though it does find some proponents among the younger parents also. There is rather more emphasis on this viewpoint from the South-West, from the lower middle class, and from the most prosperous compared with other sections of the community. Many of the proponents of this view seem to take an attitude analogous to that judicially upheld in the McNaghten rules, that guilt lies not in the act, but in knowing that the act was wrong; since the child's intentions are not evil, its act is not 'really bad'. Thus, a 37-year-old working class mother from Derby·

> Goodness only knows nowadays they do such queer things but I don't think a child of that age would do anything really wicked with evil intent.

A 33-year-old working class father from Denton, Lancs.

A small child of this age can't do anything really bad. Stealing perhaps? cruelty to animals? A tiny mind does not regard as bad things it will deplore in later life.

A 43-year-old middle class father from Swinton, Yorks·

Probably something not really bad at all Maybe something due to an attempt to enlarge personal experience or something to draw attention to himself or herself We cannot do wrong unless we know the difference between right and wrong

A 43-year-old working class wife from Ilford·

I cannot conceive that a child that age could do anything really bad. I was beaten by my mother for a number of things until I married. The beatings never stopped me from doing the same things again

A 62-year-old middle class mother from Cottingley, Yorks.

it can't have done anything really bad at that age, the worst my boy did was bite another childs fingers whilst playing at dogs, 'my', didn't the childs Mother shout, she said she would bite him, but she had me to reckon with, he was put to bed out of harms way.

Of the different acts of aggression, theft is the one most often named; 33 per cent of the fathers and 41 per cent of the mothers name this misdeed. The balance of the sexes is reversed with the other offence against property—damage or destruction; 22 per cent of the fathers and 18 per cent of the mothers mention this. The fears that children will steal or damage property is more common in the big cities than in the small towns, among the younger parents (under 35) than among the older, and among the more prosperous members of the community This fear is comparatively little stressed by members of the lower middle and upper working classes, who tend to concentrate on more direct aggression or on other moral faults.

Thirteen per cent of the fathers and 14 per cent of the mothers fear injury or cruelty to another child, 12 per cent of the fathers and 15 per cent of the mothers injury or cruelty to an animal. These fears are particularly voiced by parents between the ages of 24 and 44, by the inhabitants of small towns and villages, and by the more prosperous members of the middle classes, particularly the lower middle and upper middle. They are comparatively seldom mentioned by people living in the Midlands or by the lower working class. A very small group, chiefly mothers of the upper working class, mention fighting as 'really bad' childish behaviour, and a few possibly facetious correspondents mention murder.

179

The unconscious connection between these different types of aggression is illustrated by a number of respondents who link them together. Thus, a working class father of 3 from Huddersfield:

Hit another child with something to cause a serious injury Of course if your informant was a woman it would most likely be some vase or plate had been broken

A father from Southend-on-Sea:

Push another child in the river etc shut the cat puppy in the oven

A 32-year-old working class mother from Barnes, Surrey:

From experience I might think the child had thrown a stone at another child or pulled the petals off every flower in someone's gardens

A remarried mother from Accrington, Lancs:

Most children of this age tend to steel things, or bite and kick other children, I think it is the developing age

A working class mother of 3 from Liverpool, aged 35:

Might run into a roadway and nearly been knocked down or hit a younger child than hisself or done something to a dumb animal or perhaps spoilt something on you you can't replace or fix

A 27-year-old working class mother from Harpenden:

Wilfully ill treated an animal. Children as young as this rarely do bad things intentionally but they are inclined to enjoy being spiteful to animals and younger children.

A poor middle class widow from Ilford, aged 65:

Probably been very cruel to an animal—children usually love animals.

A 24-year-old working class housewife from Doncaster.

I can't decide on this But my son chopped a hens head off the other day and I didnt approve at all.

A 65-year-old retired jeweller from Torquay·

If jealous of younger brother (or sister) who was made more of than itself—physical force or even murder might be attempted. Many children delight in throwing things on the fire. During the war very small children learnt to abuse their sexual organs in Air Raid Shelters —To My Knowledge

A 31-year-old father from Southend seems to typify most English parents' attitude in saying that he would suspect the child of having done 'Something destructive, rather than sexual.'

Very few English parents—a mere 3 per cent—mention childish sexuality; it is hard to tell from the evidence whether such behaviour

180

is not noticed, is not considered serious, or is considered too upsetting to be mentioned in the answers to a questionnaire. Probably all three explanations operate in some cases; but in view of the very great frankness which characterizes most of the answers, I would hazard that by and large there is relatively little parental anxiety on this score. It is however curious that the respondents of the lower middle class hardly mention this subject at all; they are also reticent about the possibility of a child making a mess, which is feared by 4 per cent of the fathers (particularly the youngest group) and 1 per cent of the mothers. Greater than either of these anxieties is the fear that the child should use 'bad' language; 9 per cent of the fathers and 3 per cent of the mothers, concentrated in the middle income groups of the upper working and working classes, fear this.

The importance given to swearing[1] and 'bad' language by the English, particularly by the men of the upper working and working classes who are themselves most likely to use the tabooed words, seems idiosyncratic and difficult to explain on a rational level. As will be seen, the bad words are for a number of respondents the equivalent or alternative to the bad act; and it also seems possible that swearing is envisaged as aggressive and that, by reflection, the sexual or excretory acts referred to acquire an aggressive tinge. If this hypothesis is correct, then the fear of the appearance of aggressive tendencies in children is even more widespread than I described it earlier.

The following are a few examples of the linking of bad language and bad acts in guessing at the 'really bad' things a child might have done. 'Wet the bed or swore' (working class father from High Wycombe); 'Swore and exposed itself as they nearly always do so at some time or other' (a working class father from Leeds, aged 31); 'Swore or become curious about the human body' (a 42-year-old working class father from Cannock); 'Having had considerable experience of children of 7–8 I should single out Insolence, Bad Language, and even stealing as being the outstanding "crimes" of children of this particular age' (a middle class schoolmaster from Cornwall); 'Used language reserved for grown-ups' (a 38-year-old working class father from Bradford). This last man says of his children 'I don't want them to swear. They think I don't'; and may perhaps give a further clue to the fear of childish swearing by linking it with precocity. Precocity itself is very seldom mentioned, a 29-year-old Hereford man writes of a child having 'Partaken in some premature form of Enjoyment. Either smoking, drinking dads beer, or some sex act'; his articulateness on this aspect of childhood development is uncommon.

Apart from swearing, quite a few respondents link excretion or sexual behaviour with aggression. A middle class father from Harrow:

> Deliberately 'wet' etc on the floor of my room as a form of nasty temper

A 30-year-old mother from Darlington.

> Perhaps tortured or hurt a dumb animal, or another child, or set fire to something—causing danger, knowing it to be wrong. Also—'sexual knowledge' makes my flesh creep

A 30-year-old father from Galgate, Lancs:

> Impossible to answer this. A child between 3-8 is unpredictable and too near the animal state to be above doing anything, from eating buns, playing with little girls/boys sexual organs. or setting house on fire

A metaphor with some odd overtones which occurs fairly regularly to describe childish masturbation is 'playing with her own personal property' or 'playing with his private property'. Quite a few respondents, particularly the older people, use this periphrasis, if it is widely spread (I had never previously encountered it) the socio-political implications are interesting.

A working class mother of one 4-year-old boy living in South-East London tells an illuminating anecdote in this connection. She writes:

> Hard to say. My own experience being that, my boy when aged 2 with another little friend aged 3 urinated in the garden several times. We were sent a letter from a solicitor complaining of 'disgraceful and disgusting conduct and threatened with notice to quit if it did not stop I understand many little boys have this phase. The neighbours who complained did not approach me at all.

Nine per cent of the fathers and 7 per cent of the mothers mention some form of disobedience as what they would suspect a naughty child to have committed. Where the disobediences are specified, they concentrate on going into forbidden places, either crossing dangerous roads or running away, or otherwise endangering themselves. It would seem that the dangers from traffic are particularly feared, for it is above all the less prosperous inhabitants of London who mention this, followed by the inhabitants of the smallest towns and villages who write of young children not coming back directly from school. Thus, a 36-year-old mother of two girls from a village near Salisbury:

If school age, they have gone for a walk, and don't come back to time and they are a hour late, its so worrying and you always think the worst as happened, when they show up you are too relieved to punish them too much.

A 48-year-old mother from Nuneaton, Warwickshire:
Swallow a safety pin and a pebble and a two inch nail which mine did and lived thats really bad while playing.

The fear that the child might have told 'a bad lie' is voiced more by mothers than by fathers (12 per cent mothers and 8 per cent fathers) particularly the older parents (over 45) of the middle, lower middle and upper working classes. A few members (2 per cent) of the same groups suggest that the child might have 'followed a bad example' without being more specific.

Another small group of 2 per cent, somewhat concentrated in the upper middle and lower working classes consider that children are capable of any misdemeanour so that they would not be surprised whatever they heard. Thus, a 47-year-old professional man from London:
Shot Grandma dead, or said 'Dash!' according to the informant.

A 40-year-old working class father from East Ham·
Goodness knows? they have more tricks than a monkey at that age.

A 72-year-old middle class father from Clacton:
Called the Parson a B—— when he was caressing the dear child or letting the Canary out.

I think it can be fairly stated that the typical English view of childish nature is that the young child is inadequately human and that, unless the parents are careful and responsible, it will revert to, or stay in, a 'wild' or 'animal' state, aggressive, destructive, without proper respect of property or sense of shame. To transform the child into a proper human being, a good English man or woman, undesirable or retrogressive tendencies must be eradicated by appropriate punishment Desirable tendencies may also be fostered by appropriate reward; but as far as my evidence goes there is less articulate feeling about this. It seems possible that the 'ordinary life' of a boy or girl of good character is considered sufficiently rewarding by itself.

Nearly all English parents have very decided views on what punishments are appropriate, and what inappropriate, for naughty boys and girls. Only 4 per cent of the population failed to name some punishment they approve of, and 8 per cent some punishment

183

EXPLORING ENGLISH CHARACTER

they disapprove of, for boys; in the case of girls the corresponding figures are 8 per cent and 12 per cent. These abstainers are predominantly the elderly and the widowed. There is also a tiny group of less than one in a hundred who don't think children should be punished at all. All the remainder approve of some form of punishment, and, in most cases, of more than one form; the base line is 149 per cent in the case of boys and 141 per cent in the case of girls. The list of disapproved-of punishments is somewhat fewer· 125 per cent of punishments are disapproved of for boys, 116 per cent for girls.

There are a couple of generalizations which seem worth making before the subject is discussed in more detail. With the single exception of physical punishment for girls in their teens (when this is approved of for boys of this age) English parents, especially in the middle and working classes, appear very unwilling to make a distinction in the treatment of boys and girls, to elaborate more than the minimum necessary on the basic physiological differences in sex. 'I do not believe sex should be stressed, even in punishments' (written by a 42-year-old Liverpool father) is a constantly recurring theme. With some fathers, this statement is made with a faint touch of resentment at female privilege· 'I don't see why girls should have it easier, just because they're girls' (a young father from London). Rather a surprising number of parents appear aware of the pathological potentialities implicit in physical punishment.

It also seems to be worth noting that among the less educated groups the phrase 'corporal punishment' is quite consistently misunderstood to mean 'cruel or brutal punishments.' Numerous respondents write to the effect 'a naughty boy should be given a good caning but I don't approve of corporal punishment.' This misunderstanding was so consistent that I found it necessary to create a special category for it; at least one parent in six misuses the term. It follows that any statements about the attitude of the English public, or at any rate the less educated sections of it, toward corporal punishment should be accepted with the very greatest suspicion.

Nearly all the punishments mentioned with either approval or disapproval by English parents fall into five main groups· deprivation, restraint, verbal punishments (such as lectures), manual punishments (slapping or spanking) and physical punishments with instruments. There are a few, however, mentioned by small groups, which fall outside these categories; they can be dealt with fairly summarily.

The setting of household tasks as a punishment is mentioned with

184

approval by 2 per cent of the parents for boys and 5 per cent for girls and is considered inappropriate by 1 per cent for both sexes. In the case of girls it finds its greatest number of advocates in the lower middle and lower working classes. Thus, an 'ordinary working class' mother from Leicester advises for older children.

For a boy, stay in and help in the house that day, a girl should be made to do some mending or clean her own bedroom.

A 46-year-old working class father from Exeter advises

Age under 10—go to bed early with no light to read in bed Over 10 —forfeit his pocket money if issued weekly If pocket money not in issue—then made to do menial job in the house—chopping sticks, getting coal etc so depriving him of his companionship of a good book or his boy friends for an hour or so.

A working class painter from Sandwich, Kent, disapproves of this type of punishment because:

To regard small household jobs as punishment, I believe this tends to make hatred of ordinary household jobs later in life

This man is not so cunning as the 29-year-old lower middle class father of three girls from Chigwell, who writes·

Most girls like to help around the house, if refused this way of play this checks them, because I find that a girl who finds she can be done without, soon try to make amends

There are three types of punishment which are mentioned almost entirely by the upper middle class and high income groups· lines, making the child apologize (as sole punishment), and psychiatric treatment. A few members of the other groups in the community mention psychiatric treatment with disapproval ('There is far too much talk about "psychology"' writes a lower middle class mother from Shrewsbury); but by and large these concepts play no significant rôle in the thinking of English parents.

Various techniques of shaming a child by holding it up to ridicule by exposing its punishment to others, by 'sending it to Coventry', by dressing boys in girls' clothes or girls in ragged clothes or by exposing its nakedness are mentioned with disapproval by 9 per cent of the parents for both boys and girls. with some concentration of this disapproval in the rural South-West. A very small group (2 per cent for boys and 3 per cent for girls) approve of shaming techniques, which, in some other societies, would almost certainly be a major device for inducing conformity in the young Such approval as there is is somewhat concentrated among the elderly; and a reading of Victorian novels (for example *David Copperfield*) suggests that this

185

may have been a much more widespread pattern in earlier times, when 'breaking a child's spirit' was an avowable educational aim. When such devices are advocated by younger parents they leave a rather unpleasant overtone; for example a working class father of three from Headcorn (who finds no punishments to disapprove of) advocates for both sexes· 'Tan bottom in front of other children to hurt his or her pride', a 57-year-old father from Wolverhampton: 'Dress boys in girls clothes'; or a 31-year-old working class father from Crawley. Sussex·

If picture going is usual, stop it for a time let her go to the club when its half over, its really horrible to arrive late then have to explain to your friends why

There is a moderately sized group (12 per cent in the case of boys and 10 per cent in the case of girls) who advocate 'letting the punishment fit the crime' without, in most cases, giving any idea how this operation is to be performed. This is somewhat more favoured by fathers than by mothers, especially in the upper middle and lower middle classes. Some of these parents show considerable understanding; a miner with three children from Cullercoats, Northumberland writes 'One cannot generalize, the punishment must take into consideration the childs temperament'; or a 36-year-old working class father from Maidstone:

The question cannot be answered honestly, it depends entirely on the childs character the boy is a human being and not a standard piece of machinery.

Although the views of such respondents may commend themselves to those interested in personality development and individual psychology, they are in sharp contrast with the great majority of English parents who have most decided views on the suitability or unsuitability of specific punishments, quite regardless of any difference in the children's temperaments or characters

Some type of deprivation is the form of punishment which meets with the greatest approval and least disapproval from English parents. Somewhat more than half the parents (58 per cent for boys and 54 per cent for girls) recommend either 'withdrawing privileges', 'forbidding or withdrawing favourite toys or pastimes', 'temporary stopping of pocket money' or 'going without food' as the most suitable and efficacious method of disciplining naughty children, if any form of punishment can be called 'typically English' it would be some aspect of deprivation With a single exception, very few parents indeed disapprove of deprivation, though one or two say

186

that stopping pocket money might make children dishonest; but 10 per cent in the case of boys and 7 per cent in the case of girls disapprove of the withdrawal of food. This disapproval is stressed somewhat more by fathers than by mothers, by younger rather than by older parents, and especially by the upper middle class. This concentration suggests that the impact of contemporary ideas on nutrition, and possibly rationing, have evoked conscious disapproval of a type of punishment formerly little regarded. Only a few people (2 per cent for both sexes) mention the withdrawal of food with approval, and these are significantly and heavily concentrated among the old, the poor, and the lower working class. It was apparently those people for whom hunger was a realistic danger who used temporary hunger as a punishment.

The phrase 'stopping privileges' seems to be worth some consideration, both for its application and implications. Its implications seem to be that all pleasure is, as it were, conditional, that children's enjoyments are not 'rights', but are granted by the benevolence of the parents while the children's conduct is satisfactory, and may be withdrawn under provocation. This concept of privilege and conditional enjoyment would appear to have a number of ramifications. It will be recalled that quite a number of the married respondents[2] referred to marital intercourse as 'sexual privilege', apparently with implications very similar to those of childish pleasure. A great deal of political discussion has been taken up with the question of 'undeserved privilege', which has served as a moral basis for the attacks on the more prosperous members of the community and on at least some aspects of the welfare state. Secondly, if pleasure is conditional, its maintenance may depend on the absence of supervision by possibly censorious authorities; and this may help account for the very high value so many of the English put on privacy, on not being overlooked, and for the fact that 'snooper' or 'busybody' is probably the characteristic most disliked by the majority of English people.

The actual phrase 'withdrawal of privileges' is used by nearly a fifth of the parents, nearly twice as often by mothers as by fathers. Women differ from men in the use of this concept much more markedly than in any other aspect of the subject; indeed, from the evidence available, it would appear to be a predominantly feminine concept, though it is applied by women to the behaviour of both sexes. As far as the more concrete types of deprivation are concerned, fathers put a trifle more emphasis than mothers on the temporary withdrawing or forbidding of favourite toys or pastimes (26 per

187

cent men and 24 per cent women in the case of boys): and 11 per cent of both sexes favour the temporary stopping of pocket money.

Punishment by deprivation is somewhat more favoured by parents of the working classes than by parents of the middle classes, by people living in the metropolises in the two Southern regions, and has fewer advocates in the medium-sized towns and the two Northern regions. Where boys are concerned there is less advocacy of this type of punishment from parents with incomes between £8 and £15 than from those with incomes below or above these sums, in the case of girls there is much less variation on income level. This may be due in part to the fact that parents in this medium income range are more in favour of spanking or caning naughty boys than of punishing naughty girls in this manner; but it does not entirely account for the discrepancy.

A number of parents specify concretely the type of deprivation they favour. Thus, a 38-year-old working class mother from Leytonstone, Essex·

Older girls being kept away from a special activity she takes part in and enjoys The younger ones not being allowed to hear their favourite programme on wireless or television.

This informant, incidentally, disapproves of father administering 'capital punishment' to his daughters

A 44-year-old middle class father from Middlesex, with one son aged 15.

I have found that what hurts him is to stop his pocket money for a week and no pictures, and give him a good talking to has so far done the trick. Up till now I have never used a cane on him

A hairdresser from Fulham:

Stop him from his pleasures, do not give him any pocket money, and do not allow him to go out with the boys to play for about one week.

Personally I do not believe in Beating them up, although I have a son myself as you have already seen and he is a tartar. But I am curing him little by little by not giving as I used to give him

A lower working class mother from Edmonton:

Depriving him of something he prizes such as a visit to Scouts for a period of 2 weeks (this I consistently threaten but alas never carry out).

A 33-year-old father from Lancashire:

Deprive her of some beloved plaything for a time, state for how long and do not return it a second before. If she pulls the cats tail then pull her hair hard.

188

The distinctions between deprivation and restraint are in many cases very slight. I made the distinction that when the parent mentioned that food or pastimes were withdrawn it should count as deprivation, and not otherwise, but I realize that this is arbitrary; and probably most of the advocacies of restraint should properly be added to the popular concept of deprivation. Statements like the following have been calculated as deprivation: 'Put to bed without food till next morning, giving them a good hiding they soon forget it' (a 41-year-old working class mother from Malmesbury); 'Locking her in the bedroom without food will soon bring her to her senses' (a 65-year-old working class mother from near Bournemouth); 'Naughty children should be sent to bed for a period of not less than 12 hours with only liquid food' (an elderly invalid father from Huddersfield); 'Stop him for a time from going out to play or pictures' (a working class father from Penge).

Statements like the following were on the other hand scored as restraint: 'I find by keeping my children indoors it cures them more than by caning them' (a 29-year-old middle class father from Bristol); 'Put in a room with nothing in it until he says he will never do it again. If he does, repeat the dose' (an 'ordinary working class' father from Leicester, aged 30); 'I find the best way to punish my boy was to make him go to bed' (a lower middle class mother from Blackfield, Southampton); 'Shut up in a room (or lock if necessary) for an hour alone to think and afterwards to be talked to kindly but firmly' (a middle class mother from Ealing), 'My boy is easy, one day locked in his bedroom with bread and water would be enough' (a 26-year-old middle class mother from Hanlow, Beds).

Sending a naughty child to bed is mentioned with approval by about a tenth of the population for both sexes, somewhat more by mothers than by fathers and with a marked concentration in the middle class, young parents mention it more than older ones. Only a very few people (under 2 per cent) mention it with disapproval; a middle class father from Bristol says 'I never send my boy to bed as a punishment, I believe it induces self-abuse as an expression of self-pity.' Keeping in is slightly more favoured by fathers than by mothers, especially from the working classes; some 5 per cent advocate it, about half that number disapprove. Solitary confinement, especially locking children up in dark rooms, finds practically no advocates (only twenty in all) and is mentioned with emphatic disapproval by some 10 per cent of the population, concentrated in the younger members of the middle classes. Fourteen fathers approve of Borstal or a reformatory for naughty boys and three

189

for naughty girls; some 5 per cent mention these institutions with disapproval, particularly parents of the lower working class, whose children, presumably, have the most chance of being sent thither. The chief argument against them is that they tend 'to make a boy more hardened than before' (a 65-year-old lower working class mother from Bournemouth). Little can safely be deduced from negative evidence; but it is interesting to note that lower middle class parents voice their disapproval of Borstals and the like less than those of any other social group; in a number of contexts members assigning themselves to this class appear to approve of representatives of the state carrying out functions which members of other classes deem more appropriate to the family.[3]

Something over a sixth of the population, with slightly more emphasis from mothers than from fathers, consider that a lecture, a 'good talking to', or threats of punishment, are appropriate punishments for both sexes. Only a tiny group mention this punishment with disapproval. It is mentioned conspicuously less often by the inhabitants of London, by members of the upper middle class, and by parents between the ages of 24 and 44 than by the rest of the community. There are small groups (less than 2 per cent in every case) who mention with approval or disapproval sarcasm, the withdrawal of love or some form of emotional blackmail Some of these devices, when mentioned with approval, are rather distasteful Thus, a 36-year-old mother from West Ham.

Give him a pet dog he'll love it. Tell him the dog will have to go if he does not behave.

A twice married woman from Accrington:
Smack hands and legs and put to bed *threaten* most loved toy or doll, to give it to some friend or put it on the fire, most affective for boys and girls.

A 49-year-old poor mother from Gainsborough, Lincs:
Talk to her and tell her she won't always have a mother, that soon does the trick, I have proved it.

A 27-year-old mother from Sunderland, Durham:
Well, I find if I say I won't speak to Doreen and keep it up its the best punishment, with Joyce I only have to shout.

A 49-year-old middle class father from Swindon, Wilts:
I found with my son that by ignoring him, not answering his questions or taking interest in him hurt him more than anything.

Some 5 per cent of the parents mention with disapproval frightening threats of bogey men, of 'God won't love him, threatening

190

police and prison' (mentioned by a middle class mother from Manchester) and such like. This is mentioned very little by the youngest parents, suggesting that it may be a disappearing technique of disciplining children. Five elderly parents speak of such threats approvingly. In a number of societies threats of this nature are very generally employed.[4]

All the techniques of disciplining children which have so far been discussed have been considered equally appropriate for boys and for girls, and, with the exception of the concept of 'withdrawal of privileges', equally approved by fathers and mothers, there is some disapproval of punishments which could frighten children—either frightening threats or locking up in dark rooms—but this does not appear to preoccupy many parents' thoughts The case is different with punishments that cause the children physical pain, and it will therefore be necessary to analyse these replies somewhat more carefully.

Nearly all English parents make a distinction between physical punishments inflicted with the open hand—spanking or slapping—and those inflicted either with an instrument—caning, whipping etc.—or with the fist or foot. The first group of punishments is approved by quite a number and disapproved of by very few (2 per cent in the case of boys and 5 per cent in the case of girls, the objectors chiefly being in the upper middle class), for the second group of physical punishments there is far more disapproval than approval, and it is a subject on which many English parents feel very strongly, whatever their views.

Slapping as an adequate punishment for naughty children is mentioned only by very few parents (2 per cent for boys, 3 per cent for girls) and these are predominantly young parents of presumably young children. Only a tiny group mention slapping with disapproval. Spanking, on the other hand, has a considerable number of advocates —21 per cent for boys and 18 per cent for girls; although it nowhere approaches the figures for the various types of deprivation, it must be considered the second choice of punishment for most English parents, especially the fathers of younger children Men advocate it quite a little more than women, and the younger parents (under 34) more than their elders, a figure which was contrary to my expectations. Londoners approve of spanking much less than the inhabitants of the rest of the country, and the poorest and best off less than those with intermediate incomes. As far as social class is concerned, there is some reversal in the approval of this form of punishment for boys and girls. For boys there is greatest approval of spanking in the middle and lower middle class, and somewhat less in the upper

191

middle and upper working classes; the upper working class also disapprove of this punishment for girls, but the upper middle class approves of it highly, as does the lower middle class Some 2 per cent of the parents, mostly elderly and from the upper middle or lower working classes, think that boys should never be spanked, disapproval rises to 5 per cent in the case of girls, with some concentration in the two Northern regions, the upper middle and upper working classes.

It is generally assumed in English broadcast, television or music hall humour that the fact that human beings possess buttocks is inexhaustibly funny, an endless source of innocent merriment; and a great number of my respondents used somewhat facetious synonyms for the area spanked—'the place nature meant for it', 'where it hurts to sit down', 'the b-t-m' 'the right place', 'the posterior' and so on. On the evidence of this survey it would seem that it is less likely to be spanking than earlier disciplines which are responsible for the remarkable amount of affect concentrated on this portion of the body.

I found it necessary to divide the more severe types of physical punishment into five categories, based on the words chosen by my respondents They are (i) caning, which includes the synonyms of hiding and tanning; (ii) thrashing, including the use of straps, belts or whips, (iii) punching, including kicking, shaking and other violent means of 'beating the kids up' without the use of instruments, (iv) birching, including the 'cat' (mentioned by very few respondents) and flogging; and (v) the afore-mentioned 'corporal' punishment, which includes punishments inflicted by teachers, the police and other people outside the family. The vague category of 'cruelty' or 'brutality' was only mentioned with disapproval. On the subject of severe physical punishment there is the greatest contrast in what is considered suitable for boys or girls, in the views of fathers and mothers, and in the amount and intensity of approval or disapproval. Before the subject is discussed in more detail, it seems useful to present a synoptic table of the percentages of views held by fathers and mothers on these punishments.

	APPROVE				DISAPPROVE			
	Boys		Girls		Boys		Girls	
	Father	Mother	Father	Mother	Father	Mother	Father	Mother
Caning	9	7	5	4	15	25	14	22
Thrashing	6	5	3	3	17	9	12	8
Punching	0	0	0	0	6	4	2	—
Birching	0	0	0	0	11	6	10	4
'Corporal'	6	2	3	1	12	9	18	12
'Cruelty'	—	—	—	—	11	6	10	4

Whether in approval or disapproval, English men seem to feel far more strongly about severe physical punishment than do English women; with the exception of caning, to which a quarter of the mothers object strongly, the fathers are far more articulate in their objection to this type of punishment; it would seem to be disapproved of by nearly half the community which has any views on the subject of children's punishments.

Twenty-one per cent of the fathers and 14 per cent of the mothers approve of some type of severe physical punishment for boys There is much more approval for caning in the Southern regions (especially in the South-West) than there is in the rest of the country, and from the upper working and lower middle classes Thrashing on the other hand has its greatest number of advocates in the North-West, followed by the Midlands, it is little advocated in the South. This is the type of punishment favoured by the lower working class, followed by the lower middle, middle and working classes; it has no advocates among the upper middle or upper working classes. It is the younger parents, under 44, who favour these more precise types of punishments, the older are more likely to advocate 'corporal' punishment without further elaboration, particularly in the lower middle and upper working classes Parents at the top and bottom of the economic scale are much less in favour of severe physical punishments than those of intermediate incomes.

For girls the figures are less in every case (11 per cent of the fathers and 8 per cent of the mothers in all) but the distribution is very similar. The South-West is particularly in favour of caning, followed by London and the South-East, and the North-West of thrashing; the upper middle, upper working and lower middle classes favour caning and are against thrashing, the younger parents are more in favour of these punishments than the older. So few parents are in favour of 'corporal' punishment for girls that little can be learned from the distribution.

Parents who approve of this type of punishment appear to do so with considerable gusto and moral self-righteousness The quotations which follow are only a small selection of those available; and I have thought it advisable not to give the exact age or the town of the informants quoted, to avoid any possibility of identification.

An elderly retired engineer from Yorkshire:
A boy should have his 'seat' slapped until he screams for mercy and make him promise never to do the same thing again.

A middle aged working class man from Lincoln:
[for a boy] Punishment by hand or strap until it hurts, administered

193

with shirt off [for girls] Same applys as to boy but layed across knees and given smacks on the back-side until she really cried

A middle-aged separated woman from Warwickshire
It is good for boys to feel through the skin because they realize how serious the crime is, I think a few strokes across the seat of the trousers is very good—performed effectively.

This informant is against such punishment for girls:
Because they can always seek sympathy from other people if marks are left.

A young upper working class mother from London with a 7-year-old girl and two younger boys
I should hesitate to use the cane on an older girl My girl of seven has had it several times and will probably again I wouldn't cane a girl over the age of nine—I hope, but might under provocation.

A young lower middle class father from Somerset:
If you are quite certain that he is naughty and understood that his act was wrong, he should be made to feel pain (cane or stick) so that before committing wrong again he will firstly consider whether it is worth a caning

A middle-aged 'manual working class' father from Middlesex:
The father should interview the lad alone—explain that the gravity of the offence demands corporal punishment—tell him he personally finds it distasteful, but its what his dad did to him, and its for his own good—and then do it

A young working class father from Yorkshire:
A good hiding never made me hate mother or father and its a good thing if administered with justice

An elderly working class mother from Hampshire:
According to the wise man in Proverbs, a good use of the rod is the best punishment.

A middle-aged father from Kent:
Same as myself, a damned good hiding I dont' agree with cruelty, such as going without meals

A young middle class mother from Herts:
I do not approve of being brutal, but a good tanning I do not frown on.

An elderly working class father from Notts·
Boys should be thrashed, but avoiding injuries other than flesh weals. Girls, as for boy, but not after the age of puberty, when exposure might be regarded as an outrage. After that age deprive them of allowances and privileges.

A middle-aged 'middle working class' father of two girls, aged 18 and 13, from Lancashire.

[For a boy] Thrashing with strap, then made to stay in at least two weeks Minimum of food during that time [For a girl] Slapping posterior with hand, whilst girl is completely naked Kept without new clothes and pocket money for three months

This father of two adolescent girls is opposed to 'striking with strap or belt or instrument of any kind'.

A fairly young school-master from Middlesex, who describes himself as 'poor middle class'.

Between the ages of 10 and 16, the most effective and convenient punishment for boys is undoubtedly a really sharp caning preferably on the bare buttocks, the latter being highly advisable in order to be able to guard against undue severity which goes unnoticed when clothes are worn or hands are caned

I strongly disapprove of all 'deprivative' punishments or any long drawn-out penalty, except any wilful damage should normally be paid for out of pocket money if possible.

For girls precisely the same as for boys, and I speak as a teacher in a co-educational secondary grammar school Indeed, the only distinction I would make is that, in certain cases, girls need the occasional corrective of a caning at home (or at school) beyond the boys age limit above of 16, in all cases where a girl's reputation and good name seem likely to be in jeopardy through headstrong or irresponsible behaviour.

I strongly deprecate allowing any girl culprit to believe that she will be dealt with any more severely (or more leniently) than her boy counterpart There must be no difference made simply because the offender happens to be a girl I have personally found the cane successful more than once with girl pupils of 17 and, even, in one case 18 years of age [5]

I have thought it desirable to present this rather long series of quotations (they could have covered a number of pages) because they appear to give insight into the reasons for the very strong and emotional opposition to severe physical punishments which is voiced by so many parents. The quotations suggest that at least some English parents find pleasure without conscious guilt in inflicting severe pain on children as punishment The majority disapprove of such behaviour, but the emphasis with which such disapproval is voiced suggests the possibility that there is an unconscious temptation against which such defences have to be erected. In many other societies, I very much doubt whether such heat and indignation would be engendered on the subject of severe punishment of children, or indeed whether the possibilities would be mentioned in answer to the vague and open question 'Are there any forms of punishment you don't approve of for boys or girls?'

If the disapproval of all types of physical punishment is lumped together, we find that this disapproval is most vehement from the metropolises and in the Midlands and London and the South-East, and from parents aged between 24 and 44 earning between £5 and £12 a week and from the upper working, working and upper middle classes. There is least objection (though it is still considerable) from the two Western regions, from people over the age of 65 and under 24, from the £12–£15 a week income group, and in the case of boys from the lower middle class. Members of this class oppose severe punishments for girls as much as any other: there is slightly less objection to severe punishment for girls from the upper middle and lower working classes. The total figures are in all cases slightly lower for girls, because the birch, or similar judicial punishments, are not envisaged in their cases.[8]

With the exception of caning and 'corporal' punishment, there are not very marked variations in the amount of disapproval. The upper middle class (which does not disapprove of caning for either boys or girls) very strongly disapproves of whipping for both sexes; the lower middle class mentions whipping very little, but may include this in 'corporal' punishment, to which it is vehemently opposed. People over 65 and with incomes over £12 do not voice many objections to whipping. The upper working class particularly objects to punching children and knocking them about; this is little mentioned by the upper middle class (who may not envisage it) or by people living in the South-West. People from this area also mention the birch very little; it is the lower working class who are the most emphatic in their disapproval of this type of punishment. Cruelty or brutality is most mentioned by members of the upper and lower middle classes living in the metropolises; it is little referred to by the young or the poor. 'Corporal' punishment is most strongly objected to in London and the South-East, in the lower middle and upper working classes (especially in the case of girls) and by parents with an income of over £12 a week. It is little mentioned by the very young, the elderly or the poor, and, in the case of girls, by parents of the upper middle class. Caning would seem to be little objected to, in suitable cases, by parents over the age of 45 earning over £12 a week; besides the upper middle class parents, who don't object at all, members of the lower middle and lower working class mention this with disapproval relatively little. Parents of the upper working

196

class on the other hand object to it very strongly; so do the youngest parents with low incomes (£5 to £8 a week) and parents from the Southern regions, particularly the South-West People from the North-West mention objections to girls being caned less than those from any other region

Where any form of physical punishment is objected to, the objection is passionate. One of the more temperate is a middle class father from Middlesex, who writes.

> I do not think savage treatment does any good at all and I would not stand for anyone knocking my boy about however good their intentions might be, and maintain that all good British men and women are built in the homes of England

A curious inversion of the use of physical punishment is told by a 27-year-old father from a small town near Doncaster

> My eldest daughter did once tell a deliberate lie I took off my belt let her hold it and forced her to beat me. She has never told a lie since The moral being that if she does wrong she hurts her parents

I don't think it is merely due to the ways in which the questions were phrased that most English parents seem much less interested in rewards for their children than they do in punishments, it seems more likely that the concept of 'privilege' implies that the ordinary life of the child is sufficiently rewarding by itself to re-enforce good, or approved-of, behaviour; though deviations from the proper course call for remedial action, conformity demands relatively little recognition.[7]

Nearly a fifth of English parents do not think children should even be praised in front of others when they have been good and

Figure XXVIII

Question 71 by Question 60

71 Should children be praised in front of others if they are good and helpful?

60 How many children have you?

Question 71	Question 60						
	1	2	3	4	5 and more	No answer	Total
Yes	33	34	16	6	6	5	100
No	38	32	13	5	7	5	100
No answer	32	21	8	6	8	25	100
Total	34	33	15	6	6	6	100

helpful. Twice as many fathers as mothers (22 per cent fathers, 12 per cent mothers) take this austere position; they are somewhat fewer in the two Southern regions, in the middle class with incomes of £12–£15 a week, and in the ages between 25 and 34 than they are in the rest of the country, but there is not a very marked difference. There is a slight tendency to withhold public praise from only children, and also from the larger families with five children or more [8]

Nearly a quarter of the parents answering the questionnaire said that they do not, or did not, give their children regular pocket money when they start going to school As might be expected, fathers and mothers are practically in agreement on this point. This is one of the fairly few situations where there is quite a marked difference between the middle and working classes (a difference in giving pocket money of 9 per cent) Income would appear to be a major determinant here; with a weekly family income of under £8 barely half the parents give their children pocket money. The number doing so thereafter increases consistently, but even in the income range of £12–£15 nearly a fifth of the parents say that they do not give their children any regular pocket money. In this situation the only child is likely to be favoured and most of them do get pocket-money; with the big families children are less likely to get any, but this may well be a direct result from the incidence of other expenses.[9]

Figure XXIX

Question 60 by Question 72

60 How many children have you?

72 Do you give your children regular pocket-money when they start going to school?

Question 60	Question 72			
	Yes	No	No answer	Total
1	58	23	19	100
2	58	31	11	100
3	64	31	5	100
4	69	28	3	100
5 and more	54	40	6	100
No answer	53	21	26	100
Total	56	26	18	100

In a number of countries, including the U.S.A., it is customary to allow children to 'earn' pocket money by doing various odd jobs round the home; and I tried to discover to what extent this custom

198

was prevalent in England Unfortunately, the question was clumsily worded and the interpretation of the answers is therefore somewhat ambiguous The question was 'Do you give your children money or other rewards when they are useful and helpful?' and the alternative answers were 'always', 'sometimes', 'occasionally', 'never'. My intention was that 'sometimes' should imply a usual, but not invariable, custom, 'occasionally' an unusual and exceptional action; but I cannot be sure that my respondents so understood the words

Mothers and fathers give almost parallel answers; the biggest contrast is that 19 per cent of the mothers and only 15 per cent of the fathers 'always' reward their children. Five per cent never do, with the concentration in the prosperous upper middle class; 26 per cent do so 'occasionally' and 40 per cent 'sometimes'. Twelve per cent. chiefly the parents of very young children, did not answer this question, which was inapplicable in their case. If one groups 'always' and 'sometimes' together, one finds there is some concentration of this practice in the middle income group, especially £12– £15 a week, and that it is less common among the poorest and the most prosperous but that it is slightly more common in the working than in the middle class. If one groups 'occasionally' and 'never' together the contrast in the practice of the social classes comes out equally strongly. it is the children of the more prosperous middle classes who do not receive any childish lessons in the connection between money and work It should however be emphasized that this is a relative, and not an absolute contrast, in all classes something more than half the children do get rewards for work The custom of rewarding children is somewhat more frequent when the families consist of three or more children.[10]

When I was a child one of the most heavily sanctioned rules of conduct was that one must *never* take money from 'strangers'; uncles and aunts, and friends of one's parents who were given such honorary titles might give one money as presents, as 'tips', but under no circumstances could one take money for services rendered.[11] I had thought that this would be an area which would show clearly differences in the upbringing of children of different social classes, and therefore asked· 'Would you let your children take money for doing jobs for neighbours such as running errands, watching babies, or helping them?'

My expectation that this question would reveal strongly marked class differences was not fully realized. There is a difference of 11 per cent between middle class parents and working class parents who would let their children earn in this way, but the absolute figures are 43 per cent and 54 per cent respectively. Just over half (51 per cent) of the parents would permit their children to earn money in such ways and a third (34 per cent) would not; 15 per cent did not answer, chiefly the very young parents, for whom the question was probably not applicable. Gross family income is at least as great a determinant as class, with permission falling markedly as income increases; and the greatest absolute contrast is between regions, with the Midlands, nearly always the most generous portion of the country, being 12 per cent above the North-West. It seems possible however that the determining factor here is religion rather than region or class; Roman Catholics are much less likely to allow their children to earn money in this way than are members of the Church of England or other Protestant sects, and the Catholics in my sample are heavily concentrated in the North-West In general, the devout, those who say prayers daily or more often, are less likely to let children earn money in the fashions described. Family size seems to make little difference to this aspect of education, though children of big families have somewhat more opportunity to do so.

Figure XXX

Question 74 by Question 60

74 Would you let your children take money for doing jobs for neighbours?

60 How many children have you?

Question 74	Question 60						
	1	2	3	4	5 and more	No answer	Total
Yes	31	35	16	8	8	2	100
No	35	34	16	5	5	5	100
No answer	41	25	8	4	3	19	100
Total	34	33	15	6	6	6	100

I also thought, perhaps over-generalizing from my own Edwardian upbringing, that another marked determinant of social class would be parental supervision of the children's playmates and the houses they visited, middle class parents trying to keep their children from the 'evil communications' which corrupt good manners In this respect too my expectations were falsified. None of the material which I have been able to secure on the less formal aspects of education and child rearing shows very marked differences in the familial upbringing of children in the different social classes My material suggests that, in nearly every possible implication of the phrase, it is

200

Figure XXXI

Question 83 by Question 74

83 Which religion or denomination are you?

74. Would you let your children take money for doing jobs for neighbours?

Question 83	Question 74			
	Yes	No	No answer	Total
'Christian'	49	35	16	100
'Protestant'	41	39	20	100
Church of England	51	34	15	100
Anglican	39	39	22	100
Roman Catholic	43	44	13	100
Methodist	52	32	16	100
Baptist	48	34	18	100
Nonconformist	51	31	18	100
Congregationalist	48	39	13	100
Presbyterian	25	25	50	100
Jewish	38	50	12	100
Spiritualist, etc	46	26	28	100
Small Protestant sects	53	36	11	100
No answer	55	32	13	100
Total	51	34	15	100

Figure XXXII

Question 74 by Question 60

74 Would you let your children take money for doing jobs for neighbours?

60 Do you say private prayers?

Question 74	Question 60						
	More than once a day	Daily	Only in peril or grief	Very seldom	Never	No answer	Total
Yes	9	29	16	30	15	1	100
No	10	37	14	29	10	0	100
No answer	10	31	14	27	14	4	100
Total	9	32	15	29	13	2	100

the 'tone of voice' rather than the content which determines class differences in England, apart from the marked differences in formal education.

Only 13 per cent of the parents who answered (17 per cent did not answer this question, predominantly the very young and the very old) say that their children 'never' play with other children whose

201

parents they don't know; these parents are mostly under 34, and therefore presumably their children are still young; though there is a little concentration in the middle class, it is only a matter of some 4 per cent more than the working class. The remaining two-thirds of the parents divide equally between the statement that their children 'often' or 'occasionally' play with other children whose parents they don't know. Seven per cent more parents of the working class say their children 'often' play with strangers compared with those of the middle class: there is no significant difference between the three middle classes in this respect; the upper working class have the fewest respondents of any class for their children often playing with strangers, the lower working class far the most. There is no significant regional difference; on income level those with incomes over £12 a week have the larger number of 'often' and the smallest number of 'never', which may possibly be a reflection on the custom of better-off children attending boarding schools or grammar schools some distance away from their homes. Parents over 35, whose children would be more likely to be of boarding school or grammar school age, show the same distribution. When there are more than three children in the family, the parents are less likely to know the parents of their children's playmates—a conclusion which can cause little surprise.[12]

One quarter of the population tell their children not to play with some of the neighbours' children; 16 per cent (again predominantly the very young, under 24, and the old, over 65) do not answer the question; the remaining three-fifths of the population do not. By a small degree, the banning parents are proportionately concentrated in the upper working class, and are fewest in the lower working class. there is no difference in working class and middle class patterns in this respect. There is some concentration of this ban among the parents aged between 25 and 44 and in the medium income groups; and there is quite a contrast between the North-West (with 29 per cent imposing this ban) and the South-West (21 per cent); the remaining regions are on the national average.

Somewhat more parents (34 per cent) forbid their children visiting some of their neighbours' houses; and this ban is imposed slightly more by the working class than by the middle class, and by parents aged between 24 and 44 with incomes of under £8 a week. Fifty-four per cent of the population do not impose such a ban; and the very young and the old, to the number of 12 per cent, do not answer this question.

Those who do forbid their children to visit neighbours' houses were asked why they did so; many gave long replies which when analysed, produced a base line of 157 per cent answers (from, of course, 35 per cent of the population). Some 40 per cent of these answers are based on sanitary grounds—that it is better for children to be in the open air rather than in houses, or that they should avoid houses where there is danger of infection. The South-West, followed by the North-West, seems particularly alive to the danger of infection; people with incomes of under £8 a week are particularly alive to the value of the open air, especially those living in big towns. A few state rationally that their children are too young; and another small group considers that such bans are ineffective. An example of this last attitude is a working class mother from Huddersfield·

> I sometimes feel I would like to forbid her on account of 'language' and 'cheek' allowed to pass unchecked, but realize she will have to meet all kinds of people when grown-up.

Apart from such straightforward considerations, the major complaints centre directly or indirectly round the adults, rather than the children—that they don't keep their house properly, that they drink or use bad language, or are sexually immoral and similar complaints. These complaints are made predominantly by the working class (44 per cent) followed by the lower middle class (38 per cent); only 31 per cent of the middle class make this complaint, and 11 per cent of the lower working class There is a concentration of these complaints from the North-West and the medium-sized towns, and from parents aged between 35 and 44 It is only a minority which tries strongly to keep their children from evil communications; but within that minority a significant group are parents of the respectable working class trying to keep their children away from the disreputable working class, particularly in the towns of the North-West. Exemplifying this attitude is a 49-year-old working class father from near Barnsley, Lancs·

> Swearing in some homes, dirtiness in others loose morals in a lot of homes too many people in this village live with other men's wives openly, and don't seem to mind who knows Lodgers sleeping with women when husband on nights etc etc.

A 46-year-old working class father from Kent:

> Having been in one or two houses I knew that they would be a bad influence, very untidy, no restraint of language, etc., this is of course exceptional and not the general thing

A father from Buckingham:

> Lack of responsibility by parents, factory shop language used in front of kiddies, children not clean Parents in my opinion, being of low

mentality by allowing their nippers to shout, swear at them This, I must hasten to add, is not general, but applies to three neighbours only Oddly enough, in each case, they found it necessary to marry in haste

Six per cent, somewhat concentrated in the rural South-West, suspect the neighbours of pumping visiting children about matters which the respondents would like to keep private, and a further 2 per cent think that children are liable to provoke quarrels between the adults, no members of the upper middle or upper working classes voice these suspicions An 'ordinary working class' father from Halifax writes.

The type of neighbours we have would ask the child questions regarding happenings in her home.

A woman from Leighton Buzzard, Beds:

This is a sticky question. Possibly the only truthful reason is because I do not wish these certain neighbours to inquire of our private affairs, nor do I wish to have more than a nodding acquaintance with them myself.

A 43-year-old working class father from Averley:

Only to get to know your business, some neighbours invite children to their homes to pump them

A working class man from London:

Their reason for inviting my oldest child into their homes is to try and find out why my wife and I separated.

A 43-year-old working class father from Wednesbury, Staffs:

My boy is what you would call artfull and if anything is amiss with their children its 10 to one they say he is the cause of it

A working class father from Slough ·

When playing with certain neighbours children, mine always seem to be in the wrong if anything untoward happens. This, according to these neighbours, necessitates their interference in the childrens squabbles As this has given rise to high words, we have forbidden children to go round these particular houses.

A working class father from Nottingham:

Some of the neighbours think their children are made of Gold and must not get Dirty. I forbid them not to visit neighbors Houses because I no they are not wanted there.

Some 21 per cent of the parents who impose a ban, considerably more mothers than fathers, consider children a nuisance, and forbid their children to visit neighbours on these grounds. The most usual phrasing is that they don't want their children to be a nuisance to

204

others; a small group say frankly that they don't want to be bothered with the neighbours' children. A few advance the maxim that one should keep oneself to oneself; and there are some complaints that the neighbours don't welcome children and are unkind to them. These attitudes are predominantly middle class; they are not mentioned at all by the upper middle class, and relatively little by the upper working class It is above all the younger parents (under 45) with incomes under £12 a week, who make such statements, there are relatively few in the North-West, or in London and the South-East.

Typical of such attitudes is the 51-year-old middle class father from Ruislip Manor:
To stop them making a nuisance of themselves to the neighbours. My kids are pushing.

A 41-year-old working class mother from West Bromwich:
Because I have enough of other people's children in my house.

A working class father from Leyton, Essex:
Children pick up little bits of information which they repeat. Also they are inclined to make a habit of visiting once started Children seem to like other people's food better than their own.   .   They invariably come home with some new habit, or a grumble after visiting neighbours, so the best cure is not to let them start it

A 33-year-old working class father from Castle Cresley, Derby·
It hurts their feelings when the neighbours shut them out when they are not wanted. In the case of my daughter they are jealous because she has a mop of curly hair and a sunny disposition.

A 36-year-old father of four girls from St. Helens, Lancs:
When I came out of the army, I was coming down the street with my pack on my back when I saw my eldest daughter standing outside one of the houses opposite to where I live. She hadn't spotted me so decided to creep behind her, as I got near I could see her look at a small doll that was in the doorway of this house, with such longing that I stopped, just then the *Lady* of the house happened to spot her and with utter ruthlessness picked the doll up and said to my daughter run home you can't have our Mary's doll, if your daddy wasn't a soldier he could buy you one like Mary's daddy's done Believe me sir, with God's help none of my girls have had to want for dolls or toys of any neighbour since that day.

Some 12 per cent of the parents say they do not want their children to follow bad examples, without, in most cases, specifying whether

205

the exemplars are adults or children. This phrasing is particularly favoured by parents aged over 45 living in big cities, and especially by the upper working class It is not a phrase which is used at all by members of the upper middle class, and little by the lower middle class or the most prosperous members of the community Some of the more prosperous parents, particularly in the middle and lower middle classes. keep their children away from neighbours because they want them to speak 'nicely', but this only accounts for 7 per cent of the people who impose a ban in these classes

Finally there are the parents who consider the children undesirable companions because they are dirty or use bad language. are rough and unruly, cheeky and undisciplined, immoral or light-fingered. These charges are made by 33 per cent of the parents imposing a ban, fathers and mothers in nearly equal numbers, though, as has already been stated, fathers are particularly concerned about swearing. There is a concentration of these complaints from the lower middle class and from people with incomes between £8 and £12, but there are also a considerable number of such complaints from the working and lower working class. The North-West once again leads with these complaints. followed by the South-West There are more complaints of children with bad characters from the smaller towns than from the metropolises

Since these complaints of undesirable behaviour provide inferentially a good deal of information about the ideals parents have about their own children, it seems worth while giving a representative selection of these explanations

A 33-year-old middle class mother from Coventry

One child in particular; goes into other people's houses when she knows they are out, tells lies, careless of other children's toys, constantly breaking and losing them. Nearly four years older than my elder girl and a bad example One house in particular; Occupants like and encourage children but unable to speak without swearing. Don't wish my children to acquire this habit

A working class father from Rochester, Kent:

Some parents have no control over their children these children in the eyes of a child have a wonderful time naturally it would disturb my own

A 43-year-old father from Kidderminster.

Because the Children, through the neglect of the parents have been to the Juvenile Courts, a number of times, the children due to their Home Life, are little rogues and run the streets at all hours, they draw my boy like a magnet, and through them he also got into trouble.

A 33-year-old working class father from Padham, near Burnley:

This is a very bad district and but for housing shortage would have moved long ago I forbid my children to visit the neighbours because they learn bad habits from them, and because their children retaliate and we have enough of our own

A young father from Leigh, Lancs:

One of the kids he plays with, his mother works and his Grandmother lets him rome about any where, he gives cheek to his elders and he will land himself in trouble, mind you I blame the grandmother.

A 41-year-old working class father from Ilkeston, Derby·

We have one boy who is easily led and very often gets into mischief with some boys We try to keep him away, but we don't always succeed. As a matter of fact just this one boy we have tried to choose his friends. We do not worry at all over the other two boys.

A young middle class mother from Hereford.

I am trying to teach my children to be clean Not to be rude and manners, but if they visit my neighbours all my teaching will be undone as they are dirty in their ways and rude and their talk is filthy Their mother does not bother with them.

A working class father from Bradford:

They might hear indecent talk or bad language. In one case they certainly would I don't want them to swear. They think I don't.

A 25-year-old mother from Leicester who describes herself as 'working class with a desperate urge to better myself'

My daughter never goes out of the front gate unless I take her, she is quite (happy) to play with her toys by herself In any case most of the children who live round here have been brought up to be rough and cheeky and I should hate my daughter to hear some of the words they use Im not blaming the children dont think that its not their fault but all the same I shouldn't like to think my little girl would be the same

A father from Fulham, earning a good income but who describes his class position as 'very modest':

Our child plays only with our friend's children, he's never allowed in the road to play The neighbour's children are not the type we want our little boy to mix with Besides being filthy they use bad language and have very bad behaviour. We speak to no one in this road, so the child does not visit any neighbours houses, with the exception of only one friend who lives in walking distance.

A 30-year-old Birmingham mother of two girls:

I do not allow them to play in streets or other people's house's till I know them, they play very well together and never ask to go elsewhere, the children are always in the Roads, the proper place is bed at six till

207

they are old enough to realize bad from good, then they can pick decent friends, I think more children stay up later than ever probably because they both work and its late when they get home, and I dont believe in pictures, only a circus or pantomime

A coal miner from West Melton, Rotherham:
There are some people who Have no control over their children, and allow them to Have too much of their own road, which is bad for Discipline, they also allow them to have Dirty Habits, therefore we as Parents must use a little Discrimination.

The implicit belief in the foregoing quotations (as well as in the very large number from which they were selected) that parents are responsible for their children's good qualities and failings is also expressed in the reasons chosen to explain the post-war increase in crime, especially among young people [13] People were asked to choose between seven popular 'explanations' of the increase in juvenile crime (more precisely, increase in police charges) Three of these reflected one way or another on parental care and responsibility, two dealt with state institutions, one with symbolic material and one with religion The statements, among which respondents were asked to choose the one which seemed to them most important were:
Modern parents aren't strict enough
Children whose fathers were in the Forces didn't have proper discipline
Children who were evacuated weren't properly looked after.
Modern schools aren't strict enough
People got into bad ways in the Forces.
Young people follow the bad example of crime films and crime stories in books and on the radio.
People are neglecting religion

Over half (56 per cent) of the respondents chose the statements imputing responsibility to the parents, the married being somewhat more insistent than the single. The most popular statement, held equally by men and women, is that modern parents aren't strict enough; 29 per cent of the population, extremely evenly distributed in every category except age, opts for this answer. The young, under 18, do not much hold this view; it is most highly approved by people between the ages of 25–34. More men than women (26 per cent men, 20 per cent women) consider that children whose fathers were in the forces did not have proper discipline, it seems understandable that men should rate the father's influence more highly This viewpoint is slightly more highly stressed by people between the ages of 18 and 34; there is some emphasis in the upper working class.

Only 4 per cent of both sexes thought that evacuated children (presumably separated from their mothers' care) were not properly looked after, it is mostly Londoners who support this notion

There is very little tendency to blame state institutions for juvenile delinquency Four per cent of the population think modern schools aren't strict enough, and 8 per cent that people got into bad ways in the forces, rather more men than women hold this view

Rather curiously, it is the young under 18, who most tend to blame the bad examples of films, books and radio, 20 per cent of this age group choose this explanation, whereas their elders vary between 10 and 12 per cent, the latter figure being the overall total. Few persons in the upper middle or upper working classes hold this view.

Twenty-one per cent of the women, compared with 14 per cent of the men blame juvenile delinquency on the neglect of religion. This view particularly commends itself to the upper middle class and the under 18's, it finds little support from the lower working class, and not

Figure XXXIII

Question 79 (first choice) by Question 64

79 One reads a lot in the papers about the post-war increase in crime, especially among young people Please mark which of the following reasons seem to you most important.

64 Who is the proper person to punish a child who has done something really bad?

Question 79	Question 64					
	Mother	Father	Teacher	Others	No answer	Total
People got into bad ways in the Forces	41	54	6	3	2	106
Children whose fathers were in the Forces didn't get proper discipline	30	67	5	2	1	105
Children who were evacuated weren't properly looked after	40	64	6	2	1	112
Modern parents are not strict enough	32	66	6	1	0	105
Modern schools are not strict enough	38	62	9	1	—	110
Young people follow the bad example of crime films and crime stories	40	57	6	2	1	106
People are neglecting religion	37	58	7	1	1	104
No answer	45	47	10	4	—	106
Total	35	61	6	2	1	105

very much from the metropolises. Quite a few respondents altered the wording to 'Religion is neglecting the people' before marking this choice [14]

A correlation between the reasons chosen for juvenile delinquency and the question where authority should reside in the family shows at least considerable internal consistency on the part of the respondents. Those who think that the father should be the chief disciplinarian emphasize that children whose fathers were in the forces did not get proper discipline, and secondly that modern parents are not strict enough; those who say that the mother should punish emphasize that evacuated children were not properly looked after, that people got into bad ways in the forces, and also the bad influence of crime films and crime stories; the small group who think that teachers should do the punishing find that modern schools aren't strict enough.

NOTES TO CHAPTER TWELVE

1 See also p 203

2 See p 133

3 See e g p 170

4 For example, the male bogeyman of France Croque-Mitaine, Lustucru, Le loup-garou, etc, etc See Metraux and Mead, *Themes in French Culture* (Stanford University Press, 1954).

5. It does not seem necessary to take this respondent's statement as referring to actual behaviour in a secondary co-educational school in Middlesex What is being studied are the views of parents, not the practice of schools Besides respondents of this nature, five male respondents (out of about 6,000) indulged in flagellation fantasies in some other portion of the questionnaire, mostly to the questions 'What do you think are the three most important qualities a wife should have?' or 'What do you think goes to make a happy marriage?'

6 It is interesting to compare these figures with those given in *A Survey of Rewards and Punishments in Schools*, a report of the National Foundation for Educational Research (Newnes, 1952) Although the absolute figures cannot be usefully compared, the areas of emphatic approval or disapproval of corporal punishment seem to be very similar

7 It seems possible that this treating of 'ordinary' life as gratifying in itself might account for the peculiar emotion called 'boredom' felt by many adults when this ordinary life is disturbed by the presence of strangers. Many people seem to consider meeting people they do not know or with whom they are not intimate 'boring', even though the alternative to these meetings is not more, but less, social activity I have on occasion discussed with people used to living in Asia or Africa the politically disastrous custom of excluding all members of the native society from the various British social clubs, intelligent people, who admit how indefensible such a policy is from nearly every point of view, excuse it on the ground of the boredom which would be evoked by the presence of strangers among one's familiar colleagues In many cases this certainly did not imply that the speaker was not interested in any people who were not English, the presence of others would disrupt the even tenor of 'ordinary' life, and the displeasure felt by this disruption is described as 'boredom'. Shyness is presumably another component in this emotion.

8 This question was also asked in the field survey with somewhat strongly contrasting results Over a third (36 per cent) of the parents interviewed said that children should never be praised publicly men and women holding these views in equal numbers The North-East and North, parents aged between 45 and 64, and members of the upper working and lower working classes emphasize particularly the undesirability of praising children Members of the upper middle and lower middle classes are in favour of praise when due

9. In the field survey, the parents once again proved themselves more severe, with 40 per cent saying they did not give their children pocket money, but there is here a marked discrepancy between the sexes (fathers 35 per cent 'no', mothers 45 per cent) which one would not expect if there were any regularity in the custom, it seems at least possible that the interview situation made the interviewees take the question too personally, and that mothers answered 'No' when not they, but their husbands, were the givers of weekly pocket money The contrast between middle and working class, and the close correlation between income and the giving of regular pocket money is quite parallel with the main survey, though the absolute figures are somewhat different In the field survey there is a marked regional contrast between the generous Midlands and the withholding North-West which has no parallel at all with the main sample

10 In the field survey the parents were much more likely to choose polar answers. Twenty-seven per cent said they 'always' gave such rewards and 18 per cent 'never', 27 per cent said 'sometimes' and 20 per cent 'occasionally', 8 per cent, again chiefly the young, did not answer If the 'always' and 'sometimes' are calculated together, in contrast with the 'occasionally' and 'never' the distribution for income and social class is fairly parallel In the field survey, once again, there is a marked regional contrast which has no parallel in the main survey, very few parents from the North-West (42 per cent) and very many parents from the South-West (70 per cent) say they give rewards 'always' or 'sometimes' Parallel figures for the main survey are 58 and 55 per cent. The discrepancy is so great that I suspect it of being an artifact of the recording of the interviews

11. An illustration of this apparently widespread attitude can be found in E. Nesbit's *The Treasure Seekers*, originally published 1899, Chapter IV, Good Hunting'

12 In the field survey once again parents tend to choose polar answers. 41 per cent say 'often', 14 per cent say 'occasionally', 35 per cent 'never' and 10 per cent do not answer The number of parents saying 'never' is so high as to seem inherently improbable, many of the respondents giving this answer were women (40 per cent, contrasted with 31 per cent men), and it seems at least possible that the mothers would think it would reflect on their maternal care if they said they did not know their children's playmates The 'often' answers follow the same class, income and age distributions as in the main survey; but once again there is a regional difference not paralleled in the main survey, with relatively far fewer parents from the two Northern regions saying they don't know their children's playmates than from the rest of the country

13 The views which follow are those of the total sample, including the unmarried and the childless All the previous portions of this chapter are based on the view of parents with living children

14. This question was also asked in the field survey, with the added refinement that a number of cards were printed with the questions in different order, in case the rank order of the questions were influential There is a marked difference in the emphasis given to two of the choices. The field survey gives less importance to the lack of discipline for children whose fathers were in the forces, this was an answer particularly chosen by men who are much less represented in the field survey than in the main sample (47 per cent and 56 per cent respectively) Secondly, much greater emphasis is placed on the corrupting influence of fantasy. This might be an artifact of the interviewing situation, which removes blame both from the interviewee and the

absent spouse Otherwise the figures are strikingly similar These are the gross figures for the field survey, the main sample figures being added in brackets and italics

People got into bad ways in the forces	5 per cent	*(8 per cent)*
Children whose fathers were in the forces didn't get proper discipline	15 ,, ,,	*(22 per cent)*
Children who were evacuated weren't properly looked after	3 ,, ,,	*(4 per cent)*
Modern parents aren't strict enough	29 ,,	*(29 per cent)*
Modern schools aren't strict enough	10 ,, ,,	*(4 per cent)*
Young people follow bad example of films, etc	20 , ,,	*(12 per cent)*
People are neglecting religion	16 ,, ,,	*(17 per cent)*
No answer	2 ,, ,,	*(3 per cent)*

CHAPTER THIRTEEN

LAW AND ORDER

I HAVE ALREADY stated that there are relatively few attitudes and beliefs or practices which are subscribed to by two-thirds or more of a population so diversified as the English Besides the attitudes to child training and childish character, already described, another subject on which three-quarters of the population, who have any views at all, are in agreement is enthusiastic appreciation of the English police

This result, I admit, came as a big surprise to me, perhaps the greatest reversal of expectations which occurred in the whole research. I had asked the question 'What do you think of the police?'[1] with the expectation that a very considerable number of the respondents would take advantage of the anonymous questionnaire to express feelings of hostility to the representatives of the state, of law and order, of the repressive aspects of society. I had also thought that a considerable number of people would give their replies a political tinge, referring to one law for the rich and another for the poor, or describing the police as the servants of the capitalist class Such replies did occur, but only from a very small proportion of the population, chiefly those describing themselves as upper working class; some 18 per cent of the population had criticisms to make of the police (5 per cent did not answer and 2 per cent gave irrelevant replies) but, as will be shown in more detail later, these criticisms were mostly on points of character or behaviour, that the police as individuals are 'no better than anybody else', on the human failings of persons in the police. There is extremely little hostility to the police as an institution.

As far as I know, no parallel survey of attitudes to the police has been undertaken in any other country; but all the evidence available to me from my own research or observations or those of others strongly suggest that the amount and extent of enthusiastic appreciation of the police is peculiarly English and a most important component of the contemporary English character. To a great extent, the police represent an ideal model of behaviour and character, an aspect about which many respondents are articulate.

An attempt was made to divide the favourable judgments into 'enthusiastic' and 'appreciative'; but the division is so subjective that little value can be put upon it. For what the figures are worth,

213

men, particularly the married, are more enthusiastic than women; there is most enthusiasm in the lower middle class, in the two Southern regions and in those with incomes of under £12 a week. When all the positive judgments are put together nearly all these differences disappear; there is, for example, only 1 per cent difference between men and women (73 and 74 per cent respectively) By nearly every criterion, the positive attitudes are most evenly distributed; the only areas in which there is a variation of 3 per cent or more from the national average are the regions with very high appreciation in the North-West (78 per cent) and low appreciation in the North-East and North (69 per cent); and in the extremes of the social classes, the upper middle having 79 per cent, and the lower working class 65 per cent, the class differences are not very surprising. Young people under 18 are also particularly enthusiastic, with 82 per cent positive; after the age of 18 there is very little variation

Only a battery of quotations can give some impression of the strength of the emotions evoked. A 28-year-old 'higher working class' married woman from Formby, Liverpool:

I believe they stand for all we English are, maybe at first appearance slow perhaps, but reliable stout and kindly, I have the greatest admiration for our police force and I am proud they are renowned abroad

A 38-year-old married man from New Malden:

The finest body of men of this kind in the world. Portraying and upholding the time tested constitution, traditions and democracy of the British Way of Life combining humble patience with high courage and devotion to duty.

A 31-year-old married working class man from Fishburn, Durham.

Overworked, underpaid body of men with a high sense of duty. One of the chief reasons why this is such a pleasant country to live in. I take my hat off to them.

A 27-year-old single working class woman from London:

They are a most useful, helpful, and necessary body of men and women, I am proud to belong to a country which has such a fine police force

An old married man aged 72, who describes himself as 'under dog (serious)' from Binfield, Bucks:

'Essential'—I would put them on a par with 'Teachers' as the absolute 1st grade for preferential human unity.

A 19-year-old youth from Brentwood, Essex, of the middle class.

I think its the best thing that civilization has done for anybody next to science.

Many of the respondents take a deep personal pride in the international reputation of the English police forces; several, particularly young men whose service careers took them overseas, proudly contrast them with the police of other lands

A working class bachelor from Norwich:
They are the best in the world. The most understanding capable and tolerant I have met Canadian, American, Indian and Malayan but our 'Bobbies' are the best.

A married upper working class man from Peckham
I have travelled abroad considerably during the war and have seen all sorts of different police forces and say that our police are much more sensible, considerate and efficient than any others I have seen.

A 19-year-old middle class youth:
Very good, if not excellent Experience in Sweden, where police are, unfortunately, slightly Gestapo-styled, strengthened my belief that the British 'cop'—friendly, understanding—is a great servant of the public —and not his master.

A 16-year-old working class girl from West Ewell:
I think they are a wonderful and unbeatable group of people, we have the best in the world, and I hope when I'm old enough to become one of them.

A young working class lad from Wolverhampton·
We're led to believe that Britain has the best police force in the world This I believe simply due to the fact that we Britishers do, and have to, respect the law, who give us a true sense of freedom and security

The psychological reassurance which the police provide is another theme which many people elaborate. A 20-year-old bachelor from Shepton Mallet, Somerset, who says of himself 'I belong to the common people', writes
Slow but efficient. The sight of a policeman gives a sense of security to every British citizen. This is often felt only subconsciously, but deep down it must be realized how much we depend on our police force in order to go about our daily activities in peace and free from friction.

A 36-year-old miner from Barnsby, Yorks·
Excellent and woe betide many people today if we were without a good Police Force and ours is only a small mining village.

A 22-year-old unmarried working class girl from Hendon·
I think the police do a wonderful job, and would never think of criticizing them. Although I have no reason at all for fearing them, I always regard them with respect and a certain amount of awe.

215

The personal character of the members of the police forces also evokes a great deal of admiration and approbation, though this is also the chief grounds for most of the criticism made of them.

A 33-year-old working class bachelor from Sutton-in-Ashfield·

A necessary body of men and women carrying out a difficult job extremely well as they themselves are human, and subject to human thoughts, envies and whims.

A 67-year-old Worthing, Sussex, widower.

In the course of my duties as a Cinema attendant, I meet members of the police force nearly every day I find them pleasant companions and interesting to talk to. As regards efficiency I consider them *superior* to those of any other country

An 18-year-old unmarried London girl.

Oh I like them (I wish I could marry one.) I think that policemen aren't any different to other men in the walks of life

A 34-year-old Birmingham bachelor who describes his social class as 'Upper Middle, Spot of decayed gentry':

They have a rotten job, which they do very well (being English) but these big clumsy men have not the feel or intelligence to deal with small crime and ordinary criminals like most of us The nice ones are very very nice and the bad ones horrid (like guardsmen)

A 30-year-old unmarried Civil Servant from Surbiton, who describes himself as a 'low paid relic of the Bourgeois intelligentsia':

Underpaid and overworked in dealing with masses of petty bureaucracy Insufficient encouragement to the enterprising types. Admire them for the results they get, and also for surprisingly little evidence of 'fiddling' among the Police force itself.

A 47-year-old married man from Greenford·

I think the police still command the respect of the general public, and they effectively uphold the dignity of the law Despite the fact that some wartime and post-war laws tend unwittingly to make criminals of us all.

Thirteen per cent of the population qualify their judgments with some criticism or hostility; another 2 per cent give brief neutral comments like 'all right'. These mixed judgments are made somewhat more by men than by women, especially in the upper working and lower middle classes with incomes of £12–£15 weekly. Typical of such mixed judgments is the 31-year-old working class wife from near Tamworth, Staffs:

They are very smart and very efficient, but knowing 2 policemen very well, and guessing they are all more or less the same, I cannot say they are altogether fair or honest

216

A small farmer from Leicester:

Having worked with them, majority decent human folk—the rest not worth a dam fortunately these are in the minority. The British Force as a whole I believe the best in the world

A 46-year-old educated middle class woman from Folkestone·

On the whole I consider them a fine body of men; though, when I go away I never tell the police, as I think when they know others (undesirable) get to know too.

A 21-year-old married working class woman from a village near Newark:

I think the police in big towns and cities do a grand job and their work is hard, but in villages such as this we become their friends and they ours, and they often turn a blind eye

A 25-year-old married man from Birmingham.

I have a very high opinion of them yet I have had one approach me (when I was working in a shop) and tell me who he was, at the same time asking for a few extra eggs.

A 29-year-old middle class London man·

I consider they are the best in the world but subject to human thoughts and failings and bribed and corrupted on many occasions by wealth, position or friends (I can prove this)

A 32-year-old single woman from Sheffield

Having worked with two ex-policemen for two years I would say I find them, slow, ponderous, niggly about detail, but they get there in the end Apart from these two specimens I have a great admiration for the force as a whole—there must be some intelligent men among them somewhere.

A 24-year-old working class mother from Birmingham:

Majority of them show off when in uniform as if everyone should be afraid of them Yet they seem kind and considerate to children My children love to say Hello to Policemen and it isn't very often they are ignored.

A 53-year-old married woman from Nottingham.

Taken on the whole they are a grand set of people The few exceptions are some youngsters who try to show some authority, which make you feel afraid.

An upper middle class bachelor aged 21 from Barnstaple, Devon:

Living with two young policemen and in the home of an ex-sgt also working in close co-operation with them, I find them to be no better than 'the man in the street'

217

A few respondents comment on the alleged class-consciousness of the police without any marked bitterness; for example, a 37-year-old working class man from Gosport

> Very helpful, but I do object to the way they speak to the different classes Upper or Middle Class it is 'Excuse me, Sir', Working Class it is 'Oi'

A 39-year-old working class Londoner.

> On the whole a fine body of men, but are inclined to judge the clothes and not the man, i e a poorly dressed man, carrying a suitcase late at night would be challenged, not so a well-dressed one.

A 39-year-old lower middle class wife from Birmingham.

> I think they have two sets of laws (or rules), one for the rich and one for the poor, both in and out of prison The average policeman is a 'scrounger' but otherwise very capable of carrying out his duties.

A fairly common theme in the criticism of the police is criticism of the activities they undertake, or fail to undertake, as if (in the eyes of these respondents) the individual police man or woman, or at most the local authority were responsible, not only for the action taken, but for the law itself When the questionnaire was being answered, in January 1951, newspapers and wireless news bulletins were much taken up with the attempt to recover the Coronation Stone (the Stone of Scone) which had been removed from Westminster Abbey by Scottish nationalists This police search for the Coronation Stone was mentioned by a very considerable number of correspondents, and with unanimous disapproval; the police, they averred, should give up such nonsense and concentrate on catching serious criminals Since the incident is now very much past history, it does not seem worth while giving any *verbatim* quotations; but as far as my respondents are indicative, not a single English man or woman stated that the search for this symbolic piece of masonry was worth the trouble and hullabaloo, and a very considerable number stated definitely that it was not.

Apart from this incident, the greater number of such complaints centred around the enforcement of the traffic laws. There appears to be a fairly widespread feeling that the laws about the speed limit, parking of vehicles, lights on vehicles and the like are devices for petty persecution, and with no relevance to the convenience or safety either of the respondents or of the community as a whole. This sentiment is sufficiently widespread to suggest that a very indifferent job of public relations has been performed, and to allow the suspicion that this may be one cause of the extremely high accident rate on the English roads.

218

A few examples will illustrate a fairly general trend.

A 43-year-old upper working class wife from Enfield.

I think the Police pay too much attention to little offences, like car lights and riding bikes on pavements. I used to live in a house where a policeman lived, and when he was on night duty he used to slip home to bed and get back in time for his sgt to see him on his beat.

A working class woman from near Manchester:

Well they do a good job in some places such as London and the big cities but here they are never there when wanted but just catch poor people pinching a bit of coal or trying to do motorists

A 26-year-old upper working class man from Sidcup:

Not Much! If they can get promotion generally for pinching some poor little man they would gladly do so While the big offenders should be pursued more ruthlessly. Too much time is taken up with minor traffic offences on the roads. Freemasonary should be barred in the Police Force.

A 23-year-old lower middle class bachelor from Bristol.

Helpful when visiting strange towns and their presence comforting in crowds and heavy traffic conditions. They do tend however to report a case when a warning would suffice and this applies particularly to town police This is, presumably, mainly due to promotion being partially based on the number of addresses in the rate book, showing that the P.C knows his job.

A 22-year-old upper working class man from Millom, Cumberland:

A very good Force, but sometimes they close their eyes to things where action should be taken immediately, as in the case of the wholesale prostitution in some of our big cities.

Some 5 per cent of the population is really hostile to the police and with about 1 per cent of these the hostility reaches an almost pathological level. With such small numbers there is little that can be usefully said about distribution; there is a little concentration in the Midlands and the North-East and North of such hostility, which is very little voiced in South-West; few members of the upper middle, and rather a larger number of the lower working class voice such feelings.

The pathological hatred occasionally reaches appalling lengths; this can be exemplified by a 64-year-old professional woman from Polegate who writes:

I'd like to murder every one I meet. (This is not a joke). I laugh every time I hear or read of a policeman battered. My experience is that a large proportion are a BAD LOT.

More frequently this hatred is a symptom of a political philosophy based on hatred, whose proponents consider themselves leaders of the working class. In the words of Saki's epigram, though they may consider themselves born leaders, they have found very few people born to follow them, as far as this survey is an indication. A 55-year-old married man from Gretton, Northants, 'upper working class':

> I hate the Police and all they stand for, which among other things is the subjugation of the working classes so that the idle rich can live their useless lives in comfort and security.

A 27-year-old married man from Stoke Newington, 'militant working class':

> As at present constituted, they are the most vicious anti-working class body of people in the whole country. They seem to be biased in favour of the people who can *afford* to pay fines as an alternative to jail.

More usually, the small group who are hostile to the police base this hostility on the belief that they misuse their power, are unscrupulous, avaricious or dishonest, suspicions which I believe would be much more widely voiced in most other societies. A 37-year-old middle class man from a Staffordshire village writes:

> Generally speaking they are perverters of the truth with no respect for the 'oath'—governed by 'promotion complex' as a force efficient without scruple This opinion based on private associations from childhood.

A prosperous 23-year-old working class man from Lancashire·

> I am of the opinion that the majority of the police force joined for the security the job offers and not because of any thoughts of preventing crime. I dislike some of the petty offences that are reported. A policeman friend of mine once told me 'my inspector said it was about time I had a case or else pack the job'

A 28-year-old working class man from Newcastle-on-Tyne:

> Like everything and everyone they are open to a fiddle. They don't look for trouble or crime against society, but you have to bring it to them, explain about it, put it on their doorstep. Apathetic is the word. I don't think some of these young coppers even know what they are supposed to do Cant get into our Bus canteen for them swigging tea.

A 36-year-old unmarried working class man from a village near Normanton, Yorks.

> My opinion is, and six years R.N. Service to give me backing Give the majority of Englishmen the least bit of authority and they become more or less 'The Great I Am'.

A 19-year-old working class girl from Leeds:

Having had a great deal of experience with them through working in a solicitors office I find them particularly open to bribery, i e. charging people for no reason but what solicitors give them

A 42-year-old manual worker from Enfield·

Not much—they rarely solve a major crime by their own efforts—in nine cases out of ten the criminal is 'shopped' by an informer—again, I've met scores in private life, and on the field of play, and I've rarely met a good fellow. (lastly, once a policeman, *always* a policeman—that's true!)

A 59-year-old working class man from Pembridge, Herefordshire:

Mostly they are people who are trained to be friendly with the object of 'finding out' all they can about you and when necessary using their information against you (*and I'm a Christian*).

A 26-year-old unmarried man from Birmingham:

Considering I was once—to be frank—blackmailed to bribe on the spot. Personally, police on the whole concentrate to much on petty things rather than the important crimes (ex book you on first offence such as no rear light on bike.)

In the answers they gave to this question two groups of people identified themselves with more particularity than was called for in the questionnaire: those who were themselves members of a police force or one of the police auxiliaries or who had relatives in the force; and secondly a small group who had at some time of their lives come into what might be called professional relations with the police. These seem to be sufficiently interesting in themselves, as well as for occasional insights they give into English character, to merit full quotation.

Some dozen respondents, all of them men, stated, either directly or inferentially, that they had been in trouble through police actions. Although the number is too small to be anything but suggestive, it does seem that there is a tendency for those who have broken criminal laws to be appreciative of the police force, whereas those who have been imprisoned for civil offences and the like are full of resentment. Thus, a 29-year-old unmarried middle class man from near Blackpool:

As a C.O. I refused 'medical' so went to jail for 6 months, where I learnt that police are biggest crooks of all!—'Never trust a policeman—keep out of their way and never let them pull a fast one on you' is my motto.

221

A 19½-year-old sailor from Croydon:

Personally I don't like the Police; but I suppose they have to do their job as well as anyone else But I think they go a little to far in 'booking' a matelot when he's drunk and trifles like that.

A 31-year-old working class man from Greenwich:

I have been to prison four times for arrears of maintenance, and I think that if the police gave as much time to criminals as they do to the likes of me more criminals would be in jail now.

A 24-year-old man from Birmingham:

My opinion may be biased? am now 24 years of age have been in 5 institutions since 2 years of age came out when 13½. Put on probation when 15. Sent to Borstal at 18½ for three years; Licence revoked, sentenced to 8 months etc. in all 5 homes, 5 prisons, 2 Borstals.

A 58-year-old working class man from Buckingham:

Knowing that I am one of the people they have to watch I think they are a body of wise men.

A working class man from Lincolnshire:

They are very decent to you providing you act ignorant.

A 40-year-old working class man from Rochdale Spotland, Lancs:

The police in this town are very considerate and don't booked you unless you are arkward.

A 49-year-old married man from Morden, Surrey:

Speaking as an ex civil-employee of Scotland Yard's engineer's staff and an ex tramp (two years on the toby in the great slump)—generally —very very fair.

A 75-year-old professional man from Windermere, Westmorland:

A remarkably fine body of men doing their often difficult and dangerous work well though among so many there are a few black sheep. Twice in my life I have been had up and fined and each case I agreed with the police Once for riding a cycle to the common danger and once for showing a light though I was an ARP warden.

A 44-year-old middle class man from North London·

A good body of men with a big job to do all the year round and there is nothing to beat the Bulldog British Policeman on the beat although he has pinched me for speeding 3 times. 'God Blessem'.

A 23-year-old middle class man from Maidenhead:

Although, on two occasions I have run foul of the police I do consider that our Police Force is very efficiently organized, and for that, I have great respect for them.

A 30-year-old married man from near Lancaster:

In the beginning of my life, I hated them on sight, I have been in trouble as a youth, now however with home, wife and children, I cherish, I would risk my life to help them in any circumstances

Twenty-two respondents identified themselves as being, or having been in, the regular police, ten as special or temporary police, and two as military policemen. Twenty-two people were the wife or children of policemen; six had brothers, sons or daughters in the Force, and nine more distant relatives or in-laws.[2] This is of course a comparatively large number, out of a sample of 11,000;[3] it seems possible that the familiarity of the police with paper work made the filling out of the questionnaire congenial to them I had phrased my appeal for collaborators as a request for help; and this may have elicited the helpfulness to which so many of the previous quotations have borne witness. Nobody could have known that this question was to be asked until they had expressed their willingness to collaborate by sending in the form requesting the questionnaire. Eight of the acting police men or women who identified themselves as members of the force gave that as a reason why they should not make any comment on the question 'What do you think of the police?' so that it seems improbable that any members of the police or their families sent for the questionnaire as a device for working off grudges anonymously. In their replies to all the other questions my police respondents do not differ either in fullness or frankness from comparable respondents in other walks of life. Quite a few of them admitted to some form or another of disapproved-of behaviour; but in such cases I have not thought it proper to identify the respondent as a member of the police force when I have quoted him or her.

Despite some criticism, the general morale of the police force appears to be extremely high, as the following quotations show. I shall not identify the respondents further than by age and county.

The police are terrific, their biggest task being to keep their world-wide reputation I am one (E. Yorks, 20)

The police have many arduous and difficult tasks to perform They are courteous and well-disciplined in all respects They elicit the co-operation of the public in the investigation of crime. They are a fine body of men I being an ex-police officer should know Hats off to them. (Northumberland, 66)

As a police officer I think the police are more efficient than they have ever been but there is room for improvement in conditions of service. The relations between the police and the public is better than it has ever been and is improving daily. (Lincolnshire, 24)

As I was a member for 4 years in England and 5 abroad can speak from inside and state fine body of men with public not so fine amongst themselves and in the station. Abroad, as at home, doing splendid work preventing crime, but far too much 'red tape' as in the Army. Too many young 'uns persecuting public instead of helping them (Nottinghamshire, 51)

As an ex-Policeman I think the average policeman is a most efficient and enthusiastic young man but is badly hampered by having to serve under disgruntled and often ignorant officers who have got their position through favour. (Yorkshire, 27)

As a Police Cadet I suppose I am rather biased But the Police force and the medical profession are the two most (In my opinion) important professions and may I say the most under paid. (West Riding, $16\frac{1}{2}$)

I cannot give an unbiased answer to this question, as I am a Police Officer. I do, however, think they are doing a good job, but there are still improvements to be made (Cheshire, 45)

I am in the Police Force, and I think they are a fine body of men who do a difficult job well (Warwickshire, 26)

Over worked (in the Cities only) underpaid for what we have to know and anti-social ungenial duties understaffed in (both County and City) not enough Beat Duty in County area, too much 'phone and office, typing duties, not nearly enough admin. from above (not really enough space for me to let rip here either (More so I should know!) Too many offenders 'not proceeded against'. (Monmouthshire, 33)

Being a Police Constable myself, I am therefore of the highest opinion regarding the Police Service in this Country I have travelled to quite a number of European Countries, consider ours to be the finest in the World. (Worcestershire, 20)

Some improvement in the standard of recruits is required, but will be brought about only by monetary inducement As a member for 26 years, the questions is probably unfair (Lancashire, 44)

I am a police officer! Most of us are average chaps, for the most part very fair and reasonable, and we have a very difficult job. (Surrey, 20)

No country could run smoothly without the restraining army of the law, But the men are treated like schoolboys by their superior officers. I know, I have worked as a constable (Kent, 41)

I think a considerable amount but probably biassed as I served more than 26 years in the Metropolitan Police and now in receipt of a Police pension however I consider the police do their job well and function more effectively when supported by the Courts and the public. I observe that in recent years sentences are more severe than in the 1930's and there is less probation. Police get disheartened when tiresome criminals young or old get placed on probation or given light sentences (Devonshire, 53)

Some of those who have had temporary employment with the police are much less enthusiastic. The six men quoted first consider themselves middle class, the remainder working class.

Having been a special during the last war—they stink (London, 26)

Having been an officer in the Metropolitan Special Constabulary for the past 18 months and think the Met. Police are the most unprincipled bunch of scoundrels imaginable (London, 26)

Having been a Special Constable for $3\frac{1}{2}$ years—not much. There is as much complaint inside the police force as there is outside (Devon, 53)

Having been in the Police War Reserve I find them alright. (Sussex, 57)

Being myself a member of the Metropolitan Special Constabulary I know that on the whole they carry out a difficult job extremely well but unfortunately some try to avoid 'jobs' out of sheer laziness. (Kent)

Being a special constable I think the regular police are doing a difficult job well. (Yorks 37)

Being in the (Police War Reserve) during the War I came in very close contact with all grades and found good and bad. (Kent, 47)

I spent six years as a War Reserve in the Metropolitan Police and taking them as a whole they are a fair generally impartial, decent crowd of men (Dorset, 43)

Having served 4 years as S.P during War, I am of opinion that they are one of our finest bodies of men in the country (Lancashire)

Forget it I've been an R A.F. policeman (Lancashire, 45)

A fine body of men, dealing very fairly with wrongdoers. I speak from experience, having had 6 years with the Military Police (Durham, 36)

With a few exceptions, the children of police officers regard their fathers' profession with enthusiasm; but the views of their wives and other relatives are usually more moderate.

A 66-year-old working class man from Essex:
Under present circumstances I think they do a good job of work. My father was a copper so perhaps I'm a bit biased, but with the modern equipment to help them the crime Gangs have a thin time.

225

A 44-year-old working class man from Yorkshire:

My father served 30 years in the W.R C. constabulary therefore I may be biased But I have a great admiration for the body of men. My experience of them, and particularly the young men of todays forces, is that if you treat them as human beings doing a necessary job you get their respect and co-operation.

A man from Warwickshire:

When looking back on my father's days when he was a policeman, I would say they have deteriorated in discipline and appearance.

A 35-year-old Lancashire woman:

Firstly there are not enough of them. Secondly, my Father was one for 25 years and I think the Policeman these days doesn't know he is born compared to 20 years ago, nevertheless they are helpful and courteous

A 50-year-old married woman from Norfolk:

My father was a policeman so I suppose I think they are a grand lot and I dont know what we should do without them.

A single woman, 24-year-old, from Devonshire

They are a very necessary force. But my own father who was in the police disillusioned me In private life during early childhood. He made our lives hell.

A 32-year-old married woman from Hampshire:

I come of a police family, so naturally have a healthy respect for them. I really wish my husband was a policeman. I don't know whether the modern 'copper' has quite the same courage as his grandfather though.

A 24-year-old woman from Nottingham:

This is rather an amusing question, because my husband is a policeman. However, I think they are no better and no worse than ordinary citizens. They certainly work very hard for comparatively little. I think, though, that they could spend less time filling up forms, seeing children across roads, inspecting cinemas and pestering poor motorists, and devote more time and energy to the prevention of real crime, instead of chasing people who break silly idiotic little rules.

A 30-year-old woman from East Yorkshire:

My husband is a Police Constable, so naturally I think they are quite a nice lot on the whole, but they fiddle like anybody else.

A 25-year-old woman from Middlesex.

They will always help if you ask them and children should be taught to look upon them as friends, but from personal experience of my husband who joined the Force for a time in this area keenness is not very prevalent amongst them these days

A 42-year-old woman from Middlesex:

Well, having been married to one from 1931 to 1941 I haven't a very good opinion, but of course there are sure to be good and bad in every walk of life.

A 31-year-old woman from Yorkshire:

I am prejudiced—my husband was a policeman! Knowing him and many other constables my definition is 'callous and conceited' From an impersonal view I suppose I should say 'Helpful and useful to the public'.

A young married woman from Worcester:

My twin is a policewoman—my father was a policeman and find 25% too fond of their work to ever forget it 25% seem to be law-breakers themselves

A 24-year-old bachelor from Yorkshire who describes himself as 'Working class but I dress quite decent':

Ha, ha, I have to say it is very good because my brother is one. Besides if there wasnt a police force there would be more crime than there is today.

A 53-year-old woman from Lancashire:

Don't know. My brother was one and I know they were like all other class—much differences in characters Some all out for promotion—others very considerate etc. Think on the whole they are better than 50 years ago.

A 30-year-old married man from Leicestershire:

I think they are a grand lot of men (Not because I have a brother in the Force), but I do admire them and have taught my child to ask a policeman any time in difficulty.

A 36-year-old married woman from Bedfordshire:

Most helpful in ordinary circumstances but having relatives in the force (police), I wouldn't trust that they would help me or mine, if it meant a case for themselves.

An 18-year-old girl from Norfolk:

I have relatives in the police force so cannot give an entirely unbiased view but my opinion is that they are sometimes unfair, prejudiced. People with records can never live them down.

A 42-year-old woman from Shropshire:

Several of my husband's relations and one of mine are in the 'Force' three holding fairly high rank, so I think, that as men, they're a grand crowd doing a fine job of work.

227

A 57-year-old man from Berkshire:

Having a son-in-law who is a police-constable, I can say without hesitation that it is the system not the men that is at fault. So long as aged and doddering magistrates let off juvenile delinquents with a mild caution (so that thereafter they jibe at the law instead of respecting it) and so long as promising young men are given nothing better to do than harrass the owners of parked cars and perform similar trivial tasks, so long will the British Police Force continue to be a great deal more ornamental than useful.

A 32-year-old woman from Kent·

One of my relatives is a retired policeman and from his own telling police are the biggest fiddlers They are not conscientious enough.

A 26-year-old married woman from Bedfordshire·

I think the police are great, maybe because my uncle is in the City of London police but I must add honestly even country police do a little fiddling when they can

I should like to draw attention to the number of these respondents who warn me about their possible bias or prejudice. It appears to me to constitute a striking illustration of the honesty and fair-mindedness on which so many other respondents comment.

The fairly frequent references to 'fiddling' which occur in these quotations may be partly due to the fact that the question about the police immediately followed one about 'fiddling' (Some of the police respondents stated that they 'fiddled', but since this was at least a technical misdemeanour I have not included these statements in the quotations.)

Taken in conjunction with the enthusiastic appreciation of the police shown by my respondents, their attitude to 'fiddling' illustrates one of the paradoxes of English character. These fervid respecters of the law are most of them law-breakers, at least in a technical sense.

'Fiddling', both as a word and a concept, is something new in conventional English. The word has existed for a considerable period as a cant or underworld phrase for 'making a living just within the limits of the law'[4]; at some date in the second half of the Second World War it came into general use, with (at least) two major meanings One of these seems to be practically a synonym for the World War I term 'scrounge', the stealing or appropriating usually on a small scale of articles belonging to military stores and the like, and so by extension to petty larceny from employers or from 'them'— anonymous corporations like the nationalized railways. The second

228

and, I believe, much more general use is the circumvention of various rationing and control laws, the acquiring of food, hard or soft goods, or petrol, without surrendering the appropriate coupons or having the proper permits, but usually as an open cash transaction (dealing with the 'black market'), with the proper price, or something over the odds, paid for the goods. In this sense it has some connection with the World War I phrase 'wangle'; but I think this term was more of a middle than a working class word, and was considerably less specific.

What seems to me exceptional about this phrase, at least as far as twentieth century England is concerned, is that this term for law-breaking does not carry any connotation of guilt. Much of the previous material will have shown the great strength and severity of the English conscience, but this conscience is silent about the infringement of rationing laws enforced six years after the cessation of hostilities. Barely one person in fifty, either in the main sample or in the field survey, claims that 'None of my family has ever got anything "off the ration"'.

I will venture a generalization. Any attempt to impose rationing and controls on the English people except in the face of the most patent emergency, such as a war, no matter how ethical the reasons (such as 'fair shares for all'), will almost inevitably undermine the best qualities of the English character. A strong conscience is, so to speak, self-policing, if an attempt is made to replace this self-policing by external controls, particularly by unenforceable laws of which the necessity or usefulness is not immediately obvious, the most valuable qualities of the English civic character developed over the last century or so will inevitably be sapped. Laws 'which tend unwittingly to make criminals of us all', in the words of more than one informant, are far more dangerous for the law-abiding English than for any other society of which I have detailed knowledge.

After the introduction 'There's a lot of talk about 'fiddling' nowadays. Please mark which of the following statements most nearly represent your own opinion' I presented a choice of nine statements (not precisely in the order which follows), three of which could be considered admissions of fiddling, three as rejection on ethical grounds, two as projection (it isn't me, it's them) and one as denial. The choice of statements was as follows:

(i) Nearly everybody fiddles nowadays.
(ii) Most people fiddle occasionally, but not many do regularly.
(iii) With all the rules and regulations, one can't help having to break a rule sometimes.

229

   (iv) It is unpatriotic to fiddle.
    (v) It is wrong to break the law under any circumstances.
   (vi) It is unfair to try to get more than others.
  (vii) Most fiddling is done by profiteers.
 (viii) Most fiddling is done by foreigners.
   (ix) None of my family has ever got anything 'off the ration'.

Just on two-thirds of the population (67 per cent of the men, and 61 per cent of the women) mark one of the three admissions. A considerable number more men than women consider that 'nearly everybody fiddles nowadays' (22 per cent contrasted with 15 per cent) and slightly more women than men (18 per cent men, 22 per cent women) choose the third statement. The distribution of the three admissions, taken together, is remarkably even; there are somewhat fewer admissions from the middle-aged and elderly (over 45) from the poor and the lower working class and the North-West; and the admissions are higher from the upper middle classes, from the young (between 18 and 24) from the more prosperous (over £12 a week) and from the Midlands. With the single exception of the over 65's the admissions never fall below 57 per cent nor rise above 74 per cent.

In the choice of admissions, the working and lower working classes particularly emphasize that nearly everybody fiddles nowadays; the upper middle and lower middle classes that most people fiddle occasionally, but not many do regularly; and the upper working, middle and upper middle classes that with all the rules and regulations one can't help having to break a rule sometimes, an argument which appeals relatively little to the working and lower working classes.

The three rejection sentences (iv, v, vi) are chosen much more by women than by men (22 per cent women and 16 per cent men), the major contrast appearing in the option for the statement that it is unfair to try to get more than others. This is the only statement out of these three which commands 10 per cent of the choices; it is particularly emphasized by the lower middle class and by the elderly. Only 3 per cent of either sex considers that it is unpatriotic to fiddle; this falls to 1 per cent in the upper working class and in the 18–24 group. Five per cent consider that it is wrong to break the law under any circumstances; this appeal to the sanctity of the law only rises to 7 per cent or above in the upper working class and with people aged over 45 or with incomes of under £5 a week; it falls to 2 per cent in the lower working class. Taking the three ethical rejections together, one finds that they have most appeal to the poor and widowed aged over 45, and least appeal to the young, aged between 18 and 34 and to the lower working class. They are relatively little used by the more prosperous members of the upper middle and middle classes

Only one of the projective statements commands more than a scattering 13 per cent of the men and 10 per cent of the women state that most fiddling is done by profiteers. This belief finds a very high number of supporters from the North-West region (18 per cent in the main survey and 20 per cent in the field survey); and I am some-what inclined to link this figure with the high concentration of Roman Catholics in the same region,[5] it seems likely that many of these Roman Catholics are the children of Irish immigrants; and blaming somebody else for one's troubles is almost an Irish national policy. The belief in profiteers is held by somewhat more of the lower working and working classes, and somewhat less by the upper middle and upper working classes. Only 2 per cent of the population put the blame for fiddling on foreigners, with a little concentration in the London lower working class; and, as has already been stated, only 2 per cent claim that their family have never had anything off the ration, predominantly poor old widowed women.[6]

Respondents were asked, if they agreed with more than one statement, to number them in the order of their importance; and 72 per cent took advantage of this to mark more than one answer. As I was reading through the questionnaires, it had seemed that a number of respondents so to speak 'hedged their bets', following an admission by a rejection or projection and conversely. I therefore had a table made showing which were the second choices of each first choice. The tabulation did not altogether bear out my impression. Less than a quarter of those whose first choice was an admission sentence and who made a second choice chose a rejection or pro-jection sentence; and those who consider fiddling unpatriotic and law-breaking wrong are similarly consistent More than half of those whose first choice was the statement 'It is unfair to try to get more than others' selected one of the admission statements as second choice; but what is perhaps most revealing is that nearly two-thirds of those who stated that most fiddling was done by profiteers or foreigners selected an admission statement as second choice. I think this may derive from a rather particular interpretation of the word 'most' in the two statements; these people may consider that the 'big fiddles' are performed by profiteers and foreigners, even though the little men, among whom they count themselves, fiddle in their own little way. If this interpretation be correct, my respondents are

231

more consistent than my impressions had suggested, though there is a confused minority.

A number of writers[7] have suggested that there is a direct correlation between the increase in petty law-breaking, such as fiddling, and the 'decline of religion', and I therefore correlated the answers

Figure XXXIV

Question 81

81 There's a lot of talk about 'fiddling' nowadays Please mark which of the following statements most nearly represents your opinion.

FIRST CHOICE	SECOND CHOICE									
	1	2	3	4	5	6	7	8	9	
	Nearly everybody fiddles nowadays	Most people fiddle occasionally but not many do regularly	With all the rules and regulations one can't help breaking a rule sometimes	It is unpatriotic to fiddle	None of my family has ever got anything 'off the ration'	It is wrong to break the law under any circumstances	Most fiddling is done by profiteers	It is unfair to try to get more than others	Most fiddling is done by foreigners	Total
	%	%	%	%	%	%	%	%	%	%
1. Nearly everybody fiddles nowadays	—	28	46	5	—	3	11	4	3	100
2. Most people fiddle occasionally but not many do regularly	6	—	55	5	1	4	16	11	2	100
3. With all the rules and regulations one can't help having to break a rule sometimes	19	45	—	6	1	4	14	8	3	100
4. It is unpatriotic to fiddle	8	18	9	—	8	19	10	26	2	100
5 None of my family has ever got anything 'off the ration'	5	7	9	7	—	32	12	26	2	100
6. It is wrong to break the law under any circumstances	7	8	14	15	5	—	15	34	2	100
7 Most fiddling is done by profiteers	9	32	19	5	1	3	—	20	11	100
8 It is unfair to try to get more than others	4	30	20	18	6	12	8	—	2	100
9 Most fiddling is done by foreigners	18	16	25	2	—	4	22	13	—	100

It is necessary when reading this table to bear in mind the very great differences in first choices about fiddling with membership of any religious denomination, with the extent of attendance at Church or religious services, and with the frequency of prayer or other private devotions, which can roughly be considered three increasingly accurate measures of religious practice The answers are far from conclusive. Membership of a religious denomination does not appear to make any significant difference. Those who go to church once a week or more often are slightly more likely to choose one of the ethical rejection sentences than those who never go, or only for weddings and funerals; but there is only 10 per cent difference in admissions between the most fervent church-goers and the total abstainers (52 and 62 per cent respectively). With the saying of private prayers the pattern is very similar: those who say prayers daily or more often are slightly more likely to choose the ethical rejections (and also, though to a less degree, to project guilt on to profiteers and foreigners) than those who say they seldom or never; 57 per cent of those who pray more than once a day choose admission sentences compared

Figure XXXV

Question 81 by Question 82

81 There's a lot of talk about 'fiddling' nowadays Please mark which of the following statements most nearly represents your opinion

82 Would you describe yourself as being of any religion or denomination?

Question 81	Question 82			
	Yes	No	No answer	Total
Nearly everybody fiddles nowadays	71	27	2	100
Most people fiddle occasionally, but not many people do regularly	74	24	2	100
With all the rules and regulations one can't help having to break a rule sometimes	78	20	2	100
It is unpatriotic to fiddle	77	20	3	100
None of my family has ever got anything 'off the ration'	78	21	1	100
It is wrong to break the law under any circumstances	80	19	1	100
Most fiddling is done by profiteers	74	23	3	100
It is unfair to try to get more than others	77	19	4	100
Most fiddling is done by foreigners	74	25	1	100
No answer	74	18	8	100
Total	75	23	2	100

with 70 per cent of those who never do. The active practice of religion does make a slight difference in the attitudes towards minor law-breaking, but the influence is negligible compared with its influence on pre-marital chastity.[8] To the extent that these figures are reliable (and the sample is far the largest, to my knowledge, dealing with these two questions) if the whole population were suddenly to become extremely devout, the reduction in fiddling and similar petty offences would only be in the neighbourhood of 10 per cent. The majority of English men and women break the rationing and control laws in peace time because these laws do not command the respect and allegiance either of their intellects or of their strict consciences.

Figure XXXVI

Question 84 by Question 81

84 Do you attend church or religious services?

81 There's a lot of talk about 'fiddling' nowadays Please mark which of the following statements most nearly represents your opinion

Question 84	Question 81									
	Nearly everybody fiddles nowadays	Most people fiddle occasionally, but not many do regularly	With all the rules and regulations one can't help breaking a rule sometimes	It is unpatriotic to fiddle	None of my family has ever got anything 'off the ration	It is wrong to break the law under any circumstances	Most fiddling is done by profiteers	It is unfair to try to get more than others	Most fiddling is done by foreigners	No answer	Total
More than once a week	14	22	16	4	1	10	14	16	1	2	100
Once a week	15	22	18	4	3	7	11	14	2	4	100
Less than once a week, but more than once a month	14	27	21	3	1	5	11	12	2	4	100
Less than once a month	16	26	20	4	2	5	13	11	2	1	100
Once or twice a year	18	15	22	3	2	5	11	9	2	3	100
Only for weddings and funerals	23	27	19	3	1	5	12	7	3	0	100
Never	22	24	16	3	2	5	14	7	2	5	100
No answer	—	—	20	—	13	—	—	27	—	40	100
Total	19	26	20	3	2	5	12	10	2	1	100

234

Figure XXXVII

Question 85 by Question 81

85 Do you say private prayers?

81 There's a lot of talk about 'fiddling' nowadays Please mark which of the following statements most nearly represents your opinion.

Question 85	Question 81										
	Nearly everybody fiddles nowadays	Most people fiddle occasionally, but not many do regularly	With all the rules and regulations one can't help breaking a rule sometimes	It is unpatriotic to fiddle	None of my family has ever got anything 'off the ration'	It is wrong to break the law under any circumstances	Most fiddling is done by profiteers	It is unfair to try to get more than others	Most fiddling is done by foreigners	No answer	Total
More than once a day	16	21	18	3	4	9	9	14	2	4	100
Daily	16	24	19	4	2	6	14	11	3	1	100
Only in peril or grief	21	26	23	2	1	4	10	8	3	2	100
Very seldom	19	28	20	3	2	5	12	9	2	0	100
Never	24	28	18	3	1	4	12	8	2	0	100
No answer	12	22	14	2	—	3	10	22	3	12	100
Total	19	26	20	3	2	5	12	10	2	1	100

NOTES TO CHAPTER THIRTEEN

1 Four blank lines were provided for the answer

2 See Chapter Three, p 35, for a discussion of the class position to which these people assigned themselves

3 Since there is approximately one policeman to every 720 citizens, it is only slightly above expectation from a random sample

4 See Eric Partridge, *A Dictionary of the Underworld* (Routledge and Kegan Paul, 1950) It has existed as an army slang term at least from 1910 (personal communication from Mr Partridge)

5. See Chapter Fourteen, p 239

6. The same question was asked in the field survey, with the added refinement that a number of cards were printed with the sentences arranged in various orders, to prevent any possibility of the order influencing the choice This was one of the questions where I expected a marked difference between the replies given in face-to-face interviews and those from anonymous questionnaires, I thought the interviewees would make much more use of the rejection and projection sentences As has been explained, men and women differ quite markedly in the sentences they choose, since the proportion of the sexes is different in the two samples, I am giving the answers of the field survey by sexes, rather than as totals, with the corresponding percentages from the main sample in brackets and italics.

235

	Men	Women
(i) Nearly everybody fiddles nowadays	23 (22)	17 (15)
(ii) Most people fiddle occasionally but not many do regularly	14 (27)	13 (24)
(iii) With all the rules and regulations one can't help having to break a rule sometimes	22 (18)	18 (22)
(iv) It is unpatriotic to fiddle	5 (3)	5 (3)
(v) It is wrong to break the law under any circumstances	6 (5)	8 (6)
(vi) It is unfair to try to get more than others	6 (8)	14 (13)
(vii) Most fiddling is done by profiteers	14 (13)	14 (10)
(viii) Most fiddling is done by foreigners	7 (2)	5 (2)
(ix) None of my family has ever got anything 'off the ration'	2 (1)	4 (2)
No answer	1 (1)	2 (3)

As can be seen, the choices of the two samples are remarkably similar, with the exception of the answers to (ii) and (viii) The few people choosing the intermediate 'admission' in the interview confirms the pattern which has been noted several times that interviewees tend to give all-or-none answers while people filling in a questionnaire and, at least presumably, giving more thought to their answers, tend to choose shaded answers The greater number choosing to give the 'projective' answer that most fiddling is done by foreigners is in accordance with my preliminary expectations This answer was not given at all by members of the upper middle or upper working classes. There is some concentration in the lower working and working classes from the two Northern regions. It seems noteworthy that the two samples are in such close agreement that (by 1951) it was not unpatriotic or wrong to break the rationing and control laws and that practically none would claim that they or their families had never done so

7 See especially R Seebohm Rowntree and G R Lavers, *English Life and Leisure* (Longmans, London, 1951).

8 See Figures VIII, IX, X, XI, in Chapter Eight.

236

CHAPTER FOURTEEN

RELIGION AND OTHER BELIEFS

NEARLY A QUARTER of the population of England, according to this sample, do not consider that they belong to any religion or denomination, not even the minimal self-ascription of 'Church of England—only to distinguish myself from Roman Catholic or other denomination', in the typical words of a 40-year-old upper working class man from Ramsbottom, Lancs Twenty-six per cent of the men and 18 per cent of the women have no religious affiliation at all. A further 2 per cent did not answer this question.

This non-religious group is unevenly distributed throughout the country. It is most numerous in the metropolises (29 per cent) and least so in the small towns and villages (19 per cent), it is much less represented in the two Western regions (South-West 16 per cent, North-West 17 per cent) than in the rest of the country. It seems possible that this regional variation springs from two main causes: the South-West is the most rural of the regions and (as will be shown subsequently) the practice of religion is more frequent in the small towns and villages; and the North-West has the greatest concentration of Roman Catholics (14 per cent of the total acknowledging adherence to any denomination) Age appears to make no appreciable difference to non-religion; nor does marriage, while the partners are alive and living together. The divorced or separated have the highest proportion (30 per cent) of those claiming no religious affiliation, and the widowed the lowest (18 per cent). Income appears to be a determining factor, with the percentage of non-adherents consistently rising as income rises, from 20 per cent of those with incomes of under £5 a week, through 23 per cent for those in the £8–£12 weekly income bracket, to 26 per cent of those with incomes of over £15 weekly Members of the middle and of the lower working classes, with 18 and 19 per cent respectively, have markedly fewer non-religious than do the remaining classes. Those who cannot place themselves in the English social system also tend not to place themselves in a religious denomination.

Three-quarters of the population assign themselves to some religion or denomination; of this group 2 per cent do not give further details; 3 per cent, slightly concentrated in the young and prosperous, say 'Christian' without further elaboration; and another 4 per cent, again somewhat concentrated in the under 18's and over 65's and

237

the lower working class call themselves 'Protestant'. The remainder are more precise; they all claim membership in some Protestant communion, with the exception of 8 per cent who are Roman Catholics, 3 per cent belonging to such modern sects as Spiritualists, Christian Scientists and Theosophists, and slightly less than 1 per cent (25 individuals) who are Jewish. Eighty per cent of those English people who claim any church membership belong to some organized Protestant Church.

Of these far the largest group is Church of England, comprising 58 per cent of all the English people claiming allegiance to some denomination Members of the Church of England are somewhat heavily concentrated in the two Southern regions, and are relatively fewer in the two Northern ones, particularly the North East and North; and they are also fewer in the large towns (between a million and a hundred thousand inhabitants) and most numerous in the small towns and villages. There is some concentration in the younger (25–34) married groups, and there are comparatively fewer among the aged. With an income of over £5 a week money makes very little difference to this ascription; the very poor are slightly more likely to belong to other denominations There is a larger proportion of members of the Church of England among people calling themselves middle class or working class without modifiers than in the remaining social classes.

Although doctrinally there is no difference between those calling themselves Church of England, and those calling themselves Anglican, there appeared to be so much difference in practice that I had this small group of less than 2 per cent (48 people) classified separately. They come predominantly from the two Southern regions and tend to consider themselves upper middle class; no member of the lower working class describes him or her self in such a way.

The most sizable Protestant group after the Church of England are the Methodists with 10 per cent of the religious population. There is a heavy concentration of these in the North-East and North (18 per cent of the population of the region) followed by the Midlands (12 per cent). There are relatively few in London and the South-East, and in the metropolises; they are concentrated in the medium sized towns. Few of the most prosperous people are Methodists, nor are many members of the upper middle class, they are relatively numerous in the lower middle, upper working and lower working classes. Very few Methodists are divorced or separated.

None of the other Protestant churches have more than 3 per cent of the total religious population. The Baptists have 3 per cent with some concentration in the Midlands and the upper middle and lower middle classes The Congregationalists also have 3 per cent, evenly divided regionally, but with rather a higher number of middle-aged and elderly members concentrated in the lower middle and upper working classes The Nonconformists have 2 per cent, also chiefly middle-aged and elderly with some concentration in the South-West; no members of the upper middle class belong to this denomination, which finds most of its members in the lower middle and upper working classes. There is a tiny group (less than 1 per cent) of Presbyterians, from the North-East and North, presumably chiefly people with Scottish connections Finally there is a group of adherents to small sects with only a very few representatives of each sect in the sample; among them are Christadelphians, Unitarians, Quakers, Peculiar Persons, Primitive Methodists, Toc H, Salvation Army, Plymouth Brethren, Jehovah's Witnesses, Seventh Day Adventists, Providence Particular Baptists, Andrew Jackson Davis's Teaching, British Israel World Federation and The Countess of Huntingdon's Persuasion. For convenience of tabulation I grouped all members of these and similar bodies under the rubric 'small Protestant sects'; it was perhaps not permissible to put into the same category the prosperous unmarried upper middle class lady from Chelsea who described her denomination as 'dialectical materialist'. These small Protestant sects find most of their members in those over the age of 45 and with very low incomes, otherwise the distribution is very even except that no members of the upper working class belong to such small sects.

As has already been stated, the Roman Catholics are heavily concentrated in the North-West with 14 per cent, and are very few in the South-West (3 per cent) or the small towns and villages. Most of the Catholic respondents are between the ages of 18 and 44; they are sparsely represented among the very poor and (not surprisingly) among the divorced and separated. Those who can place themselves in the English social system call themselves upper middle or working class; but a surprisingly high number fail to place themselves in any of the six social classes, which gives further likelihood to the suggestion that the majority of Roman Catholics are of Irish origin or descent and not completely assimilated into the English social structure

The small group of Jews are predominantly prosperous young students from London and the South-East who place themselves in the upper middle class, though there are representatives from all areas and social classes except the lower working class.

The 3 per cent of Spiritualists, Christian Scientists and Theosophists (most of them Spiritualists) are predominantly middle aged or elderly, poor, widowed or separated; they are fairly evenly divided though few of the young, under 24, belong to such elective groups, nor do many of the upper or lower working classes.[1]

Even on so factual a question as one's religious denomination a certain number of respondents chose to add elucidating comments. Thus, three respondents stated they were recent Catholic converts, another, a 29-year-old middle class man from Cheshire, wrote.

I was brought up Roman Catholic and still follow it so as not to hurt near relatives' feeling. I do not believe in Christianity

A widowed lady from Bardesley, who describes herself as 'By birth and breeding middle class, but by force of circumstance working class'

Christian with a strong leaning to Judaism.

A 45-year-old working class wife from Bridport:

S D A I believe wholly in the Bible, try to keep Gods law. E G. keeping Saturday Sabbath, believing Saturday to be the Seventh day, find it difficult, but do my best. No Church here S D A.

A 29-year-old 'working middle class' bachelor from Cleveleys.

Christian—but not belonging to any church as churches nowadays are mostly hypocritic.

A 43-year-old working class bachelor from Bristol:

Church of England but more of Bishop Barnes theories attract me

A 38-year-old 'hard working' married man from Croydon:

Am a version of Jehovahs Wittness But I am a weak hypocript mostly sexually

In a country in which most people inherit their religious denomination from their parents, self-ascription to one sect rather than another gives very little information of the rôle religious practices or beliefs play in their lives. In an attempt to get further insight into the extent to which religion is of importance in people's lives I asked a series of questions on religious practices and beliefs. These questions were asked of the whole sample, both those who claimed membership of some denomination and those who did not; all the answers were analysed according to the denomination of the respondents subsequently; but it should be kept in mind that only three-quarters of the population claim membership of any denomination, and also that the absolute sizes of the denominations are very different. Thus, though the Church of England, for example, may show a much smaller percentage of fervent church-goers than the Baptists, the number of members of the Church of England attending service more than once a week will be much higher than that of the Baptists doing so.

Seven alternative answers were offered to the question 'Do you attend church or religious services?': more than once a week, once a week; less than once a week but more than once a month; less than once a month; once or twice a year; only for weddings and funerals; never. I supplied the category 'only for weddings and funerals' because I thought that many respondents, either through meticulousness or some feeling of apprehension, might object to marking the alternative 'never', and indeed this category was selected by a third of the total. A few respondents wrote in 'christenings' as a third reason for entering holy premises.

Six per cent of the population visit a church more than once a week, and can be considered fervent church-goers; another 9 per cent go regularly once a week. A little less than a sixth of the population are regular or fervent in their devotions, but it seems likely that not all of these are voluntarily so; the percentages are much the highest in the upper middle class under 24, and especially under 18, and these may well be students with compulsory chapel.

Fervent church-going is relatively uncommon in the two Southern regions and in the metropolises, and with the younger married people, between 25 and 44, otherwise they are fairly evenly divided throughout the population. save for the lower working class; 5 per cent of the men and 7 per cent of the women attend religious services more than once a week.

The regular church-goers comprise markedly more women than men (11 per cent and 7 per cent respectively); they are more frequent in the small towns and villages, among the single and widowed rather than the married; they are particularly few between the ages of 25–34 Some of the young married people mention the impossibility of leaving small children alone as a reason why they do not go to church; and this may be operative in a number of cases. Certainly the married and those between the ages of 25 and 34 visit churches less than any of the other groups.[2]

Forty-five per cent of the population, just under half, can be considered intermittent church-goers, attending less than once a week, but at least once or twice a year, with the greater proportion, a quarter of the total population, falling into the least frequent category Twice as many women as men (11 per cent and 6 per cent) go more than once a month; a third more women than men (13 per cent and 9 per cent) go less than once a month; but the two sexes are nearly equal (27 per cent and 25 per cent) for a visit once or twice a year, presumably for most people Easter and Christmas.

If the figures for intermittent church-going are summated, a consistent pattern emerges. Such intermittent church-going is a middle class rather than a working class pattern, a small town and village, rather than a metropolitan pattern, and is least common in London and its conurbation. To the extent that, in a society as urban as that of modern England, country ways represent a survival of earlier patterns, it appears that attending religious services is such a survival. These intermittent church-goers represent about half the congregation of the great majority of the sects, it represents a somewhat small proportion of the Roman Catholics and Presbyterians, and a very high proportion—nearly three-quarters—of the Nonconformists and Jews, both of which groups tend to visit a place of worship once or twice a year.

The remaining two-fifths of the population do not attend churches or religious services for the purpose of worship, though all but 7 per cent do so for weddings or funerals. Nine per cent of the men and 5 per cent of the women say they 'never' go to church; they are somewhat concentrated in London and in the lower middle and lower working classes.

For most purposes it seems legitimate to consider as a single group all the people whose only visits to religious buildings are for weddings and funerals and those who never go at all. They comprise just on half (48 per cent) of the men and nearly a third (31 per cent) of the women in the sample. These non-worshippers are heavily concentrated in the metropolises (51 per cent) and in London and the South-East, they are relatively fewest (30 per cent) in the South-West and the small towns and villages. Half of the divorced and separated fall into this category, but less than a third of the unmarried; there is a difference of 12 per cent between the married and the single. Very few (20 per cent) of the under 18's fall into this category, and less than a third of those under 24; the highest total is reached by those between 25 and 34 The very poor and the most prosperous have fewer non-worshippers than those in the median income ranges; and what is perhaps more significant, the members of the middle class, with 34 per cent, have 10 per cent fewer non-worshippers than members of the working class. The upper middle class have the fewest non-worshippers with 26 per cent; the lower working class has a slightly higher proportion than the working

242

class. On the basis of these figures a married working class man living in London or Birmingham and their conurbations is unlikely to make any public profession of religion; women, particularly the unmarried or widowed, the very young, members of the upper middle and middle classes, and the inhabitants of the small towns and villages are much more likely to be at least intermittent church-goers.[3]

A variety of circumstances might either prevent people with religious convictions from attending church services or impel people without religious convictions to put in an appearance; and it seems likely that both may be occasionally operative. This is not the case with the saying of private prayers which therefore seems a more reliable criterion for religious feeling.

I offered five alternative answers to the question 'Do you say private prayers?': more than once a day; daily; only in peril and grief; very seldom; never. The category 'very seldom' was chosen for the same purpose as the category 'only for weddings and funerals' in relation to church-going, for the benefit of the meticulous, who might wonder how childhood prayers should be reckoned, and for the superstitious; it was a widely used rubric.

If those who 'very seldom' and 'never' say private prayers are treated as a single group they form very much the same size population (42 per cent, contrasted with 40 per cent) as those who never go to church or only for weddings and funerals. The composition of this group is however somewhat different, and the differences appear revealing. The differences between region and town size become very much less, as do the differences between the married and the single, which suggests that quite a number of married town-dwellers are prevented by force of circumstances from visiting places of worship despite their belief; and, on the other hand, quite a number of people who never pray attend church with some regularity in the small towns and villages where their absence would be marked by censorious neighbours The difference between the middle class and the working class is maintained almost unaltered (38 per cent of the middle and 45 per cent of the working class seldom or never say prayers); but there is a marked reversal with the upper middle class who had the smallest proportion of non-church-goers (26 per cent) but the highest proportion (47 per cent) of non-prayers. Over half (53 per cent) of the men but less than a third (29 per cent) of the women seldom or never pray The greatest absence of prayer is found in the groups aged between 18 and 34 earning between £8 and £15 a week, the absence is least with the old, the poor and the widowed. The general picture of the younger, married, prosperous working class English man having no, or only residual, religious feelings is maintained. This non-religious group is to a considerable extent the group which served in the Forces in the last war; it is possible that this experience in one way or another (for example, compulsory church parades) turned them away from religion; but since this group is the most sceptical on non-religious subjects also[4] this hypothesis is certainly a very tentative one.

It was with wartime experiences in mind that I provided the category 'only in peril or grief'; and this category is marked somewhat more by men than women (17 per cent contrasted with 14 per cent), by people under 34 more than those above that age, and by the working class slightly more than by the middle class. A few respondents added to this category 'in thankfulness'; an upper working class mother from Brighton elaborated 'usually in gratitude for my husband and babies.'

Two-fifths of the English population make prayer a regular part of their lives, precisely one-third saying prayers daily, and 11 per cent more frequently. Nearly twice as many women as men make use of constant prayer; 16 per cent of the women and 6 per cent of the men pray more than once a day; 42 per cent of the women and 25 per cent of the men say daily prayers. If daily prayer be taken as a sign of religious faith, the picture, typical of so many Catholic countries, of women being the more fervent in their public devotions, is reproduced in the private devotions of the English.

The North-West, with its high concentration of Roman Catholics, has the greatest number of regular pray-ers, and the Midlands the fewest; by the standards of private prayer, rather than church going, Birmingham has even fewer devout people than London. The inhabitants of the small towns and villages pray somewhat more than people in the rest of the country. Area however in this connection seems to be much less of a determinant than age and poverty; the high concentrations of daily or more frequent praying occur in those aged over 45 with low incomes. Social class makes comparatively little difference in the case of the devout praying more than once a day, save that these people are few in the upper working class; with daily prayers there are some 8 per cent more in the middle than in the working class. Relatively few members of the lower working and upper middle classes say daily prayers.[5]

Quite a number of English parents who do not go to church or pray themselves teach their children to do so; but something like a quarter of English parents do not teach their children to say prayers or send them to Sunday school.[6] The relative vagueness of this statement is due to the fact that 17 per cent of the parents did not answer the question 'Do you teach your children to say prayers?' and 19 per cent 'Do you send your children to Sunday school?'; these non-answerers are predominantly parents for whose children the questions are not appropriate, the very young whose children are not old enough to learn these activities, and the old whose children have long since passed the appropriate age. Only 7 per cent of the parents aged between 35 and 44 failed to answer the questions.

There is also a further ambiguity about the answers to the question 'Do you teach your children to say prayers?' in that some parents may have taken the question extremely personally and. when they have answered 'No' may have meant, not that their children were not taught prayers, but that they were taught by the other spouse. Seventeen per cent of the mothers and 32 per cent of the fathers say they do not teach their children to say prayers; 52 per cent of the fathers and 66 per cent of the mothers say they do The pattern for not teaching children to say prayers is the same as that for not praying or visiting a place of worship oneself, it is most concentrated in London and Birmingham among parents earning £8–£12 a week; such parents are fewer in the middle class and (slightly anomalously) the upper working class

No comments were called for on this question; but nevertheless a few parents added them, mostly suggesting a rather marked abdication of parental responsibility. Thus, the wife of a sailor from Leeds: 'Taught to say prayers up to 3, now I leave it to the children'. A 32-year-old middle class mother from Hereford: 'I taught my child to say prayers, just going through a 'funny' phase and does not want to say them.' A 37-year-old working class father from Portslade, Sussex: 'I do not believe in cramming religion down anyone's throat.'

The 27 per cent of the parents who do not send their children to Sunday school are evenly divided by sex; the pattern of abstention is the same for region, town size, age and income as it is for not teaching to say prayers, but the class composition is slightly different. The greatest number of abstentions is in the upper middle class, followed by the lower middle class; there is only 1 per cent difference in the habits of the middle and working classes in this practice (the only practice connected with religion where the middle class is not markedly more observant than the working class); and the lower working and upper working classes have the smallest proportion of abstentions. In this case too, the occasional comment suggests that parents will not force the unwilling child; for example the 41-year-old working class mother from Barking who writes 'They don't wish to go (I don't like this)': or the 30-year-old mother from Hebburn, Durham: 'The older boy went to Sunday school for a few weeks, says he doesn't like it'.

Just over half of all the parents (54 per cent) and two-thirds of those aged between 35 and 64 send or sent their children to Sunday school. This can be considered a national custom, apart from the very young parents, the figure only falls to under 50 per cent in the metropolises and in the upper middle class; it rises to 59 per cent or above in the North-East and North, in the £12–£15 a week income group, in the upper working and lower working classes. The high figure for the lower working class, which is not otherwise particularly devout, may derive from the concentration of large families in that group. When there are more than four children in the family the children are very likely to attend Sunday school; when there are two or three children the chances are even whether they be sent or not; with an only child there is a slight probability (28 per cent of them go, 36 per cent do not) that it will not be sent

Figure XXXVIII

Question 87 by Question 60
87. Do your children go to Sunday School?
60 How many children have you?

Question 87	Question 60						
	1	2	3	4	5 or more	No answer	Total
Yes	28	36	17	8	9	2	100
No	36	37	18	5	4	0	100
No answer	48	20	6	2	3	21	100
Total	34	33	15	6	6	6	100

The high concentration in the North-East and North would appear to result at least in part from the high concentration of Methodists and members of other Nonconformist denominations in this area, for these sects appear to attach much more importance to attendance at Sunday school than does the Church of England.[7]

Two-thirds of the parents whose children attend Sunday school say that they allow their children to go because they (the children) wish to; one-third say that they send them. This was a badly worded question, because the two attitudes are not incompatible; but it does seem a possible explanation for the fact that there is so little correlation between the parents' own church-going habits and their children's attendance at Sunday schools. Just on half the parents who never attend church themselves send their children to Sunday school; and a slightly higher proportion of those who only do so for weddings and funerals; greater devoutness makes very little difference in the proportion of children who go to Sunday school, except for those fervent worshippers, going to church more than once a week, who have a slightly higher proportion of children going to Sunday school.

Figure XXXIX

Question 84 by Question 87

84 Do you attend church or religious services?

87 Do your children go to Sunday school?

Question 84	Question 87			
	Yes	No	No answer	Total
More than once a week	69	11	20	100
Once a week	61	21	18	100
Less than once a week but more than once a month	65	13	22	100
Less than once a month	64	18	18	100
Once or twice a year	59	23	18	100
Only for weddings and funerals	46	36	18	100
Never	41	43	16	100
No answer	48	21	31	100
Total	54	27	19	100

The saying of private prayers is similarly relatively uninfluential in determining whether children shall go to Sunday school or no; there is only a 5 per cent difference between the children of those who say prayers daily, and those who say them 'very seldom'. Even with the small group of adults who 'never' say prayers themselves more than half of them send their children to Sunday school [8]

With the teaching of children to say prayers, the praying habits of the parents play a somewhat larger rôle; three-quarters of those who say prayers daily or more often, slightly more than half of those who say them 'very seldom', but only a fifth of those who 'never' say them teach their children to pray.[9] It is probable that all these figures underestimate the proportion of children taught to

Figure XL

Question 85 by Question 87

85. Do you say private prayers?

87. Do your children go to Sunday School?

Question 85	Question 87			
	Yes	No	No answer	Total
More than once a day	61	21	18	100
Daily	59	23	18	100
Only in peril and grief	49	29	22	100
Very seldom	54	27	19	100
Never	43	41	16	100
No answer	55	18	27	100
Total	54	27	19	100

Figure XLI

Question 86 by Question 85

86 Do you teach your children to say prayers?

85 Do you say private prayers?

Question 86	Question 85						
	More than once a day	Daily	Only in peril or grief	Very seldom	Never	No answer	Total
Yes	13	41	12	28	5	1	100
No	3	12	19	31	33	1	100
No answer	7	29	18	31	13	2	100
Total	9	32	15	29	13	2	100

say prayers because of the meticulousness, referred to above, of respondents who replied in the negative when it was the other spouse who actually taught the children to say their prayers.

The beliefs of the parents seem to have greater influence than their practices in whether they will teach their children to say prayers or no. Four-fifths of those who believe in an after-life teach their children to say prayers, a third of those who are uncertain on this subject, but only half of those who do not believe in life after death. Beliefs are relatively uninfluential in determining whether children shall attend Sunday school or no. Those who do not believe in an

248

Figure XLII

Question 92 by Question 86

92 Do you believe in an after-life?

86. Do you teach your children to say prayers?

Question 92	Question 86			
	Yes	No	No answer	Total
Yes	67	17	16	100
No	41	41	18	100
Uncertain	56	26	18	100
No answer	50	11	39	100
Total	58	25	17	100

Figure XLIII

Question 92 by Question 87

92 Do you believe in an after-life?

87. Do your children go to Sunday School?

Question 92	Question 87			
	Yes	No	No answer	Total
Yes	57	24	19	100
No	48	35	17	100
Uncertain	55	27	18	100
No answer	50	11	39	100
Total	54	27	19	100

after-life send their children to Sunday school slightly less than those who do, but the difference is only 9 per cent.

Much more indicative of parental piety, and inferentially of the religious atmosphere of the home, are the occasions on which prayers are said by the children, rather than the saying of childish prayers If the children say prayers at any other time than before going to bed it is a strong presumption that the parents themselves are actively religious. Prayers before going to bed are part of the ritual of the end of the day for most English children, almost independently of whether their parents ever say a prayer or attend a church service or no. But the 8 per cent of the children who are taught to say prayers in the morning are almost certain to be children of pious parents.[10] Rather inexplicably, this also appears to be

249

the case where children are taught to say grace before meals, but much less so with grace after meals. although the same proportion (19 per cent in each case) of those parents who teach their children to pray teach grace before as grace after meals Grace before meals correlates markedly and positively with frequent public and private devotions by the parents; grace after meals does so to a very much less marked degree.

Figure XLIV

Question 84 by Question 89

84. Do you attend church or religious services?

89 If you teach your children to say prayers, when do they say them?

Question 84	Question 89					
	Before going to bed	Morning and evening	Grace before meals	Grace after meals	No answer	Total
More than once a week	80	23	40	23	2	168
Once a week	85	21	28	20	1	155
Less than once a week but more than once a month	90	9	21	16	2	138
Less than once a month	92	8	12	24	1	137
Once or twice a year	87	6	16	21	1	131
Only for weddings and funerals	92	3	13	16	2	126
Never	88	5	24	15	—	132
No answer	79	5	16	11	—	111
Total	89	8	19	19	1	136

Figure XLV

Question 85 by Question 89

85 Do you say private prayers?

89. If you teach your children to say prayers, when do they say them?

Question 85	Question 89					
	Before going to bed	Morning and evening	Grace before meals	Grace after meals	No answer	Total
More than once a day	78	20	27	25	1	155
Daily	91	9	22	18	1	141
Only in peril or grief	90	5	12	16	2	125
Very seldom	89	4	14	19	1	127
Never	85	2	11	11	6	115
No answer	100	—	17	33	—	150
Total	89	8	19	19	1	136

The distribution of the teaching of the two graces appear strongly contrasted. Grace before meals is most taught in the two Southern regions in the metropolises, by the older parents over 45 (especially the widowed) at the top or bottom of the economic scale. and in the lower middle and upper middle classes. It is little practiced by the upper or lower working classes. Socially, the pattern of grace after meals is almost the reverse of this, most frequent in the lower working, upper working and middle classes and relatively uncommon in the upper middle and lower middle classes. The poor, the old and the widowed are again the most frequent teachers of this practice, but the contrast between people of different ages and incomes is very much less than with grace before meals. Not very many parents in the South-West teach their children to say grace after meals, but this pattern is comparatively common in London and the South-East. Relatively few parents in the two Northern regions teach grace either before or after meals [11]

Public and private worship, and the religious education of children, are activities which are found in a great number of societies; information about them can give some indication of the rôle played by religion in the lives of the members of the society, but very little of the content of that religion. With insignificant exceptions (the very small group of Jews and Theosophists, and somewhat less clearly, the Spiritualists) all my respondents who claimed membership of any denomination were members of some Christian church or communion; how much of the dogma of Christianity did they believe?

When I devised the questionnaire. I thought it would be useless to ask my respondents whether they believed in God or the Divinity of Jesus Christ, for I imagined that, where there was no faith, superstition would stop people giving negative answers. I think now that I probably misjudged the courage and candour of my respondents, and would have got significant answers to such questions. However the questions I did ask on religious belief were more indirect.

I assume that (with the possible exception of some of the very small Protestant sects) Christians of all denominations should believe in the Trinity and in the Incarnation, Passion and Resurrection of Jesus Christ. They should also believe that the soul survives after the death of the body and comes to Judgment; those who have led good lives on earth are rewarded by heaven, while unrepentant evil-doers are punished by consignment, either temporarily or eternally, to some other and painful place or condition designated

251

as hell or purgatory. Belief in hell and purgatory is a matter of dogma for Roman Catholics, most Protestant sects do not use the concept of purgatory; but whatever the definition, it would seem that a Christian must believe in the existence of hell as well as of heaven, though it may not be necessary to believe that any soul is permanently damned. The dogmatic position of belief in the devil would seem to be rather more obscure; but there are numerous references to his existence in the Gospels.[12]

Precisely three-fifths of the English population state definitely that they believe neither in hell nor in the devil. The remainder are almost evenly divided between belief and uncertainty; 20 per cent say they believe in the devil and 18 per cent in hell; the figures for uncertainty are just the reverse, 18 per cent uncertain about the devil and 20 per cent about hell, 2 per cent did not answer the question. Those who believe in the devil but not in hell are almost entirely women, predominantly from the small villages in the South-West, very young or elderly. The sex and location of these believers in the devil could perhaps be interpreted as a faint survival of the witch cult in the West country. The lower working class is the only group in the community having more believers in hell than in the devil.

The patterns of belief and disbelief follow those for church attendance and prayer. though the negative figures are higher in every case. Two-thirds of the men, but only one-half of the women express disbelief in these two concepts; the greatest concentration of disbelief is in the younger married men living in London or Birmingham and earning a weekly income of £12 a week or more. The believers, and those who are uncertain, are predominantly women; but whereas apart from sex, the uncertain are fairly evenly distributed throughout the community, the believers tend to come from the two Western regions, to be either under 18 or over 45, and to be poor with incomes under £8 a week.[13]

A certain number of people stated a purely metaphorical belief in the devil and hell; typical is a 28-year-old married woman from Ayrdale, Yorks, who writes· 'I believe both the devil and hell are inside each one of us; we make our own.' In contrast to this a 72-year-old widower from a small town near Rudesy, Yorks, does not believe in hell fires, but is

> absolutely certain about the existence of the devil. At the age of 18 I attended a Methodist Chapel. The preacher said there is no such things as a personal devil I went home and challenged the Almighty and he sent him and by his help I withstood him for about 5 minutes. I asked the Almighty to send him to hell. He growled like a roaring lion and departed.

Although the evidence from the past is not strictly comparable, it seems reasonable to suppose that the belief in hell, and, consequently, of possible damnation, was held by a much larger proportion of the population than the 18 per cent of today. With its virtual disappearance it could be argued that the major supernatural sanctions of Christianity have also disappeared, for, implicitly, if there is no belief in hell the concept of Judgment also becomes meaningless; and then all that is left of Christianity is a system of ethics with closer resemblance to such a system as Confucianism than to any of the major historical religions As will be developed subsequently, belief in Judgment is very uncommon even in that portion of the English population who believes in a future life.

Just on half the population—47 per cent—state that they do believe in a future life; a third—30 per cent—state that they are uncertain; a little under a quarter—22 per cent—state that they do not believe in an after-life. One per cent did not answer this question.

As in all matters of religious belief there is a very marked contrast between men and women; 39 per cent of the men and 56 per cent of the women believe in an after-life; 28 per cent of the men and 14 per cent of the women do not; 31 per cent of the men and 29 per cent of the women are uncertain. The 'uncertain' group is extremely evenly divided throughout the population, no section of it going more than 3 per cent above the national average of 30 per cent; the only groups which fall more than 3 per cent below it are the elderly (over 45) the widowed, the very poor and, slightly surprisingly, the upper middle class.

These are also the groups with the greatest amount of positive belief, belief is also relatively high in the small towns and villages and in the South-West, among the under 18's, and in the middle, lower middle and upper working classes, in comparison with the working and lower working classes. The distribution of disbelief is already familiar, highest among the younger men living in the metropolises and earning an income around £12 a week The contrast between the social classes is relatively slight, except for the comparative scarcity of non-believers in the upper middle, lower middle and upper working classes.[14]

The 47 per cent of the population who said they believed in an after-life were asked 'What do you think it will be like?' and just on half of these gave detailed answers Thirty-five per cent of the men and 45 per cent of the women predominantly those under 35, left the question unanswered, and approximately a further 10 per cent of both sexes replied that they had no idea, or didn't know. The detailed answers consequently derive only from a portion of a minority, about half of the people who believe in an after-life; but these respondents are extremely evenly divided among the total population, and follow very closely the proportions of the membership of the different denominations,[15] they can, I think, be considered a representative cross-section of the total sample population.

The views expressed on the nature of the after-life are extremely varied; in order to make any sort of tabulation possible I had to establish ten categories based on the presence or absence of certain phrases in the replies Since some people offer alternatives there is a certain amount of overlapping. There was also a small group of 4 per cent whose belief in the after-life was purely metaphorical; one survived in the memory of others, transformed into flowers and so on Typical of such views is that of a 25-year-old man from Watford:

When a body is buried, and subsequently rots, the germs, or what other matter is left, could act as a food or fertiliser in the soil, people or animals would eventually eat the 'germs', thus a likeness of the deceased person, possibly could exist in any future generation of man or animal.

The holders of this metaphorical belief appear to be mostly the middle-aged and elderly.

The ten categories into which the responses were divided are as follows.

> (i) *Scriptural Heaven and Hell and/or Purgatory.*
> (Direct references to the Bible and/or Judgment: the good rewarded, the bad punished)
> (ii) *Scriptural Heaven.*
> (References to God, Jesus, the Holy Family, but *no* reference to Judgment or punishment for the wicked.)
> (iii) *Not like Scriptural Heaven.*
> (Explicit disbelief in angels, harps, etc)
> (iv) *Beauty, Rest, Peace, etc.*
> (Stated positively; no reference to God)
> (v) *Absence of evil, pain, worry, inequality, etc.*
> (Stated negatively; no reference to God.)
> (vi) *Rejoining loved ones.*
> (vii) *Watching over loved ones*
> (viii) *Like this life*
> (ix) *Reincarnation.*
> (Implicitly or explicitly on this earth)
> (x) *Life on another planet.*

The criteria by which the believers in the after-life were placed in the first category (Scriptural Heaven and Hell) were very generously interpreted. The quoting of any Biblical verse[16] or any reference

254

to punishment for, or expiation of, sin place people in this category, even if the phrasing is far from orthodox. Thus, for example, a 17-year-old student from Morecambe, Lancs·

A paradise full of objective living people. A place where one must work off ones sins by being, for example, a guardian angel to some mortal being When one's sins are worked off one can take one's rest

Similarly a young girl from Bury St Edmunds·

When I die all the jobs I have ever neglected I will have to sit and do everything twice over with burning fires around.

Other respondents define the dogmatic position precisely and concisely. Thus, a 29-year-old married woman from Stockton-on-Tees, a Methodist, writes·

I believe in the Resurrection of the body at the worlds end and believe the good shall go on living as taught in our Creed

A 45-year-old married working class man from Walsall, a Roman Catholic:

I expect to go to purgatory to make amends for my sins in this world, when these have been made through my own prayers and the prayers of friends left on earth I expect to continue a spiritual life with our Lord

Even stretching every point, only 14 per cent of the men and 11 per cent of the women who believe in an after-life (which, it must be remembered is slightly less than half the sample) can be included in this category; they are extremely evenly divided throughout the population, except for a little concentration on the North-West, in the upper middle and upper working classes. This 6 per cent of the total population are all who profess belief in the full dogma of Christianity.

There is a further 5 per cent (11 per cent of the men and 7 per cent of the women believing in an after-life) who make reference to the Holy Family, or to angels or other figures from Revelations, without any reference to Judgment or expiation, as though heaven were automatically achieved by death. This view finds somewhat more proponents among the middle-aged and elderly, from the Midlands and North-West and from the lower middle class. It is little mentioned by members of the upper middle and lower working classes.

In this category, too, some very unorthodox views were included. Thus, a 19-year-old architectural student from Lancashire:

Heaven is a school where we can learn how to live the correct way without having the devil to annoy us. God is the headmaster and he is the example we shall have to emulate.

255

A 69-year-old unmarried middle class man from Kingston-upon-Hull:

I believe the soul to be infinite—and according to what one puts into the banking account of Divine Power the credit balance will be unlimited.

A man from Newcastle-on-Tyne:

A world possible Earth, peopled by everybody who ever lived, with no diseases or tragedy or wars, to mar what will be a paradisiacal, and sublime state of living God will live, in this world, to rule us, we shall be able to see Him, and his whole plan will be revealed to us. There will be no cold and no class distinctions apart from Holy Family which of course is only right

A 17-year-old girl student

I think it will be lovely with hosts of angels and good living people. No wrong doing at all. And I think it will be like walking on air, a thing that will never end.

A 25-year-old unmarried miner from Whitwick, Leicester:

I really have very little idea but I do give Our Lord shape and figure in my prayers so that I believe we shall all meet again in recognizable form

The only other references to specifically Christian beliefs about the after-life come from the small group (5 per cent men and 2 per cent women of those believing in an after-life) who define their beliefs negatively: 'NOT as described in Revelations' (an 18-year-old girl from East Croydon), 'NOT the Anglican conception' (an 81-year-old man from Bridlington, Yorks). These people choosing a negative definition tend to be young and to come from the small towns and villages.[17]

Slightly more than a quarter of those who believe in an after-life at all envisage an eternity of untroubled leisure. Twelve per cent of the men and 19 per cent of the women stress the positive features of this future, peace, rest, security etc.; 10 per cent of the men and 12 per cent of the women the absence of negative features, no more war, or want, or sex, or other undesirable characteristics of the present life. The positive features seem to appeal more particularly to the less prosperous members of the community, especially in the Midlands and to members of all social classes except the upper middle. The absence of negative features appeals less to members of the middle and working classes than to those of other social classes, and less to people in the Midlands than in other areas.[18]

Many of these eternal longings are of a very material nature. The following quotations are typical·

A 41-year-old married woman of West Bromwich, Staffs, 'just a decent working class family':
It will be a wonderful place with everything just right and there will be plenty of lovely food without rationing I hope.

A 25-year-old married Lincolnshire woman·
I think it will be nice and warm, friendly, no quarrelling, people just floating about in a hazy atmosphere, a rosy glow turning to blue then gold and so on.

An 18-year-old youth from Dunstable, Beds
A life at the age that you liked best, in the company of the people you liked most of all, and doing all the things you found most enjoyable on Earth.

A 17-year-old Lancashire girl:
I can imagine it to be something like a pleasant holiday we planned and never took, somewhere where we would be able to think things out and just relax.

A 38-year-old married woman from Keswick:
A place where I can study and travel, hear good conversation, be able to help other people on, no money troubles.

A 41-year-old divorced working class woman from Oldham:
Similar to life here but no sex life.

A 20-year-old girl from Skipton, Yorks·
I should think it will be slightly easier in the next life, because without our bodies we will not be troubled by carnal lusts of the flesh.

A middle class married woman from Berkhamsted:
More peaceful than the present one, with no cold, wars or washing up. I hope there will be animals music and no towns; a kind of ideal earth in heaven. I hope everyone will be able to remain at the age at which they were happiest on earth.

A young woman from Bishop's Stortford:
I believe it will be a very happy place, with no colour bars, no 'class' distinction, no intonation of speech, a place where everyone will have a job to do, no matter whether he was king or peasant in this world, a place where there will be a common language Jesus Christ and his twelve disciples will be a form of Government, there will be no opposition, for there will be nothing to oppose

257

A few of the men envisage this abstract after-life with something less than enthusiasm. Thus, a 25-year-old middle class man from West Byfleet.

Something I can hardly visualize, but approximating to the Yoga astral planes; just thought and meditation; although that seems dull to me at this moment

An unmarried working class man from East Moseley:

Not as good as the present as far as physical enjoyment is concerned, but more advanced and developed mind power as of the spirit. It remains to be seen, however.

For a further 6 per cent of the total (14 per cent of the women and 9 per cent of the men who believe in any sort of after-life) human love is stronger than death, and they envisage the after-life as rejoining their loved ones, or, in the case of 3 per cent of each sex, 'watching over' their loved ones, without any considerable precision as to where this operation takes place or the conditions of the watcher. These beliefs, understandably, appeal to the middle-aged and elderly rather than to the young, to the married and especially the widowed, rather than to the single The lower middle and upper working classes hold this belief somewhat less than the other social classes; otherwise it is very evenly divided.[19]

Most of the respondents expressed this belief fairly tersely, but a few of them elaborate. Thus, a 26-year-old married woman from a village near Hitchin:

A meeting of friends and relations, possibly as one knew them when they 'passed over', or if they were very old—to become younger about 50–60 I imagine a kind of sphere where the Spirit World still works, such as tending gardens and doing good deeds for the people left behind.

A married woman from Little Snoring, near Fakenham, Norfolk:

I was always taught as a child to believe in God even though the road through which we travel might not be smooth. This I do and hope when I draw my last fleeting breath I shall be re-united with my mother, sister and baby daughter, in the land where there is no pain.

A 65-year-old general foreman from Essex:

My personal belief is that although I shall not be seen, I shall be able to be near those I have loved in life and may be able to communicate with them sometimes as my mother often does when I am peaceful in bed. She has been gone since 1914, but has told me many things since.

A betrothed middle class girl from a small Leicestershire town:

The journey into affinity through clouds, coloured rays, beyond the stars to the celestial throne All have work guardians for mortals, helpers to the spirits of music, love, poetry, emissionaries of all the worlds virtues One does not loose the true love of one's mate on earth, Love being the greatest thing in heaven or earth.

A 45-year-old middle class married man from Birmingham:
When one passes over to the other side one is met by relatives friends etc. whom one recognizes because the spirit has a face form and not a material body The spirits are clothed in a colour The colour will depend upon the person's deeds on the earth plane. Red indicates evil deeds, blue good deeds, pale blue being the brightest and purest spirits. Spirits when they attain a certain colour are allowed if they wish to return to earth and help their loved ones

One respondent envisages some disadvantages to this reunion with loved ones. She is an unmarried middle class woman of 55 with a 93 year old mother whom she can only leave for very short periods. She writes: 'I do not think we shall know each other, as if one member of a family was missing the result would be very saddening.'

A quarter of all of those who believe in an after-life (an eighth of the population) do not appear to believe that this after-life will be eternal. Eleven per cent believe in future lives just like their present life, 2 per cent believe in life on another planet, and 11 per cent believe in reincarnation, either implicitly or explicitly on this earth.

The relative prevalence of the belief in reincarnation (explicit statements come from 252 individuals out of a population of 5,000) is perhaps the most surprising single piece of information to be derived from this research. Reincarnation is a belief of the major Asiatic religions, but it is contrary to the creeds of all the established religions of Europe and the Near East. The Theosophists imported it into Europe at the end of the last century, but they comprise a minute portion of my sample; and, apart from the Presbyterians, some members of every denomination subscribe to this belief, though many of its holders must be 'undenominational'.

There seem to be two possible sources from which the belief was diffused· firstly, films elaborating the 'When-I-was-a-king-in-Babylon-and-you-were-a-Christian-slave' type of fantasy; and secondly, the magazines on astrology and 'the occult' which appear to have quite a large circulation. And in some ways the concept of reincarnation is not incongruous with other themes in English life, the emphasis on, and the value given to, gradualness, and the strange complex of attitudes towards animals.

By and large the believers in reincarnation are very evenly distributed throughout the population; they are somewhat fewer in the upper middle and lower working classes, among the poor, the old, the widowed and those living in small towns and villages and in the South-West. All these groups however (with the exception of the lower working class) hold rather more strongly than the rest of the community a belief in future lives 'just like the present'; the upper working class, and people aged between 18 and 24 are the only other groups with relatively few members holding this belief. Members of the upper middle, upper working and lower working classes do not mention life on another planet.[20]

One of the themes or metaphors (it is not always easy to distinguish which is intended) in these descriptions of the future lives expected is continued education, with the present life compared to or equated with the sojourn in one school class.

Thus, a 43-year-old married man from S.E. London.

A question hard to answer, but believing this world to be a school for adults, I believe the next life will be in accordance to what we've learned and taught here.

A 25-year-old single upper middle class man from Falmouth, Cornwall:

Each 'soul' having various incarnations learning each time on earth some vital lesson in the pathway to perfection and having graduated the final 'After life' will be spent in 'University' studying to perfect a perfect civilization. The surroundings—unimaginable but probably earth like.

A 56-year-old married working class man from Derby.

A series of examinations, getting more like God would have us, with final perfection.

A professional soldier with his home in Warwick:

Divided into various stages where a person will have to pass through each stage, each one better than the other. A man will have to better himself accordingly.

An old man from Blackpool, Lancs.

New world with a higher standard of education.

A well educated married woman from Farnborough, aged 36:

A long long, peaceful rest first Then a looking back on the past mistakes and failures. A clear seeing of what went wrong and how. A complete knowing, then back to work again to do better.

An educated married man from Newcastle-on-Tyne:

It will be entirely one of 'thought-process' and extremely cultural. The appreciation of beauty and goodness will be the target of all 'spirits'. There will be a 'selection board' and some 'spirits' will be given a number of 'chances' before being condemned to destruction

A 30-year-old married man from Hanwell:

My spirit will enter another body (not necessarily on this planet) and carry on its education towards perfection.

A young woman from Herne Bay:

I am rather vague on this, loving life as I do I am inclined to sheer off such thoughts I'd prefer to think we're given a chance on another planet. Knowing the mistakes we made in this life we wouldn't make them in the other life. Heaven suggests peace, and tranquility—no trials and tribulations not even a breeze to disturb that peace. Am inclined to think would be rather dull

A working class married man from Marlborough:

A difficult question. I only feel this life cannot be the end of everything I regard life as being only one phase of preparation for something higher. After this life it may be that we pass on to another stage of our preparation.

A 30-year-old single man from Nelson, Colne, 'working class with a middle class outlook'.

That according to how you have lived your life whilst on earth, so you shall return to reach a certain standard either in a lower form (if under) or a higher form (if that standard has been attained) quite possibly on another planet

Another sizable group of respondents do not give any reasons for continuous rebirth except for a few who seem preoccupied with a celestial housing problem: thus. a divorced woman from Chesterfield writes·

If all the 'dead' over the ages are 'to live' there won't be much room.

And a 24-year-old working class married man from Stroud, Glos.·

I believe that the soul is immortal and that it returns to earth in another body when our present body dies. I don't believe in Heaven as an ever-lasting resting place of all souls as there couldn't possibly be room for all the souls that have passed on since the world began.

A 26-year-old married man from Clare, W Suffolk·

Certainly not 'stuffy' like the average Church life. I should think similar to this life but more nebulous

A 33-year-old 'respectable shopkeeper class' woman, from Maldon, Essex, separated:

My spirit will possibly slip into a body of the next generation, try to make all the changes I would make now if I could start again, and thereby probably make the life of the future body (hell).

261

A young miner from Durham:
Like life on this earth, but in a different form, they say that if a man leads a bad life when he does come back again he will be a woman.

A working class man from Nuneaton:
I think every one will change their sex.

A 59-year-old working class man from South Shields, Durham:
Reincarnation with similar existence on another planet or similar sphere of influence or on another plane differing from our present existence My belief based on the immortality of the something we term the soul and utilization of its future use.

Finally there are a number of respondents who carry their belief in reincarnation to the logical point of imagining human souls passing into animals; though, with one possible exception, none of these respondents suggested that animals contained souls which had previously been in human bodies. This possible exception is a 59-year-old married woman from South Devon who writes:
We come back as a bird, earth was made for us to walk and I feel the sky is for us also that is why I think we will be birds I often think this when I see a school of birds flying over.

A 31-year-old middle class married man from Brighton, Sussex:
I believe we return as something other than a human being I'd like to be a Seagull! Reasons I'm mad about gliding and What a wonderfully clean life a seagull has.

A 33-year-old middle class man from Haywards Heath, Sussex:
If one has been evil in life, they are reborn in an animal or insect state. If good, reborn in human form and in better station of life.

A young man from Dewsbury, Yorks:
You fall into space and all your old thoughts and memorys die and you come back as a new mind into a newborn child or animal.

An upper working class woman from Truro:
I think reincarnation is some form or other, not necessarily human.

A prosperous married man, 29-year-old, from Chigwell, Essex:
I think that if everyone has lived a good life, they will be some animal with daylight activities, to enjoy the sunshine and like, but if they have been bad they will be like mice and rates and other nocturnal animals, so under cover of darkness they can hide their shame and not enjoy the beauty of Gods world.

A 35-year-old 'lower class' married man from Newent, Glos.:
Well I think if a man's been cruel to an animal or some other creature I mean cruel to a great extent knowing full well he had been cruel I think he will come back and suffer like such.[21]

The immortality of the soul is not the only form of after-life with which the English are acquainted; there are also ghosts and hauntings, which are uncertainly connected with the soul or with the survival of consciousness. A sixth of the population say that they believe in ghosts, just under a quarter are uncertain and two-thirds do not, gross figures which are almost identical with the belief in the Christian conception of Hell. There are two men to three women among the believers in ghosts (13 per cent and 21 per cent); the uncertain are nearly evenly divided; the disbelievers have some 10 per cent more men than women. By and large the pattern of scepticism is much the same as we have seen for religious beliefs, the prosperous married working class men being the least believing, but there is one interesting reversal; scepticism increases steadily with age, with a greater concentration among those aged over 45; those between 18 and 34 have the greatest number of 'uncertain' replies. Since the number holding orthodox religious beliefs and following religious practices increase with age, these figures suggest that an active belief in Christianity and a belief in ghosts may be to a certain extent incompatible.

Quite a number of those who are 'uncertain' about ghosts possess acquaintances whom they believe have seen or heard a ghost—some 10 per cent of the total, evenly divided among the sexes. This modified credulity is slightly more widespread in the middle than in the working class. The people from the North-East and North, who have the fewest actual believers in ghosts, have the greatest number of uncertain respondents, and nearly as many acquaintances who have seen or heard ghosts as any other part of the country.

Somewhat unexpectedly, the greatest belief in ghosts comes from London and the South-East, followed by the Midlands. I had thought that the belief in ghosts would be most common in the West country and in the small towns and villages; in point of fact it is nearly as frequent in the metropolises as in the villages, and somewhat less frequent in the middle-sized towns. With few exceptions the belief in ghosts is remarkably evenly distributed throughout the population, there is slightly more belief among the poor, the widowed, the young, and the members of the upper middle class; apart from the regional differences, the only significant drop in belief comes from people aged between 25 and 34.

Those who believed in ghosts were asked if they themselves had seen or heard a ghost. Three hundred and fifty-one people (out of a total population of 5,000) replied in the affirmative; 189 in the negative; and 298 were uncertain. If 7 per cent of the total population are convinced that they have seen or heard a ghost, one is driven to one of two conclusions: either a sizable proportion of the population suffers from delusions or the country contains a great number of ghosts. Nothing in my data can indicate which conclusion is the more probable.

Although the numbers are small, it is interesting to note that the distribution for experience of ghosts is in many ways sharply contrasted with that for belief in ghosts. Thus, there is practically no significant difference in this respect between men and women; and the claimed experience mounts steadily with age, the big increase being over the age of 35, which is what one might expect theoretically if witnessing a ghost were a real but uncommon experience. Similarly, considerably more married people than unmarried (who are mostly younger) claim to have experienced a ghost. Although a higher proportion of members of the middle class than of the working class believe in ghosts, the proportions are reversed when experience is asked for. The most surprising reverse is on the regions; the traditionally credulous South-West and the traditionally hardheaded North-East and North have the same proportion of people claiming to have experienced a ghost, and these two regions are lower than the rest of the country, the Midlands being by a small degree the highest. Considerably more people who have experience of a ghost come from towns with less than 100,000 inhabitants than from larger ones.

Although most of the people who believe in ghosts believe in an after-life, the third of these believers who claim to have seen or heard a ghost are almost evenly divided between belief and disbelief in an after-life.[22]

Only very few respondents gave any details of their experience with ghosts—the lay-out of the questionnaire gave little space even to the most persistent writers of additional material. A married man, now living at Runcorn, Cheshire, gave the address of a house in Widnes, Lancs, which had ghosts in it while he lived there, and which were also seen by the succeeding residents; a married woman from Worcester Park, Surrey, says their house has its own resident spirit; and a retired black-coated worker from Southend-on-Sea, aged 74½ writes:

> I know definitely that a young brother of mine appeared to mother (in Brixton) at the precise moment of his death in Hong Kong. She awakened us at the time. The official news from the Colonial Office arrived four days later.

264

Ghosts are not necessarily outside established religion, as the perplexities of Hamlet well demonstrate; but there are also a number of devices for foreseeing the future or controlling the future which are quite unconnected with religion.

One of the simplest of these devices is the lucky mascot, the fetish (in the strict sense of the term) which will preserve its owner from misfortune, these are owned by 15 per cent of the population, one man in eight and one woman in five. This custom is very evenly distributed throughout the population; the very young (under 18) are much given to it, and there is some concentration among the poor, the widowed and the inhabitants of the South-West, but the only groups which fall to 12 per cent or below are the people aged between 25 and 34 and the lower middle class. There are proportionately somewhat more mascots in the upper middle and middle classes than in the upper working and working classes.[23]

During the war the carrying of mascots was a habit with a different distribution. Fourteen per cent of the total population—slightly more men than women—had a war-time mascot, since less than half the total population were in the services, this means that roughly one serving man or woman in three had his or her private piece of solid magic. The holding of wartime mascots reverses the general pattern of scepticism the concentration is among the married men aged 25 to 34. High proportions of the upper middle and lower working classes carried war-time mascots; there were a few more holders of wartime mascots among the middle than among the working class. The practice was once again lowest in the lower middle class.

The mascot which will bring good and avert bad fortune at least demands the minimum activity of acquiring and keeping the magical object; but something between a quarter and a fifth of the population believe that luck is controlled mechanically without any effort on the part of the individual beyond discerning the pattern. Twenty-four per cent of the population believe that some number or numbers are especially lucky or unlucky for them; 17 per cent that special days carry automatically good or bad fortune.

These beliefs are predominantly optimistic; 18 per cent believe in a lucky number, compared with 3 per cent believing in an unlucky one, and a further 3 per cent who discern both lucky and unlucky numbers; 9 per cent believe in a lucky day, compared with 5 per cent in an unlucky one and 3 per cent who discern both patterns. It seems reasonable to trace a connection between this relatively common belief in automatic luck and the very great prevalence of petty gambling in the English population in football pools and similar 'competitions'.

As usual, there are slightly more women than men believing in the supernatural, but the contrast is not very great; and as usual there is slightly more scepticism among the married moderately prosperous members of the working class aged between 25 and 34. There is most belief in the special qualities of days and numbers in the lower working class and in the middle class; in this respect the upper middle class is as sceptical as the lower middle and upper working classes. Fewer people from the North-East and North hold these beliefs than do those from the rest of the country.[24]

People may discover their lucky or unlucky days or numbers for themselves, or they may have them pointed out to them by professional fortune-tellers. Just on half the population (44 per cent) have consulted a fortune-teller at some time of their lives. Very few people go to a fortune-teller before they are 18, and not very many before they are 24, but apart from age, between 40 and 50 per cent of the population in every category of social class, income, region and town size have visited fortune-tellers, and only the very poor, the widowed and the divorced exceed 50 per cent. There is, however, a most striking difference in the sexes; two-thirds of the women, but only just over a quarter of the men, consult these professional prophets.[25]

Probably many people go once in their lives to a fortune-teller, 'just for a lark'; and that is the case for two-thirds of the men and a third of the women in the main sample. Approximately a fifth of the men and a quarter of the women had two consultations, the remainder—one-sixth of the men and nearly two-fifths of the women were more frequent addicts (some 7 per cent of the total population). There is little that can be said about this group except that most of its members are aged over 35; they are very evenly divided among the population.[26]

Just on half of those who consulted a fortune-teller—that is to say a fifth of the total population—consider that the predictions made came true, either in whole or in part! Seven per cent of the consultants did not answer, 11 per cent said they did not know or could not remember; only a little over a third said definitely that nothing at all came true.

The affirmative answers were categorized in three ways: a simple 'yes' without qualifications (accounting for 30 per cent of all the consultants). 'yes, some of it' (accounting for 15 per cent) and 'yes, all of it' (accounting for 2 per cent). The belief in accurate prophecy goes up with age, but is otherwise most evenly distributed throughout the population. As the figures show, it is one of the most widely held beliefs in the supernatural.[27]

Two hundred and seventy-five people—6 per cent of the total population—claim the ability to tell fortunes themselves. Three times as many women as men make this claim; but the numbers are so few that one can say little more about this prophetic group than that it tends to be aged over 45. One hundred and thirteen of them read cards, one hundred and one read tea-leaves, ninety-three read hands, and a further 53 use other devices. Where men claim to be fortune-tellers they are liable to use at least two of the techniques mentioned; women are more likely to be satisfied with a single mantic medium.[28]

Only a few respondents elaborated their claims to prophetic powers. Some claimed to be accurate palmists, or 'face-readers'; there were a few people who stated that they had prophetic dreams; a 'poor professional' married woman from Yorkshire writes that she is 'interested in Circle Seance sittings—emergence of secondary personalities in trance states. Have myself foretold things to friends (nothing very momentous), at the moment think it subconscious telepathy not the dear departed.' A 48-year-old middle class married man from Liverpool is rather like a character out of a novel by Arthur Machen; he is a member of 'a circle of magicians', has seen numerous ghosts and can tell fortunes; he considers that the afterlife will resemble Dante's Inferno; and considers his greatest fault to be 'Seeing things that I should not see'!

Of course, it is not necessary to go to the trouble to visit a fortune-teller to get a preview of the future, nearly all the Sunday papers, and many weekly magazines, with mass circulation carry a 'horoscope' feature, with forecasts for the coming period divided according to the zodiacal sign or birthday, but not further particularized.

Since the questionnaire was circulated by the *People*, I asked my respondents whether they read the prophecies of that paper's astrologer, who signs himself 'Lyndoe', regularly, occasionally, or never. Just half the respondents—41 per cent of the men and 62 per cent of the women—are regular readers; another two-fifths—45 per cent of the men and 31 per cent of the women—are occasional readers; a mere 10 per cent do not read him at all. It seems probable that much of this 10 per cent is composed of those respondents who were reached from other sources than the regular readers of the *People*; they are predominantly young, from prosperous families and more than twice as many men as women, a relatively high proportion claim upper middle class status.

If this be the case, then slightly more than half of the readers of the *People* are regular readers of the horoscope section, and the remainder occasional ones, a not improbable combination; though it is at least questionable whether the political or editorial pages have so many regular readers. Regular reading is in inverse relationship to income, with the dividing line at the family income of about £12 a week. It also tends to increase directly with age, but there are a couple of exceptions to this: there are fewer regular readers between the ages of 18 and 24 than above or below this age; and the apex of regular reading comes between 45 and 64, with over two-thirds of the people of this age, rather than with the aged. There is slightly more regular reading in the two western regions, and slightly less in the metropolises than in the smaller communities, but these are only minor variations The highest proportion of regular readers belong to the middle class, and the lowest to the upper middle and lower middle, all three working class groups being on the national average.

Since it was possible that people might feel constrained, out of a sense of politeness, to say they read the *People's* feature, they were also asked if they read the horoscope in any other paper or magazine? A quarter of the men and half the women did so regularly, half the men and two-fifths of the women did so occasionally, just on a quarter of the men, but less than a tenth of the women never did so. Something like four-fifths of the English population read more than one horoscope weekly.[29]

As with 'Lyndoe' the regular reading of second horoscopes varies quite consistently with income, the lower the income the higher the readership, and, between the ages of 25 and 64, tends to increase with age. There is most consistent reading in the middle class, followed by the working class; all the other classes read horoscopes less consistently. The most confirmed non-readers are found in the lower middle and lower working classes, and among the more prosperous.

People were asked which other papers they read their horoscopes in, but the answers were not tabulated. Among Sunday papers the *News of the World* and the *Sunday Express* figured most frequently; the most frequently mentioned magazines were *Woman*, *Woman's Own* and papers of similar title; and it was curious to note how many men at least glanced at papers specially designed for their wives.

268

People might read horoscopes for diversion, without taking them seriously, and that appears to be the case with something over half the men and a third of the women; but a sixth of the men and a little over a quarter of the women think 'there is something in horoscopes'; the remainder, around a third of the total for each sex, is uncertain. These figures for belief are slightly less than the figures for belief in the after-life but considerably greater than for belief in hell or the devil.[30]

The pattern of belief in horoscopes follows closely the pattern for the reading of horoscopes as far as income is concerned, the lower the income the greater the belief; and there is greater belief above the age of 35. Belief is lowest for people between the ages of 18 and 34, in the North-East and North (though this region has the greatest proportion of 'uncertain' answers) and in the lower middle and upper working classes. Disbelief is very high in the upper middle, lower middle and upper working classes; uncertainty is very evenly divided throughout the population; it is very high with the under 18's and low with the over 65's and the upper middle class.

Four per cent of the women and 2 per cent of the men say that they *regularly* follow the advice given in the horoscopes; a further 16 per cent of the men and 29 per cent of the women say that they do so occasionally. These figures strike me as quite astounding; one wonders if any other type of public communication is quite so influential when there is no emergency.[31]

The number who follow horoscope advice 'regularly' is so small that the figures of distribution give little guide. Most of these people seem to be under 18 or over 45 and of low income. If the 25 per cent of the population who say that they are influenced either regularly or occasionally by the advice of horoscopes are summated, one finds that there are very few categories where there is a variation of more than 3 per cent from the national norm; the under 18's and over 45's, the widowed and the lower working class have rather numerous followers of horoscope advice; people between the ages of 18 and 34, with incomes of over £12 a week and in the lower middle class have rather fewer; but only in the lower middle class and the £12–£15 income group does the total come to less than 20 per cent.

About a quarter of the population, it would seem, holds a view of the universe which can most properly be designated as magical; the future is, for them, pre-determined and knowable by various techniques which are not connected with either science or religion; for some the bad potentialities of the future can be avoided by the employment of mascots or following the advice of newspaper astrologers, and the good potentialities increased by the same devices; for others good or bad luck is mechanically connected with numbers or days of the week Such views are quite unconnected with any system of ethics, although the view of the universe is not materialist, it is mechanical (so to speak); there is practically no connection between effort and reward, transgression and punishment. It is above all passive; the future lies not in ourselves but in the stars.

It will not have escaped notice that, to a very considerable extent, those sections of the population who are most given to the magical view of the universe are also the most fervent in the practice of their religion; and those groups who are most sceptical about fortune-telling and horoscopes are also the least religious in belief or practice. The one exception to this generalization is the use of mascots during the war.

NOTES TO CHAPTER FOURTEEN

1 These figures can be usefully compared with those collected by the Research Section of Odhams Press in September 1947 from 3,019 interviews administered in 110 areas in England, Wales and Scotland to respondents over 18, even though the population (since it includes Wales and Scotland) and the categories employed are somewhat different This population divided as follows 54 per cent Church of England, 9 per cent Roman Catholic, 22 per cent Nonconformist (Methodist, Baptist, Congregationalist, etc), 7 per cent 'other' (Spiritualist, Salvation Army, etc), 8 per cent no denomination The low figure for those claiming no denomination in an interview is congruent with the hypothesis previously advanced that in face-to-face interviews English people will tend to give answers which they think will do them credit with the interviewer The high proportion of Nonconformists would seem to be explicable by the inclusion of Wales and Scotland in the sample. A poll taken by the British Institute of Public Opinion in January 1950 for the whole of Britain had the following figures Church of England, 51 per cent; Nonconformists, 15 per cent; Roman Catholics, 11 per cent, Scottish Church, 8 per cent; 'other', 6 per cent, no denomination, 9 per cent

2 Herewith a synoptic table of the percentages of the different denominations who attend religious services more than once a week and weekly

Denomination	Percentage attending more than once a week	Percentage attending once a week
Roman Catholic	19	35
Spiritualists, etc	18	20
Presbyterians	12	24
Anglican	21	12
Baptist	17	15
Congregationalist	16	16
Methodist	14	13
Small Protestant sects	18	11
'Christian'	4	10
Church of England	3	7
'Protestant'	4	5
Nonconformist	3	6
Jewish	—	4

The British Institute of Public Opinion asked a sample from the whole of Britain, 'What did you do last Sunday?' in September 1948 Fifteen per cent of those queried went to church on that Sunday, 18 per cent of the women and 12 per cent of the men As far as denomination was concerned, members of the Church of England had 11 per cent church-goers, the Nonconformists 25 per cent, the Roman Catholics 27 per cent; and the 'others' 18 per cent Apart from the high number of Nonconformists, who presumably include members of the Church of Scotland, the figures appear very close to those given above

3. The figures, discussed above, for non-attendance of church or religious services, include the 25 per cent who do not place themselves in any denomination, as well as some members of all the denominations discussed The following table gives a synoptic view of the proportions of the membership of the different denominations who visit places of worship only for weddings or funerals, or never The Anglicans and the Jews are the only groups who have no members at all in the 'never' category.

'Protestant'	41 per cent
Church of England	36 ,, ,,
'Christian'	32 ,, ,,
Small Protestant sects	32 ,, ,,
Jewish	24 ,, ,,
Presbyterian	22 ,, ,,
Methodist	18 ,, ,,
Baptist	17 ,, ,,
Nonconformist	17 ,, ,,
Congregationalist	17 ,, ,,
Roman Catholic	16 ,, ,,
Anglican	15 ,, ,,
Spiritualist	14 ,, ,,

The figures for church attendance given here can be usefully compared with those in *English Life and Leisure*, by R Seebohm Rowntree and G R Lavers (London Longmans, 1951), Chapter XIII Only two communities, York and High Wycombe, were studied by these investigators, but the picture is very similar.

In the poll taken by Odhams Press, referred to in note 1, the church-going habits of men and women were tabulated separately. The figures, which are considerably higher than those from my anonymous questionnaires or Rowntree and Lavers' actual count of people present, suggest that once again the tendency of interviewees to present themselves in the most favourable light is operative, the actual figures are·

	Men (44 per cent)	Women (56 per cent)
Visit church weekly	11 per cent	18 per cent
Every 2–3 weeks	6 ,, ,,	10 ,, ,,
4–8 weeks	12 ,, ,,	16 ,, ,,
Less frequently	15 ,, ,,	12 ,, ,,

This survey only distinguished three denominations, Church of England, Roman Catholic, and Nonconformist, all other denominations were grouped as 'other'. The figures for attendance by denomination are

	C of E.	R C	Nonconformist	Other
Visit church weekly	8	52	14	33
Every 2 or 3 weeks	7	9	8	6
4–8 weeks	16	9	18	11
Less often	17	9	13	9

These figures imply that 52 per cent of those calling themselves Church of England, 21 per cent of those calling themselves Roman Catholic, and 47 per cent of those calling themselves Nonconformists are not church-goers.

271

4 See under p 266.

5 The following is a synoptic table of the percentages of the members of the different sects who say prayers daily or more frequently The highest proportion of those saying prayers more frequently than once a day are the Spiritualists (32 per cent), the Roman Catholics (28 per cent), the small Protestant sects (24 per cent), the 'Christians' (18 per cent), the Anglicans (17 per cent) Church of England has 9 per cent

Spiritualists	75 per cent
Roman Catholics	67 ,, ,,
Small Protestant sects	65 ,, ,,
Anglicans	63 ,, ,,
Congregationalists	60 ,, ,,
Baptists	53 ,, ,,
'Christian'	51 ,, ,,
'Protestant'	51 ,, ,,
Methodist	49 ,, ,,
Church of England	45 ,, ,,
Nonconformists	44 ,, ,,
Presbyterians	29 ,, ,,
Jewish	20 ,, ,,

Only the very small groups of Presbyterians and Jews have more than 10 per cent of their members who 'never' say prayers, though every denomination has some non-prayers, even the elective religions like Spiritualists Here follows a synoptic table of those who claim membership of some denomination but say prayers 'very seldom' or 'never', given in percentages of membership of the denomination.

Presbyterian	64 per cent
Jewish	64 ,, ,,
Nonconformist	49 ,, ,,
Church of England	40 ,, ,,
Methodist	39 ,, ,,
'Christian'	35 ,, ,,
Baptist	35 ,, ,,
Anglican	31 ,, ,,
'Protestant'	29 ,, ,,
Congregationalists	28 ,, ,,
Small Protestant sects	27 ,, ,,
Roman Catholics	26 ,, ,,
Spiritualists	17 ,, ,,

In reading these tables it should be remembered that the numbers of Jews, Presbyterians and Anglicans are very small, so that the answers of very few individuals produce very high percentages

In January 1950, the British Institute of Public Opinion asked a sample from the whole of Britain 'Apart from children, does anyone in your home pray regularly?' and analysed the answers according to the denominations

Denomination	Yes	No	Don't know
Church of England	48	41	11
Nonconformists	43	38	14
Roman Catholics	68	24	8
'Other'	46	41	13

6 The pages which follow on the religious education of children are based on the answers given by parents of living children only, as in Chapters Eleven and Twelve

7. Fifty-seven per cent of members of the Church of England send or sent their children to Sunday School. Sixty-nine per cent of the Methodists do so, and even

greater percentages of the Baptists, Congregationalists, Nonconformists, and the small Protestant sects Only a third of the Roman Catholics and Anglicans send their children, though this figure may be due to a very literal interpretation of the question

8 Questions asked about children's attendance at church or religious services either by themselves or in company of their parents were too ambiguously phrased to be worth analysis

9 The Nonconformists, the Presbyterians, the Baptists and the members of the small Protestant sects are particularly zealous in teaching their children to pray, but this is an area where the differences between the denominations are relatively slight. There is only a difference of 5 per cent between the Roman Catholics (67 per cent) and the members of the Church of England (62 per cent)

10 The denominations with the greatest proportion of parents teaching their children to say morning prayers are the Roman Catholics, Anglicans, small Protestant sects and Nonconformists, but because of the size of its congregation the greatest numbers would be found in the Church of England, 8 per cent of whose members teach their children to say morning prayers (Roman Catholic 32 per cent)

11 Members of the small Protestant sects, the Congregationalists, the Anglicans, the 'Christians', and to a lesser extent the Baptists and Methodists, teach grace before meals rather than after The 'Protestants', the Nonconformists, and to a certain extent the members of the Church of England, tend to favour grace after meals Proportionately, Roman Catholics, Jews, small Protestant sects, Presbyterians and Congregationalists have the largest number of their members teaching the saying of grace (between 40 and 30 per cent), in the Church of England 16 per cent of the parents teach grace before, 19 per cent after, meals.

12 St Matthew Chapters IV, 1, 11; IX, 32; XV, 22, XVII, 18; XXV, 41 St Mark· Chapters V, 15, VII, 29 St Luke Chapters IV, 2 and 23; VIII, 12 and 29, XI, 14. St. John Chapters VI, 70, VII, 20; VIII, 44, XIII, 2 References to Satan occur in St Matthew, IV, 10, XII, 26, XVI, 23 St Mark, IV, 15, St Luke, X, 18, XIII, 16; XXII, 22, 23, 31, St. John, XII, 31; XIII, 27, XIV, 30, XVI, 11

13. As far as the members of the different denominations are concerned, belief in hell and belief in the devil parallel one another very closely, belief in the devil having some 2 per cent more in each case In the case of three sects only (the Anglicans, the Baptists, and the small Protestant sects) there is slightly more uncertainty about hell than there is about the devil; in the case of the Spiritualists this is reversed

The following is a synoptic table of belief, uncertainty, or disbelief in Hell, according to denomination·

Denomination	Believe	Percentage Uncertain	Disbelieve
Anglican	25	42	31
Methodist	21	27	50
Church of England	21	19	59
'Christian'	21	16	60
Jewish	20	—	80
Nonconformist	19	24	55
'Protestant'	19	18	61
Baptist	18	43	36
Congregationalist	16	17	66
Roman Catholic	15	58	25
Presbyterian	12	23	65
Small Protestant sects	11	35	53
Spiritualists	3	10	83

There were 1 or 2 per cent non-answerers for most denominations.

14 Herewith a synoptic table of the percentages of each denomination believing in, uncertain about, or not believing in, an after-life

Denomination	Believe	Percentage. Uncertain	Disbelieve
Spiritualists	90	6	1
Anglicans	70	17	10
Baptists	71	17	11
Congregationalists	68	18	13
Presbyterians	65	11	24
Small Protestant sects	62	27	9
Roman Catholic	62	22	14
'Christian'	59	26	14
Methodists	55	29	13
Nonconformists	53	35	10
'Protestant'	49	27	21
Church of England	46	33	20
Jewish	32	28	40

In most denominations there were 1 or 2 per cent who did not answer

In December 1947, the British Institute of Public Opinion asked a sample from the whole of Britain 'Do you believe in a life after death?' Forty-nine per cent replied 'Yes', 33 per cent 'No'; and 18 per cent had no opinion The beliefs of the sexes contrast quite markedly 43 per cent of the men and 55 per cent of the women expressed belief in a life after death, 38 per cent of the men and 28 per cent of the women did not believe in an after-life

15 The following synoptic table gives the percentages of the members of the different denominations who either wrote that they 'don't know' or 'have no idea' about the nature of the after-life, or just left the question unanswered This table should be compared with those in footnotes in the following pages of the members of each denomination subscribing to the various beliefs in the after-life It should be recalled that only 75 per cent of the population considers itself a member of a denomination, quite a number of the believers in an after-life are consequently excluded from these tabulations

Denomination	Don't know	Percentage writing No idea	No answer
Jewish	40	8	28
Church of England	35	5	20
Nonconformists	30	3	18
'Christian'	29	6	13
Presbyterian	28	12	6
'Protestant'	27	8	20
Roman Catholic	27	5	13
Methodists	24	4	20
Small Protestant sects	24	3	14
Baptists	19	6	10
Congregationalists	17	5	15
Anglican	8	6	21
Spiritualists	4	2	3

16 The two verses most frequently quoted were 'In my Father's House are many mansions'; and 'Eye hath not seen nor ear heard, neither doth it enter into the heart of man the things God hath prepared for those who love him '

17 The following is a synoptic table of the percentages of the members of different denominations, who profess belief in Heaven and Hell, in Heaven only, and who reject the conventional descriptions

274

Denomination	Percentage believing in		
	Heaven and Hell	Heaven only	Not conventional Heaven
Roman Catholic	17	7	1
Anglican	15	8	6
Small Protestant sects	15	13	2
Baptists	10	10	—
Congregationalists	10	6	2
Spiritualists	10	6	3
Methodists	7	6	2
'Protestant'	6	5	2
'Christian'	6	2	2
Church of England	5	4	1
Jewish	4	—	—
Nonconformist	3	6	2
Presbyterian	—	6	12

18. The following is a synoptic table of the percentages of members of different denominations envisaging a future life of positive pleasant features or without negative unpleasant features

Denomination	Percentage	
	Positive features present	Negative features absent
Presbyterian	18	6
'Christian'	14	9
Congregationalists	13	6
Roman Catholics	12	5
Spiritualists	11	13
Small Protestant sects	9	3
Nonconformists	8	11
Baptists	8	10
Jewish	8	4
Church of England	7	4
Methodists	7	7
'Protestant'	6	5
Anglicans	4	12

19 Twenty-five per cent of the Spiritualists envisage rejoining their loved ones; all the other denominations have between 6 and 8 per cent of their members believing this, except the Church of England (5 per cent) and the 'Christians', 'Protestants', Methodists and Jews who have 3 or 4 per cent

Eleven per cent of the Baptists envisage 'watching over' their loved ones; the Congregationalists, Presbyterians, Methodists and Anglicans have 6 or 7 per cent, all the remaining denominations have 3 or 4 per cent, save the Roman Catholics, with 2 per cent, and the Jews, none of whom hold this belief.

20 Herewith a synoptic table of the percentage of members of the different denominations holding this belief:

Denomination	Percentage believing in:		
	Like this life	Reincarnation	Other planet
Spiritualists	25	2	9
Anglicans	8	2	2
Baptists	7	4	1
Congregationalists	7	3	3
Small Protestant sects	7	4	—
Nonconformists	6	5	—
Roman Catholics	6	2	1

Denomination	Like this life	Percentage believing in Reincarnation	Other planet
Presbyterians	6	1	—
Church of England	5	6	1
Methodists	4	6	1
Jewish	4	—	—
'Christian'	3	6	—
'Protestant'	3	5	1

21 The British Institute of Public Opinion in December 1947 asked the 49 per cent of their respondents who said they believed in a life after death (see note 14) 'What will it be like?' Thirteen per cent said they did not know, and 2 per cent of the answers were treated as 'miscellaneous', the ideas of the remainder were

Spiritual form—spirit does not die	19 per cent
Heaven and hell according to life on earth	4 ,, ,,
Reincarnation	3 ,, ,,
Paradise	3 ,, ,,
Higher plane	2 , ,,
Similar to life on earth	2 , ,
Same as now	1 ,,

22 The number of people claiming to have seen or heard a ghost are so few that their distribution among the different denominations can only be suggestive No Presbyterians claim this experience nor do any Nonconformists, and very few of the Methodists, Roman Catholics, Anglicans, or Jews Apart from the Spiritualists, the highest proportions are found among the 'Christians', 'Protestants', Church of England and Baptists A considerable proportion of those seeing or hearing ghosts are not members of any denomination

In April 1950 the British Institute of Public Opinion asked a sample from the whole of Britain 'Do you believe in ghosts?' Eight per cent of the men and 12 per cent of the women replied in the affirmative, 84 per cent of the men and 75 per cent of the women in the negative, the remainder said they did not know Two per cent of the men and 3 per cent of the women said they had seen a ghost

23 In the field survey, the percentage holding lucky mascots is slightly lower, 12 per cent, and in this sample there is much less difference between the sexes. The poor, the young (under 24), the upper middle and the lower working classes are the greatest holders of mascots, with the lower middle class again having the lowest percentage The main difference between the replies of this group and the main sample —apart from sex—is in the regions, the two Northern regions have far fewer mascot-holders than the rest of the country

24 In the field survey there is the same proportion (9 per cent) believing in lucky days and, rather surprisingly, a rather higher percentage (7 per cent) believing in unlucky days The sexes are evenly divided There is the same marked regional contrast as was found in the case of mascots (see note 23); otherwise the distribution is very similar.

25 In the field survey the total numbers consulting fortune-tellers were quite considerably less—28 per cent in all, 14 per cent men and 40 per cent women The distribution is very similar to that of the main sample

26 The distribution of visits is very similar in the field sample to the main sample The following are the proportions of each sex visiting a fortune-teller once, twice, or more frequently, the proportions for the main sample are in brackets and italics

	Percentage of men	Percentage of women
Visit once	70 (64)	45 (35)
Visit twice	13 (19)	23 (26)
More frequently	14 (17)	28 (38)

276

27 The distribution of belief is very similar in the field survey The figures give the percentages of those consulting fortune tellers who report the different results to the question 'Did any of it come true?', percentages from the main survey in brackets and italics

Yes 29 (30), Yes, all of it 3 (2); Yes, some of it 14 (15), No, nothing 43 (35); Don't know: 11 (11), 7 per cent of the main sample, but none of the field sample, left the question unanswered

28 In the field survey, 2 per cent of the men and 3 per cent of the women claimed the ability to tell fortunes; but they were very unwilling to tell the lady interviewers what techniques they used

In March 1951 the British Institute of Public Opinion asked 'Do you believe in telling the future by . . ?' various techniques Eighty per cent of the population (88 per cent of the men and 70 per cent of the women) expressed no belief in any of the techniques named, but 'horoscopes' were not, it appears, included as such Four per cent of the men and 11 per cent of the women thought the future could be foretold by cards, 2 per cent of the men and 12 per cent of the women by palmistry, 4 per cent of the men and 10 per cent of the women by stars; 1 per cent of the men and 11 per cent of the women by tea-leaves, and 3 per cent of the women by phrenology Other (unidentified) techniques were named by 2 per cent of the men and 3 per cent of the women

29. The figures from the field survey are strictly comparable Interviewees were asked 'Do you read the horoscope in a newspaper or magazine?' without any astrologer being named Since men and women differ quite markedly in this practice the percentages will be given by sexes In brackets and italics are the percentages of the main sample reading horoscopes in 'any other paper or magazine'.

	Percentage of men	Percentage of women
Read regularly	30 (25)	53 (48)
Read occasionally	30 (49)	28 (39)
Never read	40 (23)	19 (9)
No answer	— (2)	0 (4)

Except for an odd concentration of 'regular' readers in the Midlands, the figures of distribution for the field survey and main sample are very similar.

30. There is slightly less credulity, but considerably more refusal to answer, from the field survey As previously, the answers are given by the sex of the respondents to the question 'Do you think there is something in horoscopes?', the answers from the main survey being in brackets and italics

	Percentage of men	Percentage of women
Yes	12 (15)	21 (27)
Uncertain	13 (29)	16 (37)
No	63 (53)	58 (33)
No answer	12 (2)	5 (3)

31. The figures from the field survey are not quite comparable because they are only derived from that portion of the interviewed sample who said that they read horoscopes, 71 per cent of the total For an exact comparison, the field survey percentages could be reduced by seven-tenths, but the pattern is very similar. The figures for the main sample, in brackets and italics, refer to the percentages of the total population, whether they read horoscopes or not. The question was 'Do you follow advice in the horoscope columns you read?'

	Percentage of men	Percentage of women
Regularly	3 (2)	5 (4)
Occasionally	15 (16)	20 (29)
Never	78 (75)	74 (63)
No answer	4 (6)	1 (4)

CHAPTER FIFTEEN

TO SEE OURSELVES

WHEN ENGLISH PEOPLE sit in judgment on their own characters over half name bad temper as a major defect, and over three-quarters consider that their chief quality is consideration for others Both these terms cover a number of near synonyms· bad temper, for example, includes nagging, taking offence quickly, enjoying rows, surliness and similar traits; consideration for others includes understanding, sympathy, seeing the other fellow's point of view, tolerance (a word much favoured by the working class with a general connotation of permissiveness, but without political or ethnic overtones), friendliness and so on I think an impartial observer would consider that these self-ascriptions are justified; and they can hardly have come as a surprise to the readers of the foregoing chapters

Fairly early in the questionnaire I placed the questions 'What do you consider your three best qualities?' and 'What do you consider your three worst faults?' chiefly because I thought people would enjoy answering them, and would go on to the rest of the questionnaire with greater zest. I think the questions were enjoyed, they were certainly answered with fullness and frankness. It is an interesting side-light on English character that, although 6 per cent of the population did not answer the question about their good qualities, only 3 per cent were silent about their faults. The old (over 65) and the poor were the most likely to leave both questions unanswered; young women were particularly diffident about naming their good qualities.

People were astoundingly frank in their confession of faults. Respondents accused themselves of bigamy, stealing, receiving stolen goods, lying and technical perjury, homosexuality, fetishism, sadism, masturbation[1] (in a considerable number of cases), domestic cruelty or callousness, and even, in one case, 'at times a feeling to hurt some animal (then repentance)'. Obviously every effort was made by nearly all respondents to be as truthful and co-operative as possible.

The difficulty about dealing with these answers was a mechanical one. There is a fairly easily reached technical limit to the number of categories which can go on to an I.B.M. card, or which the girl 'editors' can carry in their heads when marking the questionnaires before the cards are punched. My respondents gave such an enor-

278

mous list of qualities and faults—especially faults—that some overall categories had to be devised. Unfortunately I did not perform this job very well; I have a number of categories which include too few respondents, and a few which include too many.

The categories with very few respondents can be dealt with very summarily. Less than 1 per cent of the population pride themselves on their ambition or on their Christian principles or religious devoutness; only 3 per cent define their virtues negatively (that they don't sulk, are not jealous, are unaffected and so on), only 4 per cent claim their financial integrity or economy as a good quality. As far as faults are concerned only 1 per cent accuse themselves of cowardice, of financial meanness or inadequacy (as will be seen, quite a number accuse themselves of extravagance), or of gluttony. A similar small group, with what seems to me admirable clear-sightedness, lists prejudice against Americans, coloured people, Jews or foreigners as faults. Three per cent accuse themselves of drinking too much, the same number accuse themselves of sexual faults (unfaithfulness, over-preoccupation with sex, as well as perversions); and a further 3 per cent reproach themselves for not loving or appreciating their spouses, parents or children sufficiently.

About a third of the good qualities claimed are lumped together under two rather vague over-all labels: Qualities of Character, by which I intended to signify 'innate' or 'natural' characteristics such as tidiness, good memory, good physique, industriousness, punctuality, and similar desirable traits, and Moral Qualities, by which I intended to signify what the religious call virtues—straightforwardness, simplicity, loyalty, truthfulness, reliability, conscientiousness and the like. Nearly everybody lays claim to possessing one or another of the traits subsumed under these two rubrics, and few claim more than one; but the categories are so wide that little can be deduced from their distribution.

The remaining good qualities are sufficiently concrete. Twenty-two per cent of the population pride themselves on their good temper, their sportsmanship and similar phrases. Fourteen per cent mention their optimism, the fact that they are always cheerful, always look on the bright side of things. Thirteen per cent, overwhelmingly the young from the poorer families, mention quite concrete skills, being a good cook, a good dancer, a good athlete etc. Eleven per cent mention their love of their own family, parents, spouse or children, or just generally 'home life'; 8 per cent name love of the weak, typically children, animals and old people in that order, though sometimes one or another may be omitted; and 6 per cent

279

mention their financial integrity—their honesty, thrift, economy and
so on.

The picture which the English draw of their own good qualities
is remarkably consistent through the different categories of region,
town size, age, income and social class. The single lay considerably
more claim to optimism than the married (20 per cent and 12 per cent
respectively); the married, on the other hand, emphasize their love
for their own family much more than the single (14 per cent against
3 per cent). The greatest consistent difference is between the views
of men and women on their own character, and these differences are
in quantity, rather than rank order. The following table lists the
percentage of men and women claiming the different good qualities,
since three qualities were asked for the base line would be 300 per
cent; but I have omitted from this tabulation those qualities which
are claimed by less than 5 per cent of the total population, and also
those who didn't answer.

Quality	Percentage of men	Percentage of women
Consideration for others, understanding	73	80
Moral qualities	59	47
Qualities of character	55	42
Good temper, sportsmanship	25	20
Optimism	11	18
Concrete skills	10	15
Love of own family	10	12
Love of the weak	6	10
Financial integrity	6	4

The blanket categories used to describe faults are not quite so
unsatisfactory as those used to lump together good qualities, for
they do seem to me to be idiosyncratic and revealing. There does
seem to be an English tendency to describe one's faults indirectly
by reference to good or desirable traits, to say that one has either
not enough of, or too much of, a quality which would be desirable
if it were present in the optimum which is by implication less than
the maximum. Thus, people blame themselves for being too self-
confident or not self-confident enough ('inferiority complex'), too
independent and not strong willed; too meek and not forgiving; too
trusting and not trusting enough; too tidy and too untidy; and so on
through a considerable number of reciprocals. I am inclined to
think that this concept of good qualities having an optimum, and
turning into faults if there is present either too little or too much is
specifically English; it is congruent with the high value given to
moderation in other contexts.

The negative definition, what I have dubbed the Absence of Good Traits, is much the more common, being favoured by nearly half the population, the Excess of Good Traits is used by about half that number. Not all the qualities listed as 'too little' or 'too much' have reciprocals; people reproach themselves for not being observant enough, having no sense of humour, no concentration, no ability to plan, neglecting religion, or, on the other hand, with being too idealistic, too dogmatic, too sensitive, too frank, without these qualities appearing on more than one of the lists. But, it would seem, it is only the exceptional trait which can be overdone in only one direction.

There are two other blanket terms which apply in both cases to nearly a quarter of the population. I used 'social faults' for all the habits which tend to make other people dislike one—argumentativeness, snobbishness, rudeness, abruptness, sarcasm, and 'moral faults' for a straightforward naming of qualities generally condemned on religious or ethical grounds—vanity, pride, deceitfulness, revengefulness, suspicion, selfishness, lying, stealing and so forth.

The remaining faults are more specific. Nearly a fifth of the population blame themselves for procrastination, putting things off, dilly-dallying. Thirteen per cent blame themselves for shyness or one of its numerous synonyms, a phrase frequently used being 'backward in coming forward'; and the same number reproach themselves for financial extravagance, either as over-spending, or as being unable to save, or as gambling. A tenth of the population accuse themselves of what I have called 'compulsive traits', borrowing a phrase from clinical psychiatry; these are the people who consider themselves too exact, too thorough, too methodical, always worrying or fidgeting, too conscientious or over-cautious, excessively methodical. Half this number describe themselves as depressed or moody; with the 3 per cent who are nail-biters this gives nearly a fifth of the population who ascribe to themselves symptoms which a psychiatrist would unhesitatingly consider neurotic, a remarkably high proportion one would imagine. The remaining faults all have between 8 and 5 per cent of the population listing them. Smoking is the only one of the physical self-indulgences in this list. Domineering, with its synonyms of bossiness, always wanting one's own way, taking advantage of others, obstinacy (stubbornness, pigheadedness), and sluggishness (sloth, late rising, being too fond of bed) complete the dismal list.

With the faults, as with the qualities, the most marked differences lie between men and women, though the other distributions are

281

slightly less even than in the case of good qualities The following list shows the percentages of men and women admitting to the different types of faults, except for those with very small numbers.

Fault	Percentage of men	Percentage of women
Bad temper	45	60
Absence of good traits	50	42
Excess of good traits	19	31
Social faults	28	19
Moral faults	20	18
Procrastination	17	18
Shyness	15	10
Financial extravagance	14	11
Compulsive traits	8	15
Domineering	5	8
Smoking	10	4
Obstinacy	6	8
Sluggishness	6	7
Depression	4	6
Nail-biting	3	2

As can be seen English men present themselves as lacking in good traits, as being socially 'awkward' and shy much more than women, and also as smoking too much; English women stress their bad temper (nagging), their excess of good traits, and their compulsiveness much more than do men. Marriage seems to increase the feminine faults of bad temper (an increase of 11 per cent) and compulsiveness (an increase of 5 per cent), the unmarried are more conscious of their moral faults (an increase of 8 per cent) and of their shyness (an increase of 5 per cent).

The compulsive traits increase not only with marriage but with age; they are rare under 24, and then mount slowly as the people get older. There is a slight decrease as income rises They are markedly characteristics of the middle and lower middle classes. Nail-biting is chiefly a trait of the young; and depression or moodiness is very evenly distributed Nearly a quarter of the women in the sample, especially from the middle and lower middle classes, blame themselves for having traits which most people would consider neurotic symptoms; barely a seventh of the men are in a similar case.[2]

Some of the faults seem to be, as it were, the specialities of different age grades or special classes. Only in one instance is there a marked regional difference; a considerable number of people in the North-West reproach themselves for procrastination, which is not a marked failing in either the North-East and North or the South-West.

Moral faults are particularly named by the young, under 24, by

282

members of the upper middle class, and by people with a family income of £12–£15; it seems possible that this is a semantic point, and that the students, who must comprise most of these groups, use the precise and positive terms, whereas most of the population use periphrases The upper middle class rate themselves highly for procrastination, but low for sluggishness or shyness.

The lower middle class emphasize their absence of good traits, but name few moral faults; the upper working class their excess of good traits and their bad temper; the working class, compared with the middle class, stress their absence of good traits and their sluggishness; the lower working class stress their excess of good traits, and do not reproach themselves for sluggishness.

The very young, under 18, stress their shyness, their procrastination and their sluggishness; few of them mention their temper or their extravagance. The elderly, over 65, do not think they are shy or procrastinating, but otherwise they present much the same picture of themselves as do their potential grandchildren. The middle aged, between 45 and 64, stress most heavily their excess of good traits, and make little mention of their moral faults; they also do not consider themselves procrastinators

If one takes the ecclesiastical category of the seven deadly sins, and applies them to these self-evaluations, an interesting and revealing pattern emerges. Practically none of the English accuse themselves of gluttony; and if one thinks of the typical English cooking and English attitude to food, this seems in accordance with facts. The self-reproaches about excessive drinking or smoking seem to be based on financial grounds, or the bad effect of drink on character ('I drink because I get lonely—and become detestable when I've had too much', or 'Disagreable when one over the 8'), rather than on excessive self-indulgence; but even if these are reckoned with gluttony, it only touches a tenth of the population.

Similarly, avarice is not a vice with which English people reproach themselves, and again one would think with reason. Apart from pathological misers, avarice would seem to be the besetting sin of some peasant populations (traditionally the French and German peasants are given to hoarding) rather than of predominantly urban populations such as the English. Extravagance might perhaps be considered the opposite face of avarice, treating money and its potentialities in an irrational and irresponsible fashion, and this fault does bulk relatively more importantly; perhaps one-seventh of the population could be accused of avarice or its converse.

283

Only 3 per cent admit to lust, in any form; and this seems congruent with most of the material in the previous chapters, where ignorance of, or distaste for, sex seems a greater hazard to individual and marital happiness, rather than an excessive preoccupation with this activity

Unfortunately, I did not give pride a separate rubric; it makes up quite a considerable portion of the 'moral faults' with which a fifth of the population reproach themselves, but by no means the total; if one takes the various accusations of snobbishness, on the one hand, and of undesirable behaviour by neighbours on the other, as further evidence, one might conclude that pride is a major sin of between a fifth and a sixth of the English, pride chiefly shown in the context of social class.

The two deadly sins of which sizable proportions of the English population are conscious and with which they reproach themselves are sloth and anger. Counting both procrastination and sluggishness as aspects of sloth, a quarter of the population acknowledge this failing; and it would probably be agreed to by most of the people who in recent years have been comparing the working habits of the Englishman with his American, German or Japanese opposite number

Anger, chiefly in its manifestations of nagging, bad temper and surliness, is a self-reproach of over half the English population; if one were to add domineering and obstinacy as at least in part manifestations of anger, the total figure would rise to two-thirds. It remains to be discussed whether there is in fact a great deal of anger among the English, or whether there is so much self-conscious-ness about the expression of anger, that even minor outbursts are noted with self-condemnation.

What is remarkable in this list is that the sin of envy is completely excluded. This is not due to the employment of faulty categories, for I started with the presumption that envy was a major characteristic of many English people, and I was constantly alert to any reference to this, but there were only a couple of respondents in the whole 11,000 who put their envy into words, both of them young men: 'Envious of richer people than myself', 'Jealousness of other people with money and good luck' The conclusion seems inescapable that either the envy is not recognized, that it is unconscious, or that it is not regarded as a sin or fault. I do not think that it could be denied that in the political appeals and actions of the last decade envy has played a major rôle; that in the policy of 'fair shares for all' the desire to see that nobody has more has been at least as important as seeing that nobody has less. Perhaps envy has received so much justification that it is no longer felt to be a sin, but is regarded as an aspect of a desire for justice. A possible parallel could be found with contemporary American urban youth, for the majority of whom, I would suspect, lust is no longer a sin, but rather a manifestation of 'psychological health' and 'good adjustment'. If this be the case, the remarkable self-knowledge, self-criticism and honesty of the English, which I think this study has demonstrated, has a blind spot.

The canonical virtues of the English are less easily determined by my material. Faith, as we have seen is low, except for a minority —perhaps a sixth of the population. More people consider themselves optimists than consider themselves depressed or moody, but the numbers in both cases are small, and I doubt whether hope should be considered an English characteristic. But three-quarters of the population consider themselves understanding, considerate of others, what Mr Knightley called 'English delicacy towards the feelings of other people', and this, I think, can be considered a good part of Charity; and the very widespread acceptance of the principles of the 'welfare state', however much grumbling there may be about the means involved in achieving it, bears out the same contention on a more material level.

Of the cardinal virtues, the English are certainly temperate, though this would appear to be to a very considerable extent a development of the last thirty years or so. In the limited meaning of temperance one cannot escape the suspicion that the very high imposts on alcoholic drinks have had a greater influence on national sobriety than a change in the national character. In the more general meaning of the term, I rather feel that the great moderation in the indulgence of fleshly pleasures (which is certainly documented) comes less from the conscious control of strong appetites than from the appetites being (at least on the conscious level) extremely moderate.

Prudence? I very much doubt if it is now a national virtue. Some 10 per cent of the population pride themselves on their financial integrity, on their economy and freedom from debt; it is a somewhat smaller group than those who reproach themselves for their extravagance. In the nineteenth century, it would appear, prudence was the great characteristic of the English middle class, and the basis for Britain's spectacular economic development. In that century, and for those classes, living on capital was almost the greatest sin in the calendar; today it is a principle of national policy.

The history of the last 15 years shows beyond cavil that fortitude is a characteristic of the great majority of the English; but I should

285

be very hard put to demonstrate this from my material. An occasional comment about the representativeness of the police, a very rare self-description ('Will assist anyone in a fight if they are outnumbered and losing very badly This is done on the spur of the moment not premeditated. If I see anyone badly hurt I take his part without stopping to think why I'm doing it': a 23-year-old bachelor from Gillingham) would be all the evidence I could muster. The English are as silent about their courage and endurance as they are about envy, and I think for very similar reasons; just as they do not appear to count envy a sin, so they do not appear to count fortitude a virtue. Modesty may play some part in this reticence. but I do not think it is great; rather, I suspect, it is considered by most a national characteristic, in which individuals vary very little; when they are describing their own qualities (or defects) they do not mention the courage in which they think they do not differ from their compatriots.

The virtue most consciously and continuously manifested by the English is, I would say, undoubtedly justice. I think there is a lot of inferential evidence for this—the consensus of attitudes towards the police, the attitudes towards premarital sexuality, even many of the unconventional beliefs about the after-life carry the same underlying value.

What psychological hypotheses can unify these apparently contradictory traits, customs and attitudes which the previous chapters have documented? In this exploration of English character we have charted some of the features in this strange, yet familiar, country; now it remains to try to bring them together into the equivalent of a map.

I would make the assumption that fundamentally English character has changed very little in the last 150 years, and possibly longer; that the Roaring Boys and the Boys' Brigade, the ardent bull-baiters and the ardent anti-vivisectionists, the romantically criminal mobs and the prosaically law-abiding queues are made up of people of the same basic type of character. Underlying the enormous superficial changes, I believe that there is a basic historical continuity.

The superficial changes are enormous, of that there is no doubt. One of the most lawless populations in the world has turned into one of the most law-abiding, a society which uninhibitedly enjoyed public floggings and public executions, dog-fights and animal baiting has turned into an excessively humanitarian, even squeamish, society; a fiercely and ruthlessly acquisitive society has turned into a mildly distributive society; general corruption in government has been

286

replaced by an extraordinarily high level of honesty. What seems to have remained constant is a great resentment at being overlooked or controlled, a love of freedom, fortitude; a low interest in sexual activity, compared with most of the neighbouring societies; a strong belief in the value of education for the formation of character; consideration and delicacy for the feelings of other people; and a very strong attachment to marriage and the institution of the family.

The reversals can, I think, all be accounted for on one principle. Up till a century ago the English were openly aggressive (John Bull, in fact) and took pleasure and pride in their truculence, their readiness to fight and to endure, and, by a simple process of partial identification, in 'game' animals which would fight, in 'game' criminals who finished a slashing career fittingly on the public gallows, and in the comical spectacles afforded by the physical mishaps and pains of others There was little or no guilt about the expression of aggression in the appropriate situations; and there was no doubt, except in odd and rather comical cases, that every English man and woman had sufficient aggression for every possible event, there was always more potential strength than could be used, unless one had 'one's back to the wall'.

Today, unless 'one's back is to the wall', almost any overt expression of aggression is fused with guilt. Nearly all the amusements of our fore-fathers would provoke the greatest indignation; all visible suffering which cannot be avoided must be hidden; any form of childish aggressive behaviour is watched for and punished; and when we think of our faults we put first, and by a long way, any lapses from our standards of non-aggression, bad temper, nagging, swearing and the like. Public life is more gentle than that reported for any other society of comparable size and industrial complexity.

But I do not think the aggression has disappeared, nor even much diminished in potentiality. It is very severely controlled, so that it rarely appears in overt or public behaviour. It sometimes breaks out pathologically in the methodical murders, the excessive cruelty to children or animals, accounts of which, when prosecuted and punished, form, significantly enough, the favourite Sunday reading of about half the English population.

An analogy which I think may be suggestive can be provided by the front door of a house. Inside the house, which is the analogue of the unconscious, is a very strong and potentially destructive force, pushing against the door through which, if it could emerge, it would wreak its will and seek its pleasure. But it can never, or hardly ever,

287

emerge, for a man, the analogue of the conscience or super-ego, is holding the door closed, but using nearly all his available strength to do so. The contest is nearly life-long, for the force retains its potential strength, the man (or woman) his resolution with little alteration from childhood to old age.

If this analogy be valid, it would account for a great number of the traits and attitudes which have been described in this study. If nearly all the 'human' strength is involved in keeping the forces of aggression under control, there is relatively little energy left for other pursuits. This might account for the slowness which so many respondents think typically English, the sloth—the procrastination or laziness—for which a considerable number reproach themselves, the 'nervous fatigue' or 'night starvation' or any of the other synonyms for a feeling of inadequate energy which the manufacturers of patent foods and medicines exploit so assiduously in England. I know no statistical analyses which have been made either of the extent of advertisements for patent medicines and 'medical' foods and drinks, or of the conditions they claim to cure or ameliorate in the different Occidental countries, but I have a firm impression that the claims to restore depleted energy are much more general in England than in any society of Western Europe or North America.

By the same token, relatively very few advertisements carry explicit aphrodisiac promises, to increase sexual potentiality or 'restore lost virility'; nor do they enhance their appeal by associating their products with pictures of sexually attracted couples.[3] Even in the hopeful minds of advertisers, the English are not unduly 'worried' about sex or sexual adequacy.

It seems reasonable to assume that every human being is born with a certain potential of undifferentiated unconscious energy, perhaps varying with the individual genetic constitution. After birth this energy gets channelized into both constructive and destructive directions. If this be the case, the more energy is channelized into potential aggression, the less remains for potential sexuality. Moreover it seems likely that the habits of rigid self-control, which we have postulated in the case of aggression, would be likely to generalize to all forms of self-expression. It was only a small group, chiefly composed of tormented adolescents or the members of rigid sects, who reproached themselves for their excessive sexual feelings or behaviour; as has been shown, too little interest in sex is the major peril to contemporary English marriages.

It would seem that this diminution in the interest in sexual activity occurred during much the same period as the increased control in the expression of aggression. According to Dr Michael Sadleir[4] the underworld of mid-Victorian London seethed with every sort of sexual activity. The copious pornographic literature of the period, and the contemporary reputation of the English in Paris and other European capitals suggest that for many people sexuality became mingled with aggression and that the two impulses found clandestine relief simultaneously. In the succeeding generations both impulses came under the same strict control

Fear of one's own impulses could most probably be a component of shyness. Shyness is a type of fear; and the fear (unrealistic, in most cases) is either of what one will do to the stranger, or what the stranger will do to one [5] But what basis can there be to these fears? In actual experience, strangers may be tongue-tied but are seldom wounding. If however we unconsciously project on to others the wounding intentions we might have if we did not keep ourselves under very strict control, then there would be an explanation, though not on a conscious level a reason, for the excessive shyness which most English people think they feel.

Similar feelings might well be a component of the marked English appreciation of privacy. It seems likely that the major component of this desire not to be over-looked derives from the widespread use of deprivation as a childhood punishment· one's normal enjoyments and relaxations become dependent on the absence of supervision which is always likely to be censorious. The old joke 'See what Johnny is doing and tell him to stop it' is very near quite a lot of parental discipline; and when Johnny or Janie grow up one of their desires for a pleasant life is that nobody shall be able to see what they're doing, for fear they shall be told to stop it, or otherwise blamed, criticized and interfered with It seems improbable also that such interference with childish pleasures provokes no resentment from the children thus checked, even though they may not manifest it, or even feel it consciously; in later life the possibly censorious overlooker might also arouse the disapproved-of feelings of aggression, and so becomes a threat to one's self-control, as well as being a possible source of deprivation. One of the most marked contrasts in West Africa between the stations for Europeans in the French and British colonies is that in the former half-a-dozen buildings will be arranged to look like a portion of a provincial town, whereas in the latter each house is carefully sited so as to be invisible from any of the others.

The picture is then of potentially strong aggression under very strong control, together involving most of the will-power and most of the unconscious energy of the greater number of English men and women. But though the energy is so watchfully controlled, it is not entirely dissipated, it finds outlets in a number of different ways, many of them symbolic. I have already referred to the marked preoccupation with the prevention of cruelty.

One of the outlets is humour. A careful analysis of the most popular B.B.C. radio and television comedy and variety programmes will show to what a remarkable extent humour for mass English audiences is based on insult and humiliation either from one character to another or even to the self. Real or supposed physical defects or weaknesses—age, baldness, fatness, impediments in speech, even skin-colour—or conceit (say, about a singing voice or ability to play the fiddle) are the continuous small coin of these comedy shows, and apparently always good for a laugh, certainly with the studio audiences, and, one must presume, with the mass of listeners and viewers. The situation is defined as humorous, and therefore harmless; if most of these remarks were made in a different context they would be deeply hurtful and humiliating and might well lead to quarrels and blows In context, they serve as a safety-valve.

Some of the comedians specialize in insulting themselves either by direct self-depreciation or by ludicrous boasting This humorous self-depreciation is a fairly common English characteristic and one which is almost always misunderstood by the non-English; when the self-depreciation is more evident than the humour it is often called 'typical English understatement.' This, it would seem, is in part a protective device; boasting in the young is liable to be punished, to call forth the righteous aggression of elders and betters, and this can be averted by claiming less than one's due. But I do not think that by any means all such modesty is mock-modesty; it would seem to have in it an element of self-criticism, of self-punishment, possibly for not reaching even higher standards.

In social life speech is the chief medium by which disapproved-of aggression slips past the watchful guard. One of the most constantly recurring themes in the material which has been analysed in the previous chapters is the dislike and fear of hurtful speech. Nagging, gossip (which is presumably always malicious), sarcasm, teasing, most forms of 'bad temper', surliness and swearing (which is the nearest equivalent to physical aggression) make up the greater number of traits which people dislike in their neighbours, dread in their husbands or wives, think go to wreck marriages, try to avoid in their children and see as blemishes in their own character. Grumbling was less mentioned by my respondents; it can perhaps

290

be considered the verbal counterpart of envy, and, like envy, justified and free from guilt; few observers, I think, would question that grumbling is not infrequent in the contemporary English scene.

Another outlet for disapproved-of aggression, which seems to be somewhat gaining in popularity, is 'motiveless' destruction of property, sabotage or vandalism. While this chapter is being written (February 1954) there is considerable discussion in the papers of non-political sabotage in warships, a couple of months earlier there were announcements that Primrose Hill had to be closed after dark, because of the amount of senseless destruction which was going on. There is a public footpath or right of way through some of my fields; constantly hedges are being broken, stacks overthrown, tiles knocked off the roofs of some unguarded buildings, without profit for the perpetrators or the gratification of personal malice; it is destruction for the sake of destruction, just 'letting off steam'. All over the country farmers have a similar tale to tell, and the figures for break-ages and losses on British Railways are remarkably high. A possible explanation of these activities would be their safety: nobody gets hurt and things can't feel.

The simile which I used a few pages back of the man keeping the door shut against the emotional force implied that this was an in-variable state of affairs, that the conscience always disapproved of the release of aggression. But this is an oversimplified picture; there are occasions or situations when the conscience gives its approval to the release of aggression and then the enormous potential strength of righteous anger, of righteous indignation is released. A war in a good cause is the most obvious example: courage, daring, and the most lethal ingenuity suddenly manifest themselves in practically the whole of a most civilian population. John Citizen is transformed into John Bull with a completeness which regularly confounds our enemies and surprises our friends; instead of the strong conscience keeping the strong aggression in check, the two, in the literal as well as the metaphorical sense of the word, join forces and shape the world.

War against a wicked enemy—and the enemy must clearly be shown to be wicked by the standards the conscience normally uses— is probably the only situation nowadays which will release the forces of righteous anger for the whole (or nearly the whole) population; for sections of the population political or religious passion or indignation at injustices or mistreatment of others can have a similar effect. For individuals too severity can become a duty; as we have seen, most parents consider children need 'more discipline'; and

291

quotations have shown how, for a minority of parents and teachers, this sense of duty allows aggression to be unleashed The remarkable number of cases brought yearly to the notice of the National Society for the Prevention of Cruelty to Children and the Royal Society for the Prevention of Cruelty to Animals suggest that this is not a very uncommon phenomenon.

The position of the animal pet calls into question the generalization I should otherwise make that the checked aggression would have as its object other people, if it were released Just on half the families in England keep some sort of pet animal;[b] and I think it is safe to say that the great majority of these animals are loved and cared for, more often over-indulged than over-disciplined or neglected. Only rarely does aggression, manifesting itself as cruelty, come into play; but I think it is probable that mastery, which might be considered the constructive aspect of aggression, has an important rôle in the pleasure which so many English people get from their pets.

Mastery is also, I think, a component of the most widespread English leisure-time pursuit—gardening.[7] Energy is applied to con-structive use, the desert, or the back yard, is made to blossom. Kipling, it will be remembered, advised digging as a remedy for the 'cameelious hump', frustration or anger; and I have often found myself that operations such as pruning or weeding tend to be accom-panied by fantasies of retaliation for humiliations, slights or annoy-ances about which I have taken no action I usually finish the job in an excellent humour This may be a purely personal response to what might be called constructive destruction, I have no means of knowing whether this be so or not. Gardening is most markedly an English pursuit, engaged in more by men than by women. Any complete theory of English character would have to account for this predilection, which would not appear to be shared to the same extent by the men of any other country.

The back garden, the prize marrow or giant dahlia, represent one aspect of mastery over nature. Other Britons have 'tamed' conti-nents—significant metaphor!—controlled, organized and governed an empire which, at the end of the nineteenth century, was the most extensive history has ever recorded. Although, when travelling in the Empire and Commonwealth, one tends to get the impression that it is run and populated almost entirely by the Scots and their descendants, the English undoubtedly had some share in the enter-prise. It seems possible that voluntary emigration may have attracted those with the greatest amount of social aggression, the greatest urge to mastery, leaving a stay-at-home population with less free energy and more internal conflict, in 'this country of ours where nobody is well.'

This hypothesis of a strong conscience successfully controlling potentially strong aggression is purely descriptive; it does not attempt to explain either how these qualities are evoked in individuals, so that babies grow into English men and women, nor how they have been maintained or transformed over previous generations.

I do not feel that my evidence is sufficient to make more than very tentative suggestions on the way in which these characteristics are elicited in the life of most individuals. Good English parents impose discipline on their children very early (compared with many other societies) and very consistently, reward the children for compliance and punish them for contumacy. In most cases the earliest of these disciplines will be the gentle, patient but insistent training in cleanliness A strong conscience seems to develop through the fantasied incorporation of some aspects of the parents who impose a consistent ideal of conduct Most English parents fulfil this rôle for their children almost from the time they are born· the pattern of English family life would seem to be favourable to the development of a strong conscience.

The disciplines which the parents think it their duty to impose must inevitably in many cases thwart the infant's or child's 'natural' tendencies or desires; it does not seem that English childhood is normally a paradisal period of unlimited indulgence and freedom. Probably, all infants and children 'naturally' resent not being allowed to do or have what they desire when they desire it, or being forced to do or have things when they do not so desire. The 'natural' tendency is to express this resentment physically, by the various mechanisms of infantile or childish rage or temper tantrums or destructiveness; but such behaviour is almost universally stigmatized as 'naughtiness' by English parents and is appropriately punished. The expression of anger or hate or rage becomes dangerous in itself, quite apart from the unpleasant internal feelings which accompany these emotions, the emotions are not discharged but turned inwards. Anger and hatred probably always carry with them some fear of losing the love of the parents, which is the most precious thing in a child's life, when this fear is made realistic by parental disapproval, the expression of aggression becomes doubly dangerous These are possible mechanisms for producing the gentle, tolerant, law-abiding characters of a highly civilized people.

The strict conscience is, I think, a relatively new historical development, as far as the mass of the population is concerned, particularly the urban population. It would seem that it has for long been typical of the English country dweller, squire, yeoman and labourer alike, and probably, within the limits of contemporary mercantile practice, of the urban middle class It seems much less certain whether this can be said to be true of most of the aristocracy centred on London during the Regency and the subsequent decades; and in the early nineteenth century the mass of the population of the towns, both the new industrial towns and the greater part of London, apart from the rich residential quarters, seem to have been little troubled by conscience either in breaking the laws against property, in deviations from strict sexual morality, or in violence towards their fellow human-beings or towards animals; the figures of criminal prosecutions, quoted lower on this page, are extremely high for the size of the population

During the nineteenth and the first half of the twentieth centuries the strict conscience and self-control, which had been a feature of a relatively small part of the English population, became general throughout nearly the whole of the society, as the present study has indicated. The forces which led to this transformation in character are difficult to establish; although religious belief is not nowadays typical of the prosperous working class, it is possible that the evangelical missions of John Wesley, of whom it is said that he prevented the French Revolution reaching England, may have played a significant part in their time, particularly in the industrial Northern regions. So too may have done the gradual spread of universal education. On the basis of the evidence available to me, however, I should consider that the most significant factor in the development of a strict conscience and law-abiding habits in the majority of urban English men and women was the invention and development of the institution of the modern English police force.[8]

One of the most impressive demonstrations of the increase in the law-abiding character of the English is the following table of the number of criminal commitments in the half century between 1841 and 1891. During this period serious offences decreased 60 per cent in volume, and 80 per cent relative to the increase of population.

Table of Commitments[9]

Census year	Population in millions	Number of commitments	Proportion per 100,000
1841	15·9	27,760	174 6
1851	17 9	27,960	156 2
1861	20	18,326	91 3
1871	22 7	16,269	71 9
1881	25·9	14,704	56·6
1891	29	11,605	40·0

As can be seen, the really dramatic break in criminal commitments came in the decade 1851–1861. Police forces were first established all over England by the County and Borough Police Act of 1856. The pattern of the modern, unarmed, uniformed police force, on duty day and night, was established by Sir Robert Peel's Metropolitan Police Act of 1829, but in the first instance this Act only operated in the London area. Despite two permissive Acts for establishing police forces in the counties and boroughs 'it is a mistake to think of the years 1835 and 1839 as witnessing sudden and fundamental changes in the policing of counties and boroughs . . . Police reform outside London was gradual, patchy and unspectacular', even though the criminal classes moved in their enormous masses from London to the unpoliced boroughs after the establishment of the Metropolitan police.[10]

The very marked decrease in the number of commitments as soon as there was a network of police forces based on the same model covering the whole country would seem to demonstrate the very great effectiveness of this institution in modifying the aggressive behaviour of a very large portion of the population; for if behaviour had not altered, one would have expected a considerable increase in the number of commitments with the increased efficiency of the force for apprehending law-breakers.

Taking only the figures of commitments, it might be argued that the main motive for the drop in criminal statistics was fear. Presumably this emotion did play a part in restraining some law-breakers; but I can find no evidence that, from a few years after the first establishment of the Metropolitan police, the police were ever actively feared or disliked by the majority of the population. It is probable that the enthusiastic appreciation of the police, disclosed by this study, would have been more tempered in the latter half of the nineteenth century; but I do not think the English police have ever been felt to be the enemy of sizable non-criminal sections of the population, as has certainly been the case on some occasions with French, German and even United States police forces.

When the original Metropolitan police force was set up considerable care was taken to eschew any resemblance to the militarized police forces of the continent and only a very small proportion of the force has even been drawn from ex-army or ex-navy personnel; and with the noted exception of the Metropolitan police, all the police forces in the country were placed, and have remained, under local authorities, and only indirectly under the central government. From the first (and especially in the early critical years) every

295

complaint about the conduct of the police, however extravagant it might seem, was openly investigated.

What however was really novel about the British police was that the force was recruited entirely on the basis of character. From its origin and till this day the only automatic qualifications for recruits is a certain minimum height and age; and the age of entry is sufficiently high so that the police recruit can be virtually certain of having passed several years as a worker in civilian life before joining the force.[11] The three other qualifications laid down by the Home Secretary are all matters of opinion rather than of fact. the candidate should be 'of good character and with a satisfactory record in past employments; physically and mentally fitted to perform the duties of a constable; and sufficiently well educated' Within very wide limits, what this means is that the recruit should have a suitable character; and, with very slight exceptions in certain cases, acceptance is dependent on the interviews.

The type of character sought (probably a rare one in the classes from which recruits were drawn) was outlined in the original regulations drawn up by one of the first two Commissioners of the Metropolitan police, Mr Mayne, shortly after its foundation in 1829:

> The Constable must remember that there is no qualification more indispensible to a police officer than a perfect command of temper, never suffering himself to be moved in the slightest degree by any language or threats which may be used: if he do his duty in a quiet and determined manner, such conduct will probably induce well-disposed bystanders to assist him should he require it [12]

'No qualification more indispensible than a perfect command of temper . . .'; here, it would seem, is the model for the self-control which has now become so widespread an English characteristic. Although the policeman had certain authority and prestige, he had shared in full, and continued to share when off duty, the life of his fellows; policemen were never segregated in barracks. The policeman was not separated from the classes from which he was recruited; he was present and visible as a model of conduct, as a protector from the destructive forces of society, and, symbolically and in his own behaviour, from the destructive forces within the personality. The policeman, it would seem became for many Englishmen the ideal model of masculine strength and responsibility; as generations passed, aspects of this ideal figure became incorporated into the personality; and the English character became, to a very marked degree, 'self-policing'.

(It is tempting to think that the analogue to the rôle of the police

296

for members of the middle and upper middle classes was the creation of a permanent Civil Service 'independent of the patronage of politicians and holding office during good behaviour', with admission to the senior branches based on examinations and interviews, with the ideal character judicious, impartial, experienced and self-disciplined. The report which established this modern Civil Service was written in 1854—two years before the establishment of police forces all over the country—by Sir Stafford Northcote and Sir Charles Trevelyan; the principles were seriously implemented some 16 years later. Unfortunately, I failed to get any information on attitudes towards the Civil Service which could be compared with the material on attitudes towards the police.)

So far, while discussing English character, I have only accorded glancing notice to the different social classes [13] I should suspect that all through the nineteenth century, and even perhaps up to a generation ago, there would have been marked differences in the typical characters of members of the middle class and of the working class, but as far as my evidence goes, this is not the case today. There are very marked differences in habit, in education, accent and vocabulary, etiquette and standard of living; in January 1951 the median income of the middle class was some £4 a week higher than the median income of the working class; and 56 per cent of the middle class but only 25 per cent of the working class continued their full-time education after the minimum school-leaving age of 14. But in attitudes, as opposed to circumstances, there is only one major subject on which these two classes (making up over three-quarters of the total population) differ really significantly: this is in religion and other supernatural beliefs. The middle class is consistently more religious than the working class. It goes to religious services more, prays more, is more insistent in teaching its children to pray and has fewer members belonging to no denomination; it is also more credulous concerning fortune-tellers, horoscopes and similar devices for fore-knowing or controlling the future. Compared with the working class, the middle class has considerably more people reproaching themselves for compulsive traits and more advocates for starting infants' cleanliness training from birth. Middle class parents are more likely to give their children regular pocket money and to forbid them accepting money from strangers for services rendered. Middle class women are more likely to 'shop around' before they decide which man to marry.

In the working class the family is likely to be a closer geographical unit than in the middle class; far more working class people live

297

in the same town as their parents, compared with the middle class, and also near their in-laws. War-time and service friendships are markedly less important for the working class. Conscious interest in the opposite sex seems to develop somewhat later in the working class; and working-class men are more appreciative of the domestic skills of their wives. These exceptions apart, the two main classes which comprise the bulk of the population are quite surprisingly similar, often identical, in their views and attitudes.

The sections of the population for whom social class does seem to determine attitudes to a really marked extent are that 25 per cent who place themselves in other than the middle or working classes: the two intervening classes, the lower middle and upper working class, who tend to stress some themes that are much more lightly emphasized by the two main classes; and on the other hand the upper middle and lower working classes, who place themselves above and below the main bulk of the population, and who differ in many respects from the remainder.

The most marked characteristic of the members of the lower middle class, as shown in this survey, is the extent to which they welcome and approve of the authority of the contemporary state. They are the most enthusiastic admirers of the police, the most ready to concede authority over their children to the teachers, they are the most resolute opponents of 'fiddling', the most eager to state that laws should be obeyed under any circumstances, that it is always unfair to try to get more than others. When the questionnaire was circulated, a Labour government was in power; and the remarks of a few respondents confirm my impression that this government represented and carried out the ideals of the lower middle class more completely than it did that of any other section of the community.

Members of the lower middle class are not superstitious, few of them carry mascots in peace or war, visit fortune tellers more than once, or believe in their powers or those of astrologers. In considering the good qualities of a wife lower middle class men pay relatively little attention to her skills as cook and housekeeper; the qualities particularly valued are 'a sense of humour' (whatever may be the meaning of this phrase in the context) and fidelity. For both sexes, somewhat to my surprise, the most important factor making for happiness or unhappiness in marriage is the presence or absence of sexual compatibility; they also place much emphasis on good temper and shared interests. More than any other group, they fear the expression of aggression—stealing, destruction, and the like—in their children; and, with only surface inconsistency, they are high

298

in their advocacy of caning for naughty boys, and low in their disapproval of thrashing in appropriate cases.

In contrast to the members of the lower middle class, those prosperous and industrious people who consider that they belong to the upper working class are opposed to the authority of the state, as at present constituted. It is from this class that stem most of the criticisms of the police; and they are unwilling to allow the teacher authority over their children. More emphatically than the members of any other class they stress paternal authority; father is the head of the household, and is the proper person to discipline his children; the chief reason for juvenile delinquency, in the eyes of members of this class, is that children whose fathers were in the forces didn't have proper discipline. An interesting counterpart to this belief is that fewer members of the upper working class than of any other group in the community, consider that children need more discipline than they get nowadays; these self-reliant and self-confident men and women are quite sure that they discipline their children adequately. It is this group which exercises the greatest amount of supervision of its children's playmates and the houses they visit. Its favourite punishment for boys is the cane, for girls the stopping of pocket-money Nearly all children in this class are taught to say prayers, though the parents themselves are not likely to be assiduous church-goers.

Men of the upper working class put high value on the domestic skills of their wives. People in this class are particularly likely to marry the first person to whom they become seriously attached, and place emphasis on the importance of understanding and mutual trust to keep a marriage happy; they consider neglect the greatest cause for marital unhappiness. They will go to considerable lengths to preserve the marriage; if one of the spouses is involved in an affair with a third party, the solutions they propose is to talk the matter over with the erring spouse and try to win him or her back Members of the upper working class have little use for shyness.

The members of the lower working class present a strong contrast with those of the upper working class, and indeed with the great bulk of the English population. These people with little money or education, and with (mostly) big families seem to resemble more the 'poor', as described by such observers as Mayhew, than any other contemporary group in the country, they seem to be, in the anthropological sense of the word, 'survivals'. There is little evidence, in this group, of the strict conscience, the rigid self-restraint, which characterizes the greatest part of the population of England. They

299

are the only group with an absolute majority in favour of pre-marital sexual experience for young men, and over a third consider it desirable for young women too. it's 'human nature'. If, after marriage, they find their spouse drifting towards infidelity, their solution is to beat up or kill the intervener: no talking things over for them. Similarly, they have little fear of their children being aggressive, and by and large they try to control their children very little, don't know, or bother with, their children's playmates or the houses they visit If they feel called upon to punish their children they make little use of withdrawal of privileges or other techniques of deprivation; the boys are whipped, the girls made to work in the house Very few parents of the lower working class think it desirable to start cleanliness training at birth; they somewhat emphasize the second year of life as the best period to start such training They tend not to reward their children, either with praise or pocket money.

The lower working class tend to be both pious and superstitious; to practice religion and carry mascots and believe in the automatic luck of days and numbers. They tend to be on bad terms with their neighbours and have little reliance in their help. They nearly all admit to fiddling, and (somewhat understandably) are not very enthusiastic about the police They are the only class for whom drink is a major cause of marital unhappiness (surely, another survival) followed by neglect. They pay little attention to sexual compatibility, give-and-take or mutual trust as making for the happiness of a marriage; but they do like their spouses to be economical.

The upper middle class is the most educated and wealthiest section of the community (this sample had no members of the very small upper classes); and it too varies in very significant ways from the bulk of the population; and, to the extent that the contemporary trend is towards levelling in income and education, can perhaps, like the lower working class, be considered in some sort a survival from the generations before 1914. But whereas the lower working classes differed most from the rest of the population by their comparative lack of self-restraint in giving vent to their sexuality and their violence, the upper middle classes differ more subtly, and above all in their scale of values.

In contrast with the remaining classes in the community, local bonds are relatively unimportant for the upper middle class. It is, so to speak, a nation-wide class; its friends and its family are widely scattered, more than any other class it does not know its neighbours. Its members would appear to be more social than those of other classes; they feel shyness less and approve of it less; and few of them consider that staying in the bosom of their family is an agreeable way of spending a pleasant evening.

The views on marriage and the proper rearing of children are different in the upper middle class. Though they have a tendency to become engaged after a short acquaintance they are very likely to marry within their own class, and are almost alone in being articulately conscious of the dangers to a marriage when the couple are of different social, religious or national backgrounds A factor which members of this class stress as important to the success of marriage is community of interests; in this class this is far more important than the domestic skills or equitable temper which the bulk of the population value highly. Selfishness can be the cause of marital unhappiness for them; but the concept of give-and-take which is heavily stressed in all other classes, finds little mention in this. In the upper middle class, marriage seems to be viewed as a symmetrical relationship; in the rest of the community it tends to be a complementary relationship.[14]

With this view of the relationship of husband and wife, it seems logical that the upper middle class should on the whole be opposed to a single authority in the rearing of children, and in favour of dual (father and mother) or multiple authority, with teachers, nurses or governesses as well as parents enforcing the proper rules of behaviour; in this class the supposed legal position of the father as head of the family is very little mentioned. Members of this class are emphatic in their demand that children should have more discipline; it seems at least possible that the changed economic situation which has removed the nannies and governesses from many of the families is responsible for this demand. Withdrawal of privileges is relatively little used in this class for punishing naughty girls or boys, the favoured punishments are either sending the children to bed, or else verbal—the withdrawal of love, sarcasm and the like. As regards the earliest training of infants, parents of the upper middle class seem to fall into two groups: those who advocate training from birth, and those who would postpone it for at least six months and are conscious of the possible dangers of too early training. It seems likely that this latter group reflects current psychiatric theory.

If belief in hell, the devil and the after-life are components of a doctrinally sound Christian faith, then there is a markedly high proportion of doctrinally sound Christians in this class. Except for a rather high belief in ghosts, members of this class are not superstitious, are relatively sceptical about fortune-tellers and astrologers.

As with the classes, so with the regions; it is the relatively smaller

301

regions which show marked regional characteristics. Accent is probably the most marked regional, as it is the most marked class, characteristic; and accent, of course, is lost in written questionnaires.

In nearly every respect, the Midland region is typical of the whole of England; it is a trifle more permissive about sex, and a trifle less given to church-going and the saying of private prayers, than the rest of the country; but otherwise the Midlands reflect with very slight deviations the values and customs of the whole country, standing at the mid-point of the contrasts between some other regions. London and the South-East too, differs chiefly in the greater loneliness of its inhabitants, who are more likely to be separated from their kin and know nothing of their neighbours than are the inhabitants of the rest of the country.

The three other regions differ in their social composition The South-West is the most rural of all the English regions, the most generally religious (in so far as church going and saying prayers is a sign of being religious) and the only one which pays much attention to the problem of drunkenness Many of the lower working class come from the small villages of the West country, and to a certain, though diminished, extent, the values of that class modify the values of that region.

The difference between the North and the South is almost a cliché in all discussions on English characteristics This study bears out the cliché to a certain extent; but though the North does differ from the South, as a whole, the two Northern regions, divided by the Pennines, differ much more dramatically from one another than either differs from the rest of the country. There are some points of resemblance between the North-West and the South-West; at least in some aspects it would be as sensible to talk about the East-West division of the country as to talk about the contrast of North and South.

One of the major contrasts between the North and the South is that there are proportionately far fewer members of the Church of England in the North; but in the North-West the creed of the next most sizable group is Roman Catholicism, whereas in the North-East and North it is Methodism The major point of contrast between the two Northern regions cannot be surely connected with this difference in denomination, though it is not incongruous with it; undoubtedly the different industrial traditions also play an important part.

Put briefly, in the North-Western region women have greater authority in their family and greater independence than in any other part of England; in the North-East and North paternal

302

authority is at its highest, and there are the greatest number of all-male associations. A number of fairly self-evident traits cluster round these two images of the family; the North-East is more severe, with high demands for more discipline and fears of bad results if infant training is postponed; the North-West is more permissive, gentler, and more protective, mothers from this region are somewhat more likely to supervise their children's associations and to forbid them taking money from strangers. The North-East is highly sceptical of fortune-tellers, astrologers and the like; the North-West is not. Although women have less authority in the North-East and North than in any other region, the men are particularly appreciative of their wives' specific domestic skills; the good cook and good housekeeper receives her full meed of praise from her 'hard-headed' husband. In both Northern regions local endogamy (choosing a husband or wife from the same community as oneself) is more common than in the rest of the country, and consequently the extended family, comprising grand-parents, uncles, aunts, cousins and similar relatives, is much less broken up than it is in the Midlands and Southern regions.

As far as differences in values and attitudes are concerned, the greatest contrast between groups of English people is not that between different social classes or between different regions but between men and women Since this has been illustrated in very full detail in the earlier chapters, it does not seem necessary to recapitulate the evidence here.

In the three years during which I have been occupied with the data on which this study has been founded, I have been increasingly more impressed with the basic unity of the people of England. The upper middle and lower working classes, the mother-centred North-West and father-centred North-East and North depart to a somewhat marked extent from the habits and attitudes of the rest of the country; but in the main the English are a truly unified people, more unified, I would hazard, today than at any previous period of their history. When I was reading, with extreme care, the first batch of questionnaires which I received, I found I was constantly making the same notes: 'What dull lives most of these people appear to lead!' I remarked; and secondly, 'What good people!' I should still make the same judgments.

NOTES TO CHAPTER FIFTEEN

1 Fifteen men described themselves as practicing homosexuals, two as sadists, and three as fetishists, out of a population of about 6,000 No women accused themselves

of perversions; a very few mentioned masturbation, and a dozen or so described themselves as *allumeuses* 'I'm interested in getting a boy, but I'm not so interested when I've got him' These figures are of course no indication of the prevalence of such practices or attitudes in the population

2 In May 1952 the British Institute of Public Opinion asked a sample from the whole of Britain 'Would you say you worry a lot—a fair amount—a little—not at all?' These answers would of course include rational worries, but the differences between men and women still appear significant Twenty-nine per cent of the women but only 16 per cent of the men consider they worry 'a lot'; 31 per cent of the women and 30 per cent of the men 'a fair amount', 29 per cent of the women and 33 per cent of the men 'a little'; 11 per cent of the women but 21 per cent of the men 'not at all'. The BIPO combines social and economic status, so that it is impossible to tell whether the women who worry 'a lot' are significantly concentrated among those who consider themselves middle or lower middle class

3 In an analysis of English and American advertisements, directed by Dr Margaret Mead, it was found that the majority of English advertisements were illustrated by a single, isolated figure, the majority of American ones by a couple (man and girl) or by a family

4 M Sadleir. *Fanny by Gaslight* and *Forlorn Sunset* (London Constable, 1940 and 1947).

5 See Chapter Two, p 21

6 *Patterns of British Life*, p 100, Table 16

7 Op. cit , pp 107, 108, Tables 27 and 28

8. This theme is developed in somewhat more detail in Appendix One

9 Quoted from W L Melville Lee *A History of Police in England*, p 337 (London: Methuen, 1901)

10 J M Hart. *The British Police* (London· Allen & Unwin, 1951), p 31 Lee, op cit , p 272

11 Between 1928 and 1939 the average age of entry was a little over twenty-two *Oaksey Report on Police Conditions of Service*, 1949, H.M Stationery Office

12 Quoted by Lee, op cit , p 242

13 In this and the following paragraphs I am only dealing with the more marked contrasts between the various social classes and regions, where there are differences in the neighbourhood of 10 per cent between the highest and lowest figures

14 See Gregory Bateson. *Culture Contact and Schismogenesis in Man*, XXXV

MODIFICATION OF NATIONAL CHARACTER: THE PSYCHOLOGICAL RÔLE OF THE POLICE IN ENGLAND

(an elaboration of Chapter Fifteen pp. 294–296)

I WISH TO advance the hypothesis that one of the techniques by which the national character of a society may be modified or transformed over a given period is through the selection of personnel for institutions which are in continuous contact with the mass of the population in a somewhat super-ordinate position. If the personnel of the institution are chosen chiefly for their approximation to a certain type of character, rather than for specific intellectual or physical skills; if persons with this type of character have not hitherto been consistently given positions of authority; and if the authority of the institution is generally felt to be benevolent, protective, or succouring; then the character exemplified by the members of this institution will to a certain degree become part of the ego ideal of the mass of the population, who will tend to mould their own behaviour in conformity with this ideal, and will reward and punish the behaviour of their children in the light of this pattern which they have adopted As generations pass, the attempt to approximate to this ideal will become less and less conscious, and increasingly part of the unconscious mechanisms which determine the content of the super-ego or of the ego ideal; with the consequence that a type of character which may have been relatively very uncommon in the society when the institution was first manned will subsequently become relatively common, and even perhaps typical of the society, or of those portions of it with which the members of the institution are in most continuous contact or from which their personnel is drawn.

The institution which I propose to examine in detail is the English police forces; but the evidence which is available to me suggests that strictly analogous functions were performed by the public school teachers of the United States[1] [2] particularly during the period of the great immigrations of the half century ending in 1914, when masses of immigrants' children were transformed into '100 per cent Americans'; and that a similar attempt is being made in the U S S.R.[3] [4] where the members of the Communist Party are consciously presented as models for the mass of the population.

The modern English police force had its inception in the Metropolitan Police Act of Sir Robert Peel in 1829; it was a generation before Police Forces became mandatory all over the country, through the County and Borough Police Act of 1856.[5] In one important respect the Metropolitan Police is anomalous, it is directly responsible to the Home Secretary, to the centralized government; all the other Police forces in the country are controlled by local authorities In the counties the chief officer of police has the legal power to promote and recruit other members of the force; in the borough forces of England and Wales the power of appointment lies (at least legally; in practice it is usually the chief constable who exercises the authority) in the hands of the watch committee.[6] In its relationship to the community it serves and protects the Metropolitan Police is on a different footing to the numerous other forces in Britain (in 1857 there were 239 separate forces, a number gradually reduced by amalgamation to 129 in 1949), but its practices and standards have always served as a model to the other Police forces throughout the Kingdom.

The chief novelties in Peel's conception of the police appear to be (i) the institution of a force for the prevention of crime and maintenance of public order, rather than for the apprehension of criminals after the crime was committed; (ii) the high visibility of the police in a distinctive uniform, what Inspector J. L. Thomas has called the 'scarecrow function' of the police;[7] (iii) the fact that the police were on continuous duty during the whole 24 hours (the Bow Street runners were not in uniform and only patrolled during the evenings, invariably finishing duty by midnight),[8] (iv) the fact that the police were unarmed, except for the truncheon, which was no more formidable than the 'life-preserver' which many gentlemen of the period carried on their walks abroad; (v) the fact that every complaint against the conduct of the police was publicly investigated;[9] (vi) the fact that the police were never segregated in barracks nor treated as a para-military formation, as occurred in a number of European countries, and (vii) the fact that, apart from certain qualifications of height and age, the police were recruited entirely on the basis of their character, and not on their previous employment, or through patronage, or for the possession of any special skills beyond an unfixed minimum of education. Neither examinations nor tests have ever preceded recruitment into the police force, though new entrants are naturally given training after they have been accepted. It is this last point which I wish to examine in greater detail.

The great bulk of the police has almost continuously been drawn from the ranks of skilled and semi-skilled labour, from the working,

306

upper working and lower middle classes. In 1832, three years after its inception, Peel's Metropolitan Force was composed of former members of the following careers· 135 butchers, 109 bakers, 198 shoemakers, 51 tailors, 402 soldiers, 1,151 labourers, 205 servants, 141 carpenters, 75 bricklayers, 20 turners, 55 blacksmiths, 151 clerks, 141 shop-keepers, 141 'superior mechanics', 46 plumbers and painters, 101 sailors, 51 weavers and 8 stonemasons.[10] The heterogeneity of this list is probably typical of the composition of most of the English police forces over the last 120 years, with two exceptions: the proportion of former military and naval personnel is rather high, except for recruitment in the years immediately following a major war,[11] and in this first Metropolitan Force there is no special mention of the agricultural labourers (unless the 'labourers' without specification came from the country) who for a great part of the nineteenth century made up a very high proportion of the police recruits.[12] Agricultural labourers were considered to excel in physique and stamina, and, in the words of a former Commissioner of the Metropolitan Police to the American writer, R. B. Fosdick: 'They are slow but steady; you can mould them to any shape you please '[13] With the increasing industrialization of England, the proportion of agricultural labourers has steadily dropped; and today most police recruits were former industrial workers, office workers, commercial travellers or shop assistants.[14] It also seems probable that the type of character sought for in a police recruit was formerly much more common in the rural population than in the violent and unruly urban mobs; but with the modification of character which has been hypothesized in the mass of the English population, people of suitable temperament can be found in all strata of the English population, except possibly the lower working class.

It would seem to be worth re-quoting the only conditions laid down by the Home Secretary for the selection of police recruits. He, or she, must be (1) within certain age limits; (2) not less than a stated height; (3) of a good character and with a satisfactory record in past employments, (4) physically and mentally fitted to perform the duties of a constable; and (5) sufficiently well educated.[15] Apart from the criteria of age and height, this means in fact that the selection of recruits depends almost entirely on the result of interviews with the Chief Constable of the Force concerned; his experience and skill in assessing character by unformalized techniques of observation and interrogation replace the selection boards, psychological tests and other techniques of examination which are used for screening the entrants to most life-time careers of responsibility and authority.

In connection with the character of the members of the police force, the criterion of height may merit a little consideration. The minimum fixed by the Home Secretary is 5 ft 8 in. for men, which already excludes more than half the male population, since the average height of the British male is 5 ft $7\frac{1}{2}$ in.[16] In point of fact, only three of the country's police forces, though those are three of the largest (Metropolitan, Birmingham and Buckinghamshire) in 1949 were content with the Home Secretary's permitted minimum; about 30 forces will take men of 5 ft 9 in., and another 20 of 5 ft $9\frac{1}{2}$ in ; the remainder—somewhat more than 70 forces—insist on a minimum of 5 ft 10 in.[17] This means that most of the police recruits come from a small and, statistically speaking, physically unrepresentative section of the population, perhaps some 10 per cent of the whole; and although the connection between physique and character is still comparatively undetermined,[18] the folk observation that big men are likely to be easy-going, even-tempered, just and slow to anger may well have some foundation in fact. Although the minimum height was probably imposed with the intention of securing physically strong and impressive men, it may have had the secondary effect of securing that recruits were selected from people of constitutionally equitable temperament

From its foundation, the emphasis of the British Police force has been on the preservation of peace, on the prevention of crime and violence, rather than the apprehension of criminals and rioters. The swearing-in oath taken by each constable on entering the Force reads

> I A B. do swear that I will well and truly serve our Sovereign Lady the Queen in the office of Constable —— without Favour or Affection, Malice or Ill-will, and that I will to the best of my Power cause the Peace to be kept and preserved, and prevent all offence against the Persons and Properties of Her Majesty's Subjects, and that while I continue to hold the said Office I will to the best of my skill and knowledge discharge all the Duties thereof faithfully according to Law.[19]

Similarly the regulations drawn up by Mr Mayne, one of the two first Commissioners of the Metropolitan Police, emphasize

> The absence of crime will be considered the best proof of the complete efficiency of the police. . . . In divisions where this security and good order have been effected, the officers and men belonging to it may feel assured that such good conduct will be noticed by rewards and promotions
>
> The Constable must remember that there is no qualification more indispensible to a police officer than a perfect command of temper,

never suffering himself to be moved in the slightest degree by any language or threats that may be used: if he do his duty in a quiet and determined manner, such conduct will probably induce well-disposed bystanders to assist him should he require it [20]

This emphasis on the prevention of aggression, on the preserving of the peace by a uniformed group of powerful men demonstrating self-restraint would appear to have been a real novelty in English public life; it was not originally accepted without a great deal of opposition and abuse both from the press and from many representatives of the governing classes.[21] Prior to the coming into force of the Metropolitan Police, wearers of uniform tended to be either symbolically or potentially oppressors and exploiters rather than protectors of the mass of the population members of the armed forces, proverbially licentious and lawless, or the liveried servants of the rich and mighty. The policeman in uniform was still a member of his class in the hours off duty, had social as well as official contacts with his neighbours, and very much the same standard of living. Up to 1919 a policeman of the lowest rank was paid at roughly the same rate as an agricultural labourer,[22] but with the extra perquisites of housing and clothing allowances, security of tenure if conduct was satisfactory, and a pension on retirement at a comparatively early age. These pensions were finally established by the Police Act of 1890, but they had been part of the plan for the Police force from the earliest years; a superannuation fund was originally established in 1839. The police were disenfranchised up to the passing of the Police Disabilities Removal Bill in 1887 [23]

I have been able to find very little discussion of the motives which impel a young man or woman of superior physique and character to take up a profession or occupation which even today is not financially particularly rewarding I do not think any systematic research has been done on the subject; but Inspector J. L Thomas of the City of Bradford Police has some illuminating observations to make.[24]

In other callings (he writes) with a high age of entry, such as the Church and the teaching profession, the tyro must previously devote a number of years to studying and training for his future work, and the Police Service is probably unique in taking on men aged twenty years and upwards, who have no preliminary training whatsoever for the work they are to perform. It follows therefore that it has to attract men already engaged in an occupation, and the question which presents itself is· What were the motives that induced young men to quit a diversity of jobs to become policemen?

Among the answers he suggests are: pay steady and not subject to the caprice of trade or industry, though not high; a reasonable pension at a comparatively early age; unemployment following a 'dead end' job; lack of specialized training after a period in the armed forces; and similar circumstances.

> Minor causes, such as the power a policeman is supposed to yield, may have influenced some men. . . .
> While it is acknowledged that some men now serving did cherish over a long period an ardent desire to become policemen, it is suggested that they are in the minority, and that most policemen more or less drifted into their present job, through force of circumstances, such as those already described, rather than having been impelled by a strong sense of vocation . .
> 'How then', it may be asked, 'has the English police service succeeded in gaining such a large measure of public approbation?' This can only be attributed to the rigid observance of a number of fundamental rules . . . the principal ones are: selecting the best men available; preserving the civilian character of the Force by recruiting from the population at large and from a wide diversity of occupations, maintaining a high standard of discipline, integrity and *esprit de corps*; and observing the principle of promotion by merit.
> Consequently, the nature of the occupation previously followed by a policeman has little direct bearing on his new career . . . The motive which prompted a man to enlist is not such a vital factor as may have been thought at first. As a matter of fact it is often the men with the strongest inclination to become policemen who are the most unsuitable for the position

These perspicacious remarks omit, I think, consideration of one motive which, though it may not play a large rôle in the decision to enlist, may quite probably be influential in keeping the new recruits in the profession they have chosen: that is the respect with which the members of the police force are regarded by their peers. This is certainly the case today,[25] and although there is no comparable evidence from earlier periods, the descriptions of members of the police in novels by Charles Dickens or Wilkie Collins[26] or in music-hall songs and jokes and similar anecdotal evidence suggests that during the whole of the last century the English policeman has been regarded with respect by a considerable portion of the population.

I should like to suggest that, increasingly during the past century, the policeman has been for his peers not only an object of respect, but also a model of the ideal male character, self-controlled, possessing more strength than he ever has to call into use except in the gravest emergency, fair and impartial, serving the abstractions of

Peace and Justice rather than any personal allegiance or sectional advantage This model, distributed throughout the population (in 1949 there were 59,000 police officers, averaging one police officer for every 720 inhabitants; the force authorized was 71,000, one for every 600 inhabitants)[27] has, I suggest, had an appreciable influence on the character of most of the population during recent decades, so that the bulk of the population has, so to speak, incorporated the police man or woman as an ideal and become progressively more 'self-policing'; and with this incorporation there has been an increasing amount of identification, so that today, in the words of one typical respondent·

> I believe the police stand for all we English are, maybe at first appearance slow perhaps, but reliable stout and kindly, I have the greatest admiration for our police force and I am proud they are renowned abroad

If this hypothesis be true, then what started as an expedient to control the very great criminality and violence of large sections of the English urban population[28] has resulted in a profound modification of the character of this urban population. In a somewhat similar fashion, the need to provide a common language and literacy for the children of immigrants in the United States placed the American public school teacher in a position of prestige which was not shared by her colleagues in any European society and turned her into a model of ideal American conduct and so modified American character with an incorporated school teacher to parallel the incorporated policeman of the English. There is not yet comparable evidence to show whether the communist party member in the U.S.S.R. (or, for that matter, China) is producing analogous results in the mass of the population; this institution is much more recent than the two others hitherto discussed, but the personnel is distributed throughout the population in much the same proportions and similar relationship as the policeman and the teacher. The major contrasts are that the policy is quite self-conscious on the part of the governments, and that the Communist Party members are publicly connected with the whole apparatus of state power, in a way that neither the police nor the school teachers, both under the control of local authorities, are; and this public connection with state power may interfere with the processes of identification by the powerless; for, it would seem, it is by means of the more-or-less complete and more-or-less conscious identification with the members of an admired and succouring institution that the characters of the mass of the population are gradually modified or transformed.

311

NOTES TO APPENDIX ONE

1. Margaret Mead *And Keep Your Powder Dry* (New York, Morrow, 1942) Especially Chapter Three.

2 Geoffrey Gorer *The Americans* (London, Cresset Press, 1948) Especially Chapter Three

3 Margaret Mead *Soviet Attitudes Toward Authority* (New York, McGraw-Hill, 1951)

4. Raymond Bauer *The New Man in Soviet Psychology* (Cambridge, Harvard University Press, 1952)

5. J M Hart *The British Police* (The New Town and County Hall Series Allen and Unwin, London, 1951). pp 27–32

6 *Oaksey Report* on Police Conditions of Service (London, H M Stationery Office, 1949) Part II, p 9

7 J L. Thomas, Inspector *The Scarecrow Function of the Police* (London, *The Police Journal*, Vol XVIII, 1945)

8 J L. Thomas· op cit , p 299

9 W L Melville Lee, Captain *A History of Police in England* (London, Methuen, 1901) p 250.

10 J L Thomas, Inspector (II) *Recruits for the Police Service* (London, *The Police Journal*, Vol XIX, 1946). p 293.

11. J. L Thomas op cit II, p 297.

12 J L Thomas op cit II, p 293

13 R B Fosdick *European Police Systems.* n d.

14 J L Thomas op cit , p 152.

15 J M Hart op cit , p 152

16 W J Martin· *The Physique of Young Adult Males* (Memor. Med Res Coun. No 20, 1949, London, H M Stationery Office)

17 *Oaksey Report*, op cit , Part II, p 7. If a minimum height of 5 ft 10 in. had been insisted on by the three forces which accepted recruits of the minimum regulation height of 5 ft 8 in , the Metropolitan police would have lost 35 per cent, Buckinghamshire 52 per cent and Birmingham 65 per cent of the men recruited

18. Attempts to correlate physique and character or temperament have been made by a number of researchers, notably Kretschmer *Physique and Character* (English translation 1925) and W H Sheldon *The Varieties of Human Physique* (1940), *The Varieties of Temperament* (1942) and *Varieties of Delinquent Youth* (1949), but to date there has not been either general acceptance of their hypotheses, or convincing application of them by other researchers

19 J. M Hart· op. cit , p 10

20 Quoted by W L Melville Lee: op cit , p 242.

21. W L Melville Lee op cit , pp 245 *et seq*

22 J M Hart op cit , p 50

23 W L. Melville Lee op cit , pp 374, 400

24 J L Thomas op cit II, pp 293–6

25 See Table 80 and Chapter XIII.

26 E g Inspector Bucket in Charles Dickens' *Bleak House*, Sergeant Cuff in Wilkie Collins' *The Moonstone*

27 J. M Hart· op cit., p 8

28 Among other material, see W L. Melville Lee op. cit especially pp 196–222, J L Thomas, op. cit. I, p. 299

ON THE EMPLOYMENT OF QUESTIONNAIRES
FOR THE STUDY OF NATIONAL CHARACTER

IT APPEARS THAT it might be useful to make a few observations on the advantages and disadvantages of using questionnaires as a research technique for the study of national character, as compared with the techniques of interviewing and observation which have been used in nearly all previous studies.

The advantages are immediately obvious. Apart from the designing of the questionnaire—a point which will be returned to later—research by questionnaire is far less dependent on individual or idiosyncratic skills than research by interview or observation; consequently it is a technique of considerably wider applicability. It is probably the most satisfactory device for determining the extent of the differences between the social classes or regions of which a society is composed; and it could be used to indicate with some precision the way members of a society change their attitudes and practices over a given period.

The foremost disadvantage is that it excludes information of any depth on the interaction between individuals, between groups and between institutions. The shared elements and attitudes (in contrast to individual characteristics) which are the components of national character become most obvious in the observation or interviewing of groups of people, with the questionnaire filled up by the solitary individual, as with the psychiatrically oriented interview in privacy, a great deal of this information tends to be lost. Many of the questions which I devised (19–25, especially 24 and 25, 26–34, especially 33 and 34, 57–81 and others) were designed to get information on social inter-action; but I do not consider such information is comparable in quality to that which can be obtained from the careful and continuous observation of specific neighbourhoods or families. Metaphorically speaking, only one dimension is given of a multi-dimensional figure

A second disadvantage is that it is an extremely time-consuming technique unless the researcher has a staff of fairly highly qualified assistants The coding of the questionnaires, and the transfer of the codes to punch cards is a fairly simple (though expensive) operation with 'closed' questions in which the answers are limited by the questionnaire form; but undoubtedly most insight is derived from 'open-ended' questions, to which the respondent replies in his or her own words. To produce a small number of categories which will fit, without too much ambiguity, a great variety of answers, calls for methodological ingenuity I worked with a sample of 500 questionnaires chosen at random, each of which was analysed in very considerable detail; even so in some cases (perhaps especially tables 107 and 108) it appeared that the categories decided on were in some cases too inclusive, lumping together answers which could usefully have been analysed separately; and in others too precise, creating special categories for very small numbers of respondents In research such as this, it would probably be better to analyse 10 per cent (rather than 5 per cent) of the questionnaires before determining which categories should be applied.

Nearly every questionnaire provides a 'profile' of the respondent; if it is read with sufficient care, and attention paid to such features as hand-writing, spelling, punctuation, choice of words, the use of the space in the questionnaire, and attention to the subsidiary instructions, one can get a very good idea of the character and temperament of the individual respondent. But this is all based on faint clues; to make the evidence explicit would require a very great number of words in nearly every case, and to publish them in any fullness would be a breach of faith with one's collaborators who had filled out the anonymous questionnaire; but it is this regiment of people faintly perceived who manifest under their multifarious diversity the national character which is being analysed, only if the investigator has these thousands of individuals present in his mind can he articulate the answers to questions on many disparate topics into a whole with some sort of coherence.

It consequently seems essential that the investigator must himself read every questionnaire with analytic care to gain some picture of his respondents, and this is a considerable job. For the fullest questionnaires (those filled by parents of living children) I would reckon that I seldom took less than a quarter of an hour on each respondent, and I am a very fast worker with such material.

It is relatively seldom that a single reading of a questionnaire is sufficient Besides obtaining evidence of individual character, one also wishes to find and excerpt typical or illustrative quotations; and, as the work proceeds, one may wish to find all the respondents of a given type or category which may not have been isolated in the original coding, or determine whether a generalization be supported by the evidence. In the present study, for example, I wished

314

to gather together all the respondents who had any connection either professionally or familially, with the police (Chapter Thirteen); I wished to see if nail-biters showed any common group of characteristics (an investigation with few positive results which is not included here), and having written (Chapter Ten, p 155) 'there is practically no mention of what might be called the ethical attitude to divorce, the feeling that it is morally wrong to keep bound to one a partner who prefers another', it was necessary to check whether this was an impression due to the fact that I had not been paying attention to this aspect of the attitudes towards marriage and divorce in my previous analyses, or was firmly based on the evidence. These later searches for the presence or absence of specific material could of course be usefully carried out by research assistants, if the investigator is lucky enough to have such help available.

Because of the many extra clues provided, I consider that for this type of research written questionnaires are far more profitable than the answers to the same questions obtained from interviews. When any considerable sample is being interviewed it is necessary to employ relatively unsophisticated interviewers, and it cannot be expected that they will record the actual phrases, the hesitations or spontaneity of the interviewees which would give comparable (if fully recorded, even more reliable) insight into their personalities as well as their opinions.

The greater number of the interviewers who work for the different polls and market research organizations are young women, usually of a somewhat higher standard of education (and, in England, probably of somewhat higher social class) than most of the people they interview; and consequently, in these brief and formal sessions the interviewees will be guided in their responses by their attitudes towards young women, as well as towards people of a different social level. It seems to me that in England, at any rate, this modifies the answers given in certain quite predictable ways. Modesty becomes an important factor when the interviewees are men; and both sexes will tend to present a picture of themselves which they think would excite the interviewer's approval.

Apart from the purely factual questions concerning age, marital status and so on, 32 of the questions which were asked in the questionnaire (just under a third of the total) were simultaneously asked of a stratified sample in interviews. Thirteen of these (7, 9, 10, 17, 18, 44, 62, 79, 96, 97, 101, 102, 106) have answers which are the same as those from the questionnaire to within 2 or 3 per cent; they are all either 'neutral' questions, or, in the case of 101, 102, 106, sub-divisions of a major question, dealing with only a portion of the population.

A second group of nine questions (20, 21, 22, 23, 73, 76, 81, 104, 105) all share the common feature that they ask the respondents to choose one of a graduated series of answers—always, often, occasionally, never, or the like; in the answers to all these questions the people interviewed tended to choose the polar answers (always or never, for example) whereas people filling up the questionnaire, and presumably thinking over their answers more carefully, some-what favour the intermediate answers For all these questions the discrepancies between the questionnaire and the field survey disappear if 'always' and 'often' or other positive answers on the one hand, and 'occasionally' and 'never' or other negative answers on the other, are grouped together. Without the check of the written questionnaire the patterns of behaviour would appear to be much more strongly contrasted than they are in fact.[1]

Of the remaining ten tables, two (40 and 41) cannot be usefully compared with the answers from the questionnaire, because in the latter the instructions were not properly followed, a point discussed again below. All the remainder (19, 24, 33, 34, 63, 71, 72, 100) differed in quite a marked degree from the answers given in the questionnaire, and nearly all tended to give answers reflecting favourably on the respondents. Far more people in the interviews claimed that they found friends among their neighbours (19), and that they could rely entirely on their neighbours help in a pinch (24). This latter question (24) is the only one of those asked in the field survey which gave the possibility of expressing aggression in the answers, and nowhere is there a more marked contrast between the answers of the field survey and of the questionnaire. When asked about the company they would choose to spend a pleasant evening with (33) and the company they actually enjoyed 'last Saturday' (34) the interviewees show markedly greater fondness for their own families and markedly less interest in the company of a member of the opposite sex than do the respondents to the questionnaire; they present a picture of domestic respectability undisturbed by anything so unbecoming as an interest in sex. (The same pattern emerges in the answer to the question 'How old were you when you started being really interested in girls (boys)?' with 20 per cent of the men and 12 per cent of the women naming some age over 19, but the answers are so clumsily categorized in groups of 3 years that it has not seemed worth while reproducing the tables.) Modesty evidently made male respondents answer 'When should a child start being trained to be clean?' (63) as though the question referred to washing rather than toilet training; the habits of small babies are obviously much too indelicate for a respectable man to discuss with a strange young woman.

The remaining three tables are slightly more ambiguous. Considerably more of the parents interviewed than of those who filled the questionnaire consider that children should never be given public praise (71) and far more said they did not give their children regular pocket money when they started going to school (72); these answers could be due to the interviewed parents not wishing to present themselves as unduly 'spoiling' their children; alternatively, this may perhaps be a reflection of a changing attitude, since the interviewed sample is somewhat older than the main sample Finally, a very much smaller proportion of those interviewed said they had ever been to a fortune-teller (100), 28 per cent contrasted with 44 per cent; this may represent a real difference in practice, the readers of the *People* being more prone to believe in such techniques than the population as a whole; alternatively, interviewees may have thought that the interviewer would think less well of them if they admitted that they had done so.

The same principles—the tendency to choose 'polar' answers, and to present oneself in as favourable a light as possible—can I think be seen operating in the tables I have quoted from the Gallup Poll and Odhams Press Research Department In questions which do not offer graded choices nor reflect on the respectability of the respondents, the answers from the polls and from the written questionnaire are closely comparable; in the remainder the differences all seem to be accountable for by these two principles.

From my experience with this research, I should consider that it is most undesirable ever to alter the instructions in the course of a questionnaire. I did this in four questions, with unsatisfactory results. Two questions (79 and 81) carried the instruction:

Please mark which of the following statements most nearly represents your own opinion. If more than one do, please mark the most important '1', the next most important '2 —and so on.

A certain, though relatively small, number of my respondents marked more than one entry with a tick, which made scoring of these questionnaires impossible. Both of these questions were also asked in the field survey.

A second pair of questions (40 and 41, 53 and 54) carried the instruction:

Please mark in the first column the statement you most AGREE with and in the second column the statement you most DISAGREE with. (Only ONE statement for agree and ONE for disagree Mark with X).

Despite the capitals, barely half the respondents paid attention to this instruction, and proceeded to mark more than one statement, which is why the answers from the main sample and the field survey on questions 40 and 41 are not comparable. No matter how high the income or social class of the respondents, at least a quarter in each category marked more than one statement, though the most consistent disregard of the instructions came from the poor and old. If I were drawing up this questionnaire again I should contrive somehow to get the same information from questions so framed that they could be answered either with a simple tick or by writing.

I have already given in Chapter Two the main assumptions which I held when I drew up the questionnaire; but it may be worth noting here the principles which decided what questions should be asked to test these assumptions. Within the limits of what is practical, I think it essential that at least some information should be obtained concerning each of the basic institutions which anthropologists have discovered to be common to all societies.[2] In any study of national character, it is inevitable that major attention will be given to the institutions of the family and of education, for it is in these contexts that aspects of national character can be studied most simply. In this study I have paid some attention to the extended family as well as the nuclear family and to formal as well as informal education, though not with the completeness which would theoretically be desirable. I paid particular attention to the institution of religion, both because I considered it to be of intrinsic interest and because it is a subject which seems to me to have been unduly neglected in recent studies of national character. Questions also dealt with social control (the 'tribe-state'), defence (the armed forces, though these questions were unrewarding), the deference structure (social class), the geographical divisions of the small neighbourhood and the larger region, and neighbourhood activities. The institutions which this survey touched on more lightly than I could have wished were economics and politics. The only economic information was present family income, and I still do not know how such information can usefully be obtained by questionnaires, luckily there is a great deal of specialized material available on this aspect of English culture.

318

On politics (the 'tribe-nation') my only information is on attendance at political clubs. Were this research to be done again, I should certainly include a couple of questions on political attitudes;[3] I omitted them in this instance because I feared they might be resented; but with my greater experience of the willing co-operation of my respondents I should no longer have the same qualms.

However long and detailed the questionnaire, it is not to be supposed that adequate information on the structure and function of any institution can be obtained by such means alone; but by placing some questions in the context of each of the major social institutions one is more likely to obtain a balanced picture of the operations of the society and so to guard against the distortions which may result if all attention is focused on a single aspect of a most complex whole.

NOTES TO APPENDIX TWO

1. I asked Mr W D McClelland, director of the Research Dept. of Odhams Press, Limited, whether this observation was borne out by his great experience of questionnaires He replied 'It is our experience that, where graded choices do exist, there is a tendency to choose the extremes. One of the arts of compiling a questionnaire is to so word the possible choices as to eliminate this tendency . In general, however, in personal interviews, I think that it can be said that the emphasis tends to be placed rather more on the extremes than is the case with mail surveys '

2 See B Malinowski, *passim*, but especially his article 'Culture' in the *Encyclopedia of Social Sciences*, IV, 621–57, *Coral Gardens and Their Magic* (London, 1935); *The Group and the Individual in Functional Analysis* (The American Journal of Sociology, XLIV (1939), 938–64).

3. The questions I should ask would be. Did you vote at the last general election? If Yes, which party did you vote for? If there were an election today, would you vote the same way?

THE QUESTIONNAIRE

NOTE· This questionnaire is reproduced in one of the forms in which it was circulated; the order of the questions and the numbers attached to them are not the same as those used in the text of this book. This form is that sent to fathers of living children. All respondents were sent Questions 1 to 45, married people without children Questions 1 to 51 only Questions 42, 44, 45, 47, 48, and 49 were worded differently for men and for women.

THE "PEOPLE" SOCIAL SURVEY

This form is very easy to follow Most of the questions can be answered by placing a tick in the box opposite the answer that applies to you When the question does require you to *write in* the answer you will find dotted lines   For some of the questions special instructions have been written alongside

IT IS NOT NECESSARY TO SIGN THIS FORM

1 (a) TOWN (*Please add district number if any*)

   (b) COUNTY

2. SEX·   MALE ☐   FEMALE ☐

3 AGE

4. SINGLE ☐   MARRIED ☐   WIDOWED ☐   DIVORCED OR ☐
                                                                      SEPARATED

5. Please mark the approximate weekly *family* income (*By 'family income' we mean the total of all income earners in the family*)

    Under £5 ☐   Between £5 and £8 ☐   Between £8 and £12 ☐
                  Between £12 and £15 ☐   Over £15 ☐

6 How old were you when you finished full-time school ?

    Under 14 ☐   14 ☐   15 ☐   16 ☐   17 ☐   18 ☐   Over 18 ☐

7 If you were asked to say what class you belonged to, how would you describe yourself?

8. (a) How long have you lived at your present address?

   (b) Would you describe your home as·

       Detached—that is, standing by itself   .   .   .   ☐

       Semi-detached—one side joined to another house   .   .   ☐

       Terraced—one of a row, with both sides joined to another house   ☐

       A self-contained flat in a converted house   .   .   ☐

       A flat in a block of flats   .   .   .   ☐

       Unfurnished rooms   .   .   .   .   ☐

       Furnished rooms .   .   .   .   .   .   ☐

       Hotel or boarding house   .   .   .   .   ☐

       Other (*please specify*)

9 (a) Is your father alive?   .   .   Yes ☐   No ☐

      Is your mother alive?   .   Yes ☐   No ☐

   (b) If your father is living, does your father live in the same house as you?   .   .   Yes ☐   No ☐

      If your mother is living, does your mother live in the same house as you?   .   .   .   Yes ☐   No ☐

320

(c) If your father is living, but not in the same house as
you, does your father live in the same town as you? Yes ☐   No ☐

If your mother is living, but not in the same house as
you, does your mother live in the same town as you? Yes ☐   No ☐

10 (a) Do any of your brothers or sisters or married children
live near you—within, say, 5 minutes' walk? .   Yes ☐   No ☐

(b) Do your parents-in-law, brothers-in-law or sisters-in-
law live near you—within, say, 5 minutes' walk? .   Yes ☐   No ☐

11 Not counting relations or in-laws, do you know.

		Most	A few	Hardly any	No
	Neighbours by sight .				
Tick one box in each line	Neighbours to speak to .				
	Neighbours to drop in on without an invitation . .				
	Neighbours to visit for a meal or an evening . . .				

12. Would you say your best friends live near you (that is, within walking distance),
a short way away (say, a mile or so), or far away?

Near you ☐   Short distance away ☐   Far away ☐

Some in all three ☐

13. Are there places outside your own homes and the street where you meet neighbours
to have a chat? (*Please mark in the first column if you visit such places at all,
in the second column how often you have been this last month.*)

	A Visit at all (Tick here)	B Visit last month (number of times)
Church or chapel meeting rooms .	☐	☐
Men's club	☐	☐
Women's club or women's institute .	☐	☐
Mixed club	☐	☐
Youth club	☐	☐
Gymnasium	☐	☐
Sports ground . . .	☐	☐
Dance hall	☐	☐
Political club	☐	☐
Public house	☐	☐
Café	☐	☐
Other (*please specify*)		

14 Do you think you could rely on your neighbours in a pinch?

Entirely ☐   To a large extent ☐   To a small extent ☐

Not at all ☐   It depends ☐

321

15 What do you most disapprove of about your present neighbours?

*16 (a) Were you in the Forces?   Yes ☐   No ☐

    (b) If Yes, have you kept in touch with friends you made in the Forces?

        None ☐   One or two of them ☐   Several ☐

                The whole bunch ☐

    (c) Did you go to a Regimental or similar reunion during 1950?

              Yes ☐   No ☐

    (d) How many friends from the Forces did you see last year?

    (e) How many friends from the Forces did you write to last year?

17. What do you consider your three best qualities?

        1

        2

        3

18 What do you consider your three worst faults?

        1

        2

        3

19 One reads a lot in the papers about the post-war increase in crime, especially among young people *Please mark which of the following reasons seems to you most important, if you think more than one is important, please mark the most important '1,' the next most important '2'—and so on*

    People got into bad ways in the Forces   .   ☐

    Children whose fathers were in the Forces didn't have proper discipline .   .   .   .   ☐

    Children who were evacuated weren't properly looked after   ☐

    Modern parents aren't strict enough   .   .   ☐

    Modern schools aren't strict enough   .   .   .   ☐

    Young people follow the bad example of crime films and crime stories in books and on the radio   .   .   ☐

    People are neglecting religion   .   .   .   .   ☐

20 There's a lot of talk about 'fiddling' nowadays *Please mark which of the following statements most nearly represents your own opinion If more than one do, please mark the most important '1,' the next most important '2,'—and so on*

    Nearly everybody fiddles nowadays   .   .   .   ☐

    Most people fiddle occasionally, but not many do regularly   .   ☐

    With all the rules and regulations, one can't help having to break a rule sometimes   .   .   .   .   ☐

    It is unpatriotic to fiddle   .   .   .   .   ☐

    None of my family has ever got anything 'off the ration' .   ☐

    It is wrong to break the law under any circumstances   .   ☐

    Most fiddling is done by profiteers   .   .   .   ☐

    It is unfair to try to get more than others   .   .   .   ☐

    Most fiddling is done by foreigners   .   .   .   ☐

21. What do you think of the police?

22 (a) Have you a lucky mascot?   .   .   Yes ☐   No ☐
    (b) Did you have a lucky mascot during the war? .   Yes ☐   No ☐
    (c) Have you a specially lucky or unlucky day?   Lucky ☐   Unlucky ☐
    (d) Have you a specially lucky or unlucky number?   Lucky ☐   Unlucky ☐

*23   Can you tell fortunes?   .   .   .   Yes ☐   No ☐
      If Yes, how?   Cards ☐   Tea-leaves ☐   Reading hands ☐
      Other (please describe)

24 (a) Have you been to a fortune-teller?   .   Yes ☐   No ☐
    (b) If Yes, how often?   Once ☐   Twice ☐   Several times ☐
  *(c) When did you last go?
    (d) Did any of it come true?   .   .   .

25 (a) Do you read 'Lyndoe' in the *People*?
         Regularly ☐   Occasionally ☐   Never ☐
    (b) Do you read the horoscope in any other paper or magazine?
         Regularly ☐   Occasionally ☐   Never ☐
  *(c) If so, what paper or magazine?
    (d) Do you follow advice in the horoscope columns you read?
         Regularly ☐   Occasionally ☐   Never ☐
    (e) Do you think there is something in horoscopes?
         Yes ☐   No ☐   Uncertain ☐

26. (a) Do you believe in ghosts?   .   .   Yes ☐   No ☐   Uncertain ☐
    (b) If Yes, have you ever seen or heard
         a ghost? .   .   .   .   Yes ☐   No ☐   Uncertain ☐
  *(c) Have you ever known a person
         whom you believe has ever seen
         or heard a ghost? .   .   Yes ☐   No ☐   Uncertain ☐

27. *Please mark in the first column the statement you most* AGREE *with and in the second column the statement you most* DISAGREE *with.* (*Only* ONE *statement for agree and* ONE *for disagree. Mark with* ×.)

	A Agree	B Disagree
There is much more immorality than there used to be	☐	☐
Human nature hasn't changed, but people are not so narrow-minded as they used to be .	☐	☐
It is right and natural for young people to want to make love	☐	☐
It's other people's nasty minds which make all the mischief	☐	☐
People are really more moral today than they were thirty years ago	☐	☐

323

28. (a) Do you think English people fall in
love the way you see Americans
doing it in the films? .   Yes ☐   No ☐   Don't know ☐

   (b) Would you say you had ever been
really in love?   .   .   Yes ☐   No ☐   Don't know ☐

   (c) Do you expect to fall really in love
sometime?   .   .   Yes ☐   No ☐   Don't know ☐

29 Not counting marriage, have you ever had a real love affair?

30 Do you think a young man should have
some sexual experience before he gets
married?   .   .   Yes ☐   No ☐   Don't know ☐

  Why?

31 Do you think a young woman should
have some sexual experience before she
gets married? .   .   .   Yes ☐   No ☐   Don't know ☐

  Why?

32 In marriage do you think sexual love is very important?

Very im-   Fairly im-   Not very   Not impor-
portant ☐   portant ☐   important ☐   tant at all ☐

33 *Please mark in the first column the statement you most AGREE with and in the second
column the statement you most DISAGREE with (Only ONE statement for agree
and ONE for disagree Mark with ×)*

	A Agree	B Disagree
Most women don't care much about the physical side of sex . .	☐	☐
Women don't have such an animal nature as men .	☐	☐
Women really enjoy the physical side of sex just as much as men	☐	☐
Women tend to enjoy sex more than men . .	☐	☐

*34. Do you think a man and woman can
have a real friendship without sex
playing any part?   .   .   Yes ☐   No ☐   Don't know ☐

*35 Which of these statements do you agree with?

Friendship is more important than love .   ☐

Love is more important than friendship   .   ☐

Love and friendship are equally important   ☐

36. If you wanted to spend a pleasant evening, what sort of company would you
like to spend it in? (*Please mark in the first column the company you'd like best*

324

with '1,' next best with '2'—and so on; and in the second column mark the company which you had last Saturday evening.)

	Like best	Last Saturday
One man	☐	☐
One girl . .	☐	☐
A foursome (two couples) . .	☐	☐
A group of men .	☐	☐
A group of girls . . .	☐	☐
A mixed group . . .	☐	☐
With my own family . . .	☐	☐
Alone . . .	☐	☐
Working		☐
Was ill		☐

37. (a) Would you describe yourself as being of any religion or denomination? . . . Yes ☐ No ☐

    (b) If Yes, which?

38 Do you attend Church or religious services?

More than once a week	☐
Once a week . . .	☐
Less than once a week but more than once a month .	☐
Less than once a month	☐
Once or twice a year	☐
Only for weddings and funerals . . .	☐
Never	☐

39. Do you say prayers more than once a day? . . | ☐ |
Daily . .	☐
Only in peril and grief . . .	☐
Very seldom	☐
Never	☐

40. (a) Do you believe in the Devil? Yes ☐ No ☐ Uncertain ☐

    (b) Do you believe in Hell? . Yes ☐ No ☐ Uncertain ☐

41. Do you believe in an after-life? Yes ☐ No ☐ Uncertain ☐

If Yes, what do you think it will be like?

42. (a) Do you think it is natural for young people to be shy? Yes ☐ No ☐ Don't know ☐

    (b) Do you think you were exceptionally shy? . . . . Yes ☐ No ☐ Don't know ☐

    (c) Are you less shy than you used to be? Yes ☐ No ☐ Don't know ☐

    (d) Do you think shyness a good thing? Yes ☐ No ☐ Don't know ☐

43. How old were you when you first started being really interested in girls? (boys?)

325

44. What do you think are the three most important qualities a wife (a husband) should have?

    1

    2

    3

45. What are the three chief faults that wives (husbands) tend to have?

    1

    2

    3

The following questions were only sent to people who were or had been married

*46 How many years have you been married?

47 (a) How long had you known your wife (husband) before you were engaged?

   *(b) How long was your engagement?

48 Before you became engaged to your wife (husband) did you ever seriously consider marrying another woman (man)?

49 If a husband (wife) finds his wife (her husband) having an affair with another man (woman) what should he (she) do?

50 What do you think goes to wreck a marriage?

51. What do you think goes to make for a happy marriage?

The following questions were only sent to parents of living children

52 How many boys have you?   How many girls have you?

   *Please list your children's ages *Boys*

                              Girls

53 Generally speaking, do you consider children need more or less discipline than they get nowadays?

       More ☐   Less ☐   The same ☐

54 Who is the proper person to punish a child who has done something really bad?

   Mother ☐   Father ☐   Teacher ☐   Other ☐ *(Please specify)*

Why?

55 How should a really naughty boy be punished?

Are there any forms of punishment you don't approve of for boys?

56 How should a really naughty girl be punished?

Are there any forms of punishment you don't approve of for girls?

57 If you were told that a small child, say between 3 and 8, had done something really bad, what would you think the child had done?

58 When should a young child start being trained to be clean?

Which is worse for the child, starting training too early ☐ or too late ☐ or doesn't it make much difference? ☐

59 Should children be praised in front of others, if they are good and helpful?
     Yes ☐   No ☐   Don't know ☐

60. (a) Do you give your children regular pocket-money when they start going to school?
     Yes ☐   No ☐

    (b) Do you give your children money or other rewards when they are useful and helpful?
     Always ☐   Sometimes ☐   Occasionally ☐   Never ☐

    (c) Would you let your children take money for doing jobs for neighbours, such as running errands, watching babies, or helping them?
     Yes ☐   No ☐   Don't know ☐

61 Do your children go to Sunday School?   Yes ☐   No ☐
If Yes, do you send them ☐ or allow them to go because they themselves want to? ☐

*62 (a) If you attend a Church or other place of worship, do you take your children with you?
     Always ☐   Sometimes ☐   Occasionally ☐   Never ☐

    (b) Do your children go by themselves to Church or a place of worship?
     Always ☐   Sometimes ☐   Occasionally ☐   Never ☐

63. (a) Do you teach your children to say prayers?   Yes ☐   No ☐

    (b) If Yes, when do they say them?
     Before going to bed ☐   Morning and evening ☐
     Grace before meals ☐   Grace after meals   ☐

64. Do your children play with other children whose parents you don't know?
     Often ☐   Occasionally ☐   Never ☐

65. (a) Do you tell your children not to play with some of the neighbours' children?

           Yes ☐   No ☐

    (b) Do you forbid your children to visit some of the neighbours' houses?

           Yes ☐   No ☐

    If Yes, what are your reasons?

NOTE. All tables *except those resulting from questions or sub-questions marked with* * are reproduced in the Complete edition

The following questions were also asked in the field-survey by interviewers 1, 2, 3, 4, 5, 6, 7, 8 (a), 8 (b), 10 (a), 10 (b), 11 (a), 11 (b), 11 (c), 11 (d), 12, 14, 19, 20, 22, 22 (a), 22 (c), 22 (d), 23 (a), 23 (b), 24 (a), 24 (b), 24 (c), 24 (d), 25 (b), 25 (d), 25 (e), 27 (a), 27 (b), 28 (a), 36 (a), 36 (b), 43, 46, 52, 58 (a), 58 (b), 59, 60 (a), 60 (b), 60 (c), 62 (a), 64.